90 0388368 2

KW-206-698

New Britain:

New Elections

WITHDRAWN
FROM
UNIVERSITY OF PLYMOUTH
LIBRARY SERVICES

THE MEDIA GUIDE *to*

THE NEW

SEVEN DAY LOAN

This book is to be returned on
or before the date stamped below

- 2 OCT 2000	- 8 JAN 2002
- 9 JAN 2001	1 3 MAY 2002
2 2 FEB 2001	2 0 MAY 2002
	2 8 MAY 2002
- 8 JUN 2001	- 1 APR 2003
1 3 NOV 2001	2 8 DEC 2003
1 2 JAN 2006	2 5 FEB 2005

UNIVERSITY OF PLYMOUTH

PLYMOUTH LIBRARY
Tel: (01752) 232323
This book is subject to recall if required by another reader
Books may be renewed by phone
CHARGES WILL BE MADE FOR OVERDUE BOOKS

ISBN 0 9530664 3 6

© 1999 Vacher Dod Publishing Ltd

All rights reserved. No part of this publication may be reproduced or used in any form or by any means – graphic; electronic or mechanical, including photocopying, recording taping or information storage and retrieval systems – without written permission from the publishers.

New Britain:
New Elections

THE MEDIA GUIDE *to* THE *NEW* POLITICAL MAP *of* BRITAIN

Published by

VACHER DOD PUBLISHING LIMITED
PO Box 3700 London SW1E 5NP

Telephone: 0171 828 7256   *Fax:* 0171 828 7269
E-mail: politics@vacherdod.co.uk
www.vacherdod.co.uk

Authors' note

The material contained in this book is the result of collaboration between the BBC, ITN, the Press Association and Sky News to provide readily accessible information about the range of new elected bodies and electoral systems that will be introduced in the United Kingdom over the coming months.

Each chapter is a self-contained guide to a single set of elections, and covers the structure and functions of the body being elected; the electoral system by which it will be chosen; profiles of the character and electoral history of each constituency; and an analysis of possible election results. For the European and Scottish Parliament and Welsh Assembly elections there are also lists of the candidates being fielded by each of the major parties.

We are grateful to the staff of BBC Research, especially Bill Bush, Catherine Rimmer, Monica Soriano, and Louisa Welby-Everard, for providing additional research support; and to Eddie Green of Vacher Dod for his enthusiasm and commitment.

Professor Colin Rallings
Professor Michael Thrasher
Local Government Chronicle Elections Centre
University of Plymouth
Plymouth PL4 8AA

Tel: +44 (0)1752 233205
Fax: +44 (0) 1752 233206
email: crallings@plymouth.ac.uk

UNIVERSITY OF PLYMOUTH

Item No. 900 3883682

Date -2 JUN 1999

Class No. 324·942 NEW

Contl. No. 0953066436

LIBRARY SERVICES

Contents

Foreword by David Butler

Date of election: 10 June 1999
System: 84 Members of the European Parliament (MEPs) to be
                           elected by Regional List system (71 from 9 regions in
                           England, 8 from Scotland and 5 from Wales)
                           3 MEPs from Northern Ireland to be elected by Single
                           Transferable Vote
Deposit: £5000 per list/individual candidate not on official list.
                           2.5% threshold for return of deposit.

Parliament established following Referendum on 11 September 1997

Date of election: 6 May 1999
System: 73 Members of the Scottish Parliament (MSPs) elected by
                           simple plurality in single member constituencies
                           56 MSPs elected by Additional Member System (7 in
                           each of 8 regions)
                           Ratio of constituency to list MSPs = 57:43.
Deposit: £500 per constituency candidate/per party list.
                           5% threshold for return of deposit.

Assembly established following Referendum on 18 September 1997

Date of election: 6 May 1999
System: 40 Members of the Welsh Assembly (MWAs) elected by
                           simple plurality in single member constituencies
                           20 MWAs elected by Additional Member System (4 in
                           each of 5 regions)
                           Ratio of constituency to list MWAs = 67:33.
Deposit: £500 per constituency candidate/per party list.
                           5% threshold for return of deposit.

Chapter 4. Northern Ireland Assembly Elections

Assembly established following Referendum on 22 May, 1998

Date of election:	25 June 1998
System:	108 Members of the Northern Ireland Assembly (MNIAs) elected by Single Transferable Vote. 6 MNIAs elected in each of the current 18 parliamentary constituencies.
Deposit:	£150 per candidate. 5% threshold for return of deposit.

Chapter 5. Greater London Authority

Authority to be established following Referendum on 7 May 1998

Date of election:	4 May 2000
System:	Mayor elected in cross-London election using Supplementary Vote system
	14 Members of the Greater London Assembly (MGLAs) elected by simple plurality in single member constituencies
	11 MGLAs elected by Additional Member System on basis of total cross-London votes.
Deposit:	Amount yet to be determined for either election. 5% threshold for return of deposit.

Chapter 6. Local Government Elections

Date of election:	6 May 1999
System:	About 13,000 councillors elected by simple plurality in single or multi-member wards
	241 local authorities, including all those in Scotland and Wales, elect the entire council; 121 elect about one-third of their membership
Deposit:	none.

Chapter 7. The Jenkins Commission and the next General Election *Page 239*

Date of general election   Must be called by May 2002

System: 659 Members of Parliament (MPs) elected by simple
                                plurality in single member constituencies

Deposit: £500 per candidate. 5% threshold for return of deposit.

Reform proposals: The Independent Commission on the Voting System
                                (Jenkins Commission) recommended move towards an
                                Alternative Vote Plus electoral system.
                                A proportion of MPs (between 80-85%) would be elected
                                in single member constituencies using the alternative
                                vote and a proportion (between 15-20%) by the
                                Additional Member System on the basis of votes within
                                county- or city-wide electoral units.
                                A possibly modified and amended version of the Jenkins
                                Commission proposals is due to be put forward in a
                                Referendum 'run off' against the present electoral
                                system. The date of the Referendum has not yet been
                                fixed. The next general election will be fought under
                                current rules.

Glossary. The variety of UK electoral systems *Page 267*

Appendices *Pages 271-322*

THE VACHER DOD PUBLISHING GROUP TITLES

Dod's Parliamentary Companion 1999
Published since 1832. Parliament's leading annual reference book.
Over 1,300 pages.

The Vacher Dod House of Commons Companion
Focuses on the House of Commons. MPs' biographies,
constituency profiles and results. Government Departments,
Select Committees, Procedure and Standing Orders.
Over 1,000 pages.

Vacher's Parliamentary Companion
Published since 1832. Parliament's foremost quarterly guide.
Available in A5 or handy pocket size. 450 pages.

Handbook of House of Commons Procedure 1999
Written and now completely revised by a Clerk with fifteen years'
experience of working in the House. An essential reference work.

Vacher's European Companion
26th Anniversary. A wide-ranging European reference book.
UK MEPs and prominent European personalities' biographies.
Updated quarterly. 450 pages.

New Britain: New Elections 1999
An indispensable guide to the new constitutional and electoral
architecture of the United Kingdom.

The Prime Ministers from Walpole to Macmillan
Forty-four biographies covering 242 tumultuous years
which helped to shape the nation. 175 pages.

Vacher Dod Publishing Limited
PO Box 3700, Westminster, London SW1E 5NP
Tel: 0171-828 7256   Fax: 0171-828 7269
E-mail: politics@vacherdod.co.uk

Foreword

1999 is an altogether exceptional year in terms of elections. It sees the introduction of brand new voting systems, each different from the other, for the Scottish Parliament, the Welsh Assembly, the European Parliament, and in 2000 for the London Mayor and Assembly. It will also witness continued discussion of Lord Jenkins' proposals for an alternative to the traditional, first-past-the-post contests for Westminster. And of course, in England, Scotland and Wales there will be the old-style local elections in May.

Elections are about choosing governments or representatives and their policies. But the outcome of elections depends on the tallying up of votes. To understand election results hard facts are needed about the election system used and the way it translates votes into seats, as well as about the result last time.

In trying to understand the message given by an election it is necessary to look at the evidence about who voted for each side and why they did so. Moreover, to measure how opinion has changed it is essential to know what happened in the last comparable contest. Remember the old adage: to understand the present, study the past; to guess the future, establish the current trend and project it, with due caution, to the future.

So to master the elections of 1999 it is necessary to assemble the facts and in these pages various experts have done so.

People at every level of politics, even the highest, are confused about how the new systems will work. Mercifully most of the problems are for the protagonists and for those who count the votes and need not trouble the voters, who will have little difficulty in marking their ballot papers. But it is still important to understand how our various crosses or numbers, recorded in the polling booth, will translate into the choice of representatives who will determine the composition of governments or governing coalitions.

New electoral systems demand new political practices. Already, in selecting candidates for Scotland, Wales and Europe, the parties have had to alter their structures and to develop fresh rules. Candidates, fighting together on lists in huge multi-member constituencies, are busy devising new styles of campaigning. The media coverage and the very nature of this year's battles will see many innovations in politics.

It is almost fifty years since I first appeared in a TV election results programme. Nothing in sport seems as exciting as hearing the first results come in and making sense of them. And the broadcasters have got infinitely more skill in the art of presenting them. For those who care, 1999 is going to be a vintage year for elections. These pages are designed to help you savour the premier cru.

Dr David Butler, *Nuffield College, Oxford*

HANDBOOK
OF
HOUSE *of* COMMONS
PROCEDURE

2nd Edition 1999

This book is an essential reference work for anyone who needs to understand the procedures of the House of Commons.

Its author, a Clerk in the Commons with sixteen years' experience of working in the House, has completely revised his original guide to the procedures of the House. It describes the House, its organisation, rules and privileges; the business of the House and its committees; the role of the Speaker and chairmen; the timetables of Parliaments, sessions, weeks and days; question time; the rules of debate, procedures for bills, statutory instruments and European legislation; and the functions and procedures of the Select Committees of the House.

Also included is an extensive glossary of jargon of parliamentary procedure, and many figures and tables which summarise essential information and illustrate the text. (To be published Spring 1999).

Vacher Dod Publishing Limited
PO Box 3700, Westminster, London SW1E 5NP
Tel: 0171-828 7256   Fax: 0171-828 7269
E-mail: politics@vacherdod.co.uk

1. European Parliament Elections

New electoral system, same old public apathy?

Introduction by: **Adam Boulton**, *Political Editor, Sky News*

The European Parliament is the only directly elected trans-national assembly in the world, but its lack of powers leaves it a long way short of making up the democratic deficit generally perceived in European decision-making. In Britain at least it remains a largely unloved institution. Public suspicions of a gravy train of corruption will not have been assuaged by the failure of the Parliament effectively to discipline the Commission last January.

With few exceptions, British politicians see the European Parliament as second best: a choice for politicians on the way up to or down from Westminster. Tony Blair has not bothered to hide his contempt for many of Labour's current representatives at Strasbourg, accusing them of 'infantile incompetence' in 1995, shortly after he became party leader.

This year's European Parliament elections in Britain were trailed spectacularly at the end of 1998, when the government's plans for a closed list proportional representation system provoked a full scale constitutional clash with the House of Lords. They will now be the first ever nationwide contest in which voters will *not* elect their representative by name, having only to express a preference for a political party. Control over the order of names on the list should give party leaderships the chance to weed out trouble makers – and there have already been complaints from disappointed Labour and Conservative candidates alike.

The precise nature of the chosen electoral system was not specified in Labour's 1997 manifesto and its passage into law caused problems for all three major parties. On the Labour benches there were clashes between such luminaries as the former PM James Callaghan and his old cabinet colleague Peter Shore. The Liberal Democrats, fearing the restoration of first past the post elections, found themselves eating words which had supported an 'open list' system whereby candidates could be chosen by name. The Conservatives' fierce attacks on the 'undemocratic and unBritish' system proposed seemed unembarrassed by the fact that, in government, they had been the party to introduce closed lists to Britain for the Northern Ireland Forum election in May 1996.

The parliamentary wrangle also exposed the marked differences between the inner Shadow Cabinet and the Tory frontbench in the Lords which were to lead to the sacking of Viscount Cranborne. As Tony Blair railed against the inbuilt Tory majority of hereditary peers which had five times frustrated his legislation, Cranborne suggested that it was time to compromise. William Hague rejected this, but his power over his party in the Lords was not ultimately put to the test. When the Bill was reintroduced for the second time at the start of the 1998/99 session, the Lords short-circuited the possibility of trench warfare by rejecting it *in toto* at the earliest opportunity, thus triggering the Parliament Act which automatically enacts government legislation rejected by the Lords in two separate sessions. Appropriately the Act's conventions were drawn up by Cranborne's ancestor, Lord Salisbury, earlier in the century.

Whether the 1999 European elections campaign in Britain can match these excitements is moot. In the past public interest and voter turnout has been notoriously low with scarcely more than one-third of registered electors bothering to participate. However, elections conducted at such low blood temperature may give one of the clearest pictures of the drift in public opinion.

The 1979 European elections confirmed Mrs. Thatcher's resounding general election victory, but – interestingly – were also the last occasion on which any party has had an absolute majority of votes in a British national election. The era of regional and multi-party politics was just around the corner. In 1984 the Tories again won the most seats and votes, but they and Labour together were supported by fewer than three-quarters of voters.

In 1989 Labour came out as a pro-European party and the elections proved to be the only national contest Neil Kinnock was to 'win'. So severe was the Tory drubbing that the European Commission President Jacques Delors cancelled his British television interviews so as not to be seen to be gloating over Mrs. Thatcher's setback. The message was that the Iron Lady was not invincible. The 1989 elections also saw the unprecedented 15% vote for the British Green party, an ominous warning to the still feuding parties of the centre, the SDP and Liberal Democrats, to put their house in order.

1994 was the first national election after Black Wednesday, and the first time 'Tory meltdown' entered the lexicon of political clichés. The Conservatives took just 26.9% of the vote, the lowest figure they had recorded at any election since modern electoral politics began in 1832. So far had they sunk that it would prove impossible to recover before the 1997 general election.

The birth of the 'Euro', Agenda 2000, and the prospect of European Union enlargement to the East may make Europe more central to the campaign in 1999. Certainly the government will be scrutinizing the result carefully as it ponders its chances in a single currency referendum in Britain. But, as always, domestic issues will have an important place. The Tories will want clear evidence that William Hague can offer the party a brighter future. Voters in Scotland and Wales will be heavily influenced by the results of their own national elections 5 weeks earlier. In Northern Ireland, how will the Good Friday agreement affect the massive first place mandate given to Ian Paisley at every European election since 1979?

With the entire United Kingdom able to vote on 10 June, Europe 99 is the best measure of the national political mood we'll get this side of the general election.

Adam Boulton

Structure and functions of the European Parliament

The European Parliament has 626 members who are elected for five year terms of office. Seats are distributed amongst the 15 European Union countries. Germany has 99 seats, France, Italy and the UK have 87 seats each, Spain has 64, The Netherlands has 31, Belgium, Greece and Portugal have 25 each, Sweden has 22, Austria 21, Denmark and Finland 16, Ireland 15 and Luxembourg has six. With the prospect of European Union enlargement to include several central and eastern European countries, the total number of seats in the European Parliament has been limited to 700 in order to keep proceedings manageable.

Elections for the European Parliament are held by direct universal suffrage every five years. The last European elections were held in 1994.

The European Parliament normally meets in Strasbourg, although preparations for these meetings take place in Brussels. Parliament's Secretariat is in Luxembourg. The President of the European Parliament since January 1997 has been José Mariá Gil-Robles Gil-Delgado from Spain. There are, in addition, 14 Vice-Presidents and five Quaestors.

The European Parliament operates through a system of committees. The allocation of committee chairs and membership reflects the representation of the different party groups in the Parliament. Party groups are cross-national bodies comprising those parties from different nations who belong to the same party 'family'.

The Labour party and the Northern Ireland SDLP belong to the Party of European Socialists. The Conservatives are affiliated to the European Peoples Party and the Liberal Democrats are members of the European Liberal Democrat and Reform Party. Scottish National party MEPs sit in the European Radical Alliance and Ulster Unionists in the Independent Europe of Nations group. The sole Democratic Unionist MEP, Ian Paisley, is affiliated to no party group.

Role of the European Parliament

- The European Parliament provides a democratic forum for debate, playing the role of European Union watchdog.
- An essential function is to provide political impetus. After all the European Parliament is a melting pot of political and national sensibilities representing 373 million people. The European parliament frequently calls for new policies to be launched and existing ones to be developed or altered.
- Parliament shares the legislative function with the Council of the European Union (the main decision-making institution made up of ministers from the 15 European Union countries with the same portfolio e.g. agriculture, transport, home affairs etc.). Parliament has a hand in the drafting of directives and regulations, putting forward amendments which it invites the European Commission (the executive arm of the EU) to incorporate into its proposals.
- The European Parliament has a key role in scrutinising the activities of the Commission, and vets individual Commissioners before their appointment is confirmed.

Powers of the European Parliament

- The Parliament has joint decision-making powers with the Council of the European Union in specific areas : freedom of movement of people, freedom to set up businesses, freedom to provide services, the single market, education, research, the environment, trans-European networks, health, social and employment policy, culture and consumer protection.
- Parliament is able to reject the Council's common position and halt the legislative process provided that an absolute majority of MEPs are in favour.
- The Parliament shares budgetary powers with the European Council. It can adopt the budget or reject it - sending the whole procedure back to the drawing board. Parliament usually makes full use of its budgetary powers to try to influence policy.
- The Parliament can dismiss the entire Commission following a vote of censure.

Other European Union institutions

All the institutions complement each other, each having a specific part to play in the decision making process.

The Council of the European Union

- The main decision making institution – enacts EU legislation
- Shares legislative role and budget control with the European Parliament
- Represents the EU countries – the Council is made up of ministers from the 15 EU countries with the same portfolio of responsibilities e.g. agriculture, transport etc.
- The presidency of the Council rotates every six months between EU countries

The European Commission

- The executive arm of the EU – ensures that regulations and directives are implemented
- Intervenes to facilitate agreement between the Council and Parliament
- Represents EU interest and takes no instruction from individual countries
- Backed by a civil service located in Brussels and Luxembourg. There are 25 departments called directorates-general – divided into subject areas. There are 20 commissioners.
- Jacques Santer is President of the Commission

The Court of Justice – Sits in Luxembourg and comprises 15 judges and nine 'advocates-general'. Its role is to ensure that EU law is correctly and effectively implemented and interpreted.

The Court of First Instance – Deals with disputes between the European Commission and individuals or businesses.

The Court of Auditors – The EU financial watchdog – checks EU spending and financial dealings and produces annual reports of its findings.

The Economic and Social Committee – Assists the Council and Commission in economic and social matters. Trade, industry and unions are actively involved through this committee.

The Committee of the Regions – Consists of representatives of regional and local authorities and is consulted by the Council or the Commission.

Operation of electoral system

Elections to the European Parliament are due to take place throughout the United Kingdom on Thursday 10 June 1999. For the first time the entire country will be choosing its 87 MEPs through a system of proportional representation, but the actual method will differ as between Great Britain and Northern Ireland.

Although the total number of MEPs in England (71), Scotland (8), Wales (5) and Northern Ireland (3) will remain unchanged, territorial constituencies in the traditional sense will cease to exist. Instead there will be a number of regions returning between three and 11 MEPs each depending on the size of their electorates. The entire nations of Scotland and Wales will form single electoral regions.

Table 1.1: Electoral Regions, European Parliament Elections 1999

Region	No. of MEPs	1997 electorate	% of GB electorate	% of GB MEPs
East Midlands	6	3,134,378	7.3	7.1
Eastern	8	3,970,199	9.3	9.5
London	10	4,910,637	11.5	11.9
North East	4	1,964,407	4.6	4.8
North West	10	5,166,295	12.1	11.9
South East	11	5,904,091	13.8	13.1
South West	7	3,705,918	8.7	8.3
West Midlands	8	3,986,137	9.3	9.5
Yorkshire & The Humber	7	3,774,441	8.8	8.3
England	71	36,516,503	85.6	84.5
Scotland	8	3,949,112	9.3	9.5
Wales	5	2,203,059	5.2	6.0
Great Britain	**84**	**42,668,674**	**100**	**100**
Northern Ireland	3	1,177,969		
United Kindom	**87**	**43,846,643**		

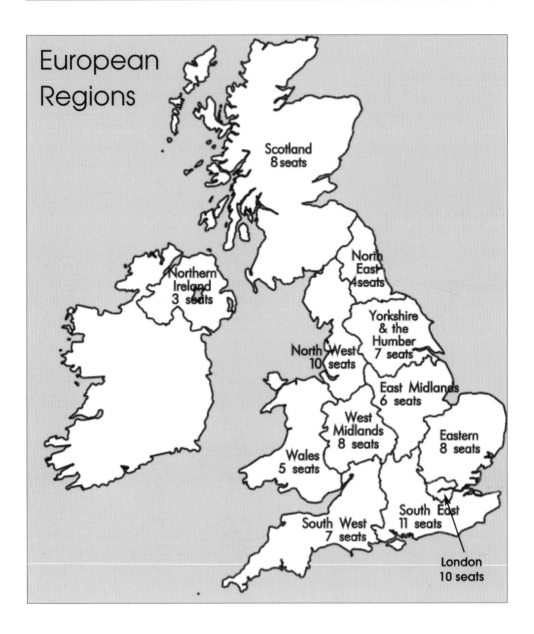

European
Regions

Scotland
8 seats

Northern
Ireland
3 seats

North
East
4 seats

Yorkshire
& the
Humber
7 seats

North West
10 seats

East Midlands
6 seats

West
Midlands
8 seats

Eastern
8 seats

Wales
5 seats

South East
11 seats

South West
7 seats

London
10 seats

In England, Scotland and Wales a list system will be used. Parties will supply a list of candidates for each region in the order in which they wish them to be elected. Electors will be able to cast their single vote either for a party or for an independent candidate. The votes of those candidates not on the list of a registered party will each be treated separately.

ELECTIONS FOR THE EUROPEAN PARLIAMENT
EAST MIDLANDS: SIX SEATS

MARK ONE "X" AGAINST A PARTY NAME	CONSERVATIVE	GREEN	LABOUR	LIBERAL DEMOCRAT	OTHERS
	1 Mark LESSING	1 Winston HELLSON	1 Annelle HUNTER	1 Graham WHITING	INDEPENDENT SOCIALIST
	2 Sam THOMAS	2 Graham ARCHER	2 William SHORTLY	2 Sally HELM	Sarah BARNETT
	3 Jeffrey POWELL		3 Mary WINDELL	3 Arnold FITZROY	
	4 Sarah DUNCAN		4 Harold BESSING	4 Calum DONALDSON	ANTI-EUROPE MOVEMENT
	5 Alistair SAUNDERS		5 John ADAMS	5 Pauline HARTLEY	Nicholas FLATLEY
	6 Anthony WRIGHT		6 Robert DAVIDS	6 BILL WINSOME	

YOU HAVE ONE VOTE ONLY

In Northern Ireland, as in every European election since 1979, the election of three MEPs will be by the Single Transferable Vote (STV) system. All candidates are listed individually and voters mark their order of preference. This allows a choice to be made among candidates and thus between parties as well.

NORTHERN IRELAND	
EUROPEAN PARLIAMENT ELECTIONS	
Mark order of preference in space below eg 1,2,3... You may number as many candidates as you wish.	
	Samuel CHAMBERS Natural Law
	Michael DONOVAN Sinn Fein
	Siobhan FERGUSON Ulster Unionist Party
	Patrick FINNEGAN Democratic Unionist Party
	Patricia MCNEAL UK Unionist
	Ian O'HARE Ulster Unionist Party
	Albert O'RYAN Democratic Unionist Party
	Philomena PATTERSON Women's Coaltion
	Peter RAFFERTY SDLP
	Laurie ROBERTSON SDLP

To be certain of securing a European Parliament seat in Great Britain a party or an individual must receive a proportion of the vote equal to 100 divided by the total number of seats in the region **plus one**. This threshold will vary from 20% (100÷4+1) in the North East region to 8.3% (100÷11+1) in the South East region. It is possible to secure a seat with a lesser share of the vote depending on the way votes are distributed between the competing parties.

In every electoral region each party which puts forward a list and each 'independent' candidate will be required to pay a deposit of £5,000. This will be returned if the party/individual receives at least 2.5% of the total valid votes cast in the region.

Votes cast in the European Parliament elections will be verified after the close of polls, but not counted until voting throughout Europe finishes on the evening of Sunday 13 June.

Electing MEPs in Great Britain: an example

In the East Midlands electoral 'region' six MEPs are to be elected. The first stage in this process will be to total the votes cast for each party list and for each individual candidate in the region. In this example we use the results of the 1997 general election and make the assumption that all electors would have cast their 'party list' votes for the same party for which they voted at constituency level. For simplicity we have summed the votes of all minor parties and individual candidates with the exception of the Referendum party. At the actual European Parliament election these will all be treated separately, not least to enable the calculation of saved and lost deposits.

Table 1.2: East Midlands - 1997 general election result

	Con	Lab	LD	Ref	Others
Votes	800,958	1,097,639	311,264	64,209	20,680
% Share	34.9	47.8	13.6	2.8	0.9

The first seat is allocated to the party with the highest vote (Labour) and to the candidate in first place on that party's list. The remaining seats are decided having taken into account the number of seats a party has already won within the region. To do this it is necessary to divide the total votes cast for each party by the number of seats it has won **plus one**. Labour's total thus becomes 1,097,639÷2 = 548,820 – see Table 1.3. Each time a party gains a seat the number by which its total vote is to be divided increases by one.

Following the initial calculation in the East Midlands the party with the highest number of remaining votes, Conservative, is awarded the second seat for its first placed candidate. The Conservative vote is now divided by two – the seat just acquired plus one – to give 400,479. Labour now has the highest remainder and its second placed candidate takes the third seat and the party's total vote is divided by three = 365,880. The Conservatives and Labour take the fourth and fifth seats, so their second and third choice candidates are also elected. The effect of dividing the total Conservative vote by three and the total Labour vote by four is to leave the Liberal Democrats with the largest remainder and thus the final seat. This is taken by the candidate in first place on that party's list.

Table 1.3: East Midlands – Allocation of members of the European Parliament

	Con	Lab	LD	Ref	Others	
Total Votes	800,958	1,097,639	311,264	64,209	20,680	
Initial divisor	0+1	0+1	0+1	0+1	0+1	*Elected (no. on list)*
1st seat	800,958	**1,097,639**	311,264	64,209	20,680	Lab (1)
2nd seat	**800,958**	548,820	311,264	64,209	20,680	Con (1)
3rd seat	400,479	**548,820**	311,264	64,209	20,680	Lab (2)
4th seat	**400,479**	365,880	311,264	64,209	20,680	Con (2)
5th seat	266,986	**365,880**	311,264	64,209	20,680	Lab (3)
6th seat	266,986	274,410	**311,264**	64,209	20,680	LD (1)

Table 1.4: East Midlands - European Parliament Membership

	Con	Lab	LD	Ref	Others
Total seats	2	3	1	—	—
% of seats	33.3	50.0	16.7	—	—

Electing MEPs in Northern Ireland: an example

The entire province of Northern Ireland forms a constituency for the purpose of electing three MEPs by Single Transferable Vote (STV). STV is also used in Northern Ireland for local council and Assembly elections.

The STV system in use requires electors to vote for at least one candidate, and then to declare their preferences for as many or as few of the other candidates as they wish. Preferences are declared numerically, with '1' being written alongside the voter's first preference candidate, '2' alongside the second choice and so on. To be elected a candidate must receive a minimum number of votes – the 'quota' – determined by a set formula. In Northern Ireland the formula known as the 'Droop quota' is used. It is calculated by dividing the total number of valid voting papers cast by the number of seats to be filled plus one.

A simple example of the way the system works can be seen from the results of the 1994 European Parliament election. The first step is to count the total number of votes cast in a constituency (559,867) and to arrive at the quota. With three seats to be filled this is $559,867 \div (3+1) = 139,967$. First preference votes are then counted and any candidate achieving the quota is elected. Both Hume and Paisley were elected on the first count because the number of first preference votes they received took them above the quota. The next stage of the count transfers the surplus votes of the candidate with the largest number of votes (Paisley) among the other candidates. The surplus is the number of votes received in excess of the number required to reach the quota, that is $163,246 - 139,967 = 23,279$.

Table 1:5. 1994 European Parliament election, Northern Ireland

Electorate	Valid votes
1,150,304	559,867

No. of seats	Quota
3	559,867÷(3+1) = 139,967

Candidate	Party	First preference votes	Elected at stage
Anderson, J.	NLP	1,418	
Boal, M. Ms.	Con	5,583	
Campion, J. Ms.	Peace	1,088	
Clark-Glass, M. Ms.	AP	23,157	
Cusack, N.	Ind Lab	2,464	
Hartley, T.	SF	21,273	
Hume, J.*	**SDLP**	**161,992**	**First**
Kennedy, M.	NLP	419	
Kerr, D.	Ind Ulster	571	
Lowry, J.	WP	2,543	
McGuinness, D. Ms.	SF	17,195	
Molloy, F.	SF	16,747	
Mooney, R.	NI Ind	400	
Nicholson, J.*	**UUP**	**133,459**	**Second**
Paisley, I.*	**DUP**	**163,246**	**First**
Ross, H.	Ulster Ind	7,858	
Thompson, S. Ms.	NLP	454	

To do this all 163,246 first preference ballots cast for Paisley are examined again to determine the distribution of second preference votes among the other candidates. Hume's votes are ignored in this procedure because he has already been elected. However, because only the surplus votes are available for redistribution, the eligible candidates receive only 23,279÷163,246 = 0.1426 of an additional vote for each recorded second preference. It transpired that 112,778 of Paisley's supporters had cast a second preference for Nicholson who thus received 112,778 x 0.1426 = 16,082 extra votes. These, added to his own 133,459 first preference votes, were sufficient to put him over the quota and he too was deemed elected at the second stage.

This is a very straightforward example. If the transfer of Paisley's votes had been insufficient to elect the third and final MEP, then Hume's surplus would have been distributed in a similar way. If no one was elected at that stage, then the bottom candidate (Mooney) would have been eliminated and his votes re-distributed. Counting would continue through as many stages as necessary to ensure that a third candidate reached the quota.

With more seats to be filled and with more candidates attracting evenly spread votes the counting procedure for STV elections can prove very protracted. At the Northern Ireland Assembly elections in June 1998 counting in the Strangford constituency went through 18 stages before the required six of the total 22 candidates were deemed elected.

The European Parliament and past election results

Although this is the fifth set of direct elections to the European Parliament to have been held in the United Kingdom, only in Northern Ireland will it be possible to make direct comparisons between 1999 and past results. In the first place, of course, previous contests in the rest of the country elected MEPs within constituencies on the basis of the first past the post electoral system. However, even making the assumption that votes cast for individual candidates at those elections can be equated with votes cast for a party, a number of difficulties concerning geographical equivalance remain.

The electoral regions to be used in 1999 are based on the new government statistical regions established in 1997. Except in Scotland and Wales they are not compatible with the former standard regional units and are not built on neat aggregations of the European Parliament constituencies used in 1994. Moreover, those European constituencies were themselves based on Westminster parliament constituencies which were abolished before the 1997 general election. These various boundary changes mean that it is impossible simply to add up the actual votes cast in either the 1992 general election or the 1994 European election – let alone any earlier contest- and translate them into the new regional boundaries. Instead we have had to re-calculate their results to provide an estimate of what might have happened. Only for the 1997 general election can the votes cast for each party and candidate in the constituencies be summed to the regional level.

Our calculations for the 1992 general election involved taking our previously published notional results for the new parliamentary constituencies and aggregating them into the government statistical regions. For the 1994 European elections the procedure was less straightforward because some of the pre-existing European constituencies are now divided between more than one electoral region. For example, the bulk of the electorate of the Bedfordshire and Milton Keynes constituency is in the Eastern region with a minority in the South East. Although it would have been easy simply to allocate the whole constituency to the region containing the majority of its electorate, this method has the potential seriously to distort the notional results. Equally, it would have been possible to add or subtract the votes cast in those parts of the former European constituencies that were being moved between regions on a proportional basis. With 26% of electors in Bedfordshire and Milton Keynes being moved into a different region, then 26% of each party's 1994 vote in that constituency could be moved as well. This too was unacceptable because the European constituencies were so large – typically eight Westminster constituencies – that there could be no guarantee that the electors being moved were a microcosm of the constituency as a whole.

More accurate, though still only capable of providing estimates, was the method adopted. This relies on identifying which Westminster constituencies or parts are being moved and calculating the required exchange of votes between regions on that basis. In the case of Bedfordshire and Milton Keynes we calculated the proportion of each party's total vote in the European constituency contributed by the two Milton Keynes parliamentary constituencies at the 1997 general election and made the assumption that the proportions would have been the same in 1994 too. The 1994 raw vote figures were then adjusted on this basis to allow the results to be aggregated to the new regional boundaries. The principle of this calculation remains the same, although the implementation becomes more difficult, where any of the Westminster constituencies affected were themselves subject to extensive boundary changes between 1992 and 1997.

On the basis of this methodology the following pages describe and map the composition of each European Parliament electoral region and indicate what the results of party list European Parliament elections might have been if they had taken place in 1992, 1994 and 1997.

East Midlands Electoral Region

1997 parliamentary electorate
3,134,378

% of G.B. electorate
7.3

No. of European Parliament seats
6

% of G.B. European Parliament seats
7.1

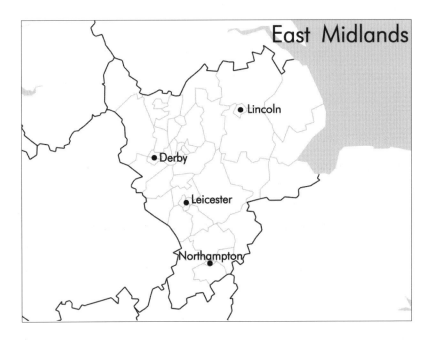

Comprising the 44 parliamentary constituencies in the counties of Derbyshire, Leicestershire, Lincolnshire, Northamptonshire and Nottinghamshire together with the unitary authorities of Derby, Leicester, Nottingham and Rutland. At the 1997 general election Labour won 30 seats and the Conservatives 14.

The East Midlands displays a pattern of political behaviour not dissimilar to that of England as a whole. The Conservatives comfortably 'won' the region in 1992 only for Labour to sweep into a commanding lead in 1997. The swing from Conservative to Labour between 1992–97 was 11% compared to a national average of 10.7%. It has been one of the Liberal Democrats' weaker regions; their best performance being 15.3% in 1992.

Under the party list system of election the Conservatives and Labour look certain to win two seats each. The remaining two seats will be determined by whichever party wins the popular vote in the region and/or the showing of the Liberal Democrats.

Votes and seats based on the 1992 general election

	Con	Lab	LD	Others
Votes	1,149,514	922,399	376,610	18,037
% share of vote	46.6	37.4	15.3	0.7
Seats on FPTP basis	5	1	0	0
Seats under list PR	**3**	**2**	**1**	**0**
% share of seats	50.0	33.3	16.7	0.0

Votes and seats based on 1994 European election

	Con	Lab	LD	Green	Others
Votes	311,479	503,695	135,567	41,950	29,657
% share of vote	30.5	49.3	13.3	4.1	2.9
Seats on FPTP basis	0	6	0	0	0
Seats under list PR	**2**	**3**	**1**	**0**	**0**
% share of seats	33.3	50.0	16.7	0.0	0.0

Votes and seats based on the 1997 general election

	Con	Lab	LD	Ref	Others
Votes	800,958	1,097,639	311,264	64,209	20,680
% share of vote	34.9	47.8	13.6	2.8	0.9
Seats on FPTP basis	0	6	0	0	0
Seats under list PR	**2**	**3**	**1**	**0**	**0**
% share of seats	33.3	50.0	16.7	0.0	0.0

Eastern Electoral Region

1997 parliamentary electorate
3,970,199

% of G.B. electorate
9.3

No. of European Parliament seats
8

% of G.B. European Parliament seats
9.5

Comprising the 56 parliamentary constituencies in the counties of Bedfordshire, Cambridgeshire, Essex, Hertfordshire, Norfolk and Suffolk together with the unitary authorities of Luton, Peterborough, Southend-on-Sea and Thurrock. At the 1997 general election the Conservatives won 33 seats, Labour 22 and the Liberal Democrats one.

The Eastern region – a considerable expansion of the old standard region of East Anglia – was one of only three regions in England where the Conservatives polled a majority of votes in 1992, and one of only two in which the party enjoyed a plurality in 1997. However, the swing from Conservative to Labour between 1992-97 was in excess of 12.5% and the Conservatives won more seats than their share of the vote 'entitled' them. The Liberal Democrats' 1997 success was in Colchester where they emerged ahead of their opponents in a tight 3-way contest.

Under the party list system of election the Conservatives and Labour are certain to win two and probably three seats each, and the Liberal Democrats will win one. The final seat will go to the major party which wins the most votes in the region.

Votes and seats based on the 1992 general election

	Con	Lab	LD	Others
Votes	1,636,990	823,743	618,106	38,503
% share of vote	52.5	26.4	19.8	1.2
Seats on FPTP basis	8	0	0	0
Seats under list PR	**5**	**2**	**1**	**0**
% share of seats	62.5	25.0	12.5	0.0

Votes and seats based on 1994 European election

	Con	Lab	LD	Green	Others
Votes	506,224	596,311	286,402	51,398	61,299
% share of vote	33.7	39.7	19.1	3.4	4.1
Seats on FPTP basis	2	6	0	0	0
Seats under list PR	**3**	**4**	**1**	**0**	**0**
% share of seats	37.5	50.0	12.5	0.0	0.0

Votes and seats based on the 1997 general election

	Con	Lab	LD	Ref	Others
Votes	1,164,777	1,137,637	504,416	98,739	41,598
% share of vote	39.5	38.6	17.1	3.4	1.4
Seats on FPTP basis	4	4	0	0	0
Seats under list PR	**4**	**3**	**1**	**0**	**0**
% share of seats	50.0	37.5	12.5	0.0	0.0

London Electoral Region

1997 parliamentary electorate
4,910,637

% of G.B. electorate
11.5

No. of European Parliament seats
10

% of G.B. European Parliament seats
11.9

Comprising the 74 parliamentary constituencies in the administrative area of Greater London. At the 1997 general election Labour won 57 seats, the Conservatives 11 and the Liberal Democrats six. There was a swing from the Conservatives to Labour in excess of 13% in London in 1997 which saw the party's parliamentary representation drop from 41 to just 11. That sort of result had already been foreshadowed in the 1994 European Parliament elections when Labour polled a majority of the votes cast, with the Conservatives managing fewer than 30%. The Liberal Democrats won six seats in the capital in 1997 – up from just one at the previous general election – despite winning a lower share of the vote.

Previous patterns of national party support suggest that Labour and the Conservatives will win nine of the ten seats in London. On current evidence these would split 5–4 or even 6–3 in favour of Labour. However, in the 1998 borough elections the Liberal Democrats polled 21% – enough to win two European Parliament seats. It is very unlikely that any minor party grouping will do sufficiently well to pass the effective 9% threshold and thereby win a seat.

Votes and seats based on the 1992 general election

	Con	Lab	LD	Others
Votes	1,630,569	1,332,456	572,432	60,747
% share of vote	45.3	37.1	15.9	1.7
Seats on FPTP basis	7	3	0	0
Seats under list PR	**5**	**4**	**1**	**0**
% share of seats	50.0	40.0	10.0	0.0

Votes and seats based on 1994 European election

	Con	Lab	LD	Green	Others
Votes	469,859	816,709	189,604	58,930	63,434
% share of vote	29.4	51.1	11.9	3.7	4.0
Seats on FPTP basis	1	9	0	0	0
Seats under list PR	**3**	**6**	**1**	**0**	**0**
% share of seats	30.0	60.0	10.0	0.0	0.0

Votes and seats based on the 1997 general election

	Con	Lab	LD	Ref	Others
Votes	1,036,082	1,643,329	485,511	68,923	87,203
% share of vote	31.2	49.5	14.6	2.1	2.6
Seats on FPTP basis	2	8	0	0	0
Seats under list PR	**3**	**6**	**1**	**0**	**0**
% share of seats	30.0	60.0	10.0	0.0	0.0

North East Electoral Region

1997 parliamentary electorate
1,964,407

% of G.B. electorate
4.6

No. of European Parliament seats
4

% of G.B. European Parliament seats
4.8

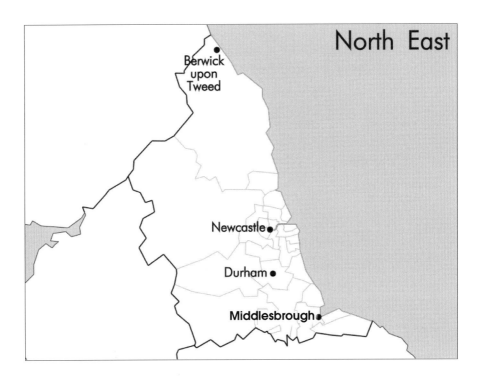

Comprising the 30 parliamentary constituencies in the counties of Durham, Northumberland and Tyne and Wear together with the unitary authorities of Darlington, Hartlepool, Middlesbrough, Redcar and Cleveland, and Stockton-on-Tees. At the 1997 general election Labour won 28 seats, the Conservatives one and the Liberal Democrats one. The North East region is Labour's strongest electoral fiefdom in the U.K. It was the only region where the party polled a majority of votes in 1992. In 1997 Labour's share of the vote (64%) was almost 10% above that anywhere else. At that election the Conservatives held on to their single constituency (Hexham) by just 222 votes. The Liberal Democrat constituency (Berwick-upon-Tweed) is rather safer with an 8,000 majority.

Labour looks certain to have three MEPs elected from the North East region and could even take all four seats if the votes of the opposition parties were evenly split. However past evidence suggests that the candidate in first place on the Conservative list will scrape home.

Votes and seats based on the 1992 general election

	Con	Lab	LD	Others
Votes	461,767	801,311	232,150	6,402
% share of vote	30.8	53.4	15.5	0.4
Seats on FPTP basis	0	4	0	0
Seats under list PR	**1**	**3**	**0**	**0**
% share of seats	25.0	75.0	0.0	0.0

Votes and seats based on 1994 European election

	Con	Lab	LD	Green	Others
Votes	115,480	446,169	65,197	17,907	14,486
% share of vote	17.5	67.7	9.9	2.7	2.2
Seats on FPTP basis	0	4	0	0	0
Seats under list PR	**1**	**3**	**0**	**0**	**0**
% share of seats	25.0	75.0	0.0	0.0	0.0

Votes and seats based on the 1997 general election

	Con	Lab	LD	Ref	Others
Votes	266,294	862,262	169,270	37,525	11,239
% share of vote	19.8	64.0	12.6	2.8	0.8
Seats on FPTP basis	0	4	0	0	0
Seats under list PR	**1**	**3**	**0**	**0**	**0**
% share of seats	25.0	75.0	0.0	0.0	0.0

North West Electoral Region

1997 parliamentary electorate
5,166,295

% of G.B. electorate
12.1

No. of European Parliament seats
10

% of G.B. European Parliament seats
11.9

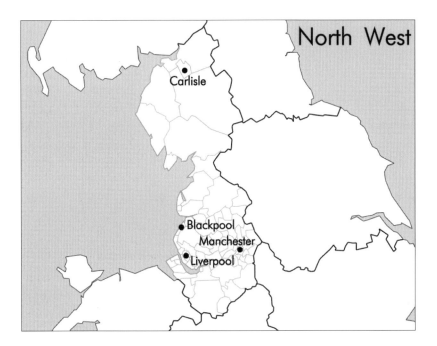

Comprising the 76 parliamentary constituencies in the counties of Cheshire, Cumbria, Greater Manchester, Lancashire, and Merseyside together with the unitary authorities of Blackburn, Blackpool, Halton and Warrington. At the 1997 general election Labour won 64 seats, the Conservatives nine and the Liberal Democrats two. In addition Martin Bell won Tatton as an Independent.

The North West is one of the three English regions where Labour polled a plurality of votes even in 1992. Although the swing to Labour in 1997 was slightly below the national average it could not save the Conservatives from losing 19 seats. The Liberal Democrats have some support based on local government success, but this is not one of their strongest regions.

Labour's solid core of support will ensure that the party wins at least four and probably five of the North West's ten European Parliament seats. The Conservatives will certainly pick up three of the others and the Liberal Democrats one. The remaining seat could be the prize for either the Conservatives or the Liberal Democrats managing sharply to improve their recent electoral performances in the region.

Votes and seats based on the 1992 general election

	Con	*Lab*	*LD*	*Others*
Votes	1,541,918	1,771,004	632,386	58,003
% share of vote	38.5	44.2	15.8	1.4
Seats on FPTP basis	4	6	0	0
Seats under list PR	**4**	**5**	**1**	**0**
% share of seats	40.0	50.0	10.0	0.0

Votes and seats based on 1994 European election

	Con	*Lab*	*LD*	*Green*	*Others*
Votes	441,362	885,931	199,750	46,566	47,906
% share of vote	27.2	54.6	12.3	2.9	3.0
Seats on FPTP basis	0	10	0	0	0
Seats under list PR	**3**	**6**	**1**	**0**	**0**
% share of seats	30.0	60.0	10.0	0.0	0.0

Votes and seats based on the 1997 general election

	Con	*Lab*	*LD*	*Ref*	*Others*
Votes	1,000,556	1,941,884	524,177	87,487	71,401
% share of vote	27.6	53.6	14.5	2.4	2.0
Seats on FPTP basis	0	10	0	0	0
Seats under list PR	**3**	**6**	**1**	**0**	**0**
% share of seats	30.0	60.0	10.0	0.0	0.0

South East Electoral Region

1997 parliamentary electorate
5,904,091

% of G.B. electorate
13.8

No. of European Parliament seats
11

% of G.B. European Parliament seats
13.1

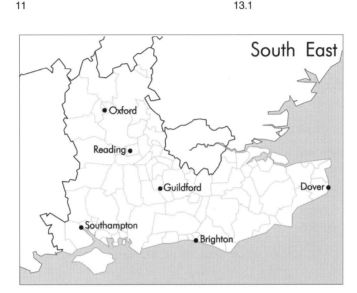

Comprising the 83 parliamentary constituencies in the counties of Buckinghamshire, East Sussex, Hampshire, Kent, Oxfordshire, Surrey and West Sussex togther with the unitary authorities of Bracknell Forest, Brighton and Hove, Isle of Wight, Medway Towns, Milton Keynes, Portsmouth, Reading, Slough, Southampton, West Berkshire, Windsor and Maidenhead, and Wokingham. At the 1997 general election the Conservatives won 54 seats, Labour 22 and the Liberal Democrats seven.

The Conservative vote in the South East region declined by 13 percentage points between 1992 and 1997 to less than 42%. In only eight individual constituencies, in this their strongest region, did they poll more than half the votes cast. Nevertheless they still managed to win two-thirds of the seats because the main beneficiary of their decline was the previously third-placed Labour party. The Liberal Democrats, as elsewhere, won a number of carefully targeted seats even though their overall share of the vote was lower than in either 1992 or 1994.

The South East is the largest European electoral region and has 11 seats. The Conservatives took nine of them in 1994 and would have won all 11 at the 1997 general election. The region will therefore provide a rare example, in the current electoral climate, of the Conservatives 'losing' seats through the exercise of proportionality. The most likely outcome is that the Conservatives will win five, with Labour and the Liberal Democrats securing three each. Minor parties need a lower share of the vote here than in any other region to gain a seat, so keep an eye on the Greens.

Votes and seats based on the 1992 general election

	Con	Lab	LD	Others
Votes	2,517,270	865,796	1,131,899	68,029
% share of vote	54.9	18.9	24.7	1.5
Seats on FPTP basis	11	0	0	0
Seats under list PR	**6**	**2**	**3**	**0**
% share of seats	54.5	18.2	27.3	0.0

Votes and seats based on 1994 European election

	Con	Lab	LD	Green	Others
Votes	829,037	598,915	586,515	83,251	121,405
% share of vote	37.4	27.0	26.4	3.8	5.5
Seats on FPTP basis	9	2	0	0	0
Seats under list PR	**5**	**3**	**3**	**0**	**0**
% share of seats	45.5	27.3	27.3	0.0	0.0

Votes and seats based on the 1997 general election

	Con	Lab	LD	Ref	Others
Votes	1,817,343	1,264,778	1,012,418	156,622	90,447
% share of vote	41.9	29.1	23.3	3.6	2.1
Seats on FPTP basis	11	0	0	0	0
Seats under list PR	**5**	**3**	**3**	**0**	**0**
% share of seats	45.5	27.3	27.3	0.0	0.0

South West Electoral Region

1997 parliamentary electorate
3,705,918

% of G.B. electorate
8.7

No. of European Parliament seats
7

% of G.B. European Parliament seats
8.3

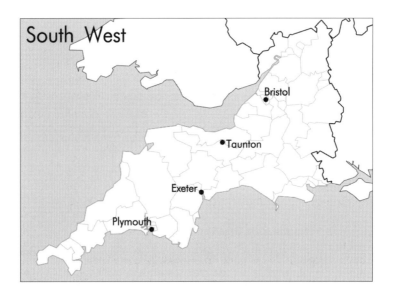

Comprising the 51 parliamentary constituencies in the counties of Cornwall, Devon, Dorset, Gloucestershire, Somerset and Wiltshire together with the unitary authorities of Bath and North East Somerset, Bournemouth, Bristol, North Somerset, Plymouth, Poole, South Gloucestershire, Torbay, Swindon and the Isles of Scilly. At the 1997 general election the Conservatives won 22 seats, Labour 15 and the Liberal Democrats 14.

The South West has developed its own style of party competition. Here Labour came third in the popular vote in 1992, 1994 and 1997, with the challenge to the Tories coming from the Liberal Democrats. Of course Labour has its own urban strongholds, but outside the cities the party often plays a minor role. The swing from Conservative to Labour at the 1997 general election was below average at 9%. The Liberal Democrats 'broke through' in the region by winning their first ever European Parliament seats, despite the handicap of the electoral system, in 1994. When the European votes are aggregated across the region it seems likely that all 3 parties – Conservatives, Labour and Liberal Democrats – will have secured sufficient, evenly distributed support for them each to claim two seats. The real battle in the South West is for the seventh seat which will almost certainly be won by the party topping the poll. The Conservatives did so in both 1992 and 1997, but they were pipped by the Liberal Democrats in 1994. Significantly the feat eluded Labour even at the time of Blair's landslide triumph.

Votes and seats based on the 1992 general election

	Con	Lab	LD	Others
Votes	1,388,330	561,917	916,955	52,199
% share of vote	47.6	19.2	31.4	1.8
Seats on FPTP basis	7	0	0	0
Seats under list PR	**4**	**1**	**2**	**0**
% share of seats	57.1	14.3	28.6	0.0

Votes and seats based on 1994 European election

	Con	Lab	LD	Green	Others
Votes	513,533	362,211	517,329	58,708	106,917
% share of vote	32.9	23.2	33.2	3.8	6.9
Seats on FPTP basis	4	1	2	0	0
Seats under list PR	**2**	**2**	**3**	**0**	**0**
% share of seats	28.6	28.6	42.9	0.0	0.0

Votes and seats based on the 1997 general election

	Con	Lab	LD	Ref	Others
Votes	1,020,635	734,361	869,486	91,134	62,430
% share of vote	36.7	26.4	31.3	3.3	2.2
Seats on FPTP basis	4	1	2	0	0
Seats under list PR	**3**	**2**	**2**	**0**	**0**
% share of seats	42.9	28.6	28.6	0.0	0.0

West Midlands Electoral Region

1997 parliamentary electorate
3,986,137

% of G.B. electorate
9.3

No. of European Parliament seats
8

% of G.B. European Parliament seats
9.5

Comprising the 59 parliamentary constituencies in the counties of Staffordshire, Shropshire, Warwickshire, West Midlands and Worcestershire together with the unitary authorities of Herefordshire, Stoke-on-Trent and Telford & the Wrekin. At the 1997 general election Labour won 43 seats, the Conservatives 14 and the Liberal Democrats one. In addition the Speaker was re-elected in West Bromwich West following a challenge only by minor party candidates.

The West Midlands region has often been seen as England's electoral cockpit. It encompasses important industrial and manufacturing centres, affluent and leafy suburbs, and unspoilt rural acres. Labour and the Conservatives, at least, have reliable areas of strength, but the voters also swing with the national mood. The Conservatives lost 17 seats – more than half their previous total – in 1997. The Liberal Democrats come a poor third in most constituencies.

The Conservatives would have won only two list seats in the West Midlands based on the 1994 European Parliament election results, but they will hope not to do as badly again. They should win at least three with the Liberal Democrats securing one. Labour seems guaranteed three and is likely to pick up the final seat as well.

Votes and seats based on the 1992 general election

	Con	Lab	LD	Others
Votes	1,390,246	1,203,349	466,226	45,124
% share of vote	44.8	38.8	15.0	1.5
Seats on FPTP basis	5	3	0	0
Seats under list PR	**4**	**3**	**1**	**0**
% share of seats	50.0	37.5	12.5	0.0

Votes and seats based on 1994 European election

	Con	Lab	LD	Green	Others
Votes	425,650	732,002	205,862	48,845	53,047
% share of vote	29.0	50.0	14.0	3.3	3.6
Seats on FPTP basis	1	7	0	0	0
Seats under list PR	**2**	**5**	**1**	**0**	**0**
% share of seats	25.0	62.5	12.5	0.0	0.0

Votes and seats based on the 1997 general election

	Con	Lab	LD	Ref	Others
Votes	953,465	1,326,822	388,807	69,626	87,105
% share of vote	33.7	47.0	13.8	2.5	3.1
Seats on FPTP basis	2	6	0	0	0
Seats under list PR	**3**	**4**	**1**	**0**	**0**
% share of seats	37.5	50.0	12.5	0.0	0.0

Yorkshire and the Humber Electoral Region

1997 parliamentary electorate
3,774,441

% of G.B. electorate
8.8

No. of European Parliament seats
7

% of G.B. European Parliament seats
8.3

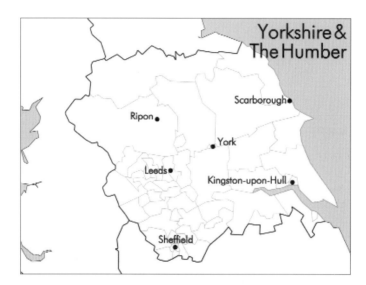

Comprising the 56 parliamentary constituencies in the counties of North Yorkshire, South Yorkshire and West Yorkshire together with the unitary authorities of Kingston upon Hull, East Riding of Yorkshire, North East Lincolnshire, North Lincolnshire and York. At the 1997 general election Labour won 47 seats, the Conservatives seven and the Liberal Democrats two.

Labour won more than three-quarters of the seats in the Yorkshire and the Humber region in 1997 with less than 52% of the vote. The Conservative vote at that election declined by less than 10 percentage points compared with 1992 – the party's 'best' performance in England. Support for the Liberal Democrats was almost unchanged, but they did manage to gain two seats from the Conservatives. In both of them (Harrogate and Knaresborough, and Sheffield Hallam) their success, unusually, was boosted by a decline in the Labour vote.

Labour looks certain to win at least three of the seven seats in Yorkshire and the Humber. The minimum Conservative return will be two and the Liberal Democrats should poll well enough to guarantee a single seat. The final seat allocation will depend on how far Labour, which will have the largest number of votes, is ahead of the Conservatives.

Votes and seats based on the 1992 general election

	Con	Lab	LD	Others
Votes	1,080,168	1,269,935	480,128	25,888
% share of vote	37.8	44.5	16.8	0.9
Seats on FPTP basis	2	5	0	0
Seats under list PR	**3**	**3**	**1**	**0**
% share of seats	42.9	42.9	14.3	0.0

Votes and seats based on 1994 European election

	Con	Lab	LD	Green	Others
Votes	300,924	645,234	181,425	44,280	28,387
% share of vote	25.1	53.8	15.1	3.7	2.4
Seats on FPTP basis	1	6	0	0	0
Seats under list PR	**2**	**4**	**1**	**0**	**0**
% share of seats	28.6	57.1	14.3	0.0	0.0

Votes and seats based on the 1997 general election

	Con	Lab	LD	Ref	Others
Votes	720,771	1,339,170	412,216	72,359	33,657
% share of vote	28.0	51.9	16.0	2.8	1.3
Seats on FPTP basis	1	6	0	0	0
Seats under list PR	**2**	**4**	**1**	**0**	**0**
% share of seats	28.6	57.1	14.3	0.0	0.0

Scotland Electoral Region

1997 parliamentary electorate
3,949,112

% of G.B. electorate
9.3

No. of European Parliament seats
8

% of G.B. European Parliament seats
9.5

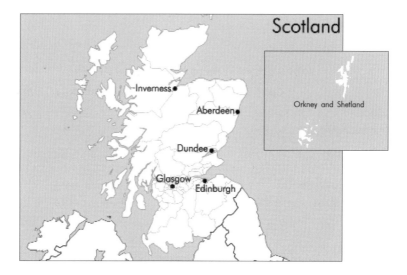

Comprising the 72 parliamentary constituencies in Scotland. At the 1997 general election Labour won 56 seats, the Liberal Democrats 10 and the Scottish National Party six.

Labour has reaped considerable advantage over the years from the operation of first past the post in Scotland. Perhaps surprisingly the party has never polled 50% of the vote (the Conservatives did manage to do so in 1955!), but has regularly taken more than half the seats. In 1997 a 45% share of the vote yielded three quarters of the total seats. The Conservatives, by contrast, have seen their decline in support in Scotland exaggerated by the operation of the electoral system. The Liberal Democrats in Scotland have tended to receive a 'fair' return for a modest national vote thanks to the concentration of their support in rural areas, while the SNP have suffered from having a more even spread of support.

Scotland forms a single region for the European Parliament elections, meaning that votes across the country will be totalled before the eight seats are allocated. The election will be held five weeks after the Scottish Parliament contests and what happened then will have an important impact on these results. The electoral procedure is likely to guarantee the Conservatives at least one seat, although the Liberal Democrats may not be so lucky. Labour seems certain to win three and the SNP two, but the SNP's performance at the equivalent elections in 1994 gives some idea of the party's potential under the right electoral circumstances.

Votes and seats based on the 1992 general election

	Con	Lab	LD	SNP	Others
Votes	751,950	1,142,911	383,856	629,564	23,417
% share of vote	25.6	39.0	13.1	21.5	0.8
Seats on FPTP basis	1	6	1	0	0
Seats under list PR	**2**	**3**	**1**	**2**	**0**
% share of seats	25.0	37.5	12.5	25.0	0.0

Votes and seats based on 1994 European election

	Con	Lab	LD	SNP	Green	Others
Votes	216,669	635,955	107,811	487,237	23,314	24,911
% share of vote	14.5	42.5	7.2	32.6	1.6	1.7
Seats on FPTP basis	0	6	0	2	0	0
Seats under list PR	**1**	**4**	**0**	**3**	**0**	**0**
% share of seats	12.5	50.0	0.0	37.5	0.0	0.0

Votes and seats based on the 1997 general election

	Con	Lab	LD	SNP	Ref	Others
Votes	493,059	1,283,350	365,362	621,550	26,980	26,447
% share of vote	17.5	45.6	13.0	22.1	1.0	0.9
Seats on FPTP basis	0	7	1	0	0	0
Seats under list PR	**1**	**4**	**1**	**2**	**0**	**0**
% share of seats	12.5	50.0	12.5	25.0	0.0	0.0

Wales Electoral Region

1997 parliamentary electorate
2,203,059

% of G.B. electorate
5.2

No. of European Parliament seats
5

% of G.B. European Parliament seats
6.0

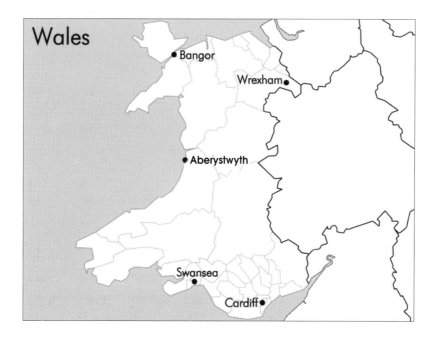

Comprising the 40 parliamentary constituencies in Wales. At the 1997 general election Labour won 34 seats, Plaid Cymru four and the Liberal Democrats two.

Wales, like Scotland, tends to produce results which disproportionally favour Labour, albeit that the party regularly receives in excess of 50% of the vote here. The Conservatives, by contrast, got no seats in 1997 despite polling almost 20% of the vote. Plaid Cymru, with its support concentrated in the Welsh-speaking north and west, picked up one in ten of both the votes and the seats, whereas the Liberal Democrats won just two seats despite a larger share of the vote.

The proportional system to be used for the European Parliament elections will correct the worst of these anomalies. However, as Wales is only electing five MEPs, the second smallest regional allocation, each individual party will require a share of the vote well into double figures to secure a seat. The Liberal Democrats look to be in particular danger of losing out. The likeliest outcome is a repeat of what the result would have been at the equivalent elections in 1994 if the list system had then been in place – three seats for Labour and one each for the Conservatives and Plaid Cymru.

Votes and seats based on the 1992 general election

	Con	Lab	LD	PC	Others
Votes	499,677	865,663	217,457	154,947	11,033
% share of vote	28.6	49.5	12.4	8.9	0.6
Seats on FPTP basis	0	5	0	0	0
Seats under list PR	**2**	**3**	**0**	**0**	**0**
% share of seats	40.0	60.0	0.0	0.0	0.0

Votes and seats based on 1994 European election

	Con	Lab	LD	PC	Green	Others
Votes	138,323	530,749	82,426	162,478	19,413	16,689
% share of vote	14.6	55.9	8.7	17.1	2.0	1.8
Seats on FPTP basis	0	5	0	0	0	0
Seats under list PR	**1**	**3**	**0**	**1**	**0**	**0**
% share of seats	20.0	60.0	0.0	20.0	0.0	0.0

Votes and seats based on the 1997 general election

	Con	Lab	LD	PC	Ref	Others
Votes	317,145	886,935	200,020	161,030	38,245	16,687
% share of vote	19.6	54.7	12.3	9.9	2.4	1.0
Seats on FPTP basis	0	5	0	0	0	0
Seats under list PR	**1**	**4**	**0**	**0**	**0**	**0**
% share of seats	20.0	80.0	0.0	0.0	0.0	0.0

England – summary of regional data

1997 parliamentary electorate
36,516,503

% of G.B. electorate
85.6

No. of European Parliament seats
71

% of G.B. European Parliament seats
84.5

Votes and seats based on the 1992 general election

	Con	Lab	LD	Others
Votes	12,796,772	9,551,910	5,426,892	372,932
% share of vote	45.5	33.9	19.3	1.3
Seats on FPTP basis	49	22	0	0
Seats under list PR	**35**	**25**	**11**	**0**
% share of seats	49.3	35.2	15.5	0.0

Votes and seats based on 1994 European election

	Con	Lab	LD	Green	Others
Votes	3,913,547	5,587,177	2,367,650	451,834	526,539
% share of vote	30.5	43.5	18.4	3.5	4.1
Seats on FPTP basis	18	51	2	0	0
Seats under list PR	**23**	**36**	**12**	**0**	**0**
% share of seats	32.4	50.7	16.9	0.0	0.0

Votes and seats based on the 1997 general election

	Con	Lab	LD	Ref	Others
Votes	8,780,881	11,347,882	4,677,565	746,624	505,760
% share of vote	33.7	43.5	18.0	2.9	1.9
Seats on FPTP basis	24	45	2	0	0
Seats under list PR	**26**	**34**	**11**	**0**	**0**
% share of seats	36.6	47.8	15.5	0.0	0.0

Great Britain

1997 parliamentary electorate
     42,668,674

Votes and seats based on the 1992 general election

	Con	Lab	LD	Nat	Others
Votes	14,048,399	11,560,484	6,028,205	784,511	407,382
% share of vote	42.8	35.2	18.4	2.4	1.2
Seats on FPTP basis	50	33	1	0	0
Seats under list PR	**39**	**31**	**12**	**2**	**0**
% share of seats	46.4	36.9	14.3	2.4	0.0

Votes and seats based on 1994 European election

	Con	Lab	LD	Nat	Green	Others
Votes	4,268,539	6,753,881	2,557,887	649,715	494,561	568,139
% share of vote	27.9	44.2	16.7	4.2	3.2	3.7
Seats on FPTP basis	18	62	2	2	0	0
Seats under list PR	**25**	**43**	**12**	**4**	**0**	**0**
% share of seats	29.8	51.2	14.3	4.8	0.0	0.0

Votes and seats based on the 1997 general election

	Con	Lab	LD	Nat	Ref	Others
Votes	9,591,085	13,518,167	5,242,947	782,580	811,849	548,894
% share of vote	31.5	44.3	17.2	2.6	2.7	1.8
Seats on FPTP basis	24	57	3	0	0	0
Seats under list PR	**28**	**42**	**12**	**2**	**0**	**0**
% share of seats	33.3	50.0	14.3	2.4	0.0	0.0

Northern Ireland Electoral Region

1997 parliamentary electorate
    1,177,969

No. of European Parliament seats
    3

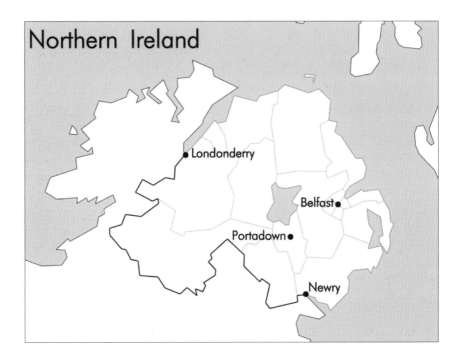

The Single Transferable Vote has been used to elect Northern Ireland's three MEPs since the first direct elections in 1979. On all four occasions the outcome has, broadly speaking, been the same. The DUP candidate, Ian Paisley, has topped the poll and been elected on the first count. The SDLP and Ulster Unionist candidates have also always been successful. Nonetheless subtle changes can be detected. In 1989 and 1994 the SDLP's John Hume was himself elected on the first count having secured more first preference votes than required by the quota. In 1994 Hume was only 1,254 first preference votes behind Paisley, compared with a gap of almost 24,000 votes in 1989. In the 1997 general election Paisley polled fewer than 50% of the vote in his Antrim North constituency for the first time since 1970. In the 1998 Northern Ireland Assembly elections the SDLP polled more votes than any other single party – the first time a nationalist party has achieved that feat. Northern Ireland is still likely to send one DUP, one SDLP and one UUP representative to Strasbourg following the 1999 elections, but there could be a new ranking in the popular vote.

The result of the 1994 European Parliament election in Northern Ireland can be found in Table 1.5.

The Likely Outcome?

The new electoral system will produce a much more proportional outcome in terms of the relationship between seats and votes. Any gross imbalance in individual regions caused by the few number of seats being filled is likely to be mitigated over the country as a whole. Nonetheless the method being used to determine which candidates are elected is one which tends to favour the larger parties and we would expect Labour and the Conservatives still to obtain more seats than their share of the vote strictly justifies. Indeed our notional results for both 1994 and 1997 show that Labour would probably have won half of all European parliament seats in Great Britain despite only polling 44% of the vote. This is, however, a considerable contrast with what actually happened in 1994 when Labour won 62 seats (73.8% of the total) and all the other parties were 'under-represented'.

Labour is certain to lose seats and the Conservatives and Liberal Democrats very likely to gain them almost regardless of the result of these inaugural party list elections. This is a consequence of the change of system and will not necessarily reflect changes in party fortunes since 1994. Commentators will therefore have a duty to use the correct benchmarks when judging each party's performance. The only true comparison with what happened four years ago is the share of the vote in each region, together with our estimates of how many seats each party would have won if the new system had then been in use – see Tables. On this basis Labour is defending 43 seats rather than 62; the Conservatives 25 (18); the Liberal Democrats 12 (2); the SNP three (2) and Plaid Cymru one (0).

There will also be a need for caution in interpreting how far the results have relevance for party competition in national elections. Previous European Parliament elections have produced sizeable, if ultimately transient shifts in political support. The reason for this is two fold. First, many voters no longer have a settled party preference and make their choice on the basis of issues which they believe are of particular relevance in the election being fought. Second, elections such as those to the European Parliament are not seen as being crucial to how the country is governed – they are second-order elections – and in those circumstances more people are prepared to cast an expressive rather than instrumental vote. The success of the Greens in polling almost 15% of the vote in 1989, only to fall away to less than 1% at the general election three years later is a clear example of this tendency. It is, of course, a moot point as to whether the adoption of a party list system will make such behaviour more or less likely.

Table 1.6: Votes for Europe

Overall result based on 1992 general election

	Con	Lab	LD	Nat	Others
% share of vote	42.8	35.2	18.4	2.4	1.2
Seats under list PR	39	31	12	2	0

Overall result based on 1994 European election

	Con	Lab	LD	Nat	Green	Others
% share of vote	27.9	44.2	16.7	4.2	3.2	3.7
Seats under list PR	25	43	12	4	0	0

Overall result based on the 1997 general election

	Con	Lab	LD	Nat	Ref	Others
% share of vote	31.5	44.3	17.2	2.6	2.7	1.8
Seats under list PR	28	42	12	2	0	0

Recent evidence about the popularity of the political parties is rather contradictory. According to the opinion polls Labour has considerably stretched its lead since the 1997 general election, with both the Conservatives and the Liberal Democrats falling back. If such results were repeated at the European Parliament elections Labour would 'gain' seats compared with 1994.

Table 1.7: Voting Intentions in Recent Opinion Polls

Fieldwork	Company	Sample	Con	Lab	LD	Others	Lab lead
Oct 1-4	ICM	1,120	29	51	15	5	24
Oct 23-26	MORI	1,775	26	53	16	5	27
Oct 29-Nov 4	Gallup	1,036	28	54	14	5	26
Nov 6-7	ICM	1,222	27	51	17	5	24
Nov 20-23	MORI	1,883	29	53	13	5	24
Nov 26-Dec 2	Gallup	1,021	29	55	11	5	26
Dec 4-7	ICM	1,123	29	49	16	6	20
Dec 11-14	MORI	1,864	27	54	12	7	27
Dec 30-Jan 3	ICM	1,209	30	50	15	5	20
Jan 4-6	Gallup	1,017	29	52	13	5	23
Jan 22-25	MORI	1,930	24	56	14	6	32
Jan 28-Feb 3	Gallup	1,069	29	53	13	5	24
Feb 5-7	ICM	1,211	28	49	16	6	21

However, the results in local elections and in the November 1998 North East Scotland European Parliament by-election paint a rather different picture. In local government Labour has been losing ground compared with the general election. In both the annual May 1998 contests and in recent by-elections it has appeared that Labour's support has fallen below the 40% level. The main beneficiary, as often in local elections, has been the Liberal Democrats. In North East Scotland Labour lost almost a third of its vote compared with the previous time the seat was contested in 1994, with the SNP increasing its majority. Although boundary changes make exact comparisons difficult, it seems that Labour support in the area has dropped by a similar amount since the 1997 general election. On the basis of these indicators Labour will 'lose' seats compared with 1994.

Table 1.8: National equivalent vote share in local elections

	Con	Lab	LD
Annual elections May 1998	33	39	23
By-elections, Oct-Dec 1998	34	37	23

Table 1.9: North East Scotland European Parliament By-election, 26 November 1998

	%share of vote	%change on 1994 election
SNP	48.0	+5.3
Con	19.9	+1.3
Lab	18.5	-9.9
LD	9.8	+1.5
SSA	2.1	+1.8
Green	1.7	+0.6

Whatever the actual result on June 10, the regional list system will bring an end to the era of electoral deserts. Instead, each region is almost guaranteed to have representation from each of the major parties. In 1994, under first past the post, 3 English regions together with Wales elected only Labour MEPs and in 3 more only one non-Labour candidate topped the poll. A re-working of those results on the basis of the new system shows that Labour and the Conservatives would have won seats everywhere, with the Liberal Democrats failing to secure representation only in the North East and in Scotland and Wales where the two nationalist parties would have been successful.

Such a pattern is also likely to prove more resistant to fluctuations in party political popularity. For example, the number of Euro-seats won by the Conservatives has varied from 60 (out of 78) in 1979 to 18 (out of 84) in 1994. Labour's high was 62 in 1994, its low 17 in 1979. However, if those two extreme elections had been fought on a regional list basis, Conservative representation would have been 42 in 1979 compared with 25 in 1994; Labour would have taken 28 seats in 1979 rising only to 43 seats in 1994. In future it will take very substantial shifts in support between the parties to produce wild variations in the number of seats they win. Stability rather than volatility is likely to characterise future British representation at the European Parliament.

A final, crucial factor affecting the fortunes of the political parties, and the subsequent democratic legitimacy of the European parliament, will be the level of turnout. In the four previous direct elections Britain's turnout has been among the lowest in the European Union, averaging just 34.2%. In fact participation in European elections has tended to be lower than in UK local elections and thereby lurks a new threat. The turnout at the 1998 local elections in England was the lowest for a quarter of a century with scarcely 3 in 10 electors bothering to go to the polls. If the European Parliament contests reflect that trend it is possible that fewer than 30% will be prepared to vote for their MEP. It is arguable that the new electoral system will make such an outcome more likely. With the ending of the link between individual candidates and identifiable geographic areas, with no opportunity to discriminate between candidates in a party's list, and with each vote having an infinitesimal impact on the final results, the rational voter may well decide to stay at home.

Table 1.10: Turnout in European Parliament elections, 1979-94

	1979	1984	1989	1994
England	31.8	31.6	35.8	35.5
Scotland	33.6	33.1	40.8	38.2
Wales	34.4	39.7	41.1	43.1
N. Ireland	55.6	64.4	48.3	48.7
Overall	32.7	32.9	36.5	36.3
EU average	63.0	61.0	58.5	56.8

Benchmarks for the 1999 European Parliament elections

Vote share   **Seats**

Labour

50%+	45+	Blair and Labour's popularity goes on growing. An extraordinary performance for a governing party.
45%-50%	42-45	More votes than at the 1997 general election. Could make one or two seat gains compared with the 1994 base.
40%-45%	38-42	Party just fails to match its 1994 and 1997 highs. Losses modest and sustainable for a mid-term government.
35%-40%	32-38	Labour looks less than omnipotent. Still the largest party, but a clear public shot across the bows to Blair.
Below 35%	<32	A performance no one in the party dare contemplate. Was the 1997 landslide so fragile after all?

Conservative

40%+	38+	A result to silence Hague's critics. The party won four general elections with this level of support.
35%-40%	30-38	A genuine step forward from the disaster of 1997. Perhaps the Tories are not destined to spend a generation out of power.
30%-35%	26-30	Only a little better than the Euro-election humiliation of 1994. Tory core support still stuck at 1997 general election levels.
25%-30%	<26	Probably the worst-ever electoral performance by a Tory opposition. A party completely out of touch with the public mood.

Liberal Democrat

20%+	16+	A real boost for Ashdown's successor. This level of support is only usually seen in local elections.
15%-20%	11-16	Only average for the party in national elections. Even so PR will produce a sizeable increase in Lib Dem MEPs.
10%-15%	<11	The party's worst result since the 1989 Euro contests. Is this a public verdict on too close Lib-Lab co-operation?

Nationalists

Likely to make little overall impact. Plaid Cymru will do well to win a single seat in Wales; the SNP will hope for three out of the eight in Scotland. It will be what happened in the national elections five weeks earlier that makes or breaks the year for the nationalist parties.

Appendix 1:1. Candidates for the European Parliament

(as known at 15 February 1999)

Candidates highlighted in **bold** are almost certain to be elected; those highlighted in *italic* could be elected if their party does well; candidates listed in plain type are unlikely to be elected.

Sitting members of the European Parliament are marked *.

East Midlands

Con	*Lab*	*LD*	*Green*
1 **Helmer, R.**	**Read M. Ms.***	**Clegg, N.**	Backhouse, G. Ms.
2 **Newton Dunn, B.**	**Whitehead, P.***	Barber, S. Ms.	Forse, G.
3 *Heaton-Harris, C.*	*Billingham, A. Ms.*	Vadher, A.	Fewster, B.
4 Arain, J.	Waddington, S. Ms.*	Gabriel, L. Ms.	Blount, S. Ms.
5 Buckle, S. Ms.	Vaz, V. Ms.	Niblett, B.	Baxter, A.
6 Latham, P. Ms.	Mann, J.	Dunbar, L. Ms.	Bullock, J. Ms.

Eastern

Con	*Lab*	*LD*	*Green*
1 **Sturdy, R.***	**McNally, E. Ms.***	**Duff, A.**	Wright, M. Ms.
2 **Beazley, C.**	**Howitt, R.***	Scott, R. Ms.	Scheimann, M.
3 **Khanbhai, B.**	**Needle, C.***	Browne, R.	Burgess, E. Ms.
4 *Van Orden, G.*	*Truscott, P.*	Spencely, L. Ms.	Powell, M.
5 *Gordon, R.*	Thomas, D.*	White, C.	Abbott, J.
6 Twitchen, K. Ms.	Buchnor, V. Ms.	Cane, C. Ms.	Berry, J. Ms.
7 Bright, G.	Kelly, B. Ms.	Burall, P.	Thomson, A. Ms.
8 Rose, C.	Bagnall, R. Ms.	Gill, R. Ms.	Holmes, A.

London

Con	*Lab*	*LD*	*Green*
1 **Villiers, T. Ms.**	**Green, P. Ms.***	**Ludford, S. Ms.**	Lambert, J. Ms.
2 **Tannock, C.**	**Moraes, C.**	*Dykes, H.*	Kortvelyessy, N. Ms.
3 **Bethell, N.**	**Evans, R.***	Kramer, S. Ms.	Jones, J. Ms.
4 *Bowis, J.*	**Balfe, R.***	Fryer, J.	Collins, S.
5 Twinn, I.	*Tongue, C. Ms.*	Leighter, H. Ms.	Bradley, J.
6 Popat, A.	*Spiers, S.*	Pinfield, N.	Olliver, V. Ms.
7 Boff, A.	Honeyball, M. Ms.	Orchard-Doughty, S. Ms.	Jago, H.
8 Steinberg, B.	Malik, M.	Wiseman, A.	Forbes, J. Ms.
9 Flack, J.	Wharfe, P. Ms.	Thomson, N. Ms.	Walton, D.
10 Harvey, A. Ms.	Elliott, M.	Facey, P.	Stimson, M.

North East

Con	Lab	LD	Green
1 **Callanan, M.**	**Donnelly, A.***	*Foote Wood, C.*	Best, N.
2 Ruff, A.	**Hughes, S.***	Hall, F. Ms.	Whiteside, R. Ms.
3 Murphy, B.	**O'Toole, M. Ms.**	Maughan, P.	Speight, B. Ms.
4 Macgregor, G.	Adam, G.*	Harvey, J. Ms.	Greveson, M.

North West

Con	Lab	LD	Green
1 **Inglewood, W.**	**McCarthy, A. Ms.***	**Davies, C.**	Whitelegg, J.
2 **Atkins, R.**	**Titley, G.***	Clucas, F. Ms.	Fitz-Gibbon, S.
3 **Sumberg, D.**	**Wynn, T.***	Farron, T.	Busby, C.
4 *Dover, D.*	**Simpson, B.***	Calton, P. Ms.	Dowding, G. Ms.
5 Foster, J. Ms.	**Cunningham, T.***	Putman, R.	Field, R.
6 Newns, D.	*Hendrick, M.*￼	Zalzala, Y. Ms.	Crookes, L.
7 Reid, A.	Turner, R. Ms.	Reid, K.	Parry, J.
8 Wiggin, B.	Nangle, C. Ms.	Fletcher, K. Ms.	Nicholls, G.
9 Pearce, A.	Ward, M.	Clayton, M.	Jones, J. Ms.
10 Carmichael, N.	Griffin, T. Ms.	Pearcey, J. Ms.	Hogg, J. Ms.

South East

Con	Lab	LD	Green
1 **Provan, J.***	**Skinner, P.***	**Nicholson, E. Ms.**	Lucas, C. Ms.
2 **Perry, R.***	**Watts, M.***	**Huhne, C.**	Woodin, M.
3 **Hannan, D.**	**Pollack, A. Ms.***	*Bowles, S. Ms.*	Francis, A.
4 **Elles, J.***	*Snellgrove, A. Ms.*	Bellotti, D.	West, P.
5 **Deva, N.**	Bodfish, K.	Hawkins, J. Ms.	Dawe, H. Ms.
6 *Bethell, B. Ms.*	Dhanda, P.	Walsh, J.	Dawe, S.
7 Kellett-Bowman, E.*	Howard, A.	Hewett-Silk, B. Ms.	Stark, A.
8 Parry, A. Ms.	Davison, A. Ms.	Vernon-Jackson, G.	Denis, J.
9 Mayhew, J.	Enright, D.	Bearder, C. Ms.	Eserrecchia, L. Ms.
10 Tanswell, B.	Armstrong, L. Ms.	Berry, C.	Littman, L.
11	Flanagan, T. Ms.	Webb, D. Ms.	Salmon, J.

South West

Con	Lab	LD	Green
1 **Jackson, C. Ms.***	**Ford, G.***	**Watson, G.***	Taylor, D.
2 **Chichester, G.***	*White, I.*￼	**Teverson, R.***	Lawson, R.
3 *Stockton, A.*	*Mallory, S. Ms.*	*Jones, T. Ms.*	Pickering, S.
4 *Parish, N.*	Knight, J.	Yates, P. Ms.	Scrase, R.
5 Martin, D.	Dewar, M. Ms.	Butt-Philip, A.	Soutar, H.
6 Cassidy, B.*	Shepherd, J.	Beasley, J. Ms.	Quinnell, J.
7 Marland, P.	Lisgo, L. Ms.	Green, S.	

West Midlands

	Con	Lab	LD	Green
1	**Corrie, J.***	**Murphy, S.***	**Lynne, L. Ms.**	Norman, F. Ms.
2	**Bushill-Matthews, P.**	**Cashman, M.**	Tilsley, P.	Woodford, G.
3	**Harbour, M.**	**Gill, N. Ms.**	Juned, S. Ms.	Baptie, P.
4	*Bradbourn, P.*	**Tappin, M.***	Bennion, P.	Clawley, H. Ms.
5	Normington, R.	*Hallam, D.**	Walmsley, J. Ms.	Mountford, R.
6	Taylor, V. Ms.	Davis, P.	Marwa, S.	Clawley, A.
7	Greenburgh, M.	Oddy, C. Ms.*	Calder, J.	Holtham, A.
8	Burnett, M.	O'Kane, N. Ms.	Cordwell, J.	Stanton, E. Ms.

Yorkshire and The Humber

	Con	Lab	LD	Green
1	**McMillan-Scott, E.***	**McAvan, L. Ms.***	**Wallis, D. Ms.**	Alexander, P. Ms.
2	**Kirkhope, T.**	**Bowe, D.***	Pitts, M.	Hill, M.
3	*Goodwill, R.*	**Corbett, R.***	Harris, A. Ms.	Smith, V. Ms.
4	Adamson, C. Ms.	*Barton, R.**	Ross, C.	Martin, A.
5	Dartmouth, W.	Seal, B.*	Anginotti, S. Ms.	D'Agrone, A.
6	Nuttall, D.	Hardstaffe, V. Ms.*	Adamson, R.	Otten, J.
7	Najabat Hussain, R.	Shellard, D.	Kirk, M. Ms.	Clark, J. Ms.

Scotland

	Con	Lab	LD	SNP	Green
1	**Stevenson, S.**	**Martin, D.***	*Attwooll, E. Ms.*	**Hudghton, I.***	Harper, R.
2	*Purvis, J.*	**Miller, B.***	Aldridge, R.	**MacCormick, N.**	Allan, K. Ms.
3	Harper, A. Ms.	**Taylor, C. Ms.**	Mitchison, N.	*Gillies, A. Ms.*	Scott, E. Ms.
4	Buchanan C.	*May, C. Ms.*	Lyall, H. Ms.	Wilson, G.	Coyne, M. Ms.
5	Leslie, S.	McMahon, H.	Hughes Hallett, D.	Law, J. Ms	O'Brien, P.
6	Mitchell, I.	Paton, J.	Sneddon, C.	Seaton, S. Ms.	Farmer, G.
7	Ramsay, P.	Clifford, J.	Skene, D.	Brown, K.	Hendry, L. Ms.
8	Gilbey, A.		Freel, K. Ms.	Goldie, I.	Ballance, C.

Wales

	Con	Lab	LD	PC	Green
1	**Evans, J.**	**Kinnock, G. Ms.***	*Roberts, R.*	*Evans, J. Ms.*	Scott Cato, M. Ms.
2	Butler, C.	**Morgan, E. Ms.***	Price, P.	Wyn, E.	Armstrong-Braun, K.
3	Williams, O.	**Wilson, J.***	Cameron, A.	Phillips, M.	Walker, S. Ms.
4	Buckland, R.	Hutt, J. Ms.	Hughes, J. Ms.	Perkins, S. Ms.	Kaleta, R. Ms.
5	Hayward, E.		Dixon, J.	Llywelyn, O.	Ainley, S.

Northern Ireland

DUP: **Paisley, I.***; SDLP: **Hume, J.***; UU: **Nicholson, J.***
Other party candidates to be announced.

Appendix 1.2: Electing MEPS in European Union countries

Country	No. of MEPs	Electoral unit	Voting system
Austria	21	Nation	List system

Single vote cast either for a list *or* for a candidate on a list. 4% of the total vote is the threshold for qualifying to win a seat.

Belgium	25	4 Regions	List system

Votes can be cast either for a list *or* for candidates on a list. An electoral college system guarantees representation for Flemish, French and German communities.

Denmark	16	Nation	List system

Single vote cast either for a list *or* for a candidate on a list.

Finland	16	Nation	List system

Single vote cast either for a list *or* for a candidate on a list.

France	87	Nation	List system

Single votes cast for a list. 5% of the total vote is the threshold for qualifying to win a seat.

Germany	99	Nation and Region	List system

Votes may only be cast for a list. 5% of the total vote is the threshold for qualifying to win a seat.

Greece	25	Nation	List system

Votes may only be cast for a list.

Ireland	15	4 Regions	Single Transferable Vote

Votes are cast for individual candidates in order of preference.

Italy	87	5 Regions	List system

Votes can be cast either for a list *or* for candidates on a list.

Luxembourg	6	Nation	List system

Each elector has as many votes as there are seats. Votes can be cast for a whole list or distributed among individual candidates.

Netherlands	31	Nation	List system

Single vote cast either for a list *or* for a candidate on a list.

Portugal	25	Nation	List system

Votes may only be cast for a list.

Spain	64	Nation	List system

Votes may only be cast for a list.

Sweden	22	Nation	List system

Votes can be cast either for a list *or* for candidates on a list. 4% of the total vote is the threshold for qualifying to win a seat.

Country	No. of MEPs	Electoral unit	Voting system
United Kingdom			
Great Britain	84	11 Regions	List system

Votes may only be cast for a list.

Country	No. of MEPs	Electoral unit	Voting system
N. Ireland	3	Nation	Single Transferable Vote

Votes are cast for individual candidates in order of preference.

2. Scottish Parliament Elections

Anything but Dreich?

Introduction by: **Brian Taylor**, *Political Editor, BBC Scotland*

As those who have followed every turn of the Scottish constitutional debate can attest, politics can be 'gey dreich' – a splendid Scots phrase inadequately rendered in English as 'somewhat dull'. Scotland's new Parliament will undoubtedly have its dreich moments – but the emotions in advance range from enthusiasm to apprehension to uncertainty. Enthusiasm over Scotland's first democratically elected Parliament. Apprehension over the political challenge involved for each of Scotland's parties. Uncertainty over the final destination of reform.

The politicians who will muster in Edinburgh after the May 6 elections will form the first Scottish legislative assembly elected by universal franchise. But not of course the first Parliament. Before the 1707 Union with England, Scotland was governed by an independent Parliament combining, post-Reformation, the three Estates of the burghs, the shires and the aristocracy in a single body. In keeping with the style of the times, only the shire representatives had to endure direct elections. After the Union, the Scottish and English Parliaments were both discontinued and formally merged.

Now – nearly three hundred years later – the calculation by Labour (and the Liberal Democrats, their partners in the cross-party Constitutional Convention) is that the Union settlement requires reform to survive and thrive. Put simply, people in Scotland have a strong and growing sense of Scottish identity – and they want that reflected in political structures. The devolved Parliament is the Labour government's specific answer to a general feeling. Devolution is a political safety valve.

Crucially, this will be a Parliament with the power to make laws. It will legislate for those areas already administratively devolved to the Scottish Office. It is argued that a distinctive Scottish Parliament – with a clear Scottish mandate – will be able to operate more efficiently and effectively in this field than the present set-up whereby the law of Scotland is determined by a UK mandate and occasionally settled in the watches of the night at Westminster. The Parliament will also supervise and allocate the Scottish budget which will be broadly determined by block grant from the Treasury as at present. In addition, the new MSPs will have the power to vary the standard rate of income tax in Scotland by a maximum of three pence in the pound. Any additional money thus raised would be added to Scottish spending. Any cash foregone by a cut in income tax would be returned to the UK Treasury. Few expect the tax power to be implemented in the early years of the Parliament.

The bigger unknown, of course, is what will be the political make-up of the new Parliament? Opinion polls have consistently suggested that voters in Scotland might be more inclined to back the SNP in elections to a distinctively Scottish Parliament than they are in Westminster contests. Arguably, some voters might be seeking a uniquely Scottish voice for discussion – and possibly conflict – with London.

The Nationalists have deliberately sought to foster this apparent trend by styling themselves 'Scotland's Party' – an appeal ostensibly beyond partisan politics – and by stressing that they would strive to make the devolved Parliament work while sustaining their campaign for a fully independent Scotland.

Labour has counter-attacked by describing the SNP as 'wreckers', arguing that they are out to overturn the settlement endorsed by Scotland through their stated aim of holding a referendum on the question of Scottish independence in the first four-year term of the new Parliament. The Labour strategy has been to talk up the alleged threat of independence, targeting SNP policy in areas like defence which remain reserved to Westminster.

The Labour/SNP conflict is the core fault line in Scottish politics, with the polls suggesting that the two parties are running neck and neck. A close fight – and the voting system – could add up to a coalition or minority government in the first Scottish Parliament. Many observers have forecast a Labour/LibDem pact or arrangement – especially given the two parties' co-operation in the Convention. But the LibDems in Scotland have been anxious to avoid the impression that they occupy a comfortable niche in Labour's pocket. The more Paddy Ashdown has consorted with Tony Blair at Westminster, the more the Scottish LibDems have been determined to display their independence. For example, they have floated the notion of a deal with the SNP – although the Scottish LibDem leader Jim Wallace stresses that the party could not support an independence referendum.

The Tories now endorse devolution after years of opposition – but that very history of hostility means they are highly unlikely to be the coalition partners of choice for any of their rivals. However the Tories took heart from their second place behind the SNP in the recent North East Scotland Euro by-election and the proportional electoral system gives the Scottish Tories an opportunity to begin the process of rebuilding.

In the longer term the crucial question is will the devolution settlement content the Scots? Or will there be further moves towards independence? Legally, only Westminster could call a full referendum on independence. In reality, however, if the Scots at some point vote demonstrably and incontestably for independence – as the SNP want – then that process will be under way. If they do not – as the SNP's rivals forecast – then the referendum issue does not arise. These elections then are partly infused by the debate over Scotland's future relationship with the rest of the UK. But primarily they are about the politics of devolution, settling the direction of the new domestic governance for Scotland herself.

Brian Taylor

Structure and functions of the Scottish Parliament

The Parliament is being established following a referendum held in Scotland on 11 September 1997. At the referendum 2,391,268 valid votes were cast, representing 60.2% of the Scottish electorate. Voters were asked two questions.

First, 1,775,045 (74.3%) agreed that there should be a Scottish Parliament and 614,400 (25.7%) did not agree. A 'Yes' majority of almost three to one. There were 11,986 spoilt ballot papers. Second, 1,512,889 (63.5%) agreed that the Scottish Parliament should have tax-varying powers and 870,263 (36.5%) did not agree. A 'Yes' majority of 642,626. On this question there were 19,013 spoilt ballot papers.

Table 2.1: Result of Referendum on Scottish Parliament, 11 September 1997

i. Question on establishing a Scottish Parliament

Council	% Turnout	Yes	%	No	%
Aberdeen	53.4	65,035	71.8	25,580	28.2
Aberdeenshire	56.7	61,621	63.9	34,878	36.1
Angus	60.0	33,571	64.7	18,350	35.3
Argyll & Bute	64.6	30,452	67.3	14,796	32.7
Clackmannan	65.8	18,790	80.0	4,706	20.0
Dumfries & Galloway	63.1	44,619	60.7	28,863	39.3
Dundee	55.3	49,252	76.0	15,553	24.0
East Ayrshire	64.5	49,131	81.1	11,426	18.9
East Dunbartonshire	72.3	40,917	69.8	17,725	30.2
East Lothian	64.9	33,525	74.2	11,665	25.8
East Renfrewshire	68.0	28,253	61.7	17,573	38.3
Edinburgh	59.8	155,900	71.9	60,832	28.1
Falkirk	63.4	55,642	80.0	13,953	20.0
Fife	60.9	125,668	76.1	39,517	23.9
Glasgow	51.2	204,269	83.6	40,106	16.4
Highland	60.3	72,551	72.6	27,431	27.4
Inverclyde	60.0	31,680	78.0	8,945	22.0
Midlothian	64.9	31,681	79.9	7,979	20.1
Moray	57.5	24,822	67.2	12,122	32.8
North Ayrshire	63.1	51,304	76.3	15,931	23.7
North Lanarkshire	60.4	123,063	82.6	26,010	17.4
Orkney	53.2	4,749	57.3	3,541	42.7
Perthshire & Kinross	62.7	40,344	61.7	24,998	38.3
Renfrewshire	62.4	68,711	79.0	18,213	21.0
Scottish Borders	64.4	33,855	62.8	20,060	37.2
Shetland	51.3	5,430	62.4	3,275	37.6
South Ayrshire	66.4	40,161	66.9	19,909	33.1
South Lanarkshire	62.8	114,908	77.8	32,762	22.2
Stirling	65.5	29,190	68.5	13,440	31.5
West Dunbartonshire	63.4	39,051	84.7	7,058	15.3
West Lothian	62.3	56,923	79.6	14,614	20.4
Western Isles	55.3	9,977	79.4	2,589	20.6
Scotland	**60.2**	**1,775,045**	**74.3**	**614,400**	**25.7**

ii. Question on the Parliament having tax-varying powers

Council	Yes	%	No	%
Aberdeen	54,320	60.3	35,709	39.7
Aberdeenshire	50,295	52.3	45,929	47.7
Angus	27,641	53.4	24,089	46.6
Argyll & Bute	25,746	57.0	19,429	43.0
Clackmannan	16,112	68.7	7,355	31.3
Dumfries & Galloway	35,737	48.8	37,499	51.2
Dundee	42,304	65.5	22,280	34.5
East Ayrshire	42,559	70.5	17,824	29.5
East Dunbartonshire	34,576	59.1	23,914	40.9
East Lothian	28,152	62.7	16,765	37.3
East Renfrewshire	23,580	51.6	22,153	48.4
Edinburgh	133,843	62.0	82,188	38.0
Falkirk	48,064	69.2	21,403	30.8
Fife	108,021	64.7	58,987	35.3
Glasgow	182,589	75.0	60,842	25.0
Highland	61,359	62.1	37,525	37.9
Inverclyde	27,194	67.2	13,277	32.8
Midlothian	26,776	67.7	12,762	32.3
Moray	19,326	52.7	17,344	47.3
North Ayrshire	43,990	65.7	22,991	34.3
North Lanarkshire	107,288	72.2	41,372	27.8
Orkney	3,917	47.4	4,344	52.6
Perthshire & Kinross	33,398	51.3	31,709	48.7
Renfrewshire	55,075	63.6	31,537	36.4
Scottish Borders	27,284	50.7	26,497	49.3
Shetland	4,478	51.6	4,198	48.4
South Ayrshire	33,679	56.2	26,217	43.8
South Lanarkshire	99,587	67.6	47,708	32.4
Stirling	25,044	58.9	17,487	41.1
West Dunbartonshire	34,408	74.7	11,628	25.3
West Lothian	47,990	67.3	23,354	32.7
Western Isles	8,557	68.4	3,947	31.6
Scotland	**1,512,889**	**63.5**	**870,263**	**36.5**

Arrangements for the operation of the Scottish Parliament are as follows:

- **Elections:** first elections to the Scottish Parliament will be held on Thursday 6 May 1999, and will then occur every four years.
- **Membership:** 129 Members of the Scottish Parliament (MSPs) will be elected under a system of proportional representation called the Additional Member System (AMS).
- **Seat of the Parliament:** The Parliament will meet in the Assembly Hall on the Mound in Edinburgh, until its permanent home at Holyrood in Edinburgh is completed in autumn 2001. Enric Miralles of Barcelona is designing an innovative creation in conjunction with Edinburgh architects.
- **Sessions:** it has been proposed that the Scottish Parliament should sit for 30-33 weeks a year, with its sessions mirroring the Scottish school holidays, and should follow normal working business hours of 9.30am – 5.30pm. These arrangements are subject to the agreement and alteration of the Scottish Parliament once elected.

- **First sitting:** it is yet to be confirmed when the Scottish Parliament will first meet, but it will probably be on the 12 or 13 May 1999. The initial duties faced by the Parliament include the election of the Presiding Officer and deputies, the appointment of the First Minister and Executive and various pieces of secondary legislation.
- **Official opening:** the Scottish Parliament will take up its full powers on the 1 July 1999, and will also be officially opened by the Queen on that day.
- **The First Minister:** the leader of the main party in the Scottish Parliament will be appointed as First Minister, and will possess similar powers to those of the Prime Minister in relation to Westminster. The First Minister will appoint Scottish Ministers, subject to the approval of the Scottish Parliament.
- **The Scottish Ministers:** the Scottish Ministers will each be responsible for the functions of a departmental area, as specified by the First Minster.
- **The Scottish Executive:** the Scottish Ministers will form Scotland's domestic government, which will be called the Scottish Executive. The Scottish Executive will be accountable to the Scottish Parliament for the development of policy and the delivery of services. The actual number of Ministers and composition of the Scottish Executive will be determined by the main party in the Scottish Parliament.
- **Presiding Officer:** the Scottish Parliament will appoint a Presiding Officer and deputies to fulfil a similar role to that of the Speaker in the House of Commons. This role includes overseeing debates in the Parliament and offering advice on procedure and Standing Orders.
- **Committees:** a central function in the Scottish Parliament will be performed by committees, and it is envisaged that they will have a broad role gathering evidence and considering legislation. The number of committees and subjects which they shall address will be decided by the Scottish Parliament.
- **Financial arrangements:** Westminster will allocate a budget to the Scottish Parliament. In addition to this, the Scottish Parliament will be able to increase or decrease its overall budget by varying the basic rate of income tax for residents of Scotland by up to three pence. The Scottish Parliament will also control local authority expenditure, non-domestic rates and other local taxation.

The Scottish Parliament will be responsible for and be able to make primary legislation in all the following areas:

- **Health:** NHS in Scotland; public and mental health.
- **Education and Training:** pre-5, primary, secondary, further and higher education, training, policy and programmes.
- **Local Government:** social work and housing; local government structure, finance, electoral arrangements; voluntary sector; area regeneration; building control and statutory planning framework.
- **Economic Development and Transport:** economic development of Scotland; assistance and support for Scottish business and industry, promotion of trade and exports; inward investment; tourism; functions in relation to the energy sector; administration of European Structural Funds; road, rail, air, sea transport and inland waterway matters.

- **Law and Home Affairs:** civil and criminal law; criminal justice and prosecution system including police, prison, fire services, legal aid, parole, release of life-sentence prisoners and alleged miscarriages of justice; certain Crown, church, ceremonial and local government electoral matters; civil defence and emergency planning.
- **Environment:** environmental protection policy; matters relating to air, land, water pollution; natural and built heritage; water supplies; sewerage; flood prevention; coastal protection.
- **Agriculture, Fisheries and Forestry:** the Scottish Office's existing responsibilities for promoting agriculture and fisheries in Scotland; the Forestry Commission in Scotland's existing responsibilities.
- **Sports and the Arts:** Scottish Sports Council, Scottish Arts Council; national institutions.
- **Research and Statistics:** relating to all of the devolved matters, that is all of the areas listed above.

Relations between the Scottish Parliament and Westminster

The Scottish Parliament will not be able to make primary legislation in the following areas:

- UK Constitution
- UK foreign policy and relations with Europe
- UK defence and national security
- stability of UK's fiscal, economic and monetary system
- common markets for UK goods and services
- employment
- social security
- most aspects of transport safety and regulation
- broadcasting policy
- national lottery

There will be arrangements, yet to be finalised, for resolving disagreements about whether or not legislation is within the powers of the Scottish Parliament.

- **Secretary of State and the UK Government:** the Secretary of State for Scotland will work with the Scottish Parliament and represent Scottish interests within the UK Government. The Scottish Executive will also work closely with the UK Government at Ministerial and official levels.
- **Transfer of Functions:** Westminster will be able to transfer further functions and powers on to the Scottish Parliament by making Orders in Council.
- **Scotland's MPs:** Scotland's MPs will continue to play a full and constructive part at Westminster, although the number of Scottish seats will be reviewed.

Operation of electoral system

The elections for the first four year term of the new Scottish Parliament are due to be held on Thursday 6 May 1999 – the same day as elections for all 32 Scottish councils (see chapter 6).

The Parliament will comprise 129 members. They will be chosen in one of two ways:

i) 73 members will represent individual constituencies. 71 of the current 72 Scottish Westminster parliamentary constituencies will elect a single member by the traditional first past the post method. The constituency of Orkney and Shetland will be split into two, with each island group electing its own member of the Scottish Parliament.

ii) Each of eight electoral regions in Scotland (the regions are coterminous with the outgoing European parliament constituency boundaries) will elect seven additional members in order to provide a counter to any disparity between votes gained and seats won in the region through the operation of simple plurality. A total of 56 members will be elected by this 'topping up' process.

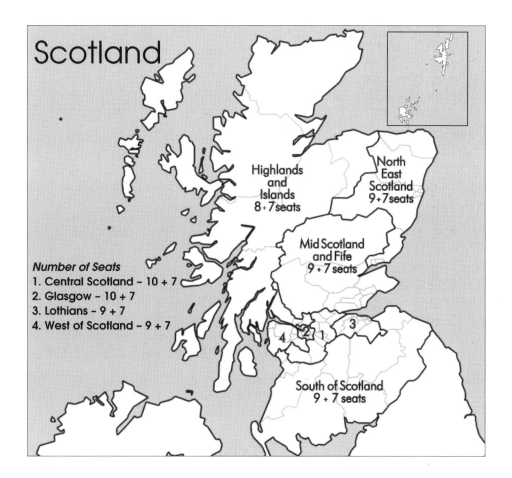

Scotland

North East Scotland 9+7 seats

Highlands and Islands 8+7 seats

Mid Scotland and Fife 9+7 seats

South of Scotland 9 + 7 seats

Number of Seats
1. Central Scotland – 10 + 7
2. Glasgow – 10 + 7
3. Lothians – 9 + 7
4. West of Scotland – 9 + 7

Electors will have two votes. One for a candidate within their Scottish (Westminster) parliamentary constituency, and one for a 'party list' within their electoral region. There is nothing to stop electors choosing a constituency candidate who represents a different party to the one for which they vote at regional level.

Scottish Parliament Region: Lothians
YOU HAVE ONE VOTE ON THIS PAPER — Put **X** in one box

THE CONSERVATIVE AND UNIONIST PARTY	1 Ann Archer 4 Donald Smith 7 Gordon Grant 2 Brian Scott 5 Eric Pender 3 Colin Brown 6 Frances Smart	☐
THE LABOUR PARTY	1 John McGregor 4 Ellen Jackson 7 Alan Somerville 2 Scott Fowler 5 Jim McWilliam 3 Alan Cuningham 6 Sharon McEwan	☐
LIBERAL DEMOCRATS	1 Paul Williams 4 Neil Firman 7 Frank Selkirk 2 Roy Rowan 3 Emma Sinclair 3 Hugh McWilliam 6 George Ross	☐
NORTH EAST REGIONAL ALLIANCE	1 Anna Hood 3 Don McDougall 2 Lesley Holloway	☐
THE SCOTTISH GREEN PARTY	1 Peter Loudon 3 Stuart Grantham 2 Lorimer Jackson 4 Anita Brown	☐
SCOTTISH NATIONAL PARTY	1 Callum Master 4 Lionel O'Connell 7 Saeed Khan 2 Jack Sword 5 Liam Johnstone 3 Lynsey Lines 6 Sonia Wilson	☐
SCOTTISH SOCIALIST ALLIANCE	1 Hamish Tavish 3 Heather Wood 5 Cameron Scott 2 Angus Brown 4 Rory Sharp	☐
BARLEY Robert Anthony	Save the Environment	☐
MACLEOD Andrew	Independent	☐

Scottish Parliament Constituency: Livingston
VOTE FOR ONE CANDIDATE ONLY

1	BROWN William Ian	23 High Street, Anytown	The Green Party
2	CRANSTON Helen	912 Main Street, Anytown	LiberalDemocrat
3	FRAME Donald Alexander	4 Elgin Avenue, Anytown	The Labour Party
4	GORDON Peter Martin	93 Holyrood Road, Anytown	The Conservative Party
5	MacDONALD Michael Gordon	45 Easter Road, Anytown	Independant
6	WALLACE Walter Alan	112 South Gyle Avenue, Anytown	Scottish National Party

The total number of list votes cast for each party in all the constituencies in each region will be aggregated to form the basis for calculating the allocation of the additional seats. Parties will supply a list of candidates for each region in the order in which they wish them to be elected. Individuals may simultaneously be candidates both in a constituency and on *one* regional list, but those who win a constituency seat will no longer be eligible to be an additional member. 'Independent' candidates are entitled to stand in either a constituency or a region or both, but the votes of candidates not on the list of a registered party will each be treated separately.

To be certain of securing a Scottish Parliament seat a party or individual must receive a proportion of the vote equal to 100 divided by the total number of seats in the region **plus one**. This threshold will vary from 6.3% (100÷15+1) in Highlands and Islands to 5.6% (100÷17+1) in Glasgow and Central Scotland. It is possible to secure a seat with a lesser share of the vote depending on the way votes are distributed between the competing parties.

Each candidate nominated in a constituency and each party and individual which appears on a regional list must pay a deposit of £500. This will be returned if the candidate/party receives at least 5% of the total valid votes cast in the constituency/region.

Votes cast in the Scottish Parliament elections will be counted and the results announced overnight on 6/7 May. It is possible that the full result in Highlands and Islands will be delayed if counting in the Argyll & Bute constituency does not begin until Friday 7 May.

Electing Additional Members in Scotland: an example

In the Lothians electoral 'region' there are nine parliamentary constituencies. This region, like all the others, has been allocated seven additional members, making a total of 16 Parliament representatives. In this example we use the results of the 1997 general election and make the assumption that all electors would have cast their 'party list' votes for the same party or group for which they voted at constituency level.

Table 2.2: Lothians – 1997 general election result

	Con	Lab	LD	SNP	Others
Votes	73,363	175,354	56,957	70,353	5,719
% Share	19.2	45.9	14.9	18.4	1.5
Seats	—	8	1	—	—

Additional members are chosen having taken into account the number of seats a party has already won within the region. Therefore, to begin allocating the seven additional seats it is necessary to divide the total votes cast for each party by the number of constituencies it has won **plus one**. Each time a party gains a seat the number by which its total vote is to be divided increases by one.

Following the initial calculation the party with the highest number of remaining votes, Conservative, is awarded a seat – see Table 2.3. That seat is taken by the candidate in first place on the Conservative regional list, assuming that he/she has not already been elected as a constituency member. The Conservative vote is now divided by two – the seat just acquired plus one – to give 36,682. The SNP now has the highest remaining vote (70,353) and its top candidate takes a seat. On the third and fourth allocations the Conservatives and the SNP each take one further seat and their total vote is now divided by three – the two seats won plus one. At the fifth stage the party with the largest remaining vote total (28,479) is the Liberal Democrats, whose first eligible candidate on the list becomes a member of the Parliament. With the Liberal Democrat vote now itself divided by three, the Conservatives and the SNP share the final two seats.

Table 2.3: Lothians – allocation of additional members

	Con	Lab	LD	SNP	Others	
Total votes	73363	175354	56957	70353	5719	
Initial divisor	0 + 1	8 + 1	1 + 1	0 + 1	0 + 1	*Elected (no. on list)*
1st seat	**73,363**	19,484	28,479	70,353	5,719	Con (1)
2nd seat	36,682	19,484	28,479	**70,353**	5,719	SNP (1)
3rd seat	**36,682**	19,484	28,479	35,177	5,719	Con (2)
4th seat	24,454	19,484	28,479	**35,177**	5,719	SNP (2)
5th seat	24,454	19,484	**28,479**	23,451	5,719	LD (1)
6th seat	**24,454**	19,484	18,986	23,451	5,719	Con (3)
7th seat	18,341	19,484	18,986	**23,451**	5,719	SNP (3)

The operation of this process has awarded three of the additional seats to the Conservatives, three to the SNP and one to the Liberal Democrats. The total representation of Lothians in the Scottish Parliament would therefore be:

Table 2.4: Lothians – Parliament Membership

	Con	Lab	LD	SNP	Others
Constituency members	—	8	1	—	—
'Top up' seats	3	—	1	3	—
Total	3	8	2	3	—

The Scottish Parliament and past election results

As this is the first election to the Scottish Parliament there are no past contests with which to make comparisons. However, there are three sets of elections which can be used to give a flavour of what might happen.

The 'notional' results of the 1992 general election and the actual results of the 1997 general election throughout the country provide information on the number of votes cast and the winning party in the 73 constituencies. On the assumption that all electors would have cast their 'party list' votes for the same party or group for which they voted at constituency level, they also allow the aggregation of the votes for each party in each region in order to calculate the allocation of the additional seats.

Unlike in Wales the effect of recent Westminster parliamentary boundary changes means that the regional (European Parliament) constituencies in Scotland do not coincide with those constituencies used at the 1994 European Parliament elections. However, we have been able to construct 'notional' 1994 results for the new regional areas by taking the actual votes cast for each party in the old constituencies in 1994 and adjusting them according to which Westminster constituencies, or parts of constituencies, have been added or subtracted. Individual constituency results are not available, but may themselves be estimated by making the assumption that the proportion of a party's total vote in the region contributed by each constituency at a general election will be the same as at the 'notional' European election. For example, if Aberdeen Central contributed 7% of the total North East Scotland Conservative vote in 1997, it is reasonable to assume that it also did so in 1994. In this way we can gauge which party would have won each of the constituencies within each region.

The results of Scottish local elections are of little help in estimating the outcome of national or regional elections. At the inaugural contests for the Scottish unitary authorities in 1995 only 285 of the 1161 (24.5%) wards featured a candidate from each of the four major parties and candidates were elected unopposed in 52 (4.5%) wards. Moreover, because both the parliamentary constituencies and regional areas were drawn on the basis of the pre-1995 configuration of Scottish local government, they frequently cross current council boundaries.

The following pages describe and map the composition of each Scottish Parliament electoral region and indicate what the results of the Scottish Parliament elections might have been if they had taken place in 1992, 1994 and 1997.

Central Scotland Electoral Region

1998 parliamentary electorate
554,494

% of Scottish electorate
13.9

No. of Parliament seats
10 + 7

% of Parliament seats
13.2

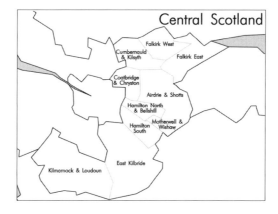

Comprising the constituencies of:	1992	Won by 1994*	1997	% maj. 1997	Second party 1997
Airdrie & Shotts	Lab	Lab	Lab	37.4	SNP
Coatbridge & Chryston	Lab	Lab	Lab	51.3	SNP
Cumbernauld & Kilsyth	Lab	Lab	Lab	30.9	SNP
East Kilbride	Lab	Lab	Lab	35.6	SNP
Falkirk East	Lab	Lab	Lab	32.2	SNP
Falkirk West	Lab	Lab	Lab	35.9	SNP
Hamilton North & Bellshill	Lab	Lab	Lab	44.9	SNP
Hamilton South	Lab	Lab	Lab	48.0	SNP
Kilmarnock & Loudoun	Lab	Lab	Lab	15.3	SNP
Motherwell & Wishaw	Lab	Lab	Lab	34.9	SNP

The individual results for 1994 are estimates based on the pattern of voting at the European Parliament election.

The electoral picture in the Central Scotland region appears to be one of almost unrelieved uniformity. Labour won every seat at both the 1992 and 1997 general elections and almost certainly recorded the largest number of votes in each constituency at the 1994 European Parliament elections too. In only one seat, Kilmarnock and Loudoun, is the party's majority over the universally second-placed SNP less than 30%. Nonetheless, there have been danger signs for the party. The Labour-dominated North Lanarkshire council – which covers five of the region's constituencies – has been in the teeth of allegations about local authority corruption, and Labour suffered a 1998 local by-election defeat at the hands of the SNP following a 32% swing. Voter reaction of that level of intensity could seriously dent Labour's representation in the Scottish parliament.

Votes and seats based on the 1992 general election

	Con	*Lab*	*LD*	*SNP*	*Others*
Votes	70,240	224,558	27,583	98,061	146
% share of vote	16.7	53.4	6.6	23.3	0.0
Seats (FPTP)	0	10	0	0	0
% share of seats	0.0	100.0	0.0	0.0	0.0
Seats ('Top up')	2	0	1	4	0
Total	**2**	**10**	**1**	**4**	**0**
% share of seats	11.8	58.8	5.9	23.5	0.0

Votes and seats based on the 1994 European election

	Con	*Lab*	*LD*	*SNP*	*Others*
Votes	16,579	117,709	7,104	64,461	1,868
% share of vote	8.0	56.7	3.4	31.0	0.9
Seats (FPTP)	0	10	0	0	0
% share of seats	0.0	100.0	0.0	0.0	0.0
Seats ('Top up')	1	0	0	6	0
Total	**1**	**10**	**0**	**6**	**0**
% share of seats	5.9	58.8	0.0	35.3	0.0

Votes and seats based on the 1997 general election

	Con	*Lab*	*LD*	*SNP*	*Others*
Votes	41,583	236,667	20,624	93,291	6,527
% share of vote	10.4	59.4	5.2	23.4	1.6
Seats (FPTP)	0	10	0	0	0
% share of seats	0.0	100.0	0.0	0.0	0.0
Seats ('Top up')	2	1	0	4	0
Total	**2**	**11**	**0**	**4**	**0**
% share of seats	11.8	64.7	0.0	23.5	0.0

Glasgow Electoral Region

1998 parliamentary electorate
515,320

% of Scottish electorate
12.9

No. of Parliament seats
10 + 7

% of Parliament seats
13.2

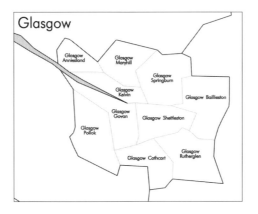

Comprising the constituencies of:	1992	Won by 1994*	1997	% maj. 1997	Second party 1997
Glasgow Anniesland	Lab	Lab	Lab	44.7	SNP
Glasgow Baillieston	Lab	Lab	Lab	46.6	SNP
Glasgow Cathcart	Lab	Lab	Lab	38.8	SNP
Glasgow Govan	Lab	SNP	Lab	9.0	SNP
Glasgow Kelvin	Lab	Lab	Lab	29.6	SNP
Glasgow Maryhill	Lab	Lab	Lab	48.0	SNP
Glasgow Pollok	Lab	Lab	Lab	42.0	SNP
Glasgow Rutherglen	Lab	Lab	Lab	42.2	SNP
Glasgow Shettleston	Lab	Lab	Lab	59.2	SNP
Glasgow Springburn	Lab	Lab	Lab	54.9	SNP

*The individual results for 1994 are estimates based on the pattern of voting at the European Parliament election.

Glasgow provides the perfect illustration of why a Scottish Parliament hoping to be seen as legitimate by all sections of the community had to be elected by other than simple first past the post. In both the 1992 and 1997 general elections Labour won all ten seats in Glasgow, leaving some four in ten voters feeling that their visit to the polling booth had been wasted. The SNP will be a threat to Labour in the still divided Govan constituency, and the nationalists could also win four of the seven 'top up' seats if their share of the total vote in the city reaches 25%. Both the Conservatives and Liberal Democrats are likely to secure representation in Glasgow for the first time in decades thanks to the Additional Member System. Nor should the Scottish Socialist Alliance be completely discounted. In the 1994 European Parliament elections Tommy Sheridan came third and would have won a 'top up' seat.

Votes and seats based on the 1992 general election

	Con	*Lab*	*LD*	*SNP*	*Others*
Votes	51,016	198,228	30,197	72,905	8,872
% share of vote	14.1	54.9	8.4	20.2	2.5
Seats (FPTP)	0	10	0	0	0
% share of seats	0.0	100.0	0.0	0.0	0.0
Seats ('Top up')	2	—	1	4	0
Total	**2**	**10**	**1**	**4**	**0**
% share of seats	11.8	58.8	5.9	23.5	0.0

Votes and seats based on the 1994 European election

	Con	*Lab*	*LD*	*SNP*	*Others*
Votes	12,407	95,131	8,357	45,004	17,532
% share of vote	7.0	53.3	4.7	25.2	9.8
Seats (FPTP)	0	9	0	1	0
% share of seats	0.0	90.0	0.0	10.0	0.0
Seats ('Top up')	1	1	0	4	1
Total	**1**	**10**	**0**	**5**	**1**
% share of seats	5.9	58.8	0.0	29.4	5.9

Votes and seats based on the 1997 general election

	Con	*Lab*	*LD*	*SNP*	*Others*
Votes	27,366	193,427	23,352	61,633	14,677
% share of vote	8.5	60.4	7.3	19.2	4.6
Seats (FPTP)	0	10	0	0	0
% share of seats	0.0	100.0	0.0	0.0	0.0
Seats ('Top up')	1	2	1	3	0
Total	**1**	**12**	**1**	**3**	**0**
% share of seats	5.9	70.6	5.9	17.6	0.0

Highlands and Islands Electoral Region

1998 parliamentary electorate
329.297

% of Scottish electorate
8.2

No. of Parliament seats
8 + 7

% of Parliament seats
11.6

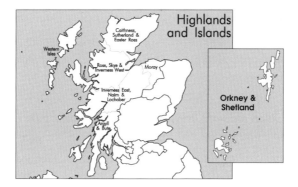

Comprising the constituencies of:	1992	Won by 1994*	1997	% maj. 1997	Second party 1997
Argyll & Bute	LD	SNP	LD	17.0	SNP
Caithness, Sutherland & Easter Ross	LD	SNP	LD	7.7	Lab
Inverness East, Nairn & Lochaber	LD	SNP	Lab	4.9	SNP
Moray	SNP	SNP	SNP	14.0	Con
Orkney & Shetland†	LD	SNP	LD	33.7	Lab
Ross, Skye & Inverness West	LD	SNP	LD	10.1	Lab
Western Isles	Lab	SNP	Lab	22.2	SNP

*The individual results for 1994 are estimates based on the pattern of voting at the European Parliament election.

†Orkney and Shetland each have a Scottish Parliament seat. Both are allocated to the party winning the Westminster seat.

The pattern of politics in the Highlands and Islands differs considerably from that found in the Scottish central belt. All parties, except perhaps the Conservatives, have pockets of local strength and most elections show a relatively even split in party support across the region. The exception to this has been in European Parliament elections when the long-standing MEP, the Scottish National Party's Winnie Ewing, has built up a commanding majority. The SNP has been less successful in parliamentary elections, but will hope that Ewing's coat-tails will ensure it a strong performance at least in 'top up' votes. It is likely that many sitting Westminster MPs have strong personal votes in the singular political circumstances of the Highlands and some constituency seats could also prove vulnerable to the SNP. Indeed the SNP held Western Isles for nearly 20 years until 1987.

Votes and seats based on the 1992 general election

	Con	*Lab*	*LD*	*SNP*	*Others*
Votes	57,158	44,174	65,688	59,624	2,014
% share of vote	25.0	19.3	28.7	26.1	0.9
Seats (FPTP)	0	1	6	1	0
% share of seats	0.0	12.5	75.0	12.5	0.0
Seats ('Top up')	3	1	0	3	0
Total	**3**	**2**	**6**	**4**	**0**
% share of seats	20.0	13.3	40.0	26.7	0.0

Votes and seats based on the 1994 European election

	Con	*Lab*	*LD*	*SNP*	*Others*
Votes	15,335	19,730	12,871	72,578	4,758
% share of vote	12.2	15.7	10.3	57.9	3.8
Seats (FPTP)	0	0	0	8	0
% share of seats	0.0	0.0	0.0	100.0	0.0
Seats ('Top up')	2	2	1	2	0
Total	**2**	**2**	**1**	**10**	**0**
% share of seats	13.3	13.3	6.7	66.7	0.0

Votes and seats based on the 1997 general election

	Con	*Lab*	*LD*	*SNP*	*Others*
Votes	37,206	61,974	63,362	61,189	5,421
% share of vote	16.2	27.0	27.7	26.7	2.4
Seats (FPTP)	0	2	5	1	0
% share of seats	0.0	25.0	62.5	12.5	0.0
Seats ('Top up')	2	2	0	3	0
Total	**2**	**4**	**5**	**4**	**0**
% share of seats	13.3	26.7	33.3	26.7	0.0

Lothians Electoral Region

1998 parliamentary electorate
537,993

% of Scottish electorate
13.5

No. of Parliament seats
9 + 7

% of Parliament seats
12.4

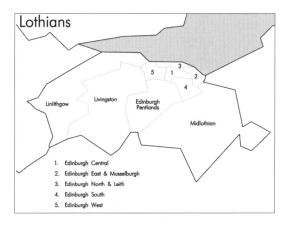

| | | | | | |
| Edinburgh | | | | | |

1. Edinburgh Central
2. Edinburgh East & Musselburgh
3. Edinburgh North & Leith
4. Edinburgh South
5. Edinburgh West

Comprising the constituencies of:	1992	Won by 1994*	1997	% maj. 1997	Second party 1997
Edinburgh Central	Lab	Lab	Lab	25.9	Con
Edinburgh East & Musselburgh	Lab	Lab	Lab	34.5	SNP
Edinburgh North & Leith	Lab	Lab	Lab	26.8	SNP
Edinburgh Pentlands	Con	Lab	Lab	10.6	Con
Edinburgh South	Lab	Lab	Lab	25.5	Con
Edinburgh West	Con	LD	LD	15.2	Con
Linlithgow	Lab	Lab	Lab	27.3	SNP
Livingston	Lab	Lab	Lab	27.4	SNP
Midlothian	Lab	Lab	Lab	28.0	SNP

The individual results for 1994 are estimates based on the pattern of voting at the European Parliament election.

Labour did well in Lothians at the 1997 general election, especially in Edinburgh itself. The party turned several marginal seats into safe ones and comfortably won Pentlands from the Conservatives. The Conservatives also lost their other seat in the capital, West, to the Liberal Democrats. Labour should win the bulk of the first past the post seats in the Scottish Parliament elections, with the SNP scooping the majority of the 'top ups'. The nationalists will be handicapped in their quest to win individual seats by their low base in 1997– their best showing was 27.5% of the vote in Livingston. The Liberal Democrats have a strong local organisation in Edinburgh West and will be helped by the city council elections being held on the same day. The Conservatives only need a 5% swing to retake Pentlands, but there is no evidence that their support has recovered sufficiently since the general election.

Votes and seats based on the 1992 general election

	Con	Lab	LD	SNP	Others
Votes	105,269	148,889	53,545	73,873	7,231
% share of vote	27.1	38.3	13.8	19.0	1.9
Seats (FPTP)	2	7	0	0	0
% share of seats	22.2	77.8	0.0	0.0	0.0
Seats ('Top up')	2	0	2	3	0
Total	**4**	**7**	**2**	**3**	**0**
% share of seats	25.0	43.8	12.5	18.8	0.0

Votes and seats based on the 1994 European election

	Con	Lab	LD	SNP	Others
Votes	33,966	90,960	17,736	52,680	6,200
% share of vote	16.9	45.1	8.8	26.1	3.1
Seats (FPTP)	0	8	1	0	0
% share of seats	0.0	88.9	11.1	0.0	0.0
Seats ('Top up')	3	0	0	4	0
Total	**3**	**8**	**1**	**4**	**0**
% share of seats	18.8	50.0	6.3	25.0	0.0

Votes and seats based on the 1997 general election

	Con	Lab	LD	SNP	Others
Votes	73,363	175,354	56,957	70,353	5,719
% share of vote	19.2	45.9	14.9	18.4	1.5
Seats (FPTP)	0	8	1	0	0
% share of seats	0.0	88.9	11.1	0.0	0.0
Seats ('Top up')	3	0	1	3	0
Total	**3**	**8**	**2**	**3**	**0**
% share of seats	18.8	50.0	12.5	18.8	0.0

Mid Scotland and Fife Electoral Region

1998 parliamentary electorate
511,437

% of Scottish electorate
12.8

No. of Parliament seats
9 + 7

% of Parliament seats
12.4

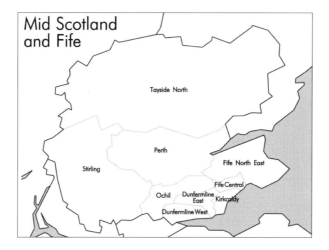

Comprising the constituencies of:	1992	Won by 1994*	1997	% maj. 1997	Second party 1997
Dunfermline East	Lab	Lab	Lab	51.3	SNP
Dunfermline West	Lab	Lab	Lab	33.9	SNP
Fife Central	Lab	Lab	Lab	33.6	SNP
Fife North East	LD	LD	LD	24.8	Con
Kirkcaldy	Lab	Lab	Lab	30.6	SNP
Ochil	Lab	SNP	Lab	10.6	SNP
Perth	Con	SNP	SNP	7.1	Con
Stirling	Con	Lab	Lab	14.9	Con
Tayside North	Con	SNP	SNP	9.1	Con

The individual results for 1994 are estimates based on the pattern of voting at the European Parliament election.

All three SNP gains at the 1997 general election came at the expense of the Conservatives and two of them – Perth and Tayside North – were in the Mid Scotland and Fife electoral region. The party's majority in both seats is in single figures, but it should be able to hang on. Four of Labour's six seats look very safe, but the SNP advanced strongly in Ochil in 1997 – a constituency in which they probably polled a majority of the votes cast in the 1994 European Parliament elections – and will have it firmly in their sights this time. The Conservatives could run Labour close in Stirling – they secured an impressive victory in a local by-election in Dunblane in June 1998. The Liberal Democrats are strong locally as well as at parliamentary level in Fife North East – an oasis for them in a region which is otherwise something of an electoral desert.

Votes and seats based on the 1992 general election

	Con	Lab	LD	SNP	Others
Votes	113,258	125,377	49,218	86,562	789
% share of vote	30.2	33.4	13.1	23.1	0.2
Seats (FPTP)	3	5	1	0	0
% share of seats	33.3	55.6	11.1	0.0	0.0
Seats ('Top up')	2	0	1	4	0
Total	**5**	**5**	**2**	**4**	**0**
% share of seats	31.3	31.3	12.5	25.0	0.0

Votes and seats based on the 1994 European election

	Con	Lab	LD	SNP	Others
Votes	29,306	73,540	16,238	61,692	3,547
% share of vote	15.9	39.9	8.8	33.5	1.9
Seats (FPTP)	0	5	1	3	0
% share of seats	0.0	55.6	11.1	33.3	0.0
Seats ('Top up')	2	2	0	3	0
Total	**2**	**7**	**1**	**6**	**0**
% share of seats	12.5	43.8	6.3	37.5	0.0

Votes and seats based on the 1997 general election

	Con	Lab	LD	SNP	Others
Votes	77,495	146,988	46,436	92,901	3,660
% share of vote	21.1	40.0	12.6	25.3	1.0
Seats (FPTP)	0	6	1	2	0
% share of seats	0.0	66.7	11.1	22.2	0.0
Seats ('Top up')	3	1	1	2	0
Total	**3**	**7**	**2**	**4**	**0**
% share of seats	18.8	43.8	12.5	25.0	0.0

North East Scotland Electoral Region

1998 parliamentary electorate
524,523

% of Scottish electorate
13.1

No. of Parliament seats
9 + 7

% of Parliament seats
12.4

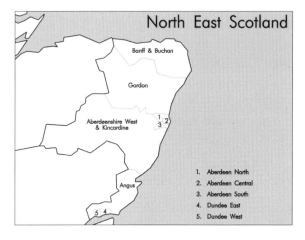

Comprising the constituencies of:	1992	Won by 1994*	1997	% maj. 1997	Second party 1997
Aberdeen Central	Lab	Lab	Lab	30.3	Con
Aberdeen North	Lab	Lab	Lab	26.1	SNP
Aberdeen South	Con	Lab	Lab	7.6	LD
Aberdeenshire West & Kincardine	Con	Con	LD	6.2	Con
Angus	SNP	SNP	SNP	23.7	Con
Banff & Buchan	SNP	SNP	SNP	32.0	Con
Dundee East	Lab	Lab	Lab	24.6	SNP
Dundee West	Lab	Lab	Lab	30.6	SNP
Gordon	Con	SNP	LD	16.6	Con

The individual results for 1994 are estimates based on the pattern of voting at the European Parliament election.

In the context of their woeful performances in the nation as a whole, North East Scotland is one region where the Conservatives can mount a respectable electoral challenge. They topped the poll and won three of the eight seats at the 1992 general election and came second in no fewer than five of them in 1997. Such underlying support guarantees them a number of 'top up' seats, but the real measure of the party's ability to rebuild its appeal to middle-class voters in Scotland will be victory at the constituency level. Both Aberdeenshire West & Kincardine and Gordon present opportunities, but the Conservatives will need to rely on those seats being insulated from any swing to the SNP across Scotland. Aberdeen South is an interesting three-way marginal with the SNP, who polled less than 10% of the vote in 1997, the only party not in contention.

Votes and seats based on the 1992 general election

	Con	Lab	LD	SNP	Others
Votes	120,051	94,133	61,770	95,779	1,793
% share of vote	32.1	25.2	16.5	25.6	0.5
Seats (FPTP)	3	4	0	2	0
% share of seats	33.3	44.4	0.0	22.2	0.0
Seats ('Top up')	2	0	3	2	0
Total	**5**	**4**	**3**	**4**	**0**
% share of seats	31.3	25.0	18.8	25.0	0.0

Votes and seats based on the 1994 European election

	Con	Lab	LD	SNP	Others
Votes	35,324	60,159	17,135	82,612	4,213
% share of vote	17.7	30.2	8.6	41.4	2.1
Seats (FPTP)	1	5	0	3	0
% share of seats	11.1	55.6	0.0	33.3	0.0
Seats ('Top up')	2	0	1	4	0
Total	**3**	**5**	**1**	**7**	**0**
% share of seats	18.8	31.3	6.3	43.8	0.0

Votes and seats based on the 1997 general election

	Con	Lab	LD	SNP	Others
Votes	82,079	113,021	69,164	95,503	6,362
% share of vote	22.4	30.9	18.9	26.1	1.7
Seats (FPTP)	0	5	2	2	0
% share of seats	0.0	55.6	22.2	22.2	0.0
Seats ('Top up')	4	0	1	2	0
Total	**4**	**5**	**3**	**4**	**0**
% share of seats	25.0	31.3	18.8	25.0	0.0

South of Scotland Electoral Region

1998 parliamentary electorate
514,077

% of Scottish electorate
12.9

No. of Parliament seats
9 + 7

% of Parliament seats
12.4

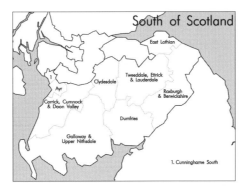

Comprising the constituencies of:	1992	Won by 1994*	1997	% maj. 1997	Second party 1997
Ayr	Lab	Lab	Lab	14.6	Con
Carrick, Cumnock & Doon Valley	Lab	Lab	Lab	42.8	Con
Clydesdale	Lab	Lab	Lab	30.4	SNP
Cunninghame South	Lab	Lab	Lab	42.0	SNP
Dumfries	Con	Lab	Lab	19.5	Con
East Lothian	Lab	Lab	Lab	32.7	Con
Galloway & Upper Nithsdale	Con	SNP	SNP	13.4	Con
Roxburgh & Berwickshire	LD	Con	LD	22.6	Con
Tweeddale, Ettrick & Lauderdale	LD	Lab	LD	3.8	Lab

*The individual results for 1994 are estimates based on the pattern of voting at the European Parliament election.

None of Labour's six Westminster seats in the South of Scotland should be seriously threatened in the Scottish Parliament elections. The party has a comfortable lead over the Conservatives in the two most marginal, Ayr and Dumfries, and the SNP can only challenge from a considerable distance in all of them. Indeed this was one of the nationalists' weakest regions in the country in terms of share of the vote in 1992, 1994 and 1997. The SNP will expect to cling on to their general election gain in Galloway and Upper Nithsdale, but otherwise will rely on perhaps three 'top up' seats for their representation. Roxburgh & Berwickshire should be safe for the Liberal Democrats, but Tweeddale, Ettrick and Lauderdale promises a tighter contest. The Conservatives are actually closer to victory there than in any of the seats in which they are formally second.

Votes and seats based on the 1992 general election

	Con	*Lab*	*LD*	*SNP*	*Others*
Votes	126,355	139,642	57,810	72,984	1,297
% share of vote	31.7	35.1	14.5	18.3	0.3
Seats (FPTP)	2	5	2	0	0
% share of seats	22.2	55.6	22.2	0.0	0.0
Seats ('Top up')	3	1	0	3	0
Total	**5**	**6**	**2**	**3**	**0**
% share of seats	31.3	37.5	12.5	18.8	0.0

Votes and seats based on the 1994 European election

	Con	*Lab*	*LD*	*SNP*	*Others*
Votes	45,155	90,311	13,510	45,677	6,303
% share of vote	22.5	44.9	6.7	22.7	3.1
Seats (FPTP)	1	7	0	1	0
% share of seats	11.1	77.8	0.0	11.1	0.0
Seats ('Top up')	2	1	1	3	0
Total	**3**	**8**	**1**	**4**	**0**
% share of seats	18.8	50.0	6.3	25.0	0.0

Votes and seats based on the 1997 general election

	Con	*Lab*	*LD*	*SNP*	*Others*
Votes	86,769	166,354	51,312	73,110	6,147
% share of vote	22.6	43.4	13.4	19.1	1.6
Seats (FPTP)	0	6	2	1	0
% share of seats	0.0	66.7	22.2	11.1	0.0
Seats ('Top up')	4	1	0	2	0
Total	**4**	**7**	**2**	**3**	**0**
% share of seats	25.0	43.8	12.5	18.8	0.0

West of Scotland Electoral Region

1998 parliamentary electorate
505,361

% of Scottish electorate
12.7

No. of Parliament seats
9 + 7

% of Parliament seats
12.4

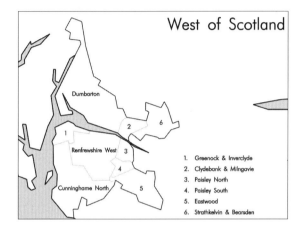

	West of Scotland
1.	Greenock & Inverclyde
2.	Clydebank & Milngavie
3.	Paisley North
4.	Paisley South
5.	Eastwood
6.	Strathkelvin & Bearsden

Comprising the constituencies of:	1992	Won by 1994*	1997	% maj. 1997	Second party 1997
Clydebank & Milngavie	Lab	Lab	Lab	34.1	SNP
Cunninghame North	Lab	Lab	Lab	26.8	Con
Dumbarton	Lab	Lab	Lab	26.4	SNP
Eastwood	Con	Lab	Lab	6.2	Con
Greenock & Inverclyde	Lab	Lab	Lab	37.6	SNP
Paisley North	Lab	Lab	Lab	37.5	SNP
Paisley South	Lab	Lab	Lab	34.1	SNP
Renfrewshire West	Lab	SNP	Lab	20.1	SNP
Strathkelvin & Bearsden	Lab	Lab	Lab	32.8	Con

*The individual results for 1994 are estimates based on the pattern of voting at the European Parliament election.

Although Labour won all nine seats in the West of Scotland region at the 1997 general election, its position is less dominant than in Central Scotland. The party did not poll a majority of votes cast in either 1992 or 1994 and the region contains what was the safest Conservative seat in Scotland – Eastwood. Success in the prosperous Glasgow commuter suburbs of Giffnock and Newton Mearns is crucial to the resurgence of Scottish Conservatism. Certainly the electors of East Renfrewshire, the council covering the Eastwood constituency, appeared sceptical of constitutional change when they recorded one of the lowest 'Yes' votes and one of the highest turnouts in the September 1997 devolution referendum. Labour has suffered from factional infighting in the Paisley area and the MP for Renfrewshire West, Tommy Graham, has been expelled from the party. Such events can only help the SNP.

Votes and seats based on the 1992 general election

	Con	*Lab*	*LD*	*SNP*	*Others*
Votes	108,603	167,910	38,045	69,776	1,275
% share of vote	28.2	43.5	9.9	18.1	0.3
Seats (FPTP)	1	8	0	0	0
% share of seats	11.1	88.9	0.0	0.0	0.0
Seats ('Top up')	3	0	1	3	0
Total	**4**	**8**	**1**	**3**	**0**
% share of seats	25.0	50.0	6.3	18.8	0.0

Votes and seats based on the 1994 European election

	Con	*Lab*	*LD*	*SNP*	*Others*
Votes	28,598	88,416	14,860	62,533	3,804
% share of vote	14.4	44.6	7.5	31.5	1.9
Seats (FPTP)	0	8	0	1	0
% share of seats	0.0	88.9	0.0	11.1	0.0
Seats ('Top up')	2	0	1	4	0
Total	**2**	**8**	**1**	**5**	**0**
% share of seats	12.5	50.0	6.3	31.3	0.0

Votes and seats based on the 1997 general election

	Con	*Lab*	*LD*	*SNP*	*Others*
Votes	67,198	189,565	34,155	73,570	4,914
% share of vote	18.2	51.3	9.2	19.9	1.3
Seats (FPTP)	0	9	0	0	0
% share of seats	0.0	100.0	0.0	0.0	0.0
Seats ('Top up')	3	0	1	3	0
Total	**3**	**9**	**1**	**3**	**0**
% share of seats	18.8	56.3	6.3	18.8	0.0

SCOTLAND

1998 parliamentary electorate
3,992,502

% of Scottish electorate
100.0

No. of Parliament seats
73 + 56

% of Parliament seats
100.0

Votes and seats based on the 1992 general election

	Con	Lab	LD	SNP	Others
Votes	751,950	1,142,911	383,856	629,564	23,417
% share of vote	25.6	39.0	13.1	21.5	0.8
Seats (FPTP)	11	50	9	3	0
% share of seats	15.1	68.5	12.3	4.1	0.0
Seats ('Top up')	19	2	9	26	0
Total	**30**	**52**	**18**	**29**	**0**
% share of seats	23.2	40.3	14.0	22.5	0.0

Votes and seats based on the 1994 European election

	Con	Lab	LD	SNP	Others
Votes	216,669	635,955	107,811	487,237	48,225
% share of vote	14.5	42.5	7.2	32.6	3.2
Seats (FPTP)	2	52	2	17	0
% share of seats	2.7	71.2	2.7	23.3	0.0
Seats ('Top up')	15	6	4	30	1
Total	**17**	**58**	**6**	**47**	**1**
% share of seats	13.2	45.0	4.7	36.4	0.8

Votes and seats based on the 1997 general election

	Con	Lab	LD	SNP	Others
Votes	493,059	1,283,350	365,362	621,550	53,427
% share of vote	17.5	45.6	13.0	22.1	1.9
Seats (FPTP)	0	56	11	6	0
% share of seats	0.0	76.7	15.1	8.2	0.0
Seats ('Top up')	22	7	5	22	0
Total	**22**	**63**	**16**	**28**	**0**
% share of seats	17.1	48.8	12.4	21.7	0.0

The Likely Outcome?

It is unlikely that Labour will secure the 65 seats required for an overall majority in the Scottish Parliament. The party's dominance of Scottish politics at Westminster, where it currently holds 56 of the 72 seats, has rarely been reflected in its share of the vote. Indeed Labour has not won 50% of the vote at any general election in Scotland. Its best result was 49.9% in 1966 when the SNP contested just 23 seats for a total 5% share of the vote. Moreover, because a relatively large proportion of Scottish Parliament seats will be elected by regional 'top up' – 56 out of a total Parliament membership of 129 – any imbalance in seats and votes between the parties at constituency level is likely to be much more fully redressed than will be the case in Wales. In each of the years for which we compiled notional results – 1992, 1994, and 1997 – Labour would have been the largest party in a 'hung' Parliament. Nonetheless Labour does appear to have one huge electoral advantage. Because it won 43 of its 56 seats at the 1997 general election with majorities in excess of 25%, the party is likely to retain a substantial bloc of representatives in the Scottish Parliament however badly it may perform in terms of the popular vote.

Table 2.5: Scotland Votes

Overall result based on the 1992 general election

	Con	Lab	LD	SNP	Others
% share of vote	25.6	39.0	13.1	21.5	0.8
Seats (FPTP)	11	50	9	3	0
Seats ('Top up')	19	2	9	26	0
Total	**30**	**52**	**18**	**29**	**0**

Overall result based on the 1994 European election

	Con	Lab	LD	SNP	Others
% share of vote	14.5	42.5	7.2	32.6	3.2
Seats (FPTP)	2	52	2	17	0
Seats ('Top up')	15	6	4	30	1
Total	**17**	**58**	**6**	**47**	**1**

Overall result based on the 1997 general election

	Con	Lab	LD	SNP	Others
% share of vote	17.5	45.6	13.0	22.1	1.9
Seats (FPTP)	0	56	11	6	0
Seats ('Top up')	22	7	5	22	0
Total	**22**	**63**	**16**	**28**	**0**

Estimating the exact outcome of the Parliament elections is complicated by two uncertainties about how voters will behave. First, there may be a tendency – as noted earlier – for people to split their constituency and party list votes between different candidates/parties. Second, and probably of greater significance, many electors may put aside their 'normal' – i.e. general election – party preferences and cast their vote specifically to reflect their preferences about the composition, operation and likely policies of the Scottish Parliament.

This habit of choosing 'horses for courses' seems to be becoming more widespread in Britain. For example, we have shown that among voters in England who were able to cast local as well as general election votes on May 1 1997 at least 10% and perhaps as many as 1 in 5 chose different parties on the same visit to the polling booth. Similarly, a survey study in 1997 of how people may cast their vote under different electoral systems found that about a quarter of Scottish voters reported that they would support a different party at the Parliament elections to the one they voted for at the 1997 general election. The aggregate impact of such switching was relatively modest, but did suggest that the SNP would be a net beneficiary and win more 'top up' seats. The Conservatives suffered a clear net defection among their general election supporters and the number of their likely 'top up' seats was sharply reduced.

More generally, previous second order elections in Britain have seen significant if transient shifts in party support. The SNP took nearly a third (32.6%) of the vote in the 1994 European Parliament elections, some 10 percentage points more than the party achieved in either the 1992 or 1997 general elections. In the same set of elections in 1989 the SNP also did better than at recent general elections (25.6%) and the Greens recorded 7.2% of the vote in Scotland compared with just 0.3% at the 1992 general election.

Recent evidence from polls and by-elections appears to support each of these contentions. The monthly series of System 3 polls published in *The Herald* show a clear and consistent difference between how electors say they would cast their vote in a Scottish Parliament as opposed to United Kingdom general election. Labour comfortably remains the most popular party in the UK context, but the gap between it and the SNP narrows considerably when putative behaviour at Scottish elections is examined. Labour is further disadvantaged by the fact that a small proportion of its potential constituency supporters appear to be prepared to use their regional list vote for another party. In a close election such defections could cost Labour vital 'top up' seats.

Table 2.6: System 3 opinion polls, July 1998 onwards

Voters were asked how they would vote in a United Kingdom general election, how they intended to cast their constituency vote in the Scottish Parliament election and how they intended to cast their regional vote at the same contest.

	Con	Lab	LD	SNP
1997 gen. election result	17.5	45.6	13.0	22.1
July 1998				
UK general election	14	43	9	33
Scottish constituency	9	37	8	45
Scottish regional list	11	32	12	43
August 1998				
UK general election	13	48	8	28
Scottish constituency	10	40	9	41
Scottish regional list	9	36	12	41
September 1998				
UK general election	13	46	8	31
Scottish constituency	11	41	8	38
Scottish regional list	10	39	10	40
October 1998				
UK general election	13	45	10	31
Scottish constituency	12	39	9	39
Scottish regional list	12	37	12	38
November 1998				
UK general election	14	43	12	29
Scottish constituency	12	39	12	37
Scottish regional list	11	37	14	35
December 1998				
UK general election	13	42	13	31
Scottish constituency	11	38	12	37
Scottish regional list	12	35	16	35
January 1999				
UK general election	13	46	11	28
Scottish constituency	11	38	11	38
Scottish regional list	11	37	12	38

Polls conducted by ICM and published in The Scotsman have arrived at materially similar results. Indeed, it is now a year since extrapolations from the two series of polls have shown either Labour or the SNP attracting the support necessary for an overall majority in the Parliament.

SNP hopes of running Labour very close in the Parliament elections have received a further boost from the results of recent local government by-elections and from the North East Scotland European Parliament by-election on 26 November 1998. The SNP held the latter seat with an increased majority compared with the 1994 contest, whereas Labour was beaten into third place by the Conservatives and saw its share of the vote fall by over a third. The outcome was in sharp contrast to an opinion poll published on the eve of the election which forecast a victory for the SNP over Labour by a margin of just four percentage points.

Table 2.7: North East Scotland European Parliament By-election, 26 November 1998

	%share of vote	%change on 1994 election
SNP	48.0	+5.3
Con	19.9	+1.3
Lab	18.5	-9.9
LD	9.8	+1.5
SSA	2.1	+1.8
Green	1.7	+0.6

At the local level Labour has not gained a single seat in Scotland since the general election and has suffered 11 losses, some following adverse swings of as much as 33%. The party has proved particularly vulnerable to the SNP in places such as Glasgow and North Lanarkshire where controversy has dogged the activities of the Labour-dominated councils serving deprived communities. Overall, and mirroring the result in North East Scotland, Labour's local vote appears to have declined by about one third. The Conservatives have picked up three seats in comfortable, middle-class wards, but such gains have to be seen in the context of the 1995 local elections when the party did even worse than at the subsequent general election.

Table 2.8: Local government by-elections in Scotland, May 1997 – January 1999

	Gains	Held	Lost	Net
Conservative	3	1	–	+3
Labour	–	9	11	−11
Liberal Democrat	3	4	1	+2
SNP	7	5	2	+5
Independent	3	1	2	+1

	%share (all 36 contests)	%change on 1995	%share (6 four-party contests)	%change on 1995
Conservative	17.9	+8.5	23.2	+5.5
Labour	27.2	−14.3	17.5	−12.4
Liberal Democrat	15.4	+3.5	32.8	+6.9
SNP	29.3	+1.0	21.9	−3.1

As the votes are counted overnight on 6/7 May all attention will be focused on two questions. Has Labour or the SNP won the largest number of seats in the Parliament? Has either party secured sufficient seats for an overall majority? On the answers to those questions hinge the whole future of Scottish politics and, very possibly, the place of Scotland in the Union. Three months before the election a 'hung Parliament' looks the most likely outcome, in which case the precise division of seats between the parties will be crucial. If Labour should require the votes of Liberal Democrats in order to sustain Donald Dewar as first minister it could usher in an era of coalition politics which eventually would spread beyond Edinburgh. If the SNP are able almost to command a majority on their own they will interpret the result as a mandate for the further pursuit of an independent Scotland. The Liberal Democrats may relish a role as the make weights in the Parliament, but for the Conservatives there is little to which they can look forward. Restricted, at best, to two dozen MSPs, they will be left to snipe from the side lines and wait – like Mr Micawber – for something to turn up.

Benchmarks for the Scottish Parliament elections

The exact number of seats won for any given share of the vote will depend on how electors use their two ballots. The analysis below assumes that the large majority will vote for the same party at both constituency and 'top up' level.

Vote share   Seats

Labour

50%+	65+	A significant advance compared with 1997 general election. Labour could win 60 of the 73 first past the post seats.
45%-50%	60-65	Labour close to an overall majority as support hardens. Threat from the SNP appears to have been held at bay.
40%-45%	54-60	A modest decline on 1997. Probably still sufficient for Labour to be largest party.
35%-40%	46-54	Party likely to be neck and neck with SNP. Balance of constituency and 'top up' votes will be critical.
Below 35%	<46	Labour's worst result in Scotland since 1931. Party faces struggle to prevent SNP grabbing the reins of power.

Conservative

20%+	26+	In context this would represent a considerable Tory comeback. The party might even win a first past the post seat.
15%-20%	20-26	This now appears to be the core unionist vote – cf. 17.5% in 1997. Tories yet to add an effective Scottish dimension to their appeal.
10%-15%	12-20	Yet another record low in electoral support. Real risk that Tories will be fourth party in Scottish Parliament.

Liberal Democrat

15%+	20+	Best 'centre' party result since the days of the Lib/SDP alliance. Able to bargain strongly with the Parliament's largest party.
10%-15%	13-20	On a par with recent general election scores -13% in 1992 and 1997. Seat total depends on polling heavily in Westminster strongholds.
Below 10%	<13	A poor result – cf. 7.2% in 1994 Euro elections. How can the new leader re-position the party in Scotland?

SNP

45%+	58+	Spectacular result for the SNP, though still just short of a majority. Support bound to be used to advance the case for independence.
40%-45%	52-58	Depending on overall pattern of results, SNP could be largest party. Scottish politics will never be the same again.
35%-40%	46-52	Likely to be neck and neck with Labour in both votes and seats. A new high for SNP national level support.
30%-35%	38-46	No better than the party got at the 1994 Euros – 32.6%. Suggests that it is still hard fully to translate sentiment into votes
25%-30%	32-38	Swing to the SNP since 1997 election, but a bitter disappointment. Labour would comfortably be the largest party and in control.
Below 25%	<32	The good news: no worse than the party's recent general elections. The bad news: a disaster compared with expectations.

Candidates for the Scottish Parliament

(as known at 15 February 1999)

In the constituency section candidates highlighted in **bold** are almost certain to be elected; those highlighted in *italic* could be elected if their party does well; candidates listed in plain type are unlikely to be elected.

The election of candidates from the lists depends on how many seats their party wins at constituency level. A party with a significant share of the vote in a region but no constituency seats could win as many as four 'top up' seats.

In some cases parties have named more list candidates than there are seats to be filled. Here we list only the first seven names on each party's list. The Greens are fielding a single list candidate in each region. The possibility of minor parties winning a 'top up' seat – e.g. the Scottish Socialist Alliance in Glasgow – should not be discounted. The Labour MP for Falkirk West, Dennis Canavan, is likely to stand as an Independent in that constituency.

Members of the House of Commons are marked *.

Central Scotland
Constituencies

	Con	Lab	LD	SNP
Airdrie & Shotts	Ross-Taylor, W.	**Whitefield, K. Ms.**	Miller, D.	*Paterson, G. Ms.*
Coatbridge & Chryston	Lind, G.	**Smith, E. Ms.**	....	Kearney, P.
Cumbernauld & Kilsyth	Slack, R.	**Craigie, C. Ms.**	O'Donnell, H.	*Wilson, A.*
East Kilbride	Stevenson, C.	**Kerr, A.**	Hawthorn, E.	Fabiani, L. Ms.
Falkirk East	Orr, A.	**Peattie, C. Ms.**	MacDonald, G.	Brown, K.
Falkirk West	Miller, G.	**Martin, R.**	Smith, A.	Matheson, M.
Hamilton North & Bellshill	Thomson, S.	**MacMahon, M.**	....	McAlorum, K. Ms.
Hamilton South	Mitchell, M. Ms.	**McCabe, T.**	....	Ardrey, A.
Kilmarnock & Loudoun	McIntosh, L. Ms.	*Jamieston, M. Ms.*	Stewart, J.	*Neil, A.*
Motherwell & Wishaw	Gibson, W.	**McConnell, J.**	Spillane, R.	*McGuigan, J.*

Regional list candidates

	Con	Lab	LD	SNP
1	....	Tynan, B.	Gorrie, D.*	Neil, A.
2	....	Sutherland, L. Ms.	Stewart, J.	Wilson, A.
3	....	....	Waddell, R.	Matheson, M.
4	....	....	MacFarlane, I.	Paterson, G. Ms.
5	....	....	MacDonald, G.	Fabiani, L. Ms.
6	....	....	Spillane, R.	Brown, K.
7	....	....	....	Neary, K. Ms.

Glasgow
Constituencies

	Con	Lab	LD	SNP
Glasgow Anniesland	Aitken, W.	**Dewar, D.***	Brown, I.	Stewart, K.
Glasgow Ballieston	Pickering, C. Ms.	**Curran, M. Ms.**	....	Elder, D. Ms.
Glasgow Cathcart	Leishman, M. Ms.	**Watson, M.**	....	Whitehead, M. Ms.
Glasgow Govan	Ahmed-Sheikh, T. Ms.	*Jackson, G.*	....	*Sturgeon, N. Ms.*
Glasgow Kelvin	Rasul, A.	**McNeill, P. Ms.**	Craig, M. Ms.	White, S. Ms.
Glasgow Maryhill	Fry, M.	**Ferguson, P. Ms**.	....	Wilson, B.
Glasgow Pollok	O'Brien, R.	**Lamont, J.**	....	Gibson, K.
Glasgow Rutherglen	Starbuck, M.	**Hughes, J. Ms**	Brown, R.	Chalmers, T.
Glasgow Shettleston	Bain, C.	**McAveety, F.**	Fryer, J. Ms.	Byrne, J.
Glasgow Springburn	Roxburgh, M.	**Martin, P.**	....	Brady, J.

Regional list candidates

	Con	Lab	LD	SNP
1	....	Dewar, D.*	Brown, R.	Sturgeon, N. Ms.
2	....	Fitzpatrick, B.	Craig, M. Ms.	Elder, D. Ms.
3	....	....	Aslam Kahn, M.	Gibson, K.
4	....	....	Paris, M. Ms.	White, S. Ms.
5	....	....	Hook, J. Ms.	Whitehead, M. Ms.
6	....	....	....	Brady, J.
7	....	....	....	Wilson, B.

Highlands and Islands
Constituencies

	Con	Lab	LD	SNP
Argyll & Bute	Petrie, D.	Raven, H.	**Lyon, G.**	*Hamilton, D.*
Caithness, Sutherland & Easter Ross	Jenkins, R.	*Hendry, J.*	*Stone, J.*	*Urquhart, J. Ms.*
Inverness East, Nairn & Lochaber	Scanlon, M. Ms.	*Aitken, J. Ms.*	Fraser, D.	*Ewing, F.*
Moray	Findlay, A.	Farquharson, A. Ms.	Kenton, P. Ms.	**Ewing, M. Ms.***
Orkney	Zawadski, C.	....	**Wallace, J.***	Mowat, J.
Ross, Skye & Inverness West	Scott, J.	*Munro, D.*	*Farquhar-Munro, J.*	*Mather, J.*
Shetland	Robinson, G.	....	**Scott, T.**	Ross, W.
Western Isles	McGrigor, J.	*Morrison, A.*	Horne, J.	*Nicholson, A.*

Regional list candidates

	Con	Lab	LD	SNP
1	....	Peacock, P.	Foxley, M.	Ewing, W. Ms.
2	....	McMillan, M. Ms.	Thurso, J.	Ewing, M. Ms.*
3	....	....	Fraser, D.	Hamilton, D.
4	....	....	Currie, R.	Ewing, F.
5	....	....	Kenton, P. Ms.	Mather, J.
6	....	....	McKie, A.	Nicholson, A.
7	....	....	Mair, R.	Crawford, D.

Lothians
Constituencies

	Con	Lab	LD	SNP
Edinburgh Central	Low, J. Ms.	**Boyack, S. Ms.**	Myles, A.	McKee, I.
Edinburgh East & Musselborough	Balfour, J.	**Deacon, S. Ms.**	Thomas, M. Ms.	MacAskill, K.
Edinburgh North & Leith	Sempill, J.	**Chisholm, M.***	Tombs, S.	Dana, A. Ms.
Edinburgh Pentlands	*McLetchie, D.*	**Gray, I.**	Gibson, I.	Gibb, S.
Edinburgh South	Whyte, I.	**MacKay, A.**	Pringle, M.	MacDonald, M. Ms.
Edinburgh West	*Selkirk, Lord*	Fox, C. Ms.	**Smith, M. Ms.**	Sutherland, G.
Linlithgow	Lindhorst, G.	**Mulligan, M. Ms.**	Barrett, J.	*Stevenson, S.*
Livingston	Younger, D.	*Muldoon, B.*	Oliver, M.	*McCarra, G.*
Midlothian	Turnbull, G.	**Brankin, R. Ms.**	Elder, J.	*Robertson, A.*

Regional list candidates

	Con	Lab	LD	SNP
1	....	Shiels, L. Ms.	Steel, D.	MacDonald, M. Ms.
2	....	McLean, B.	Pringle, M.	MacAskill, K.
3	....	....	MacLaren, M. Ms.	Hyslop, F. Ms.
4	....	....	Myles, A.	Dana, A. Ms.
5	....	....	Gibson, I.	Scott, P.
6	....	....	Utting, K. Ms.	Gibb, S.
7	....	....	....	McKee, I.

Mid Scotland and Fife
Constituencies

	Con	Lab	LD	SNP
Dunfermline East	Ruxton, C. Ms.	**Eadie, H. Ms.**	....	McCarthy, D.
Dunfermline West	Buchan, G.	**Barrie, S.**	....	Chapman, D.
Fife Central	Harding, K.	**McLeish, H.***	Liston, J-A. Ms.	Marwick, T. Ms.
Fife North East	Brocklebank, E.	Milne, C.	**Smith, I.**	Welsh, C.
Kirkcaldy	Scott-Hayward, M.	**Livingston, M. Ms.**	Mainland, J.	*Hosie, S.*
Ochil	Johnston, N.	*Simpson, R.*	Mar & Kellie, J.	*Reid, G.*
Perth	Stevenson, I.	Richards, J. Ms.	Brodie, C.	**Cunningham, R. Ms.***
Stirling	*Monteith, B.*	*Jackson, S. Ms.*	MacFarlane, I.	Ewing, A. Ms.
Tayside North	Fraser, M.	....	Regent, P.	**Swinney, J.***

Regional list candidates

	Con	Lab	LD	SNP
1	....	McLeish, H.*	Raffan, K.	Swinney, J.*
2	....	Miller, M. Ms.	Arbuckle, A.	Reid, G.
3	....	....	Harris, E. Ms.	Marwick, T. Ms.
4	....	....	Robertson, J. Ms.	Cunningham, R. Ms.*
5	....	....	Mar & Kellie, J.	Crawford, B.
6	....	....	Brodie, C.	Ewing, A. Ms.
7	....	....	Regent, P.	Welsh, C.

North East Scotland
Constituencies

	Con	Lab	LD	SNP
Aberdeen Central	Mason, T.	**MacDonald, L.**	Anderson, E. Ms.	Lochhead, R.
Aberdeen North	Haughie, I.	**Thomson, E. Ms.**	....	*Adam, B.*
Aberdeen South	*Milne, N. Ms.*	*Elrick, M.*	*Stephen, N.*	McGugan, I. Ms.
Aberdeenshire West & Kincardine	*Wallace, B.*	....	*Rumbles, M.*	Watt, M. Ms.
Angus	Harris, R.	McFatridge, I.	Speirs, D.	**Welsh, A.***
Banff & Buchan	Davidson, D.	Harris, M. Ms..	Mackie, M.	**Salmond, A.***
Dundee East	Mitchell, I.	**McAllion, J.***	Lawrie, R.	*Robison, S. Ms.*
Dundee West	Buchan, G.	**MacLean, K. Ms.**	Dick, E. Ms.	Cashley, C.
Gordon	*Johnstone, A.*	....	**Radcliffe, N. Ms.**	*Stronach, S.*

Regional list candidates

	Con	Lab	LD	SNP
1	....	McAllion, J.*	Stephen, N.	Salmond, A.*
2	....	Glenn, M. Ms.	Mackie, M.	Welsh, A.*
3	....	Sewel, Lord	Ford, M.	Adam, B.
4	....	....	Rumbles, M.	Lochhead, R.
5	....	....	Yuill, I.	Robison, S. Ms.
6	....	....	Dick, E. Ms.	McGugan, I. Ms.
7	....	....	Anderson, E. Ms.	Stronach, S.

South of Scotland
Constituencies

	Con	Lab	LD	SNP
Ayr	*Gallie, P.*	**Welsh, I.**	Bell, J. Ms.	Mullin, R.
Carrick, Cumnock & Doon Valley	Scott, J.	**Jamieson, C. Ms.**	....	Ingram, A.
Clydesdale	Cormack, C.	**Turnbull, K. Ms.**	Grieve, S. Ms.	Winning, A. Ms.
Cunninghame South	Tosh, M.	**Oldfather, I. Ms.**	....	Russell, M.
Dumfries	Mundell, D.	**Murray, E. Ms.**	Wallace, N.	Norris, S.
East Lothian	Richard, C. Ms.	**Home Robertson, J.***	Hayman, J. Ms.	Millar, C.
Galloway & Upper Nithsdale	Fergusson, A.	....	Mitchell, J. Ms.	**Morgan, A.***
Roxburgh & Berwickshire	Hutton, A.	McLeod, S. Ms.	**Robson, E.**	Crawford, S.
Tweeddale, Ettrick & Lauderdale	....	*McGregor, G.*	*Jenkins, I.*	Creech, C. Ms.

Regional list candidates

	Con	Lab	LD	SNP
1	....	Geddes, K.	Ross Scott, J.	Morgan, A.*
2	....	Beamish, C.	Hannay, D.	Russell, M.
3	....	....	Hayman, J. Ms.	Ingram, A.
4	....	....	Grieve, S. Ms.	Creech, C. Ms.
5	....	....	Bell, J. Ms.	Norris, S.
6	....	....	Napier, C. Ms.	Higgins, K. Ms.
7	....	....	....	Mullin, R.

West of Scotland
Constituencies

	Con	Lab	LD	SNP
Clydebank & Milngavie	Luckhorst, D. Ms.	**McNulty, D.**	Ackland, R.	Yuill, J.
Cunninghame North	Johnston, M.	**Wilson, A.**	....	Ullrich, K. Ms.
Dumbarton	Reece, D.	**Baillie, J. Ms.**	Coleshill, P.	*Quinan, L.*
Eastwood	*Young, J.*	*McIntosh, K.*	McCurley, A. Ms.	Findlay, R. Ms.
Greenock & Inverclyde	Wilkinson, R.	**MacNeil, D.**	Finnie, R.	Hamilton, I.
Paisley North	Ramsey, P.	**Alexander, W. Ms.**	....	MacKay, I.
Paisley South	Laidlaw, S. Ms.	**Henry, H.**	....	*Martin, B.*
Renfrewshire West	Goldie, A. Ms.	*Godman, P. Ms.*	Ascherson, N.	*Campbell, C.*
Strathkelvin & Bearsden	Ferguson, C.	**Galbraith, S.***	....	McLeod, F. Ms.

Regional list candidates

	Con	Lab	LD	SNP
1	....	Galbraith, S.*	Finnie, R.	Campbell, C.
2	....	Wilson, N. Ms.	McCartin, E. Ms.	Ullrich, K. Ms.
3	....	....	Ackland, R.	Quinan, L.
4	....	....	Tough, A.	McLeod, F. Ms.
5	....	....	Hamblen, C. Ms.	Yuill, J.
6	....	....	Morrison, J.	Hamilton, I.
7	....	....	McInnes, C. Ms.	Findlay, R. Ms.

Green Party Candidates – No. 1 on list

Central Scotland, Falconer, M.; Glasgow, Allan, K. Ms.; Highlands & Islands, Scott, E. Ms.; Lothian, Harper, R.; Mid Scotland & Fife, Farmer, G.; North East Scotland, Baird, S. Ms.; South of Scotland, Coyne, M. Ms.; West of Scotland, Ballance, C.

3. Welsh Assembly Elections

History in the making

Introduction by: **Aled Eurig**, *Head of News and Current Affairs, BBC Wales*

The narrowness of the devolution vote made the night of 18/19 September 1997 one of high political drama in Wales. The result meant that it was also one of profound historical significance. To base one's judgement of the significance of this vote purely on the detailed nature of the Government's proposals is to miss the point. John Davies, the author of the Penguin History of Wales, described it as 'the most important night in the national history of Wales since the defeat of Owain Glyndwr six centuries ago'. The then Welsh Secretary, Ron Davies, claimed that the Welsh people had shown that they believed in themselves.

The only all-Wales Parliament was established by Glyndwr in 1404. His defeat killed any hope for Wales to establish its own Parliament and constitution. It was to be subsumed and annexed within England, and the following centuries saw Welsh ambition manifest itself in gaining recognition for individual effort rather than in developing any sense of statehood to accompany Welsh patriotism.

The Liberal party, and the efforts of a small band of MPs – 'Cymru Fydd' – led by the young Lloyd George did raise the flag of Welsh nationalism at the end of the 19th century. Lloyd George himself was warmly received in both Welsh speaking districts and the industrial south, but opposition within the Liberal party from the north-east and the industrial south-east led to the movement's failure. The Welsh nationalist party – Plaid Cymru – was established in 1924, but failed politically until the seventies and even then its strength was largely confined to the Welsh-language heartlands.

It is therefore remarkable that in spite of the absence of a coherent institutional framework for the nation over such a lengthy period of time, the idea of Wales has persisted. In contrast to Scotland, whose identity has been underpinned by a Scottish Parliament until comparatively recently in historical terms, Wales's political identity has focused more on language and culture.

The one significant institutional impetus in this period was the establishment of the Welsh Office by the Labour government in 1964 and the gradual transfer of powers from Whitehall to Cardiff. Arguably this helped lay the foundations of a consensus about the desirability of taking more responsibility for Welsh affairs. Ironically, following the decisive rejection of devolution in 1979, such a consensus was boosted by the experience of Conservative government in the 1980s and 1990s. The various Secretaries of State for Wales, ranging from the conciliatory David Hunt and Peter Walker to the combative John Redwood, encouraged the creation of a 'quango' state based on the appointment of Conservative supporters to run the work of government in Wales. This factor, perhaps more than any other, revived the growth of the movement for devolution within the Labour party in Wales in this period.

One critical issue for the referendum vote in Wales was whether it was simply about constitutional reform or was it more related to a sense of Welsh identity? Unsurprisingly the 'Yes' camp in particular believed it to be an affirmation of nationhood and of Welsh patriotism. The 'Nos' took a rather more sceptical view. The fact that only a quarter of the electorate had voted in favour meant, in the words of Tim Williams, that the Assembly 'will be born in doubt'.

Indeed, at first sight, the geographical distribution of the vote reflected the linguistic splits and political cleavages within Wales. Such a map bears a remarkable similarity to the separation between the more Welsh areas – the 'Principality' – which were the ancient kingdoms of the North and West held by the native princes up until the 13th century, and the 'Marches' – the more Anglicised areas of Wales comprising the Norman domains along the Eastern border together with south Pembrokeshire.

However, such a picture can be misleadingly simple. There was a substantial vote for both camps in all districts and in no area did the vote for either side drop below 30% of those voting. People under 45 voted in favour of the Assembly by a factor of 3:2, while the reverse was the case with those over 45. A majority of those born in Wales and watching Welsh-based media were in favour, while those born outside Wales and tuned into English media voted against. Welsh speakers supported the Assembly by more than 7:2. Party support was also significant. Labour supporters backed the proposals by a margin of 3:2 and Plaid supporters by 12:1. Conservatives opposed by a margin of 9:1, and Liberal Democrat voters – despite the formal stance of the party – were 7:3 against.

Ron Davies famously stated that devolution is a 'process', not an event. His 'walk on the wild side' on Clapham Common, and the consequent bitter battle for the Labour leadership in Wales is proof that Assembly politics will be at least unpredictable. The manner in which Labour conducts itself in the Assembly will be a litmus test of how effectively the new politics, and the influence of the Blair project, has permeated the workings of the party in Wales.

Any suggestion that Wales is less significant or relevant in some way than Scotland should be banished. Although the Assembly will not have primary legislative powers, the significance of its powers over secondary legislation is underestimated. Indeed it may be considered as the model for any extension of regional government in England.

Aled Eurig

Structure and functions of the Welsh Assembly

The Welsh Assembly is being established following a referendum held in Wales on 18 September 1997. At the referendum 1,112,117 valid votes were cast, representing 50.1% of the Welsh electorate. There were 3,999 spoilt ballot papers. Of those voting, 559,419 (50.3%) agreed that there should be a Welsh Assembly and 552,698 (49.7%) did not agree. A 'Yes' majority of just 6,721. The results of the referendum were counted and announced for each Welsh local authority area. The detailed outcome was as follows:

Table 3.1: Result of Referendum on Welsh Assembly, 18 September 1997

Council	% Turnout	Yes	%	No	%
Anglesey, Isle of	56.9	15,649	50.9	15,095	49.1
Blaenau Gwent	49.3	15,237	56.1	11,928	43.9
Bridgend	50.6	27,632	54.4	23,172	45.6
Caerphilly	49.3	34,830	54.7	28,841	45.3
Cardiff	46.9	47,527	44.4	59,589	55.6
Carmarthenshire	56.4	49,115	65.3	26,119	34.7
Ceredigion	56.8	18,304	59.2	12,614	40.8
Conwy	51.5	18,369	40.9	26,521	59.1
Denbighshire	49.7	14,271	40.8	20,732	59.2
Flintshire	41.0	17,746	38.2	28,707	61.8
Gwynedd	59.8	35,425	64.1	19,859	35.9
Merthyr Tydfil	49.5	12,707	58.2	9,121	41.8
Monmouthshire	50.5	10,592	32.1	22,403	67.9
Neath Port Talbot	51.9	36,730	66.5	18,463	33.5
Newport	45.9	16,172	37.4	27,017	62.6
Pembrokeshire	52.6	19,979	42.8	26,712	57.2
Powys	56.2	23,038	42.7	30,966	57.3
Rhondda Cynon Taff	49.9	51,201	58.5	36,362	41.5
Swansea	47.1	42,789	52.0	39,561	48.0
Torfaen	45.5	15,756	49.8	15,854	50.2
Vale of Glamorgan	54.3	17,776	36.7	30,613	63.3
Wrexham	42.4	18,574	45.3	22,449	54.7
Wales	**50.1**	**559,419**	**50.3**	**552,698**	**49.7**

Arrangements for the operation of the Welsh Assembly are as follows:

- **Elections:** First elections to the Welsh Assembly take place on Thursday 6 May 1999, and will then occur every four years.
- **Membership:** 60-member Assembly, elected by a form of proportional representation called the Additional Member System (AMS).
- **Seat of the Assembly:** the Assembly will sit in Crickhowell House in Cardiff until autumn 2001, when the permanent Assembly Building at Pier Head in Cardiff is ready.
- **Sessions:** the Secretary of State for Wales has accepted proposals that the Assembly should have a three-day week and keep normal business hours. It will be for the Assembly itself to decide the final arrangements relating to its sessions.
- **First Sitting:** the Assembly will sit for the first time within a few of days of the election on the 6 May 1999, the exact date is yet to be confirmed. The Assembly will be able to exercise its full powers from this time.

- **Official Opening:** the Official Opening will be on 26 May 1999.
- **First Secretary:** the political leader of the Assembly will be elected by a majority vote of the 60 members, and will be called the First Secretary.
- **Assembly Secretaries:** the First Secretary will appoint Assembly Secretaries, who will each have responsibility for a field in which the Assembly has functions. Each Assembly Secretary will be accountable to the Assembly.
- **Executive Committee:** the Executive Committee will be made up of the First Secretary and all of the Assembly Secretaries. The First Secretary will be the effective head of the Executive Committee, and will be accountable to the Assembly for all of the Executive Committee's actions.
- **Specialist Committees:** the Assembly will establish specialist committees for each of the fields in which it has functions. All of the parties will be represented in these committees, with majority representation for the main party in the Assembly. The relevant Assembly Secretary will also be a member of each committee. These committees will report to the Executive Committee.
- **Presiding Officer:** the Assembly will elect a Presiding Officer and a deputy to perform a similar role to that of the Speaker in the House of Commons, chairing and keeping order during Assembly meetings.
- **Financial Arrangements:** the Assembly will be allocated a budget by Westminster of a similar level to the budget currently given to the Secretary of State for Wales, approximately £7 billion in 1998.

The Welsh Assembly will have responsibilities and powers as follows:

- **Transfer of functions:** the Secretary of State for Wales will transfer functions to the Welsh Assembly through Transfer Orders. All of the functions which are going to be transferred are already within the ambit of the Secretary of State.
- **Assembly powers to make secondary legislation:** the Assembly will be able to make secondary legislation in the following areas, in accordance with primary legislation enacted by Westminster.

  - economic development
  - agriculture, forestry, fisheries and food
  - industry and training
  - education
  - local government
  - health and personal social services
  - housing
  - environment
  - town and country planning
  - transport and roads
  - arts, culture and the Welsh language
  - the built heritage
  - sport and recreation
  - tourism
  - water and flood defence

- **Assembly's power over quangos:** the Assembly will have the power to question, monitor and reduce the number of unelected public bodies.
- **Assembly's power to debate:** the Assembly will be able to debate matters which it does not directly control.

Relations between the Welsh Assembly and Westminster

- **Westminster's retained powers:** Westminster will retain full primary legislation powers in all areas and control over the following:
  - Foreign Affairs
  - Defence
  - Taxation
  - Macro-economic Policy
  - Fiscal and Common Markets Policy
  - Broadcasting Policy
  - The Justice System and Prisons
  - Police and Fire Services
  - National Lottery and Related Matters
  - Social Security Benefits
  - Competition Policy
  - Labour Market Policy

- **Secretary of State for Wales:** The Secretary of State for Wales will continue to represent Welsh interests in the UK Cabinet. There will be a close working relationship between the Assembly and the Secretary of State, but the Secretary of State will not be bound by the Assembly's views. The Secretary of State will be able to attend meetings of the Assembly to participate in debates, but will not be able to vote.
- **Welsh MPs:** Welsh MPs will continue to play a full and constructive role at Westminster.
- **Future transfer of power:** the procedures which have been set down for the transfer of functions from the Secretary of State to the Assembly could be used in the future to expand further the powers of the Assembly. This would be subject to the consent of Westminster.

Operation of electoral system

The elections for the first four year term of the new Welsh Assembly are due to be held on Thursday 6 May 1999 – the same day as elections for all 22 Welsh local councils (see chapter 6).

The Assembly will comprise 60 members. They will be chosen in one of two ways:

i) Each of the 40 Welsh parliamentary constituencies will elect a single Assembly member by the traditional first past the post method.

ii) Each of five electoral regions in Wales (the regions are coterminous with the European parliament constituencies drawn up for the 1994 elections) will elect four additional members in order to provide a counter to any disparity between votes gained and seats won in the region through the operation of simple plurality. A total of 20 members will be elected by this 'topping up' process.

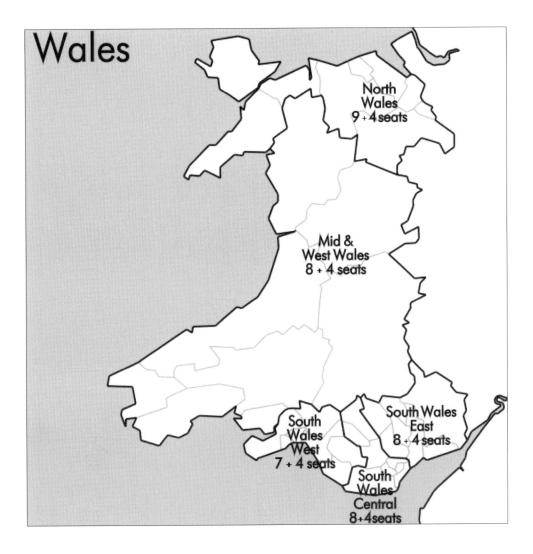

Wales

North
Wales
9 + 4 seats

Mid &
West Wales
8 + 4 seats

South Wales
East
8 + 4 seats

South
Wales
West
7 + 4 seats

South
Wales
Central
8+4seats

Electors will have two votes. One for a candidate within their Assembly (parliamentary) constituency, and one for a 'party list' within their electoral region. There is nothing to stop electors choosing a constituency candidate who represents a different party to the one for which they vote at regional level.

Welsh Assembly Region: North Wales
YOU HAVE ONE VOTE ON THIS PAPER

Put X in one box ▶

THE CONSERVATIVE AND UNIONIST PARTY	☐
1 Huw Williams 2 David Jones 3 Peter Green 4 Sarah Smith	
THE LABOUR PARTY	☐
1 Tony Jacobs 2 Mary O'Brien 3 Harry Reynolds 4 Elsa Phillips	
LIBERAL DEMOCRATS	☐
1 Jean Roberts 2 David Williams 3 Rhodri Black 4 Joe Moss	
PLAID CYMRU	☐
1 Rhodri Evans 2 Nigel Bristow 3 Ruth Middleton 4 Maria Parks	
SOCIALIST LABOUR PARTY	☐
1 James Jones 2 Robert Evans 3 Rebecca Smith	
WELSH GREEN PARTY	☐
1 Luke James 2 Dennis Peters 3 Ronald Poole	
DAVIES Colin Save the Environment	☐
JONES Alun Independent	☐

Welsh Assembly Constituency: Conwy
VOTE FOR ONE CANDIDATE ONLY

1	**BRISTOW Rhodri David** 23 High Street, Anytown Plaid Cymru	
2	**DAVIES Sarah** 912 Main Street, Anytown The Conservative Party	
3	**REES Alun** 4 Elgin Avenue, Anytown The Labour Party	
4	**SULLIVAN Huw Peter** 93 Holyrood Road, Anytown Independent	
5	**WIGLEY Rhondda Anne** 45 Easter Road, Anytown Liberal Democrat	
6	**WILLIAMS Aled David** 112 South Gyle Avenue, Anytown The Green Party	

The total number of list votes cast for each party in all the constituencies in each region will be aggregated to form the basis for calculating the allocation of the additional seats. Parties will supply a list of candidates for each region in the order in which they wish them to be elected. Individuals may simultaneously be candidates both in a constituency and on *one* regional list, but those who win a constituency seat will no longer be eligible to be an additional member. 'Independent' candidates are entitled to stand in either a constituency or a region or both, but the votes of candidates not on the list of a registered party will each be treated separately.

To be certain of securing a Welsh Assembly seat a party or an individual must receive a proportion of the vote equal to 100 divided by the total number of seats in the region **plus one**. This threshold will vary from 8.3% (100÷11+1) in South Wales West to 7.1% (100÷13+1) in North Wales. It is possible to secure a seat with a lesser share of the vote depending on the way votes are distributed between the competing parties.

Each candidate nominated in a constituency and each party and individual which appears on a regional list must pay a deposit of £500. This will be returned if the candidate/party receives at least 5% of the total valid votes cast in the constituency/region.

Votes cast in the Welsh Assembly elections will be counted and the results announced overnight on 6/7 May.

Electing Additional Members in Wales: an example

In the North Wales electoral 'region' there are nine parliamentary constituencies. This region, like all the others, has been allocated four additional members, making a total of 13 Assembly representatives. In this example we use the results of the 1997 general election and make the assumption that all electors would have cast their 'party list' votes for the same party or group for which they voted at constituency level.

Table 3.2: North Wales – 1997 general election result

	Con	Lab	LD	PC	Other
Votes	85,554	166,144	41,517	49,904	10,765
% Share	24.2	46.9	11.7	14.1	3.0
Seats	–	7	–	2	–

Additional members are chosen having taken into account the number of seats a party has already won within the region. Therefore, to begin allocating the four additional seats it is necessary to divide the total votes cast for each party by the number of constituencies it has won **plus one**. Each time a party gains a seat the number by which its total vote is to be divided increases by one.

Following the initial calculation the party with the highest number of remaining votes, Conservative, is awarded a seat – see Table 3.3. That seat is taken by the candidate in first place on the Conservative regional list, assuming that he/she has not already been elected as a constituency member. The Conservative vote is now divided by two – the seat just acquired plus one – to give 42,777. Because the Conservative vote is still the highest the party secures a further seat for its second placed eligible candidate and its total vote is now divided by three = 28,518. The party with the largest remaining vote total (41,517) is now the Liberal Democrats, whose top candidate takes the third available seat. Their vote is divided by two to leave a remainder of 20,759. With Labour, Plaid Cymru and Others still unchanged from the original calculations, the Conservatives secure the final seat because their remainder of 28,518 is now the largest. The third eligible candidate on the party's list thus also becomes a member of the Assembly.

Table 3.3: North Wales - allocation of additional members

	Con	Lab	LD	PC	Others	Elected (no. on list)
Total votes	85,554	166,144	41,517	49,904	10,765	
Initial divisor	0 + 1	7 + 1	0 + 1	2 + 1	0 + 1	Elected (no. on list)
1st seat	85,554	20,768	41,517	16,635	10,765	Con (1)
2nd seat	42,777	20,768	41,517	16,635	10,765	Con (2)
3rd seat	28,518	20,768	41,517	16,635	10,765	LD (1)
4th seat	28,518	20,768	20,759	16,635	10,765	Con (3)

The operation of this process has awarded three of the additional seats to the Conservatives and one to the Liberal Democrats. The total representation of North Wales in the Assembly would therefore be:

Table 3.4: North Wales - Assembly Membership

	Con	Lab	LD	PC	Others
Constituency members	–	7	–	2	–
'Top up' seats	3	–	1	–	–
Total	3	7	1	2	–

The Welsh Assembly and past election results

As this is the first election to the Welsh Assembly there are no past contests with which to make comparisons. However, there are three sets of elections which can be used to give a flavour of what might happen.

The 'notional' results of the 1992 general election for North Wales and for Mid and West Wales, the actual results in the other three regions and the actual results of the 1997 general election throughout the country provide information on the number of votes cast and the winning party in the 40 constituencies. On the assumption that all electors would have cast their 'party list' votes for the same party or group for which they voted at constituency level, they also allow the aggregation of the votes for each party in each region in order to calculate the allocation of the additional seats.

Because the European Parliament constituencies and the Assembly regions are coterminous, the results of the 1994 European Parliament elections can be used to show the distribution of support in each region at that time. Individual constituency results are not available, but may be estimated by making the assumption that the proportion of a party's total vote in the region contributed by each constituency at a general election will be the same as at the European election. For example, if Alyn and Deeside contributed 10% of the total North Wales Conservative vote in 1997, it is reasonable to assume that it also did so in 1994. In this way it is possible to compile 'notional' 1994 results for each constituency and to gauge which party would have won them.

The results of Welsh local elections are of little help in estimating the outcome of national or regional elections. At the inaugural contests for the Welsh unitary authorities in 1995 candidates were elected unopposed in 208 of the 865 wards (24%) and in only 48 wards (5.5%) did each of the four major parties field a candidate. Moreover, because both the parliamentary (Assembly) and European constituencies were drawn on the basis of the pre-1995 configuration of Welsh local government, they frequently cross current council boundaries.

The following pages describe and map the composition of each Welsh Assembly electoral region and indicate what the results of the Welsh Assembly elections might have been if they had taken place in 1992, 1994 and 1997.

Mid and West Wales Electoral Region

1998 parliamentary electorate
408,157

% of Welsh electorate
18.3

No. of Assembly seats
8 + 4

% of Assembly seats
20.0

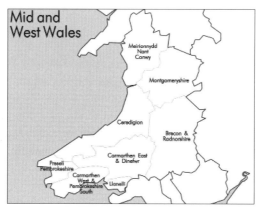

Comprising the constituencies of:	1992	Won by 1994*	1997	% maj. 1997	Second party 1997
Brecon & Radnorshire	Con	Lab	LD	11.9	Con
Carmarthen East & Dinefwr	Lab	Lab	Lab	8.3	PC
Carmarthen West & Pembrokeshire South	Lab	Lab	Lab	22.6	Con
Ceredigion	PC	PC	PC	17.3	Lab
Llanelli	Lab	Lab	Lab	38.9	PC
Meirionnydd Nant Conwy	PC	PC	PC	27.7	Lab
Montgomeryshire	LD	LD	LD	19.7	Con
Preseli Pembrokeshire	Con	Lab	Lab	20.6	Con

*The individual results for 1994 are estimates based on the pattern of voting at the European Parliament election.

Mid and West Wales is the most rural of the five Welsh electoral regions and the one where support is most evenly divided between the political parties. Nonetheless six of the eight individual constituencies look safe for the party which won them at the 1997 general election. Brecon and Radnorshire has been a perpetual marginal since a by-election in 1985 and presents the Conservatives with their only realistic target in the region. Labour cannot be entirely discounted here either. In Carmarthen East and Dinefwr Plaid Cymru ran Labour surprisingly close in 1997 and must stand a chance of winning the seat in the context of a Welsh Assembly election. The top two Conservative list candidates are almost certain to gain seats, albeit as a reflection of the party's failure to secure sufficient votes to win an individual constituency on a first past the post basis.

Votes and seats based on the 1992 general election

	Con	Lab	LD	PC	Others
Votes	93,324	105,298	65,445	57,089	2,014
% share of vote	28.9	32.6	20.3	17.7	0.6
Seats (FPTP)	2	3	1	2	0
% share of seats	25.0	37.5	12.5	25.0	0.0
Seats ('Top up')	2	1	1	0	0
Total	**4**	**4**	**2**	**2**	**0**
% share of seats	33.3	33.3	16.7	16.7	0.0

Votes and seats based on the 1994 European election

	Con	Lab	LD	PC	Others
Votes	31,606	78,092	23,719	48,858	10,462
% share of vote	16.4	40.5	12.3	25.3	5.4
Seats (FPTP)	0	5	1	2	0
% share of seats	0.0	62.5	12.5	25	0.0
Seats ('Top up')	2	1	0	1	0
Total	**2**	**6**	**1**	**3**	**0**
% share of seats	16.7	50.0	8.3	25.0	0.0

Votes and seats based on the 1997 general election

	Con	Lab	LD	PC	Others
Votes	63,769	116,151	56,479	61,777	9,378
% share of vote	20.7	37.8	18.4	20.1	3.0
Seats (FPTP)	0	4	2	2	0
% share of seats	0.0	50.0	25.0	25.0	0.0
Seats ('Top up')	3	1	0	0	0
Total	**3**	**5**	**2**	**2**	**0**
% share of seats	25.0	41.7	16.7	16.7	0.0

North Wales Electoral Region

1998 parliamentary electorate	**% of Welsh electorate**
481,345	21.6

No. of Assembly seats	**% of Assembly seats**
9 + 4	21.7

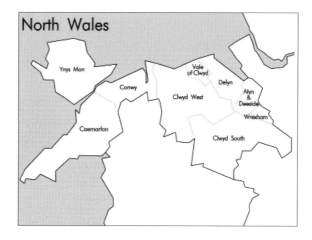

Comprising the constituencies of:	Won by 1992	1994*	1997	% maj. 1997	Second party 1997
Alyn & Deeside	Lab	Lab	Lab	39.1	Con
Caernarfon	PC	PC	PC	21.6	Lab
Clwyd South	Lab	Lab	Lab	35.1	Con
Clwyd West	Con	PC	Lab	4.6	Con
Conwy	Con	Lab	Lab	3.8	LD
Delyn	Lab	Lab	Lab	31.2	Con
Vale of Clwyd	Con	Lab	Lab	22.9	Con
Wrexham	Lab	Lab	Lab	32.3	Con
Ynys Mon	PC	PC	PC	6.2	Lab

The individual results for 1994 are estimates based on the pattern of voting at the European Parliament election.

North Wales is a socially and politically mixed constituency containing traditional Labour industrial areas, prosperous resort and retirement suburbs, and rural Welsh speaking communities. Of all the Welsh electoral regions it offers the most hope to the Conservatives, but their 24% of the vote in 1997 was not sufficient to win any parliamentary seats. Plaid Cymru do not poll strongly outside their heartlands at Westminster elections, but they ran Labour a fairly close second at the 1994 European contests. If electors treat the Assembly elections in a similar way, Plaid could win four out of the 13 seats. The Conservatives and Liberal Democrats will secure some representation thanks to the 'top up', but the Tories in particular need to win some first past the post seats – Clwyd West is easiest – to provide evidence that they can have a future in middle-class Wales.

Votes and seats based on the 1992 general election

	Con	*Lab*	*LD*	*PC*	*Others*
Votes	135,537	141,593	49,242	50,634	2,403
% share of vote	35.7	37.3	13.0	13.3	0.6
Seats (FPTP)	3	4	0	2	0
% share of seats	33.3	44.4	0.0	22.2	0.0
Seats ('Top up')	2	1	1	0	0
Total	**5**	**5**	**1**	**2**	**0**
% share of seats	38.5	38.5	7.7	15.4	0.0

Votes and seats based on the 1994 European election

	Con	*Lab*	*LD*	*PC*	*Others*
Votes	33,450	88,091	14,828	72,849	6,538
% share of vote	15.5	40.8	6.9	33.8	3.0
Seats (FPTP)	0	6	0	3	0
% share of seats	0.0	66.7	0.0	33.3	0.0
Seats ('Top up')	2	0	1	1	0
Total	**2**	**6**	**1**	**4**	**0**
% share of seats	15.4	46.2	7.7	30.8	0.0

Votes and seats based on the 1997 general election

	Con	*Lab*	*LD*	*PC*	*Others*
Votes	85,554	166,144	41,517	49,904	10,765
% share of vote	24.2	46.9	11.7	14.1	3.0
Seats (FPTP)	0	7	0	2	0
% share of seats	0.0	77.8	0.0	22.2	0.0
Seats ('Top up')	3	0	1	0	0
Total	**3**	**7**	**1**	**2**	**0**
% share of seats	23.1	53.8	7.7	15.4	0.0

South Wales Central Electoral Region

1998 parliamentary electorate
482,980

% of Welsh electorate
21.7

No. of Assembly seats
8 + 4

% of Assembly seats
20.0

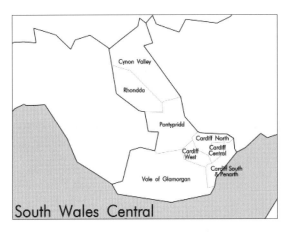

Comprising the constituencies of:	1992	Won by 1994*	1997	% maj. 1997	Second party 1997
Cardiff Central	Lab	Lab	Lab	18.8	LD
Cardiff North	Con	Lab	Lab	16.8	Con
Cardiff South & Penarth	Lab	Lab	Lab	32.7	Con
Cardiff West	Lab	Lab	Lab	38.8	Con
Cynon Valley	Lab	Lab	Lab	59.1	PC
Pontypridd	Lab	Lab	Lab	50.4	LD
Rhondda	Lab	Lab	Lab	61.1	PC
Vale of Glamorgan	Con	Lab	Lab	19.5	Con

The individual results for 1994 are estimates based on the pattern of voting at the European Parliament election.

Although Labour won all eight seats in South Wales Central at the 1997 general election the Conservatives have had some recent success in the suburbs and hinterland of Cardiff. They held Cardiff North, and its predecessor constituency, from 1974 until 1992 and Cardiff Central until 1987. The prosperous Vale of Glamorgan was lost at a 1989 by-election, but regained at the 1992 general election. Each of these constituencies will be a useful gauge of whether the Conservatives have recovered any lost ground in south Wales, but the omens do not look favourable. Polling evidence suggests that the Tories are no more popular now than at the general election. Their one crumb of comfort is that they were the only major party to oppose devolution at the referendum and they may attract some additional support from the nearly 50% of voters who agreed with them. Nonetheless it is highly likely that all their representation from the home area of the new Assembly will come in the form of 'top up' seats.

Votes and seats based on the 1992 general election

	Con	Lab	LD	PC	Others
Votes	109,692	201,701	38,689	18,838	2,362
% share of vote	29.5	54.3	10.4	5.1	0.6
Seats (FPTP)	2	6	0	0	0
% share of seats	25.0	75.0	0.0	0.0	0.0
Seats ('Top up')	2	1	1	0	0
Total	**4**	**7**	**1**	**0**	**0**
% share of seats	33.3	58.3	8.3	0.0	0.0

Votes and seats based on the 1994 European election

	Con	Lab	LD	PC	Others
Votes	29,314	115,396	18,417	18,857	5,964
% share of vote	15.6	61.4	9.8	10.0	3.2
Seats (FPTP)	0	8	0	0	0
% share of seats	0.0	100	0.0	0.0	0.0
Seats ('Top up')	2	0	1	1	0
Total	**2**	**8**	**1**	**1**	**0**
% share of seats	16.7	66.7	8.3	8.3	0.0

Votes and seats based on the 1997 general election

	Con	Lab	LD	PC	Others
Votes	70,502	201,900	41,037	19,382	14,615
% share of vote	20.3	58.1	11.8	5.6	4.2
Seats (FPTP)	0	8	0	0	0
% share of seats	0.0	100	0.0	0.0	0.0
Seats ('Top up')	3	0	1	0	0
Total	**3**	**8**	**1**	**0**	**0**
% share of seats	25.0	66.7	8.3	0.0	0.0

South Wales East Electoral Region

1998 parliamentary electorate
462,959

% of Welsh electorate
20.8

No. of Assembly seats
8 + 4

% of Assembly seats
20

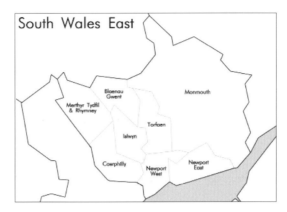

Comprising the constituencies of:	Won by 1992	1994*	1997	% maj. 1997	Second party 1997
Blaenau Gwent	Lab	Lab	Lab	70.7	LD
Caerphilly	Lab	Lab	Lab	57.1	Con
Islwyn	Lab	Lab	Lab	65.7	LD
Merthyr Tydfil & Rhymney	Lab	Lab	Lab	69.2	LD
Monmouth	Con	Lab	Lab	8.5	Con
Newport East	Lab	Lab	Lab	36.3	Con
Newport West	Lab	Lab	Lab	36.2	Con
Torfaen	Lab	Lab	Lab	56.7	Con

The individual results for 1994 are estimates based on the pattern of voting at the European Parliament election.

South Wales East is another region where Labour votes can as well be weighed as counted. The party received two-thirds of the total votes here at the 1997 general election and almost three-quarters of them at the 1994 European Parliament election. Indeed MEP Glenys Kinnock's 120,247 majority in 1994 was the largest ever recorded at an election in Britain. The Liberal Democrats regularly get less than 10% of the vote here, with Plaid Cymru struggling to reach even half that figure. Plaid have made some inroads into the Labour hegemony at recent local elections, but are unlikely to be serious competitors at the Welsh Assembly level. With the opposition vote thinly divided across the region among three very weak opponents it is perfectly possible that Labour will even win 'top up' seats here. Monmouth, just across the border from England, is the exception to this pattern and the Tories' number two target in Wales. It is the sort of seat the party should win in all normal electoral circumstances.

Votes and seats based on the 1992 general election

	Con	*Lab*	*LD*	*PC*	*Others*
Votes	87,559	227,060	35,397	12,440	2,347
% share of vote	24.0	62.2	9.7	3.4	0.6
Seats (FPTP)	1	7	0	0	0
% share of seats	12.5	87.5	0.0	0.0	0.0
Seats ('Top up')	2	1	1	0	0
Total	**3**	**8**	**1**	**0**	**0**
% share of seats	25.0	66.7	8.3	0.0	0.0

Votes and seats based on the 1994 European election

	Con	*Lab*	*LD*	*PC*	*Others*
Votes	24,660	144,907	9,963	9,550	6,806
% share of vote	12.6	74.0	5.1	4.9	3.5
Seats (FPTP)	0	8	0	0	0
% share of seats	0.0	100	0.0	0.0	0.0
Seats ('Top up')	1	3	0	0	0
Total	**1**	**11**	**0**	**0**	**0**
% share of seats	8.3	91.7	0.0	0.0	0.0

Votes and seats based on the 1997 general election

	Con	*Lab*	*LD*	*PC*	*Others*
Votes	55,142	218,276	30,897	13,998	11,861
% share of vote	16.7	66.1	9.4	4.2	3.6
Seats (FPTP)	0	8	0	0	0
% share of seats	0.0	100	0.0	0.0	0.0
Seats ('Top up')	2	1	1	0	0
Total	**2**	**9**	**1**	**0**	**0**
% share of seats	16.7	75	8.3	0.0	0.0

South Wales West Electoral Region

1998 parliamentary electorate
395,011

% of Welsh electorate
17.7

No. of Assembly seats
7 + 4

% of Assembly seats
18.3

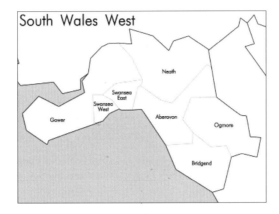

Comprising the constituencies of:	Won by 1992	1994*	1997	% maj. 1997	Second party 1997
Aberavon	Lab	Lab	Lab	60.0	Con
Bridgend	Lab	Lab	Lab	35.2	Con
Gower	Lab	Lab	Lab	30.0	Con
Neath	Lab	Lab	Lab	64.8	Con
Ogmore	Lab	Lab	Lab	64.2	Con
Swansea East	Lab	Lab	Lab	66.1	Con
Swansea West	Lab	Lab	Lab	35.7	Con

The individual results for 1994 are estimates based on the pattern of voting at the European Parliament election.

The size of the Labour majorities in its heartland constituencies of South Wales West tell their own story. The party is unchallenged and should win all seven first past the post seats with ease. The goal for the Conservatives will be to hang on to second place sufficiently convincingly to garner the bulk of the 'top up' seats. To do that the Tories need to poll in excess of 20% of the total vote in the region – a tall order given their showing in 1994 and 1997. Luckily for them both the Liberal Democrats and Plaid Cymru are weak here, with one 'top up' seat each being the realistic limit of their ambitions.

Votes and seats based on the 1992 general election

	Con	Lab	LD	PC	Others
Votes	73,565	190,011	28,684	15,946	1,907
% share of vote	23.7	61.3	9.2	5.1	0.6
Seats (FPTP)	0	7	0	0	0
% share of seats	0.0	100.0	0.0	0.0	0.0
Seats ('Top up')	3	0	1	0	0
Total	**3**	**7**	**1**	**0**	**0**
% share of seats	27.3	63.6	9.1	0.0	0.0

Votes and seats based on the 1994 European election

	Con	Lab	LD	PC	Others
Votes	19,293	104,263	15,499	12,364	6,332
% share of vote	12.2	66.1	9.8	7.8	4.0
Seats (FPTP)	0	7	0	0	0
% share of seats	0.0	100.0	0.0	0.0	0.0
Seats ('Top up')	1	1	1	1	0
Total	**1**	**8**	**1**	**1**	**0**
% share of seats	9.1	72.7	9.1	9.1	0.0

Votes and seats based on the 1997 general election

	Con	Lab	LD	PC	Others
Votes	42,178	184,464	30,090	15,969	8,313
% share of vote	15.0	65.6	10.7	5.7	3.0
Seats (FPTP)	0	7	0	0	0
% share of seats	0.0	100.0	0.0	0.0	0.0
Seats ('Top up')	2	1	1	0	0
Total	**2**	**8**	**1**	**0**	**0**
% share of seats	18.2	72.7	9.1	0.0	0.0

WALES

1998 parliamentary electorate
2,230,452

% of Welsh electorate
100.0

No. of Assembly seats
40 + 20

% of Assembly seats
100.0

Votes and seats based on the 1992 general election

	Con	*Lab*	*LD*	*PC*	*Others*
Votes	499,677	865,663	217,457	154,947	11,033
% share of vote	28.6	49.5	12.4	8.9	0.6
Seats (FPTP)	8	27	1	4	0
% share of seats	20.0	67.5	2.5	10.0	0.0
Seats ('Top up')	11	4	5	0	0
Total	**19**	**31**	**6**	**4**	**0**
% share of seats	31.7	51.7	10.0	6.7	0.0

Votes and seats based on the 1994 European election

	Con	*Lab*	*LD*	*PC*	*Others*
Votes	138,323	530,749	82,426	162,478	36,102
% share of vote	14.6	55.9	8.7	17.1	3.8
Seats (FPTP)	0	34	1	5	0
% share of seats	0.0	85.0	2.5	12.5	0.0
Seats ('Top up')	8	5	3	4	0
Total	**8**	**39**	**4**	**9**	**0**
% share of seats	13.3	65	6.7	15	0.0

Votes and seats based on the 1997 general election

	Con	*Lab*	*LD*	*PC*	*Others*
Votes	317,145	886,935	200,020	161,030	54,932
% share of vote	19.6	54.7	12.3	9.9	3.4
Seats (FPTP)	0	34	2	4	0
% share of seats	0.0	85.0	5.0	10.0	0.0
Seats ('Top up')	13	3	4	0	0
Total	**13**	**37**	**6**	**4**	**0**
% share of seats	21.7	61.7	10.0	6.7	0.0

The Likely Outcome?

The Welsh Assembly is likely to be dominated by Labour. Since the war Labour has secured less than 45% of the vote only in 1983 (37.5%) and has always been the most successful single party in Wales. As the largest party it will also receive an advantage from the operation of the particular electoral system that has been adopted for the Assembly. The limited number of 'top up' seats – 20 out of a total Assembly membership of 60 – mean that any imbalance in seats and votes between the parties at constituency level is unlikely to be fully redressed. Moreover, the method being used to determine which candidates are elected at regional level is also one which tends to favour the larger parties. Labour would have won an overall majority in the Assembly in each of the years for which we compiled notional results – 1994, 1997 and, even though it did not achieve a majority of the votes cast, 1992.

Table 3.5: Wales Votes

Overall result based on the 1992 general election

	Con	Lab	LD	PC	Others
% share of vote	28.6	49.5	12.4	8.9	0.6
Seats (FPTP)	8	27	1	4	0
Seats ('Top up')	11	4	5	0	0
Total	19	31	6	4	**0**

Overall result based on the 1994 European election

	Con	Lab	LD	PC	Others
% share of vote	14.6	55.9	8.7	17.1	3.8
Seats (FPTP)	0	34	1	5	0
Seats ('Top up')	8	5	3	4	0
Total	8	39	4	9	**0**

Overall result based on the 1997 general election

	Con	Lab	LD	PC	Others
% share of vote	19.6	54.7	12.3	9.9	3.4
Seats (FPTP)	0	34	2	4	0
Seats ('Top up')	13	3	4	0	0
Total	13	37	6	4	**0**

However, estimating the exact outcome of the Assembly elections is complicated by two uncertainties about how voters will behave. First, there may be a tendency – as noted earlier – for people to split their constituency and party list votes between different candidates/parties. Second, and probably of greater significance, many electors may put aside their 'normal' – i.e. general election – party preferences and cast their vote specifically to reflect their preferences about the composition, operation and likely policies of the Welsh Assembly.

This habit of choosing 'horses for courses' seems to be becoming more widespread in Britain. For example, we have shown that among voters in England who were able to cast local as well as general election votes on 1 May 1997 at least 10% and perhaps as many as one in five chose different parties on the same visit to the polling booth. Similarly, a survey study in 1997 of how people may cast their vote under different electoral systems found that a quarter of Welsh voters reported that they would support a different party at the Assembly elections to the one they voted for at the 1997 general election. The aggregate impact of such switching was relatively modest, but did suggest that Plaid Cymru would be a net beneficiary and win more 'top up' seats.

More generally, previous second order elections in Britain have seen significant if transient shifts in party support. Plaid Cymru took 17.1% of the vote in the 1994 European Parliament elections – nearly twice as large a share as the party achieved in either the 1992 or 1997 general elections. In the same set of elections in 1989 the Greens recorded 11.1% of the vote in Wales compared with just 0.4% at the 1992 general election.

Recent evidence from polls and local by-elections appears to support each of these contentions. The two Beaufort Research polls conducted for the BBC show only a small difference between how electors say they would cast their vote in a Welsh Assembly as opposed to United Kingdom general election. Labour retains clear majority support in both contexts. However, a sizeable proportion of Labour constituency voters appear to be prepared to use their regional list vote for another party. The main beneficiaries of this shift are the Liberal Democrats and Plaid Cymru. Plaid, in particular, are well placed to win a sizeable number of 'top up' seats and to push the Conservatives into third place in the Assembly.

Table 3.6: BBC/Beaufort Research opinion polls, July 1998 and November 1998

Voters were asked how they would vote in a United Kingdom general election, how they intended to cast their constituency vote in the Welsh Assembly election and how they intended to cast their regional vote at the same contest.

	Con	Lab	LD	PC
1997 gen. election result	19.6	54.7	12.3	9.9
July 1998				
UK general election	16	62	8	13
Welsh constituency	14	57	9	20
Welsh regional list	13	44	18	23
November 1998				
UK general election	15	62	8	14
Welsh constituency	12	62	7	18
Welsh regional list	12	48	14	24

Labour's position looks less buoyant according to the results of recent local government by-elections. The party has made a net loss of nine seats since the general election and its share of the vote is considerably lower than in the previous round of local contests in 1995. The number of contests involving all four major Welsh parties has been too small to draw firm conclusions, but they certainly hold out some hope for both the Conservatives and the Liberal Democrats that the poll findings underestimate the true level of their support.

Table 3.7: Local government by-elections in Wales, May 1997 – January 1999

	Gains	*Held*	*Lost*	*Net*
Conservative	2	4	–	+2
Labour	2	6	11	-9
Liberal Democrat	5	1	3	+2
PC	5	–	2	+3
Independent	2	3	–	+2

	%share (all 27 contests)	*%change on 1995*	*%share (5 four-party contests)*	*%change on 1995*
Conservative	16.0	+3.5	36.4	+14.0
Labour	34.5	−11.5	27.2	−19.0
Liberal Democrat	23.5	+9.4	13.9	+0.2
PC	12.7	−0.8	19.6	+5.3

Although the detail may be a little contradictory, the overall picture suggests that Labour certainly has enough in hand to win a majority of seats in the Assembly even if the party suffers the shock of not polling a majority of votes. In addition to a favourable electoral system, Labour has the advantage, certainly compared with the situation in Scotland, that support for the nationalist party in Wales is concentrated geographically and that Plaid Cymru's areas of greatest strength tend to be those of Labour's greatest weakness – and vice-versa. Moreover, Labour won 24 of its 34 parliamentary seats in 1997 by majorities in excess of 30%, and in 17 of those cases the Conservatives were in second place. Such margins would take an earthquake to overturn, and no such seismic disturbances have been felt.

Plaid Cymru does, however, seem well-placed to mount a challenge for second place in both votes and seats. The party simply needs to replicate its 1994 European election performance and, in the context of a specifically Welsh election, should manage to do so. Such a result would be bad news for the Conservatives. Although Wales has never been fruitful territory for the party, it is unlikely to win a UK general election without the support of at least one in four electors in the Principality. That target currently seems rather distant. The polls show the Liberal Democrats to be trailing badly. The party remains capable of making surprising gains at local level from carefully targeted campaigns, but its hope of winning more than half a dozen Assembly seats will rest on attracting a disproportionate 'top up' vote.

Benchmarks for the Welsh Assembly elections

The exact number of seats won for any given share of the vote will depend on how electors use their two ballots. The analysis below assumes that the large majority will vote for the same party at both constituency and 'top up' level.

Vote share	Seats	
Labour		
60%+	40+	Labour confirmed as the pre-eminent party in Wales. Opposition in the Assembly can be happily ignored.
55%-60%	37-40	Small swing to Labour compared with the general election. Few governments have enjoyed such a long honeymoon.
50%-55%	32-37	Fewer votes than in 1997 – probably to Plaid's benefit. Nonetheless a reasonable mandate for the new party leader.
Below 50%	<32	Internal party disputes appear to have damaged public support. Labour's majority in the Assembly threatened.
Conservative		
20%+	15+	Maybe enough for a couple of first past the post seats. Still way below Tory support at the 1992 election – 28.6%.
15%-20%	10-15	No sign of any recovery in Tory fortunes. Party cannot be happy if this is now their core support level.
10%-15%	6-10	Tories came third in Wales in the 1994 Euros and do so again. Vote now concentrated in Anglo middle-class areas.
Below 10%	<6	Tories relegated to minor party status in Wales. Their few Assembly members will make little impact.
Liberal Democrat		
15%+	8+	Best performance in Wales since days of Lib/SDP alliance. Likely to have attracted a large number of 'top up' votes.
10-15%	5-8	On a par with both the 1992 and 1997 general elections. Will probably be the smallest party group in the Assembly.
Below 10%	<5	A clear setback for both party morale and the new leader. Lib Dems must go back to building from the grass-roots.
Plaid Cymru		
20%+	11+	This result firmly puts Plaid in second place in Wales. By some distance the party's best ever election performance.
15%-20%	8-11	The target to beat is the 17.1% scored at the 1994 Euro elections. A clear success for the new 'the Party of Wales' strategy.
10%-15%	5-8	Above recent general elections, but falls short of a breakthrough. Unlikely to add to its four 'safe' first past the post seats.
Below 10%	<5	A poor performance for a specifically Welsh election. Party has been unable to attract support outside its heartlands.

Candidates for the Welsh Assembly

(as known at 15 February 1999)

In the constituency section candidates highlighted in **bold** are almost certain to be elected; those highlighted in *italic* could be elected if their party does well; candidates listed in plain type are unlikely to be elected.

The election of candidates from the lists depends on how many seats their party wins at constituency level. If, as at the 1997 general election, the Conservatives top the poll in none of the 40 Welsh Assembly constituencies they may pick up as many as three 'top up' seats in North Wales, Mid and West Wales and South Wales Central. In most other cases the maximum number of list candidates likely to be elected for one party from any one list is two.

In some cases parties have named more list candidates than there are seats to be filled. Here we list only the first four names on each party's list.

Members of the House of Commons are marked*

Mid and West Wales
Constituencies

	Con	*Lab*	*LibDem*	*PC*
Brecon & Radnorshire	*Bourne, N.*	*Janes, I.*	*Williams, K. Ms.*	Peterson, D.
Carmarthen East & Dinefwr	Stoddart, H. Ms.	*Llewelyn, C.*	Hughes, J. Ms.	*Thomas, R.*
Carmarthen West & South Pembrokeshire	Edwards, D.	**Gwyther, C. Ms.**	Williams, R.	Llewelyn, R.
Ceredigion	Lloyd Davies, H.	Battle, M. Ms.	Evans, D.	**Jones, E. Ms.**
Llanelli	Harding, B.	**Garrard, A. Ms.**	Dumper, T.	Jones, H. Ms.
Meirionnydd Nant Conwy	Williams, O.	Jones, D. Ms.	Worley, G.	**Elis Thomas, D.**
Montgomeryshire	Davies, G.	Hewitt, C.	**Bates, M.**	Senior, D.
Preseli Pembrokeshire	Aubel, F.	**Edwards, R.**	Lloyd, D.	Bryant, C.

Regional list candidates

	Con	*Lab*	*LibDem*	*PC*
1	Bourne, N.	Michael, A.*	Williams, R.	Jones, H. Ms.
2	Davies, G.	Evans, D. Ms.	Hughes, J. Ms.	Dafis, C.*
3	Williams, O.	Gething, V.	Brown, G.	Richards, D. Ms.
4	Aubel, F.	Richards, S. Ms.	Lloyd, D.	Huxley, L.

North Wales

Constituencies

	Con	Lab	LibDem	PC
Alyn & Deeside	Formstone, N.	**Middlehurst, T.**	Clarke, J.	Owen, A. Ms.
Caernarfon	Naish, B. Ms.	Jones, T.	Shankland, D.	**Wigley, D.***
Clwyd South	Jones, D.	**Sinclair, K. Ms.**	Harris, K.	Williams, H.
Clwyd West	*Richards, R.*	*Pugh, A.*	Feeley, R. Ms.	Williams, E. Ms.
Conwy	Jones, D.	*Sherrington, C. Ms.*	*Humphreys, C. Ms.*	Jones, G.
Delyn	Lumley, K. Ms.	**Halford, A. Ms.**	Burnham, E. Ms.	Elis, M. Ms.
Vale of Clwyd	Andrew, S.	**Jones, A. Ms.**	Lloyd, P.	Brynach, S.
Wrexham	Elphick, F. Ms.	**Marek, J.***	O'Toole, C. Ms.	Ryder, J. Ms.
Ynys Mon	Rogers, P.	*Owen, A.*	Clarke, J.	**Jones, I.***

Regional list candidates

	Con	Lab	LibDem	PC
1	Richards, R.	Jones, T.	Humphreys, C. Ms.	Ryder, J. Ms.
2	Rogers, P.	Pritchard, M. Ms.	Burnham, E. Ms.	Brynach, S.
3	Jones, D.	Williams, E.	Lloyd, P.	Roberts, F. Ms.
4	Lumley, K. Ms.	Roberts, N. Ms.	Feeley, R. Ms.	Owen, G.

South Wales Central

Constituencies

	Con	Lab	LibDem	PC
Cardiff Central	Jones, S.	**Drakeford, M.**	Randerson, J. Ms.	Thomas, O.
Cardiff North	*Morgan, J.*	**Essex, S. Ms.**	Meikle, A.	Mann, C.
Cardiff South & Penarth	Davies, M. Ms.	**Barrett, L. Ms.**	Maw-Cornish, J. Ms.	Rowlands, J.
Cardiff West	Greenwood, J. Ms.	**Morgan, R.***	Dixon, J.	Bush, E. Ms.
Cynon Valley	Hayward, E.	**Chapman, C. Ms.**	Willott, A. Ms.	Richards, P.
Pontypridd	Inglefield, S. Ms.	**Davidson, J. Ms.**	Orsi, G.	Hancock, B. Ms.
Rhondda	Hobbins, P.	**David, W.**	Williams, M. Ms.	Davies, G.
Vale of Glamorgan	*Melding, D.*	**Hutt, J. Ms.**	Little, F.	Franks, C.

Regional list candidates

	Con	Lab	LibDem	PC
1	Morgan, J.	Morgan, R.*	Randerson, J. Ms.	Jarman, P. Ms.
2	Melding, D.	Essex, S. Ms.	Orsi, G.	Thomas, O.
3	Jones, S.	Hopkins, K.	Gasson, J. Ms.	Bush, E. Ms.
4	Inglefield, S. Ms.	Morgan, W. Ms.	Willott, A. Ms.	Hancock, B. Ms.

South Wales East
Constituencies

	Con	Lab	LibDem	PC
Blaenau Gwent	Thomas, D.	**Law, P.**	Rogers, K.	Williams, P.
Caerphilly	Taylor, M. Ms.	**Davies, R.***	German, M.	Gough, R.
Islwyn	Stevens, C.	**Williams, S.**	....	Hancock, B.
Merthyr Tydfil & Rhymney	Hyde, C. Ms.	**Lewis, H.**	Jones, E.	Cox, A.
Monmouth	*Davies, D.*	*Short, C. Ms.*	Lines, C.	Hubbard, M.
Newport East	Bone, P.	**Griffiths, J.**	Cameron, A.	Holland, C.
Newport West	Graham, W.	**Butler, R. Ms.**	Watkins, V. Ms.	Vickery, B.
Torfaen	Thomas, K. Ms.	**Neagle, L. Ms.**	Gray, J. Ms.	Turner, N.

Regional list candidates

	Con	Lab	LibDem	PC
1	Davies, D.	Ash, A. Ms.	German, M.	Davies, J.
2	Graham, W.	Smith, B.	Watkins, V. Ms.	Williams, P.
3	Hyde, C. Ms.	Short, C. Ms.	Cameron, A.	Jones, G. Ms.
4	Taylor, M. Ms.	Al-Nuaimi, M.	Gray, J. Ms.	Whittle, L. Ms.

South Wales West
Constituencies

	Con	Lab	LibDem	PC
Aberavon	Davies, M. Ms.	**Gibbons, B.**	Davies, K.	Davies, J. Ms.
Bridgend	Cairns, A.	**Jones, C.**	Humphreys, R.	Canning, J.
Gower	Jones, A.	**Hart, E. Ms.**	Evans, H.	Rhys Jones, D.
Neath	Chambers, J. Ms.	**Thomas, G. Ms.**	Davies, D.	Jones, T.
Ogmore	Smart, C.	**Gregory, J. Ms.**	Waye, S. Ms.	Rogers, J.
Swansea East	Hughes, B.	**Feld, V. Ms.**	Black, P.	Ball, J.
Swansea West	Valerio, P.	**Davies, A.**	Newbury, J.	Lloyd, D.

Regional list candidates

	Con	Lab	LibDem	PC
1	Cairns, A.	Francis, M. Ms.	Black, P.	Davies, J. Ms.
2	Smart, C.	Francis, H.	Humphreys, R.	Lloyd, D.
3	Hughes, B.	Smith, R.	Evans, H.	Reid, S. Ms.
4	Valerio, P.	Griffiths, P.	Davies, K.	Bowen, D.

Green Party Candidates – No. 1 on list

Mid and West Wales, Bradney, D.; North Wales, Killock, J.; South Wales Central, Jakeway, K.; South Wales East, Coghill, R.; South Wales West, Grigg, B.

4. Northern Ireland Assembly Elections

There's No Going Back

Introduction by: **Denis Murray**, *Ireland Correspondent, BBC*

A recipe for government in Northern Ireland – take nine political parties, put into a 108 seat assembly. Add ten government departments in an executive whose members get their places as of right by electoral support, plus committees to supervise each department whose chairman must be from a different party to the minister. Blend in cross-border implementation bodies, and a British Irish Council. Stir vigorously, and by mid-1999 you will have a successful form of devolution, co-operation with the Irish Republic, and closer links between the component political parts of the British Isles. Well, that's the idea.

If 1998 taught us anything about Northern Ireland, it is that nothing should surprise us any more. But of course, the place will. Already, this year has seen the formation of the tenth party at Stormont – four members of the UK Unionist Party who split from their leader Bob McCartney in acrimonious circumstances have become Northern Ireland Unionists. That now makes for six pro-Good Friday Agreement parties, and four anti. Implementation of the Agreement, as senator George Mitchell predicted in his closing remarks on Good Friday, is proving as difficult as doing the deal in the first place.

In a sense, the groundwork for the Agreement began a decade ago, when the SDLP met Sinn Fein for private talks. One of the SDLP team later described the experience as like meeting a sect – Sinn Fein had spoken to no outsiders before. It took several more years to get to the point where all parties could sit in the same room (via the Brooke and Mayhew talks to September 1997 when the second IRA cease-fire gave Sinn Fein their place at the latest negotiations, and the Ulster Unionists agreed to stay at the table with them). Then, in just a few months, with US involvement, and the energy of the British and Irish governments, there was the Agreement.

That left the electorate a five week referendum campaign to travel the same course that had taken the politicians years to complete. The referendum on the Agreement was, and is, crucial. The difference between 71.1 per cent in favour and 69.9 repeating per cent was an awful lot more than just a couple of percentage points. Seventy-anything meant that even if unionist opinion was divided roughly fifty-fifty, there was no challenging that a majority of the people wanted to give the deal a whirl.

The election to the new Assembly threw up some surprises – not least that the nationalist SDLP ended up as the largest party in terms of percentage share of the vote. The first time the catholic community had exercised its suffrage muscle to such an extent. However, with 24 seats, they had four fewer than the Ulster Unionists – that's the vagaries of the single transferable vote for you. It was not a good result for the UUP, especially as up to seven of their number are less than utterly devoted to the Good Friday Agreement.

But much more splintered – and it has continued to fragment – is the opposition to the Agreement, led by Ian Paisley's Democratic Unionist Party. Initially saying he would go into the Assembly to wreck it, the referendum majority meant that even Paisley had to accept that the people had spoken, and to realise that the election result had guaranteed his party two seats in the new executive.

Now here's where our recipe starts to simmer. With ten departments, the seats are as follows – three UUP, three SDLP, two Sinn Fein, and two DUP. It's power-sharing, but not as we know it. This is not voluntary coalition, but enforced responsibility-sharing. The Ulster Unionists have been adamant that they won't sit in the executive with Sinn Fein until the IRA has at least begun the decommissioning of paramilitary weapons. The IRA, of course, won't hand over as much as a used cartridge case or an empty Semtex wrapper before Sinn Fein is at the heart of government, if then. Square that circle.

If and when it happens, there is a huge culture shock on the way for Northern Ireland politicians. For the first time ever they will be held accountable for closing hospitals, amalgamating education boards and so on. And imagine the poor Northern Ireland Civil Service, who have for years dealt with one direct rule British minister who had maybe three different responsibilities, coming to terms with a local member of the executive, his deputy, and a committee.

All of this leaves Mo Mowlam and the Northern Ireland Office with the nasties – security, the marching season (resolve Drumcree and you'll have gone two thirds of the way to cracking an awful lot more of the divisions in this society than just one Orange Order parade), and the reform of the RUC. I believe that if the process works security will ultimately become the responsibility of the devolved government – without it, in Seamus Mallon's memorable phrase, the set-up is 'a two-legged stool'. That, clearly, is still some way off.

But let's neither forget nor under-estimate what has been achieved – what was politically unthinkable just a few years ago has, largely, come to pass. And while the last mile can be the longest, most politicians believe the landscape has changed for ever, that there's no going back, and that the process is here to stay. As much as it ever can be, genuinely, the war is over.

Denis Murray

Structure and functions of the Northern Ireland Assembly

The creation of a Northern Ireland Assembly was envisaged as Strand One of the Good Friday agreement of 10 April 1998. Following acceptance of the agreement in referendums in both Northern Ireland and the Republic of Ireland on 22 May 1998, elections for 108 Assembly members were held on 25 June 1998.

Electors in Northern Ireland were asked whether they supported 'the agreement reached at the multi-party talks on Northern Ireland and set out in command paper 3883?'. At the referendum 951,845 valid votes were cast, representing 81% of the electorate. There were 1,738 spoilt ballot papers. Of those voting, 676,966 (71.1%) voted 'Yes' and 274,879 (28.9%) voted 'No'. A 'Yes' majority of 42.2%.

Electors in the Republic of Ireland were asked whether they approved of 'the proposal to amend the Constitution contained in the 19th Amendment of the Constitution Act 1998?'. At the referendum 1,528,331 valid votes were cast, representing 55.6% of the electorate. There were 17,064 spoilt ballot papers. Of those voting, 1,442,583 (94.4%) voted 'Yes' and 85,748 (5.6%) voted 'No'. A 'Yes' majority of almost 17 to one.

Arrangements for the operation of the Northern Ireland Assembly are as follows:

- **Membership:** 108-member Assembly, elected by proportional representation (Single Transferable Vote) from existing 18 Westminster constituencies (6 members from each constituency).
- **Seat of the Assembly:** the Assembly is currently sitting at Parliament Buildings, Stormont, but the Assembly is yet to decide where its permanent seat will be. This will be decided when the Assembly assumes its powers. It is likely that it will decide to sit permanently at Stormont.
- **Elections:** First elections to the Northern Ireland Assembly took place on 25 June 1998. The next election shall take place on 1 May 2003. Subsequent elections to the Assembly shall take place on the first Thursday in May in the fourth calendar year following that in which its predecessor was elected.
- **Sessions:** the practical arrangements are still to be confirmed and will be decided upon when the Assembly assumes its powers. The current thinking is that the Assembly will sit for two days a week, but that the committees will meet more frequently.
- **Transitional Arrangements:** The Assembly will meet first in a 'shadow' capacity, without its legislative or executive powers, and for the purpose of setting up the North-South Ministerial Council and associated cross-border bodies, and the British-Irish Council. The powers of the Assembly will come into effect once it has set up the other bodies, with all bodies (encompassing all three strands) coming into effect at the same time. It was envisaged that this would happen in February 1999, but the deadline is now 10 March.
- **Chair/Deputy Chair:** at present, because the Assembly is sitting in its 'shadow' form, the Chair and Deputy Chair of the Assembly have not been elected. Once the Assembly assumes its powers, they will be elected on a cross-community basis by parallel consent (one from each community). At present, Lord Alderdice (former leader of the Alliance

Party) is the Presiding Officer of the shadow Assembly. He was appointed by the Secretary of State for Northern Ireland.

- **Voting:** Key decisions to be taken on a cross-community basis either by parallel consent (i.e. a majority of those voting, including a majority of unionists and nationalists), or by a weighted majority (60%) of members voting, including at least 40% of nationalists and 40% of unionists. Members entering the Assembly have registered as nationalist, unionist or other (this would apply to the Alliance Party). Key decisions requiring cross-community support are designated in advance, including election of the Chair and Deputy Chair of the Assembly, the First Minister and Deputy First Minister, and budget allocations. In other cases such decisions could be triggered by a petition of concern brought by a significant minority (30 out of 108) of Assembly members.
- **First Minister and Deputy First Minister:** elected by the Assembly voting on a cross-community basis (i.e. by parallel consent, with one post per community). On 1 July 1998 David Trimble of the Ulster Unionist Party was elected First Minister and Seamus Mallon of the SDLP Deputy First Minister.
- **The Executive:** referred to as the Executive Committee, headed by the First Minister and Deputy First Minister, plus ten Northern Ireland Ministers with Departmental responsibilities.
- **Ministers:** posts of Ministers to be allocated to parties in proportion to party strength in the Assembly. With ten Ministerial posts, the UUP and the SDLP would get three each, and Sinn Fein and the Democratic Unionist Party two each. Ministers will have full executive authority in their respective areas of responsibility, within any broad programme agreed by the Executive Committee and endorsed by the Assembly as a whole. The Agreement states that: 'those who hold office should use only democratic, non-violent means, and those who do not should be excluded or removed from office.' The decision to exclude a minister would be a key decision requiring parallel consent.
- **Committees:** there will be a Committee of the Assembly for each of the main executive functions of the Northern Ireland Administration. Committee Chairs and Committee membership will be allocated in proportion to party strengths in the Assembly. The Committees will have a scrutiny, policy development and consultation role with respect to the Department with which each is associated, having the power to: consider and advise on Departmental budgets; approve relevant secondary legislation and approve the Committee stage of primary legislation; initiate enquiries and make reports; and consider and advise on matters brought to the Committee by its Minister.
- **Review:** after a period (not specified), there will be a review of all the arrangements (including the Executive) with a view to agreeing any adjustments necessary.

The Northern Ireland Assembly will have the power to pass primary legislation, referred to as Acts of the Northern Ireland Assembly, in the following devolved areas currently under the remit of the six Northern Ireland government departments:

- Finance and Personnel
- Economic Development
- Education

- Health and Social Services
- Environment
- Agriculture

The Assembly will not as yet have tax-raising powers, but this has not been ruled out for the future.

Relations between the Northern Ireland Assembly and Westminster

- **Role of the Secretary of State for Northern Ireland:** the Secretary of State to remain responsible for Northern Ireland Office matters not devolved to the Assembly, subject to regular consultation with the Assembly and Ministers.
- **Role of Westminster Parliament:** to legislate for non-devolved (i.e. reserved) issues.

Non-devolved matters include the following:
- security, policing, prisons and criminal justice; broadcasting; minimum wage, Competition Policy; National Lottery; some specific elements of health which are UK-wide (e.g. surrogacy, human fertilisation and genetics).

Under Strand 2 of the Good Friday agreement a **North-South Ministerial Council** is being established formally to link the Assembly with the Irish Parliament. The Ulster Unionists, the SDLP and the Irish Government have already identified and agreed six areas for formal co-operation through new cross-border implementation bodies which will be led by relevant ministers in both jurisdictions. These are:

- Trade and Business Development
- Special European Union Programmes
- Inland Waterways
- Aquaculture and Marine Matters
- Food Safety
- Language (Irish and Ulster Scots).

A further six areas of co-operation will be dealt with through existing institutions. These are Transport, Agriculture, Education, Health, Environment, and Tourism

Strand 3 provides for a **British-Irish Council**. Membership will be comprised of the British and Irish Governments, the assemblies in Northern Ireland, Scotland and Wales and possibly elsewhere in the UK, together with representatives from the Isle of Man and the Channel Islands. The BIC will try to establish common policies or action on issues like transport links, agriculture, environment, culture, and approaches to EU issues.

Operation of electoral system

Elections for the 108 members of the Northern Ireland Assembly were held on Thursday 25 June 1998. Each of Northern Ireland's 18 Westminster parliamentary constituencies elected 6 members by Single Transferable Vote (STV). STV is also used in Northern Ireland for local council and European Parliament elections.

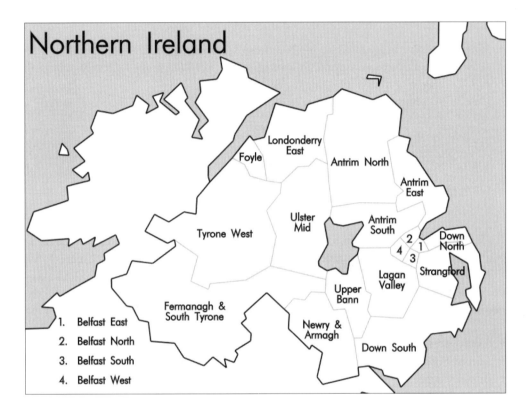

The STV system in use requires electors to vote for at least one candidate, and then to declare their preferences for as many or as few of the other candidates as they wish. Preferences are declared numerically, with '1' being written alongside the voter's first preference candidate, '2' alongside the second choice and so on. To be elected a candidate must receive a minimum number of votes – the 'quota' – determined by a set formula. In Northern Ireland the formula known as the 'Droop quota' is used. It is calculated by dividing the total number of valid voting papers cast by the number of seats to be filled **plus one**.

A simple example of the way the system works can be seen from the results of the 1989 European Parliament election. The first step is to count the total number of votes cast in a constituency (534,811) and to arrive at the quota. With 3 seats to be filled this is $534,811 \div 3 + 1$ = 133,703. First preference votes are then counted and any candidate achieving the quota is elected. Both Hume and Paisley were elected on the first count because the number of first preference votes they received took them above the quota. The next stage of the count transfers the surplus votes of the candidate with the largest number of votes (Paisley) among the other candidates. The surplus is the number of votes received in excess of the number required to reach the quota , that is 160,110–133,703 = 26,407.

Table 4.1: 1989 European Parliament election, Northern Ireland

Electorate	Valid votes
1,106,852	534,811

No. of seats	Quota
3	$534,811 \div 3 + 1$ = 133,703

Candidate	Party	No. of 1st preference votes	Elected at stage
Alderdice	Alliance	27,905	
Caul	Labour '87	1,274	
Hume	SDLP	136,335	**First**
Kennedy	Conservative	25,789	
Langhammer	Labour	3,540	
Lynch	Workers	5,590	
Morrison	Sinn Fein	48,914	
Nicholson	Ulster Unionist Party	118,785	**Second**
Paisley	Democratic Unionist	160,110	**First**
Samual	Green	6,569	

To do this all 160,110 first preference ballots cast for Paisley are examined again to determine the distribution of second preference votes among the other candidates. Hume's votes are ignored in this procedure because he has already been elected. However, because only the surplus votes are available for redistribution, the eligible candidates receive only $26,407 \div 160,110$ = 0.165 of an additional vote for each recorded second preference. It transpired that 138,170 of Paisley's supporters had cast a second preference for Nicholson who thus received 138,170 x 0.165 = 22,798 extra votes. These, added to his own 118,785 first preference votes, were sufficient to put him over the quota and he too was deemed elected at the second stage.

This is a very straightforward example. If the transfer of Paisley's votes had been insufficient to elect the third and final MEP, then Hume's surplus would have been distributed in a similar way. If no one was elected at that stage, then the bottom candidate (Caul) would have been eliminated and his votes re-distributed. Counting would continue through as many stages as necessary to ensure that a third candidate reached the quota.

With more seats to be filled and with more candidates attracting evenly spread votes the counting procedure for STV elections can prove very protracted. At the Northern Ireland Assembly elections counting in the Strangford constituency went through 18 stages before the required six of the total 22 candidates were deemed elected.

The results

The results of the Assembly elections in each constituency and for Northern Ireland as a whole are set out in the following pages. The Assembly subsequently elected David Trimble (UUP) as First Minister and Seamus Mallon (SDLP) as Deputy First Minister. Their two parties topped the poll in terms of both first preference votes and seats, with the SDLP receiving more votes but winning fewer seats than the UUP.

Northern Ireland Assembly Elections – Overall results

Party	First Preference Votes	% Share	Number of Seats
SDLP	177,963	22.0	24
UUP	172,225	21.3	28
DUP	146,917	18.1	20
SF	142,858	17.6	18
AP	52,636	6.5	6
UKU	36,541	4.5	5
PUP	20,634	2.5	2
NIWC	13,019	1.6	2
UDP	8,651	1.1	0
Union	8,332	1.0	1
United	8,152	1.0	1
UU	2,976	0.4	1
Others	19,341	2.4	0
Total	**810,245**		**108**

The following abbreviations have been used for the Northern Ireland parties throughout this chapter.

Abbreviation	Party Name
AP	Alliance Party
Con	Conservative
DUP	Democratic Unionist Party
Ind	Independent
Lab	Labour
Nat	Nationalist
NIWC	Northern Ireland Women's Coalition
NLP	Natural Law Party
PUP	Progressive Unionist Party
SDLP	Social Democratic and Labour Party
SF	Sinn Fein
Soc	Socialist
UDP	Ulster Democratic Party
UKU	United Kingdom Unionist Party
Union	Unionist
United	United Unionist
UU	Ulster Unionist
UUP	Ulster Unionist Party
WP	Workers' Party

Antrim East

A unionist stronghold encompassing the district councils of Carrickfergus and Larne. The main nationalist parties mustered just 5.9% of the vote between them at the 1997 general election. The Alliance Party had one of its candidates elected at the first count in the Assembly elections, an achievement matched only by the sitting UUP MP. One of five UKU Assembly members was elected here.

Electorate	Valid votes
59,313	35,610

No. of seats	Quota
6	35,610÷7 = 5,088

Candidate	Party	First Preference Votes	Elected at Stage
Beggs, R.	**UUP**	**5,764**	First
Brown, J.	Union	1,571	
Dick, T.	Con	233	
Dickson, S.	AP	1,921	
Greer, W.	PUP	1,432	
Hilditch, D.	**DUP**	**4,876**	Eighth
Hutchinson, R.	**UKU**	**2,866**	Thirteenth
Kirkham, T.	UDP	596	
Mason, R.	Ind	424	
McAuley, Ms. C.	SF	746	
McKee, J.	DUP	3,013	
McKissock, J.	NLP	32	
Neeson, S.	**AP**	**5,247**	First
O'Connor, D.	**SDLP**	**2,106**	Thirteenth
Robinson, K.	UUP	2,384	
Steele, Ms. M.	**UUP**	**2,399**	Twelfth

1997 general election

Candidate	Party	Votes	Share
Beggs, R.	**UUP**	**13,318**	**38.8**
Neeson, S.	AP	6,929	20.2
McKee, J.	DUP	6,682	19.5
Dick, T.	Con	2,334	6.8
Donaldson, B.	PUP	1,751	5.1
O'Connor, D.	SDLP	1,576	4.6
Mason, R.	Ind	1,145	3.3
McAuley, Ms. C.	SF	543	1.6
McCann, Ms. M.	NLP	69	0.2
		6,389	18.6

Antrim North

This large rural and coastal constituency has been Ian Paisley's heartland since 1970. All three DUP candidates were elected at the Assembly elections – Paisley on first preference votes and his son, Ian junior, with transfers from his father at the second count. The SDLP managed to secure a single Assembly seat and so prevent a unionist white-wash.

Electorate	Valid votes
73,247	49,697

No. of seats	Quota
6	49,697÷7 = 7,100

Candidate	Party	First Preference Votes	Elected at Stage
Cahill, J.	SF	2,021	
Campbell, Ms. M.	UUP	2,199	
Coulter, R.	**UUP**	**5,407**	**Tenth**
Dunlop, Ms. J.	AP	2,282	
Farren, S.	**SDLP**	**6,433**	**Sixth**
Kane, G.	**DUP**	**3,638**	**Twelfth**
Leslie, J.	**UUP**	**3,458**	**Twelfth**
McAllister, J.	UDP	400	
McCamphill, M.	SDLP	1,982	
McCarry, J.	SF	2,024	
McCaughan, C.	Ind	194	
McMullan, O.	Nat	478	
Paisley, I. Snr.	**DUP**	**10,590**	**First**
Paisley, I. Jnr.	**DUP**	**4,459**	**Second**
Palmer, T.	Ind U	38	
Rogers, R.	PUP	641	
Wright, J.	NLP	156	
Wright, W.	United	3,297	

1997 general election

Candidate	Party	Votes	Share
Paisley, I.	**DUP**	**21,495**	**46.5**
Leslie, S.	UUP	10,921	23.6
Farren, S.	SDLP	7,333	15.9
McCarry, J.	SF	2,896	6.3
Alderdice, D.	AP	2,845	6.2
Hinds, Ms. B.	Ind	580	1.3
Wright, J.	NLP	116	0.3
		10,574	22.9

Antrim South

A unionist stronghold bordering the north west of Belfast and stretching west to Lough Neagh. The UUP have not faced a DUP general election challenge here since 1983, though each party's most popular candidate at the Assembly elections polled a similar number of votes. In fact three varieties of unionist were returned as the UKU also picked up a seat. The Alliance Party squeezed in on the final count.

Electorate	Valid votes
69,426	43,991

No. of seats	Quota
6	43,991÷7 = 6,285

Candidate	Party	First Preference Votes	Elected at Stage
Boyd, N.	**UKU**	**4,360**	**Seventh**
Burns, T.	SDLP	3,474	
Clyde, S.	**DUP**	**6,034**	**Sixth**
Cosgrove, Ms. J.	NIWC	1,108	
Dalton, D.	**UUP**	**4,147**	**Ninth**
Deignan, S.	DUP	2,816	
Ford, D.	**AP**	**3,778**	**Tenth**
Frawley, O.	Lab	137	
Hunter, N.	UUP	2,337	
McClelland, D.	**SDLP**	**4,309**	**Eighth**
Meehan, M.	SF	3,226	
Stidolph, G.	NLP	28	
Wilkinson, K.	PUP	1,546	
Wilson, J.	**UUP**	**6,691**	**First**

1997 general election

Candidate	Party	Votes	Share
Forsythe, C.	**UUP**	**23,108**	**57.5**
McClelland, D.	SDLP	6,497	16.2
Ford, D.	AP	4,668	11.6
Smyth, H.	PUP U	3,490	8.7
Cushinan, H.	SF	2,229	5.5
Briggs, Ms. B.	NLP	203	0.5
		16,611	41.3

Belfast East

A strongly Protestant seat, ranging from the loyalist inner city to the middle-class suburbs of Knock and Belmont. Peter Robinson's majority at the 1997 general election was dented by UUP intervention, but he had strong first preference support at the Assembly contests. The Alliance Party's John Alderdice was also elected at the first count in 1998.

Electorate	Valid votes
60,562	39,593

No. of seats	Quota
6	39,593÷7 = 5,657

Candidate	Party	First Preference Votes	Elected at Stage
Adamson, I.	**UUP**	**3,447**	**Fifteenth**
Alderdice, J.	**AP**	**6,144**	**First**
Bell, J.	WP	79	
Bleakley, D.	Lab	369	
Collins, D.	NLP	22	
Donaldson, Ms. L.	Con	203	
Empey, R.	**UUP**	**5,158**	**Twelfth**
Ervine, D.	**PUP**	**5,114**	**Seventh**
Girvan, R.	UDP	516	
Good, R.	AP	1,000	
John, L.	Energy 106	15	
Jones, P.	SDLP	1,025	
Norris, J.	DUP	373	
O'Donnell, J.	SF	917	
Purvis, Ms. D.	PUP	271	
Robinson, P.	**DUP**	**11,219**	**First**
Rodgers, J.	UUP	1,015	
Sagar, Ms. P.	NIWC	711	
Vitty, D.	UKU	1,362	
Wilson, S.	**DUP**	**633**	**Twelfth**

1997 general election

Candidate	Party	Votes	Share
Robinson, P.	**DUP**	**16,640**	**42.6**
Empey, R.	UUP	9,886	25.3
Hendron, J.	AP	9,288	23.8
Dines, Ms. S.	Con	928	2.4
Corr, D.	SF	810	2.1
Lewsley, Ms. P.	SDLP	629	1.6
Dougan, A.	Ind	541	1.4
Bell, J.	WP	237	0.6
Collins, D.	NLP	70	0.2
		6,754	17.3

Belfast North

The Unionists are in the majority here, but there is also a strong nationalist minority. The UUP won convincingly in 1997, facing no opposition from the DUP and with the nationalist vote split between the SDLP and Sinn Fein. At the Assembly elections, however, it was the DUP which topped the poll – the SDLP coming second and SF third in terms of first preference votes.

Electorate	Valid votes
62,541	41,125

No. of seats	Quota
6	41,125÷7 = 5,876

Candidate	Party	First Preference Votes	Elected at Stage
Agnew, W.	**UU**	**2,976**	**Eleventh**
Blair, K.	NLP	76	
Browne, D.	UUP	2,064	
Cobain, F.	**UUP**	**2,415**	**Eleventh**
Cooper, S.	UKU	748	
Dodds, N.	**DUP**	**7,476**	**First**
Doran, S.	WP	155	
Emerson, P.	Green	257	
Hutchinson, B.	**PUP**	**3,751**	**Eleventh**
Kelly, G.	**SF**	**5,610**	**Tenth**
Maginness, A.	**SDLP**	**6,196**	**First**
McAughtry, S.	Lab	255	
McIlkenny, Ms. M.	SF	3,165	
Morgan, M.	SDLP	2,465	
Quinn, Ms. D.	Ind Nat	50	
Roberts, G.	AP	1,267	
Smyth, E.	DUP	1,288	
White, J.	UDP	911	

1997 general election

Candidate	Party	Votes	Share
Walker, C.	**UUP**	**21,478**	**51.8**
Maginness, A.	SDLP	8,454	20.4
Kelly, G.	SF	8,375	20.2
Campbell, T.	AP	2,221	5.4
Emerson, P.	Green	539	1.3
Treanor, P.	WP	297	0.7
Gribben Ms. A.	NLP	88	0.2
		13,024	31.4

Belfast South

A middle-class Protestant constituency stretching out of the city into Castlereagh. The UUP majority was dented by a Progressive Unionist candidate at the general election, and first preference votes were widely spread among the candidates at the Assembly contests. The Alliance came third at the first count, but picked up few transfer votes and failed to have their candidate elected.

Electorate	Valid votes
61,209	40,724

No. of seats	Quota
6	40,724÷7 = 5,818

Candidate	Party	First Preference Votes	Elected at Stage
Adams, D.	UDP	1,745	
Anderson, J.	NLP	73	
Birnie, J.	**UUP**	**2875**	Eighth
Black, B.	Lab	231	
Chambers, Ms. M.	DUP	2,449	
Clarke, J.	UUP	1,720	
Cusack, N.	Lab	62	
Dickson, W.	Union	437	
Dillon, G.	UKU	1,496	
Hanna, Ms. C.	**SDLP**	**3,882**	Tenth
Hayes, S.	SF	2,605	
Lomas, R.	Con	97	
Lynn, P.	WP	176	
McBride, S.	AP	4,086	
McDonnell, A.	**SDLP**	**4,956**	Sixth
McGimpsey, M.	**UUP**	**4,938**	Fifth
McWilliams, Ms. M.	**NIWC**	**3,912**	Tenth
Purvis, E.	PUP	2,112	
Robinson, S.	**DUP**	**2,872**	Eighth

1997 general election

Candidate	Party	Votes	Share
Smyth, W.	**UUP**	**14,201**	**36.0**
McDonnell, A.	SDLP	9,601	24.3
Ervine, D.	PUP	5,687	14.4
McBride, S.	AP	5,112	12.9
Hayes, S.	SF	2,019	5.1
Campbell, Ms. A.	Ind	1,204	3.0
Boal, Ms. M.	Con	962	2.4
Cusack, N.	Ind Lab	292	0.7
Lynn, P.	WP	286	0.7
Anderson, J.	NLP	120	0.3
		4,600	11.7

Belfast West

A nationalist dominated seat which has yo-yoed between Sinn Fein and the SDLP at recent general elections. Gerry Adams has won three times out of four against Joe Hendron. The two parties judged their pattern of contestation at the Assembly elections just right. All four SF and both SDLP candidates were elected, with the final success in each case coming on the last count.

Electorate	Valid votes
60,669	41,794

No. of seats	Quota
6	41,794÷7 = 5,971

Candidate	Party	First Preference Votes	Elected at Stage
Adams, G.	**SF**	**9,078**	**First**
Attwood, A.	**SDLP**	**4,280**	**Tenth**
Cahillane, Ms. M.	Soc	128	
Dalzell-Sheridan, T.	UKU	666	
De Brun, Ms. B.	**SF**	**4,711**	**Ninth**
Ferguson, M.	SF	2,585	
Ferris, Ms. M.	DUP	1,345	
Hendron, J.	**SDLP**	**6,140**	**First**
Kennedy, M.	NLP	29	
Lowry, J.	WP	607	
Maskey, A.	**SF**	**4,330**	**Tenth**
McGimpsey, C.	UUP	1,640	
McGuinness, D.	AP	129	
Ramsey, Ms. S.	**SF**	**3,946**	**Eighth**
Smyth, H.	PUP	2,180	

1997 general election

Candidate	Party	Votes	Share
Adams, G.	**SF**	**25,662**	**55.9**
Hendron, J.	SDLP	17,753	38.7
Parkinson, F.	UUP	1,556	3.4
Lowry, J.	WP	721	1.6
Kennedy, L.	Ind	102	0.2
Daly, Ms. M.	NLP	91	0.2
		7,909	17.2

Down North

A strongly protestant middle-class constituency on the southern shore of Belfast lough. Robert McCartney won the parliamentary seat as a U.K. Unionist at a 1995 by-election and retained it in 1997. On both occasions the DUP chose not to stand against him. In the Assembly contests he topped the poll, but his UKU running mate received a derisory vote. All three UUP candidates were elected.

Electorate	Valid votes
62,942	37,313

No. of seats	Quota
6	37,313÷7 = 5,331

Candidate	Party	First Preference Votes	Elected at Stage
Baird-Gunning, Ms. V.	Lab	212	
Bell, Ms. E.	**AP**	**3,669**	**Ninth**
Carter, C.	Ind	72	
Chambers, A.	Ind U	1,382	
Currie, S.	PUP	1,376	
Farrell, Ms. M.	SDLP	2,048	
Fee, A.	Con	337	
Gorman, J.	**UUP**	**4,719**	**Sixth**
Graham, R.	DUP	1,558	
Gribben, Ms. A.	NLP	39	
Lindsay, T.	UDP	265	
McAlister, S.	DUP	1,013	
McCartney, R.	**UKU**	**8,188**	**First**
McFarland, R.	**UUP**	**4,653**	**Sixth**
Morrice, Ms. J.	**NIWC**	**1,808**	**Twelfth**
Roche, Ms. E.	UKU	173	
Walker, G.	AP	1,699	
Weir, P.	**UUP**	**2,775**	**Twelfth**
Wilson, B.	Ind	1,327	

1997 general election

Candidate	Party	Votes	Share
McCartney, R.	**UKU**	**12,817**	**35.1**
McFarland, A.	UUP	11,368	31.1
Napier, O.	AP	7,554	20.7
Fee, A.	Con	1,810	5.0
Farrell, Ms. M.	SDLP	1,602	4.4
Morrice, Ms. J.	Ind	1,240	3.4
Mullins. T.	NLP	108	0.3
Mooney, R.	Ind	57	0.2
		1,449	4.0

Down South

There have been considerable boundary changes since Enoch Powell was returned as a UUP MP for a seat of the same name from 1974 until 1987. The nationalist community now produces a handsome Westminster majority for the SDLP's Eddie McGrady, and he comfortably topped the poll at the Assembly contests too. He pulled two colleagues through on his coat-tails with SF also taking a seat.

Electorate	Valid votes
71,000	51,353

No. of seats	Quota
6	51,353÷7 = 7,337

Candidate	Party	First Preference Votes	Elected at Stage
Bradley, P.	SDLP	5,571	Tenth
Carr, H.	SDLP	3,731	
Carr, Ms. A.	NIWC	1,658	
Cunningham, Ms. A.	AP	1,502	
Curran, M.	Lab	498	
Graham, G.	Union	1,562	
Hanna, N.	UUP	1,939	
McGrady, E.	SDLP	10,373	First
Mullins, T.	NLP	33	
Murphy, M.	SF	6,251	Sixth
Nesbitt, D.	UUP	5,480	Eighth
O'Connor, P.	Ind Lab	121	
O'Fachtna, G.	SF	1,520	
O'Hagan, D.	WP	130	
O'Neill, E.	SDLP	3,582	Twelfth
Wells, J.	DUP	4,826	Twelfth
Wharton, F.	UKU	2,576	

1997 general election

Candidate	Party	Votes	Share
McGrady, E.	SDLP	26,181	52.9
Nesbitt, D.	UUP	16,248	32.8
Murphy, M.	SF	5,127	10.4
Crozier, J.	AP	1,711	3.5
McKeon, Ms. R.	NLP	219	0.4
		9,933	20.1

Fermanagh and South Tyrone

A constituency evenly split between the two communities in terms of population. The current MP, Ken Maginnis, has benefited from never having faced a unionist opponent since his election in 1983, whereas all four general elections have featured SDLP and SF candidates. At the Assembly elections three unionists and three nationalists were returned, with the SDLP topping the poll.

Electorate	Valid votes
65,383	51,043

No. of seats	Quota
6	51,043÷7 = 7,292

Candidate	Party	First Preference Votes	Elected at Stage
Carson, Ms. J.	**UUP**	**4,400**	**Tenth**
Crawley, Ms. M.	NIWC	1,729	
Dixon, W.	UKU	4,262	
Farry, S.	AP	614	
Foster, S.	**UUP**	**5,589**	**Fifth**
Gallagher, T.	**SDLP**	**8,135**	**First**
Gildernew, Ms. M.	**SF**	**4,703**	**Ninth**
Gillan, S.	NLP	63	
Johnston, R.	DUP	3,095	
Kerr, B.	UUP	2,583	
McHugh, G.	**SF**	**5,459**	**Seventh**
Morrow, M.	**DUP**	**3,987**	**Tenth**
Mullen, Ms. O.	SDLP	2,872	
Treanor, P.	SF	3,552	

1997 general election

Candidate	Party	Votes	Share
Maginnis, K.	**UUP**	**24,862**	**51.5**
McHugh, G.	SF	11,174	23.1
Gallagher, T.	SDLP	11,060	22.9
Farry, S.	AP	977	2.0
Gillan, S.	NLP	217	0.4
		13,688	28.3

Foyle

The boundaries of this seat are coterminous with the district of Derry, situated in the historic county of Londonderry. It takes its name from the river flowing through the city, and thereby offends neither community. Nationalists avoid, but unionists insist on the prefix 'London'. This is John Hume's home territory – he got twice as many first preference votes as anyone else in 1998.

Electorate	Valid votes
68,888	48,794

No. of seats	Quota
6	48,794÷7 = 6,971

Candidate	Party	First Preference Votes	Elected at Stage
Adams, K.	Lab	345	
Allen, J.	UUP	4,669	
Brennan, D.	NLP	32	
Cavanagh, C.	AP	1,058	
Courtney, Ms. A.	SDLP	2,560	
Durkan, M.	**SDLP**	**4,423**	**Sixth**
Fleming, Ms. L.	SF	1,360	
Gurney, B.	PUP	287	
Hay, W.	**DUP**	**6,112**	**Eighth**
Hume, J.	**SDLP**	**12,581**	**First**
Mackenzie, P.	Green	253	
McLaughlin, M.	**SF**	**5,341**	**Fifth**
Nelis, Ms. M.	**SF**	**3,464**	**Eighth**
O'Heara, G.	SF	2,531	
Tierney, J.	**SDLP**	**3,778**	**Seventh**

1997 general election

Candidate	Party	Votes	Share
Hume, J.	**SDLP**	**25,109**	**52.5**
McLaughlin, M.	SF	11,445	23.9
Hay, W.	DUP	10,290	21.5
Bell, Ms. H.	AP	817	1.7
Brennan, D.	NLP	154	0.3
		13,664	28.6

Lagan Valley

A heavily protestant, residential constituency to the south west of Belfast. The sitting Westminster UUP MP, Jeffrey Donaldson, was barred by his party from standing in the Assembly elections because of his opposition to the Good Friday agreement. The Alliance party, fielding a single candidate, topped the poll, with the UUP only winning two seats despite putting up four candidates.

Electorate	Valid votes
71,661	46,510

No. of seats	Quota
6	46,510÷7 = 6,645

Candidate	Party	First Preference Votes	Elected at Stage
Bell, W.	**UUP**	**5,965**	**Fifth**
Bleakes, W.	Con	702	
Butlet, P.	SF	2,000	
Calvert, C.	DUP	3,111	
Campbell, R.	UUP	3,158	
Campbell Ms. A.	NIWC	955	
Close, S.	**AP**	**6,788**	**First**
Collins, J.	NLP	43	
Davis, I.	**UUP**	**3,927**	**Ninth**
Hull, K.	UUP	1,289	
Lewsley, Ms. P.	**SDLP**	**4,039**	**Ninth**
McCarthy, Ms. F.	WP	208	
McMichael, G.	UDP	3,725	
Poots, E.	**DUP**	**5,239**	**Seventh**
Roche, P.	**UKU**	**5,361**	**Eighth**

1997 general election

Candidate	Party	Votes	Share
Donaldson, J.	**UUP**	**24,560**	**55.4**
Close, S.	AP	7,635	17.2
Poots, E.	DUP	6,005	13.6
Kelly, Ms. D.	SDLP	3,436	7.8
Sexton, S.	Con	1,212	2.7
Ramsey, Ms. S.	SF	1,110	2.5
McCarthy, Ms. F.	WP	203	0.5
Finlay, H.	NLP	149	0.3
		16,925	38.2

Londonderry East

This constituency sits entirely outside the City of Derry itself. It takes in a substantial section of the north coast of the province towards Antrim. Unionist voters are in the majority here, but a split in the vote between the UUP and the DUP slashed William Ross's majority in 1997. It was the DUP which topped the poll at the Assembly elections, with the SDLP doing well to take two seats.

Electorate	Valid votes
59,370	39,564

No. of seats	Quota
6	39,564÷7 = 5,653

Candidate	Party	First Preference Votes	Elected at Stage
Armitage, Ms. P.	**UUP**	**3,315**	**Ninth**
Campbell, G.	**DUP**	**6,099**	**First**
Dallat, J.	**SDLP**	**4,760**	**Sixth**
Dempsey, Ms. B.	AP	2,395	
Doherty, A.	**SDLP**	**4,606**	**Eighth**
Douglas, B.	**Union**	**3,811**	**Ninth**
Gilmour I.	PUP	582	
McCann Ms M.	NLP	46	
McLarty, D.	**UUP**	**5,108**	**Fifth**
McElhinney, J.	SF	1,339	
McPherson, R.	UUP	1,531	
Nicholl, D.	UDP	171	
O'Kane, M.	SF	2,521	
Robinson, G.	DUP	3,280	

1997 general election

Candidate	Party	Votes	Share
Ross W.	**UUP**	**13,558**	**35.6**
Campbell, G.	DUP	9,764	25.6
Doherty, A.	SDLP	8,273	21.7
O'Kane M.	SF	3,463	9.1
Boyle, Ms. Y.	AP	2,427	6.4
Holmes, J.	Con	436	1.1
Gallen, Ms. C.	NLP	100	0.3
Anderson, I.	Nat Dem	81	0.2
		3,794	10

Mid Ulster

A much changed constituency formed from territory in which Sinn Fein had not performed well at the 1992 general election. The nationalists are in the majority here, and Martin McGuinness scored a personal triumph in 1997 by winning despite there also being an SDLP candidate. The DUP's William McCrea was the MP until 1992 and easily topped the poll at the Assembly elections.

Electorate	Valid votes
59,991	49,798

No. of seats	Quota
6	49,798÷7 = 7,115

Candidate	Party	First Preference Votes	Elected at Stage
Armstrong W.	**UUP**	**4,498**	**Sixth**
Boyle, Ms. Y.	AP	497	
Daly Ms. M.	NLP	38	
Donnelly, F.	WP	207	
Haughey, D.	**SDLP**	**6,410**	**Sixth**
Hutchinson, H.	Soc	91	
Junkin, J.	UUP	2,440	
Kelly, J.	**SF**	**5,594**	**Sixth**
McCrea, R.	**DUP**	**10,339**	**First**
McGlone, P.	SDLP	4,666	
McGuinness, M.	**SF**	**8,703**	**First**
McLean, P.	DUP	307	
Molloy, F.	**SF**	**6,008**	**Sixth**

1997 general election

Candidate	Party	Votes	Share
McGuinness, M.	**SF**	**20,294**	**40.1**
McCrea, R.	DUP	18,411	36.3
Haughey, D.	SDLP	11,205	22.1
Bogues, E.	AP	460	0.9
Donnelly, Ms. M.	WP	238	0.5
Murray, Ms. M.	NLP	61	0.1
		1,883	3.7

Newry and Armagh

A constituency whose ownership depends on the nationalist majority not splitting its vote too evenly between the SDLP and Sinn Fein. Seamus Mallon was first elected in 1986 when he was the only challenger to gain a seat at the by-elections following the mass resignation of unionist MPs. Mallon had the most first preference votes at the Assembly elections, with nationalists winning 4 out of 6 seats.

Electorate	Valid votes
71,553	54,136

No. of seats	Quota
6	54,136÷7 = 7,734

Candidate	Party	First Preference Votes	Elected at Stage
Allen, Ms. M.	Ind	1,227	
Berry, P.	**DUP**	**7,214**	**Fourth**
Evans, D.	NLP	23	
Fearon, Ms. C.	NIWC	1,138	
Fee, J.	**SDLP**	**3,166**	**Eighth**
Feely, F.	SDLP	2,205	
Frazer, W.	Ind	933	
Hyland, D.	SF	4,643	
Kennedy, T.	**UUP**	**5,495**	**Sixth**
Mallon, S.	**SDLP**	**13,582**	**First**
McNamee, P.	**SF**	**4,570**	**Eighth**
Murphy, C.	**SF**	**4,839**	**Eighth**
Speers, J.	UUP	4,324	
Whitcroft, P.	AP	777	

1997 general election

Candidate	Party	Votes	Share
Mallon, S.	**SDLP**	**22,904**	**43.0**
Kennedy, T.	UUP	18,015	33.8
McNamee, P.	SF	11,218	21.1
Whitcroft, P.	AP	1,015	1.9
Evans, D.	NLP	123	0.2
		4,889	9.2

Strangford

There are more UUP than DUP votes here, but in the Assembly contests the DUP's Iris Robinson beat the sitting UUP MP John Taylor into second place on first preferences. They were each so far ahead of the field that it took eighteen counts – the largest of the elections – to determine all six Assembly members. Three types of unionist accounted for five seats, with only the Alliance breaking the monopoly.

Electorate	Valid votes
70,868	42,922

No. of seats	Quota
6	42,922÷7 = 6,132

Candidate	Party	First Preference Votes	Elected at Stage
Beattie, J.	Ind UU	2,247	
Beattie, T.	Con	263	
Benson, T.	**UUP**	**1,623**	Seventeenth
Frew, A.	Green	200	
Hamilton, T.	UUP	615	
Hanvey, B.	SDLP	1,883	
Jeffers, T.	DUP	1,007	
Johnston, R.	PUP U	1,342	
Magill, W.	Union	951	
McCarty, D.	SDLP	1,982	
McCarthy, K.	**AP**	**2,947**	Seventeenth
McGreevy, P.	SF	614	
McNally, B.	UDP	322	
McNarry, D.	UUP	1,073	
Mullins, Ms. S.	NLP	27	
Orr, Ms. A.	Ind	201	
Osborne, P.	AP	2,269	
Robinson, I.	**DUP**	**9,479**	First
Shannon, R.	**DUP**	**1,415**	Eighteenth
Stewart, J.	Lab	181	
Taylor, J.	**UUP**	**9,203**	First
Wilson, C.	**UKU**	**3,078**	Eighteenth

1997 general election

Candidate	Party	Votes	Share
Taylor, J.	**UUP**	**18,431**	**44.3**
Robinson, Ms. I.	DUP	12,579	30.2
McCarthy, K.	AP	5,467	13.1
O'Reilly, P.	SDLP	2,775	6.7
Chalk, G.	Con	1,743	4.2
O'Fachtna, G.	SF	503	1.2
Mullins, Ms. S.	NLP	121	0.3
		5,852	14.1

Upper Bann

Northern Ireland First Minister David Trimble's constituency has a unionist majority, but with a sizeable Catholic minority. The SDLP polled nearly 25% of the vote at both the general and Assembly elections, with SF winning another 12% or more. Trimble easily topped the poll, but the SDLP's Brid Rodgers was also elected at the first count. Two UUP, one DUP and one SF complete the picture.

Electorate	Valid votes
70,852	50,399

No. of seats	Quota
6	50,399÷7 = 7,200

Candidate	Party	First Preference Votes	Elected at Stage
Allen, Ms. R.	DUP	3,635	
Byrne, M.	SDLP	2,687	
Carrick, W.	**DUP**	**4,177**	Thirteenth
Evans, A.	Lab	439	
French, T.	WP	270	
Gardiner, S.	UUP	1,097	
Lyons, J.	NLP	32	
McClinton, C.	U Ind	207	
McQuaid, F.	AP	1,556	
Murray, F.	SF	2,915	
Neale, M.	UUP	455	
O'Hagan, Ms. D.	**SF**	**4,301**	Tenth
Rodgers, Ms. B.	**SDLP**	**9,260**	First
Savage, G.	**UUP**	**669**	Fourteenth
Silcock, B.	Ind	101	
Trimble, D.	**UUP**	**12,338**	First
Vance, D.	UKU	1,405	
Watson, D.	**United**	**4,855**	Fourteenth

1997 general election

Candidate	Party	Votes	Share
Trimble, D.	**UUP**	**20,836**	**43.6**
Rodgers, Ms. B.	SDLP	11,584	24.2
O'Hagan, Ms. B.	SF	5,773	12.1
Carrick, W.	DUP	5,482	11.5
Ramsay, W.	AP	3,017	6.3
French, T.	WP	554	1.2
Price, B.	Con	433	0.9
Lyons, J.	NLP	108	0.2
		9,252	19.4

West Tyrone

A largely rural constituency in the far west of the province. The UUP won it at the 1997 general election because the votes of the predominantly nationalist population were split between the SDLP and SF. MP William Thompson, an opponent of the Good Friday agreement, was not allowed to stand. In his absence the DUP topped the poll, with SF and the SDLP taking two seats each.

Electorate	Valid votes
59,081	45,951

No. of seats	Quota
6	45,951÷7 = 6,565

Candidate	Party	First Preference Votes	Elected at Stage
Byrne, J.	SDLP	**6,495**	Fourth
Devine, S.	SF	3,676	
Doherty, P.	SF	**7,027**	First
Gibson, O.	DUP	**8,015**	First
Gormley, Ms. A.	AP	1011	
Hussey, D.	UUP	**4,622**	Eighth
Johnstone, R.	NLP	40	
McDonnell, P.	SDLP	1,772	
McElduff, B.	SF	**4,963**	Ninth
McGowan, P.	Ind	1,269	
McLaughlin, J.	Soc	570	
McMenamin, E.	SDLP	**3,548**	Ninth
O'Kane, L.	Ind	171	
Owens, T.	WP	157	
Patterson, A.	UUP	2,615	

1997 general election

Candidate	Party	Votes	Share
Thompson, W.	UUP	**16,003**	**34.6**
Byrne, J.	SDLP	14,842	32.1
Doherty, P.	SF	14,280	30.9
Gormley, Ms. A.	AP	829	1.8
Owens, T.	WP	230	0.5
Johnstone, R.	NLP	91	0.2
		1,161	2.5

5. Greater London Authority Elections

The Mayor We Want, or The Mayor We Deserve?

Introduction by: **Gary Gibbon**, *Political Correspondent, Channel 4 News*

"If there isn't room for me in the party, you have to ask what is the long-term goal ?" (Ken Livingstone, 31 October, 1998).

He might well ask. And 1999 should bring Ken Livingstone an answer. By the autumn, the London Labour party will have chosen its candidate for London's first elected Mayor and the leadership will make sure it is not Ken. A trap-door has been constructed to despatch Mr Livingstone from the stage. The loyal, Blairite executive in London will veto his candidacy through what are eerily called 'special procedures' inserted into the selection process.

Mr Livingstone says that if he is left off the final ballot he will urge party members to write his name onto the voting papers anyway, and even some New Labourites seem tempted to join in such defiance. It is going to be a critical test of the Blairites' ability to get what they want two years into the government. But what – and who – do they want? Health Secretary Frank Dobson has rejected approaches to throw his hat in the ring. Lowlier ministers, like Glenda Jackson, Nick Raynsford and Tony Banks, would love to swap their Whitehall perches to become London's first citizen, but the party leadership has clearly been hoping something better will turn up. The broadcaster, Trevor Phillips, has too much of the whiff of Alun Michael about him, the man Labour centrally imposed to lead Welsh self-government. The Prime Minister had hoped that an entrepreneur from outside the political world might fight the Labour ticket, but that too looks less likely.

It will all provide plenty of scope for a stream of 'control freak' headlines, exposing New Labour as something less than instinctive devolutionists. It is bound to make the party look more divided and, at the end of it all, Labour could be left struggling with a low-key candidate, like Toby Harris, leader of Haringey council and a life peer. That would do nothing to boost the mayoral race, which opened to a dismal fanfare last year when only one in four Londoners actually supported the establishment of a mayor and assembly in the referendum. A low profile candidate, or – worse – one bruised by a bitter internal selection contest risks dampening enthusiasm for the whole business even further. The public could end up looking even less enthusiastic than Tony Blair about the brave new devolved world.

The Conservative leadership hopes to point up the Labour leadership's interference in its own selection process by giving Tory grassroots an unfettered vote. It is a gamble the leadership may come to regret, as it looks pretty likely to deliver the candidacy into the hands of Lord Archer, a man whom no Tory leader has ever thought fit for even the lowliest front-bench job. Former Transport Minister Steven Norris, who handled tabloid revelations about his private life better than most of his embarrassed Tory colleagues, may also throw his hat in the ring. The 1998 London local elections showed Conservative support in the capital stagnating at 1997 general election levels so there is a paucity of alternative candidates throwing themselves at William Hague's feet.

Whatever the outcome of the election for Mayor, both within the parties and at the formal contest in May 2000, one aspect of the Blair project does seem likely to forge further ahead. The electoral system chosen for the Greater London Assembly is virtually guaranteed to produce a coalition – and almost certainly a Lib-Lab one. Mr Blair hopes that along with the expected Lib-Lab cooperation in Scotland, that will boost realignment in Westminster politics. And the plan is that London itself will be a pilot for more mayors and more proportional representation in local government. Though the internal party machinations on candidate selection and ranking may be painful, the electoral structures being put in place in London are likely to fix consensual, coalition politics into yet another part of the British political system.

Gary Gibbon

Structure and functions of the Greater London Authority

A Greater London Authority, consisting of a directly-elected Mayor and the Greater London Assembly, is being established following a referendum held in the capital on 7 May 1998. At the referendum 1,709,172 valid votes were cast, representing 34.1% of the London electorate. There were 26,178 rejected ballot papers. Of those voting, 1,230,759 (72%) were in favour of the government's proposals for a Greater London Authority and 478,413 (28%) were not in favour. A 'Yes' majority of 44%. The results of the referendum were counted and announced for each London borough. The detailed outcome was as follows:

Table 5.1: Result of Referendum on Greater London Authority, 7 May 1998

London Borough	% Turnout	Yes	%	No	%
City of London	30.6	977	63.0	574	37.0
Barking and Dagenham	24.9	20,534	73.5	7,406	26.5
Barnet	35.3	55,487	69.6	24,210	30.4
Bexley	34.7	36,527	63.3	21,195	36.7
Brent	35.6	47,309	78.4	13,050	21.6
Bromley	40.2	51,410	57.1	38,662	42.9
Camden	32.8	36,007	81.2	8,348	18.8
Croydon	37.2	53,863	64.7	29,368	35.3
Ealing	32.5	52,348	76.5	16,092	23.5
Enfield	32.8	44,297	67.2	21,639	32.8
Greenwich	32.3	36,756	74.8	12,356	25.2
Hackney	33.7	31,956	81.6	7,195	18.4
Hammersmith and Fulham	33.5	29,171	77.9	8,255	22.1
Haringey	29.9	36,296	83.8	7,038	16.2
Harrow	36.0	38,412	68.8	17,407	31.2
Havering	33.9	36,390	60.5	23,788	39.5
Hillingdon	34.4	38,518	63.1	22,523	36.9
Hounslow	31.8	36,957	74.6	12,554	25.4
Islington	34.1	32,826	81.5	7,428	18.5
Kensington and Chelsea	27.9	20,064	70.3	8,469	29.7
Kingston upon Thames	41.0	28,621	68.7	13,043	31.3
Lambeth	31.6	47,391	81.8	10,544	18.2
Lewisham	29.3	40,188	78.4	11,060	21.6
Merton	37.5	35,418	72.2	13,635	27.8
Newham	27.8	33,084	81.4	7,575	18.6
Redbridge	34.9	42,547	70.2	18,098	29.8
Richmond upon Thames	44.5	39,115	70.8	16,135	29.2
Southwark	32.3	42,196	80.7	10,089	19.3
Sutton	34.9	29,653	64.8	16,091	35.2
Tower Hamlets	34.1	32,674	77.5	9,467	22.5
Waltham Forest	33.6	38,344	73.1	14,090	26.9
Wandsworth	38.7	57,010	74.3	19,695	25.7
Westminster	31.5	28,413	71.5	11,334	28.5
London	**34.1**	**1,230,759**	**72.0**	**478,413**	**28.0**

The detail of the structure and functions of the Greater London Authority is subject to amendment during the passage of the Greater London Authority Bill, but some key elements are likely to be:

- **Purpose and powers of the Authority:** The Greater London Authority shall have the purpose of 'promoting economic and social development in Greater London and the improvement of the environment in Greater London'. The GLA may do whatever the Mayor thinks will further its purpose, subject to a duty to consult businesses and consider the impact any policies may have on the interests of business. The GLA must ensure a 'reasonable balance' between promoting economic, social, environmental and sustainable development, and promoting wealth creation and the health of Londoners. The GLA may not incur expenditure in providing health, social services, education and housing which the boroughs may provide.

- **The Mayor of London:** It is the Mayor who produces the GLA's budget. The budget can only be amended with the support of two thirds of the Assembly members who take part in the vote. The Mayor of London must produce an Annual Report and should hold an annual State of London debate open to the public. Londoners will also be able to attend two People's Question Time events every year. The Mayor may appoint two political advisers and up to ten other advisers.

- **The Deputy Mayor:** Appointed by the Mayor from amongst the members of the Assembly. The Deputy Mayor takes over in the event of the incapacity of the Mayor or his or her resignation or death.

- **The Assembly:** The 25 members of the Assembly elect their own Chair and Deputy Chair, and the Assembly can appoint its own staff. Meetings will be held monthly, to which the Mayor should submit a written report. The Assembly can require the Mayor or other GLA employees to attend to answer questions. The Assembly can make proposals to the Mayor, but there is no duty on the Mayor to do anything about them. The Assembly prepares reports and can investigate any of the Mayor's actions and 'any other matters which the Assembly considers to be of importance to Greater London'. The Assembly can call witnesses and documents. However, no person is required to disclose advice that they have given to the Mayor.

The Secretary of State shall set the rules governing the declaration of interests for Assembly members.

Policy areas:

- **Transport:** The Mayor is required to develop and implement a Transport Strategy to encourage safe, integrated, efficient and economic transport 'to, from and within Greater London'. The Secretary of State may direct the Mayor to revise the Transport Strategy where it is 'inconsistent with national transport policy and the inconsistency is detrimental to any area outside Greater London'. A new body, Transport for London, is to be established to replace London Regional Transport. All members will be appointed by the Mayor, who may also Chair it. The Public-Private Partnership Agreement will be completed before London Underground is handed over to Transport for London.

- **London Development Agency:** The members of the London Development Agency will be appointed by the Mayor rather than by central government. At least half – including the Chair – must have experience of running a business, and at least four must be elected members of either the Assembly or of borough councils.
- **Metropolitan Police Authority:** The Metropolitan Police Authority will have 23 members, 12 of whom will be from the Assembly (including the Deputy Mayor). These 12 are appointed by the Mayor who 'shall ensure that, so far as possible, the members for whose appointment he is responsible reflect the balance of the parties for the time being prevailing among the members of the London Assembly'. The Mayor may at any time remove one of his appointees to ensure this balance is maintained. There will be seven independent members and four magistrates.
- **London Fire And Emergency Planning Authority:** The LEFPA will have 17 members – nine Assembly members appointed by the Mayor and a further eight positions filled by the Mayor on the advice of the borough councils. Both groups should reflect the balance of parties pertaining in the Assembly or the borough councils. The members of the Authority serve for one year. Their Chair is appointed by the Mayor.
- **Planning:** The Mayor must prepare a Spatial Development Strategy, which 'must only deal with matters that are of strategic importance to Greater London'. The Mayor must consult on the strategy, including any districts or counties outside of London which will be affected by it. There must be a public examination of the proposals before the Strategy is published, conducted by a person appointed by the Secretary of State. The Mayor can, 'in prescribed circumstances . . . direct the local planning authority for a London borough to refuse an application for planning permission of a prescribed description in any particular case'. In this context, 'prescribed' means prescribed in regulations issued by the Secretary of State.
- **Environment:** By the end of his or her third year in office, the first Mayor of London shall issue a State of the Environment Report. This report should deal with air quality, traffic levels, water quality, ground water levels, energy consumption, land quality, waste, noise, natural resources, litter. The Mayor will also produce a London Biodiversity Action Plan; Municipal Waste Management Strategy, under which the Mayor may make directions to the borough councils and which the Secretary of State may direct the Mayor to alter; London Air Quality Strategy; London Ambient Noise Strategy. The Mayor must also promote the 'health of Londoners'.
- **Culture Strategy:** A Cultural Strategy Group for London will submit a draft strategy for culture, media and sport. The Mayor will then draw up his or her Culture Strategy, which should be based on the draft, but modified as the Mayor sees fit. The Group should keep the strategy under review and may propose revisions to the Mayor. The Mayor shall appoint the members of the Group, having sought advice from the appropriate bodies.

Relations between the GLA and Westminster

- **Financial Provisions:** The Secretary of State will give the GLA Grant and the GLA Transport Grant after consulting the Mayor of London.
- **Limitations Imposed by Central Government**: The key restrictions on the activities of the GLA are the reserve powers held by the Secretary of State to:

  - make an order preventing the GLA from doing anything that a borough may do
  - make an order limiting expenditure
  - ensure that the Mayor of London's strategies are consistent with national ones
  - instruct the Mayor of London to publish one of the strategies required under the Bill
  - make regulations requiring a proportion of the proceeds from road user charging and the parking place levy to be handed over to central government

The Secretary of State for the Environment has additional powers mainly relating to transport, and the Home Secretary has ones mainly relating to the Metropolitan Police.

Operation of electoral system

The elections for the first four year term of the new Greater London Mayor and Assembly are to be held on 4 May 2000.

The Mayor will be chosen in a cross-London ballot using the Supplementary Vote system of election. Electors will be asked to indicate their first and their second preference from among the candidates. A candidate is elected if he/she receives more than half the total number of first preference votes. If none of the candidates reaches this threshold, the two candidates with the greatest number of first preference votes remain in the contest and all the others are eliminated.

The second preferences indicated on the ballot papers of those candidates who have been eliminated are then inspected. Where such a second preference is for one of the two candidates remaining in the contest, it is added to that candidate's first preference votes. The candidate who has the greater total number of preference votes – that is, first preference votes plus second preference votes transferred from eliminated candidates – is deemed elected.

Each candidate for Mayor will be required to pay a deposit of an amount yet to be determined. This will be returned if the candidate receives at least 5% of the total valid votes cast across London.

LONDON MAYOR ELECTION

Mark your 1st preference candidate
with an "x" in the 1st column

Mark your 2nd preference candidate
with an "x" in the 2nd column

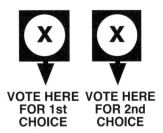

VOTE HERE VOTE HERE
FOR 1st   FOR 2nd
CHOICE   CHOICE

BRADSHAW, Michael **The Conservative Party**	○ ○
DICKENS, Jill **The Labour Party**	○ ○
LANGLEY, Oswald **Independent**	○ ○
PETTIFER, Edward **Liberal Democrat**	○ ○

The Assembly will comprise 25 members. They will be chosen in one of two ways:

i) Each of 14 constituencies whose boundaries have been drawn up and recommended by the Local Government Commission for England will elect a single Assembly member by the traditional first past the post method.

ii) Eleven additional Assembly members, to be known as London members, will be elected from the votes cast across London in order to provide a counter to any disparity between votes gained and seats won through the operation of simple plurality in the constituencies.

Electors will have two votes. One for a candidate within their Assembly constituency, and one for a 'party list'. There is nothing to stop electors choosing a constituency candidate who represents a different party to the one for which they vote at 'cross-London' level.

LONDON ASSEMBLY: ADDITIONAL MEMBER LIST
BALLOT PAPER

MARK ONE "X" AGAINST A PARTY NAME	CONSERVATIVE	GREEN	LABOUR	LIBERAL DEMOCRAT	SOCIALIST LABOUR
	1 JONES, Michael	1 KHAN, Jublyina	1 SMITH, Donald	1 MATHEWS, Sarah	1 HUSSAIN, Jahang
	2 BEGUM, Shara	2 SOUTAR, Harry	2 AHMED, Abdul	2 SEEF, Geoffrey	2 FRANCES, Joan
	3 FARRANT, Colin	3 BOXALL, Jean	3 ANDREWS, Ted	3 CATON, Shireen	3 BAKER, Jonathan
	4 DUNCAN, John	4 MILES, Susan	4 DENTON, Lindsay	4 HUGHES, Tim	4 MAHMOOD, Salim
	5 DAVIDS, Mary	5 LEONARD, Adrian	5 SINGH, Sebash	5 TRUMAN, Seb	
	6 HALL, Philip	6 JONES, Frank	6 WALTERS, Hugh	6 BRISKETT, Fred	
	7 SMITH, Malcolm	7 HEWITT, Heather	7 ADAMS, Barnaby	7 LOVING, Sybil	
	8 BARBER, Adrian	8 DICKENS, Roger	8 MAY, Rebecca	8 RYAN, Megan	
	9 WASTALL, Ann		9 LOUIS, Frances		
	10 DEPPLE, Ronald		10 BLITH, Annette		
	11 HAMILTON, Troy		11 JONES, Ken		

YOU HAVE ONE VOTE ONLY

London Assembly: Barnet and Camden VOTE FOR ONE CANDIDATE ONLY		
ALLEN, Nicholas — The Green Party	1	
FENN, Mark — The Conservative Party	2	
JACOBS, Matthew — Independent	3	
ROBERTS, Mandy — The Labour Party	4	
RUSHMOORE, Jenny — Socialist Labour	5	
TYLER, Alexander — Liberal Democrat	6	

The total number of list votes cast for each party in all the constituencies will be aggregated to form the basis for calculating the allocation of the additional seats. Parties will supply a list of candidates for the list in the order in which they wish them to be elected. It is likely to be allowable for individuals simultaneously to be candidates both in a constituency and on a party list, but those who win a constituency seat will no longer be eligible to be an additional member. 'Independent' candidates are entitled to stand either in a constituency or for election as an additional member or both, but the votes of candidates not on the list of a registered party will each be treated separately.

To be certain of securing a Greater London Assembly seat a party or an individual must receive a proportion of the vote equal to 100 divided by the total number of seats in London **plus one**. This threshold is 100÷(25+1)=3.8%. However, the Bill provides for the Secretary of State to set a 'prescribed percentage' (no higher than 5% of the vote) as a formal threshold. Any party achieving less than this prescribed percentage of votes will not be eligible for a 'top up' seat.

Each candidate nominated in a constituency and each party and individual which appears on the additional member list will be required to pay a deposit of an amount yet to be determined. This will be returned if the candidate/party receives at least 5% of the total valid votes cast in the constituency/across London.

Electing the Mayor: an example

In this example we use an entirely hypothetical case. Following the count of first preference votes cast for the candidates for Mayor, it is determined that the two candidates with the largest number were A and C. The other four candidates are eliminated. The second preferences indicated on the ballot papers of those four candidates are inspected. Where such a second preference is for one of the two candidates remaining in the contest, it is added to that candidate's first preference votes. The candidate who has the greater total number of preference votes – that is, first preference votes plus second preference votes transferred from eliminated candidates- is deemed elected. In our example the winner is candidate A.

Table 5.2: Counting first and second preferences in the election for Mayor

Candidate	1st preference votes	2nd Preference votes	Total	Result
Candidate A	300,000	200,000	500,000	Elected
Candidate B	20,000	–	Eliminated	
Candidate C	400,000	70,000	470,000	
Candidate D	100,000	–	Eliminated	
Candidate E	150,000	–	Eliminated	
Candidate F	40,000	–	Eliminated	

Electing Additional Members in London: an example

Following the counts and the declarations of the results in the 14 constituencies, the votes cast for additional members of the Greater London Assembly will be tallied. In this example we use the results of the 1994 London borough elections and make the assumption that all electors would have cast their 'party list' votes for the same party or group for which they voted at constituency level.

Table 5.3: London – 1994 borough election results

	Con	Lab	LD	Green	Others
Votes	697,427	927,557	490,519	48,798	65,267
% Share	31.3	41.6	22.0	2.2	2.9
Seats	4	9	1	—	—

Additional members are chosen having taken into account the number of seats a party has already won within the region. Therefore, to begin allocating the 11 additional seats it is necessary to divide the total votes cast for each party by the number of constituencies it has won **plus one**. Each time a party gains a seat the number by which its total vote is to be divided increases by one.

Following the initial calculation the party with the highest number of remaining votes, Liberal Democrat, is awarded a seat – see Table 5.4. That seat is taken by the candidate in first place on the Liberal Democrat list, assuming that he/she has not already been elected as a constituency member. The Liberal Democrat vote is now divided by three – the seat just acquired plus the seat won under first past the post plus one – to give 163,506. Because the Liberal Democrat vote is still the highest the party secures a further seat for its second placed eligible candidate and its total vote is now divided by four = 122630. The party with the largest remaining vote (139,485) is now the Conservatives, whose top candidate takes the third available seat. This process of dividing each party's total vote by the number of seats it has won plus one and then allocating the next available seat to the party with the highest remainder continues until all 11 seats have been determined.

Table 5.4: London – allocation of additional members

	Con	Lab	LD	Green	Others	Elected (no. on list)
Total votes	697,427	927,557	490,519	48,798	65,267	
Initial divisor	4 + 1	9 + 1	1 + 1	0 + 1	0 + 1	
1st seat	139,485	92,756	**245,260**	48,798	65,267	LD (1)
2nd seat	139,485	92,756	**163,506**	48,798	65,267	LD (2)
3rd seat	**139,485**	92,756	122,630	48,798	65,267	Con (1)
4th seat	116,238	92,756	**122,630**	48,798	65,267	LD (3)
5th seat	**116,238**	92,756	98,104	48,798	65,267	Con (2)
6th seat	**99,632**	92,756	98,104	48,798	65,267	Con (3)
7th seat	87,178	92,756	**98,104**	48,798	65,267	LD (4)
8th seat	87,178	**92,756**	81,753	48,798	65,267	Lab (1)
9th seat	**87,178**	84,323	81,753	48,798	65,267	Con (4)
10th seat	77,492	**84,323**	81,753	48,798	65,267	Lab (2)
11th seat	77,492	77,296	**81,753**	48,798	65,267	LD (5)

The operation of this process has awarded five of the additional seats to the Liberal Democrats, four to the Conservatives and two to Labour. The total representation of London in the Assembly would therefore be:

Table 5.5: London – Assembly membership

	Con	Lab	LD	Green	Others
Constituency members	4	9	1	—	—
'Top up' seats	4	2	5	—	—
Total	8	11	6	—	—

The Greater London Authority and past election results

As this will be the first election for the Greater London Authority there are no past contests with which to make direct comparisons. This is a particular problem for any attempt to extrapolate the outcome of the Mayoral contest from the results of recent elections. No single party has achieved 50% of the vote in a London-wide election since the Conservatives did so at the 1977 Greater London Council elections and it is therefore probable that voters' supplementary preferences will need to be taken into account when determining the winner. Moreover, the campaign for Mayor is likely to place considerable emphasis on the personal merits of rival candidates and their party affiliations may therefore play a secondary role in the minds of some voters when they decide whom to support. For these reasons we have decided not to calculate any 'notional' results for the Mayoralty.

As far as the Assembly contests are concerned, however, there are four sets of elections which can be used to give a flavour of what might happen. Because the Assembly constituencies proposed by the Local Government Commission are based on the amalgamation of whole London boroughs, it is possible to add up the votes cast for the parties at the 1994 and 1998 London borough elections in each of the new electoral units. This method has to assume that voters would not have behaved differently when faced with a slightly different type of contest, but is the most accurate means available for estimating outcomes. The votes of approximately 5,000 electors in the City of London, which has a different electoral system and cycle to the boroughs, are simply added to the total for the City and East constituency. The 'notional' votes likely to have been cast for each party are calculated by reference to the results in the Westminster borough ward of St James's. This ward adjoins the City and together they form part of the Cities of London and Westminster parliamentary constituency.

A similar exercise can be performed for the results in London at the 1992 and 1997 general elections. In these cases, however, somewhat greater manipulations of the basic voting figures are required. In the first place the 1992 general election was fought using different parliamentary constituency boundaries to the 1997 contest. In our analyses here we have used the 'notional' results originally calculated to show what the outcome in 1992 might have been if that election had been fought on the boundaries which were put in place in 1997. Second, five Westminster constituencies cross the boundaries of the proposed Assembly constituencies. Results are not, of course, available for sub-divisions of parliamentary constituencies, so where this happens we have had to estimate the 'notional' contribution made to the total votes cast in each constituency by those parts which are being put into different Assembly seats. We make the assumption that the proportion of a party's total vote in a constituency area contributed by each ward at a local election will be the same as at a general election. For example, if the wards forming that part of the Chingford and Woodford Green parliamentary constituency which now falls within the Havering and Redbridge Greater London Assembly seat contributed 15% of the total Conservative vote across the parliamentary constituency in the 1994 borough elections, it is reasonable to assume that they also did so in 1997. From there it is a simple matter of disaggregating the Chingford and Woodford Green general election votes and allocating them to the appropriate Assembly constituencies.

In addition, and on the assumption that all electors would have cast their 'party list' votes for the same party or group for which they voted at constituency or ward level, each of these four sets of elections allows for the aggregation of all the votes cast for each party across London in order to calculate the allocation of the additional seats.

The following pages describe and map the composition of each Greater London Assembly electoral constituency and indicate what the results of the Greater London Assembly elections might have been if they had taken place in 1992, 1994, 1997 and 1998.

Barnet and Camden Assembly Constituency

1998 local government electorate
363,027

% of London electorate
7.2

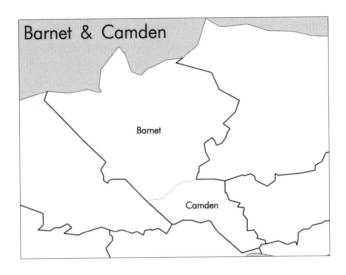

Barnet & Camden

Barnet

Camden

Comprising the boroughs of	Control 1994	Control 1998
Barnet	NOC*	NOC*
Camden	Lab	Lab

* In all these profiles NOC = No Overall Control. That is, where no single party had a majority on that council.

and the constituencies of	1992	Won by 1994	1997	% maj.	Second 1997	1998
Chipping Barnet	Con	Con	Con	2.1	Lab	Con
Finchley and Golders Green	Con	Lab	Lab	6.3	Con	Lab
Hampstead and Highgate	Lab	Lab	Lab	30.2	Con	Lab
Hendon	Con	Lab	Lab	12.3	Con	Lab
Holborn and St Pancras	Lab	Lab	Lab	47.1	Con	Lab

The Barnet and Camden electoral area stretches from Bloomsbury in the heart of the capital all the way north to the prosperous residential suburbs of Chipping Barnet on the border with Hertfordshire. The further north one goes the better the prospects for the Conservatives, although things were so bad for the party in 1997 that even Chipping Barnet was won by just 1,000 votes. Even more worrying for the Tories is the fact that their vote share actually declined between then and the 1998 local elections. The young professionals and middle-class ethnic minorities in this part of London have currently deserted the Tories for Labour. The party will not win this Assembly seat until it can persuade them back into the fold.

Votes and seats based on 1992 general election

	Con	Lab	LD	Others
Votes	116,952	89,681	31,814	4,350
% share of vote	48.2	36.9	13.1	1.8
Seat (FPTP)	1	0	0	0

Votes and seats based on 1994 London borough elections

	Con	Lab	LD	Others
Votes	47,120	64,973	29,102	9,976
% share of vote	31.2	43.0	19.3	6.6
Seat (FPTP)	0	1	0	0

Votes and seats based on 1997 general election

	Con	Lab	LD	Others
Votes	78,631	118,127	27,457	7,728
% share of vote	33.9	50.9	11.8	3.3
Seat (FPTP)	0	1	0	0

Votes and seats based on 1998 London borough elections

	Con	Lab	LD	Others
Votes	42,170	53,038	24,421	8,681
% share of vote	32.9	41.3	19.0	6.8
Seat (FPTP)	0	1	0	0

Bexley and Bromley Assembly Constituency

1998 local government electorate	% of London electorate
394,106	7.8

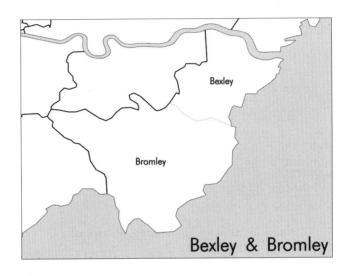

Comprising the boroughs of:	Control 1994	Control 1998
Bexley	NOC*	Con
Bromley	Con	NOC*

and the constituencies of	1992	Won by 1994	1997	% maj.	Second 1997	1998
Beckenham	Con	Con	Con	9.1	Lab	Con
Bexleyheath and Crayford	Con	Lab	Lab	7.1	Con	Lab
Bromley and Chislehurst	Con	Con	Con	21.1	Lab	Con
Erith and Thamesmead (part)	Lab	Lab	Lab	41.9	Con	Lab
Old Bexley and Sidcup	Con	Con	Con	6.9	Lab	Con
Orpington	Con	LD	Con	4.9	LD	LD

The south east boroughs of Bexley and Bromley, both with high proportions of managerial workers and/or owner-occupiers, are a safe prospect for the Conservatives even in uncertain times. The party was comfortably ahead of Labour at the 1997 general election and managed a 4% swing in its favour between then and the 1998 local elections. The Liberal Democrats did well enough to deprive the Conservatives of control of Bromley at those elections, but they show few signs of marshalling the level of support achieved across in the south west of London. Barring extraordinary events or differential turnout on an unprecedented scale Labour cannot poll a plurality of votes here.

Votes and seats based on 1992 general election

	Con	Lab	LD	Others
Votes	180,667	71,504	64,031	5,014
% share of vote	56.2	22.3	19.9	1.6
Seat (FPTP)	1	0	0	0

Votes and seats based on 1994 London borough elections

	Con	Lab	LD	Others
Votes	73,465	50,932	59,046	3,071
% share of vote	39.4	27.3	31.7	1.6
Seat (FPTP)	1	0	0	0

Votes and seats based on 1997 general election

	Con	Lab	LD	Others
Votes	119,044	95,726	59,878	16,403
% share of vote	40.9	32.9	20.6	5.6
Seat (FPTP)	1	0	0	0

Votes and seats based on 1998 London borough elections

	Con	Lab	LD	Others
Votes	63,606	39,924	42,318	1,411
% share of vote	43.2	27.1	28.7	1.0
Seat (FPTP)	1	0	0	0

Brent and Harrow Assembly Constituency

1998 local government electorate
326,254

% of London electorate
6.5

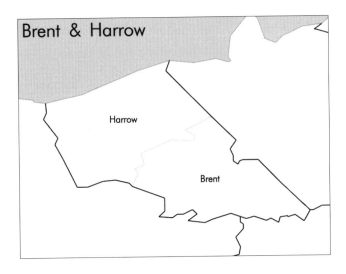

Comprising the boroughs of	Control 1994	Control 1998
Brent	NOC*	Lab
Harrow	NOC*	Lab

and the constituencies of	1992	Won by 1994	1997	% maj.	Second 1997	1998
Brent East	Lab	Lab	Lab	45.0	Con	Lab
Brent North	Con	Con	Lab	10.5	Con	Con
Brent South	Lab	Lab	Lab	57.1	Con	Lab
Harrow East	Con	Con	Lab	17.1	Con	Lab
Harrow West	Con	LD	Lab	2.4	Con	Lab

Labour swept the board in Brent and Harrow in 1997 as it ate into formerly Conservative suburban heartlands. Brent North and the two Harrow constituencies witnessed among the largest swings in the country as Tory majorities of up to 32% were over-turned. The Conservative vote picked up at the 1998 borough elections, but only Brent North would have been 'won' back. Labour will be favourites to win the Assembly seat, but a victory for the Conservatives would mark a real recovery in the party's fortunes in a part of north London where demographic as well as political change has worked against them.

Votes and seats based on 1992 general election

	Con	Lab	LD	Others
Votes	108,527	84,868	28,303	4,496
% share of vote	48.0	37.5	12.5	2.0
Seat (FPTP)	1	0	0	0

Votes and seats based on 1994 London borough elections

	Con	Lab	LD	Others
Votes	55,952	50,828	35,094	4,375
% share of vote	38.3	34.8	24.0	3.0
Seat (FPTP)	1	0	0	0

Votes and seats based on 1997 general election

	Con	Lab	LD	Others
Votes	69,439	120,005	21,349	6,638
% share of vote	31.9	55.2	9.8	3.1
Seat (FPTP)	0	1	0	0

Votes and seats based on 1998 London borough elections

	Con	Lab	LD	Others
Votes	39,899	50,840	22,421	4,215
% share of vote	34.0	43.3	19.1	3.6
Seat (FPTP)	0	1	0	0

City and East Assembly Constituency

1998 local government electorate
390,500

% of London electorate
7.7

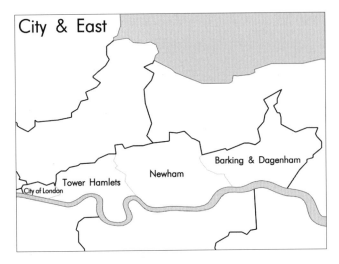

Comprising the boroughs of	Control 1994	Control 1998
Barking and Dagenham	Lab	Lab
Newham	Lab	Lab
Tower Hamlets	Lab	Lab
City of London	Ind	Ind

and the constituencies of	1992	Won by 1994	1997	% maj.	Second 1997	1998
Barking	Lab	Lab	Lab	48.2	Con	Lab
Bethnal Green and Bow	Lab	Lab	Lab	25.3	Con	Lab
Cities of London and Westminster (part)	Con	Con	Con	12.2	Lab	Con
Dagenham	Lab	Lab	Lab	47.2	Con	Lab
East Ham	Lab	Lab	Lab	48.5	Con	Lab
Poplar and Canning Town	Lab	Lab	Lab	48.2	Con	Lab
West Ham	Lab	Lab	Lab	57.9	Con	Lab

The three east London boroughs of Barking and Dagenham, Newham and Tower Hamlets are joined by 5,000 odd electors from the City of London. The City will have a neglible impact on the Labour dominance of this seat. Barking and Dagenham is traditionally working-class with a large number of skilled workers and a still high proportion of local authority housing. Newham and Tower Hamlets both have pockets of multiple deprivation and considerable ethnic minority populations. A community focused group of Liberal Democrats ran Tower Hamlets until 1994, and the British National Party has prospered in parts of the area. They gained the Millwall ward, albeit for just a few months, in 1993 and polled more than 7% of the vote both in Bethnal Green and Bow and in Poplar and Canning Town at the 1997 general election.

Votes and seats based on 1992 general election

	Con	Lab	LD	Others
Votes	74,907	133,123	40,013	4,274
% share of vote	29.7	52.8	15.9	1.7
Seat (FPTP)	0	1	0	0

Votes and seats based on 1994 London borough elections

	Con	Lab	LD	Others
Votes	16,491	93,030	31,287	20,397
% share of vote	10.2	57.7	19.4	12.7
Seat (FPTP)	0	1	0	0

Votes and seats based on 1997 general election

	Con	Lab	LD	Others
Votes	41,781	142,021	20,831	25,744
% share of vote	18.1	61.6	9.0	11.2
Seat (FPTP)	0	1	0	0

Votes and seats based on 1998 London borough elections

	Con	Lab	LD	Others
Votes	15,714	65,198	20,975	14,311
% share of vote	13.5	56.1	18.1	12.3
Seat (FPTP)	0	1	0	0

Croydon and Sutton Assembly Constituency

1998 local government electorate
358,131

% of London electorate
7.1

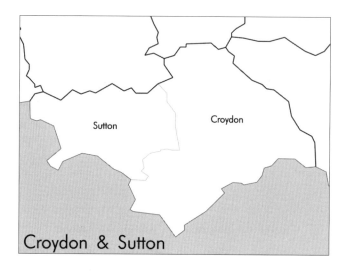

Croydon & Sutton

Comprising the boroughs of	Control 1994	Control 1998
Croydon	Lab	Lab
Sutton	LD	LD

and the constituencies of	1992	Won by 1994	1997	% maj.	Second 1997	1998
Carshalton and Wallington	Con	LD	LD	4.7	Con	LD
Croydon Central	Con	Con	Lab	7.0	Con	Con
Croydon North	Con	Lab	Lab	35.0	Con	Lab
Croydon South	Con	Con	Con	22.0	Lab	Con
Sutton and Cheam	Con	LD	LD	4.5	Con	LD

Each of the three parties have pockets of strength in Croydon and Sutton, but the Conservatives have come out on top throughout the 1990s. In 1992 they won all five constituencies, and although they managed to retain just one of them in 1997, they took second place everywhere else to beat Labour by over 5,000 votes. Liberal Democrat weakness in Croydon will make it hard for the party to get a plurality of votes across the Assembly seat area, and Labour faces a parallel problem in Sutton. However, neither party's activists are likely to concede in the battle for tactical votes, so the Conservatives should win comfortably even if their share of the poll is as little as 40%.

Votes and seats based on 1992 general election

	Con	Lab	LD	Others
Votes	149,695	68,810	60,127	1,699
% share of vote	53.4	24.5	21.4	0.6
Seat (FPTP)	1	0	0	0

Votes and seats based on 1994 London borough elections

	Con	Lab	LD	Others
Votes	59,910	50,910	51,387	6,012
% share of vote	35.6	30.3	30.5	3.6
Seat (FPTP)	1	0	0	0

Votes and seats based on 1997 general election

	Con	Lab	LD	Others
Votes	95,503	90,668	59,977	11,928
% share of vote	37.0	35.1	23.2	4.6
Seat (FPTP)	1	0	0	0

Votes and seats based on 1998 London borough elections

	Con	Lab	LD	Others
Votes	51,746	39,760	35,033	3,216
% share of vote	39.9	30.6	27.0	2.5
Seat (FPTP)	1	0	0	0

Ealing and Hillingdon Assembly Constituency

1998 local government electorate
389,339

% of London electorate
7.7

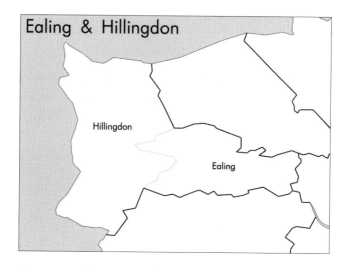

Comprising the boroughs of	Control 1994	Control 1998
Ealing	Lab	Lab
Hillingdon	Lab	NOC*

and the constituencies of	1992	Won by 1994	1997	% maj.	Second 1997	1998
Ealing Acton and Shepherd's Bush (part)	Lab	Lab	Lab	32.6	Con	Lab
Ealing North	Con	Con	Lab	16.4	Con	Lab
Ealing Southall	Lab	Lab	Lab	39.2	Con	Lab
Hayes and Harlington	Con	Lab	Lab	34.8	Con	Lab
Ruislip-Northwood	Con	Con	Con	17.4	Lab	Con
Uxbridge	Con	Lab	Con	1.7	Lab	Con

Ealing and Hillingdon together make up one of the seven Greater London Assembly constituencies which would have been won by the Tories at the 1992 general election but by Labour in 1997. There were significant swings to Labour throughout, with Ealing North and Hayes and Harlington recording two of the largest increases in the party's vote share in the country. The Conservatives did well in Hillingdon borough at the 1998 local elections, but most of their success was in winning back voters in the middle-class wards of Ruislip-Northwood and Uxbridge. Elsewhere the party seemed stuck far behind Labour. The Tories need to win here to have any chance of being the largest party in the Assembly.

Votes and seats based on 1992 general election

	Con	Lab	LD	Others
Votes	140,426	100,369	32,985	8,150
% share of vote	49.8	35.6	11.7	2.9
Seat (FPTP)	1	0	0	0

Votes and seats based on 1994 London borough elections

	Con	Lab	LD	Others
Votes	71,236	84,944	22,997	4,201
% share of vote	38.8	46.3	12.5	2.3
Seat (FPTP)	0	1	0	0

Votes and seats based on 1997 general election

	Con	Lab	LD	Others
Votes	93,453	134,961	27,900	10,786
% share of vote	35.0	50.5	10.4	4.0
Seat (FPTP)	0	1	0	0

Votes and seats based on 1998 London borough elections

	Con	Lab	LD	Others
Votes	50,046	57,897	19,015	5,986
% share of vote	37.6	43.5	14.3	4.5
Seat (FPTP)	0	1	0	0

Enfield and Haringey Assembly Constituency

1998 local government electorate
348,335

% of London electorate
6.9

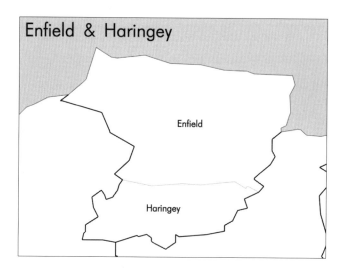

Enfield & Haringey

Enfield

Haringey

Comprising the boroughs of:	Control 1994	Control 1998
Enfield	Lab	Lab
Haringey	Lab	Lab

and the constituencies of	1992	Won by 1994	1997	% maj.	Second 1997	1998
Edmonton	Con	Lab	Lab	30.0	Con	Lab
Enfield North	Con	Lab	Lab	14.3	Con	Lab
Enfield Southgate	Con	Con	Lab	3.1	Con	Con
Hornsey and Wood Green	Lab	Lab	Lab	39.8	Con	Lab
Tottenham	Lab	Lab	Lab	53.6	Con	Lab

Labour won all five parliamentary seats in Enfield and Haringey in 1997, but the loyalties of the boroughs tended to favour the Conservatives during the 1980s. Indeed only Tottenham escaped their grasp in both 1983 and 1987. However, the 1998 local elections can have given the Tories little hope of a quick reversal in fortunes. They narrowly 'won back' Enfield Southgate but remained behind everywhere else. Rather, as in other North London areas, there is evidence of a growing Labour core vote here. Labour will only fail to win the Assembly seat if the party has begun to fall behind the Tories across the nation as a whole.

Votes and seats based on 1992 general election

	Con	Lab	LD	Others
Votes	113,439	105,016	27,496	3,857
% share of vote	45.4	42.0	11.0	1.5
Seat (FPTP)	1	0	0	0

Votes and seats based on 1994 London borough elections

	Con	Lab	LD	Others
Votes	48,031	76,434	19,794	7,080
% share of vote	31.7	50.5	13.1	4.7
Seat (FPTP)	0	1	0	0

Votes and seats based on 1997 general election

	Con	Lab	LD	Others
Votes	67,234	129,660	21,935	9,402
% share of vote	29.5	56.8	9.6	4.1
Seat (FPTP)	0	1	0	0

Votes and seats based on 1998 London borough elections

	Con	Lab	LD	Others
Votes	33,522	55,203	15,786	7,084
% share of vote	30.0	49.5	14.1	6.3
Seat (FPTP)	0	1	0	0

Greenwich and Lewisham Assembly Constituency

1998 local government electorate
328,656

% of London electorate
6.5

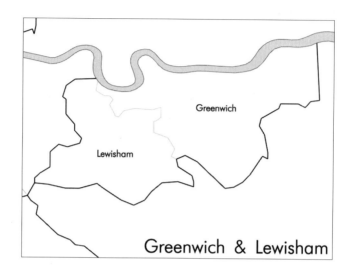

Greenwich

Lewisham

Greenwich & Lewisham

Comprising the boroughs of	Control 1994	Control 1998
Greenwich	Lab	Lab
Lewisham	Lab	Lab

and the constituencies of	1992	Won by 1994	1997	% maj.	Second 1997	1998
Eltham	Con	Lab	Lab	23.4	Con	Lab
Erith and Thamesmead (part)	Lab	Lab	Lab	41.9	Con	Lab
Greenwich and Woolwich	Lab	Lab	Lab	44.9	Con	Lab
Lewisham Deptford	Lab	Lab	Lab	56.1	Con	Lab
Lewisham East	Lab	Lab	Lab	32.4	Con	Lab
Lewisham West	Lab	Lab	Lab	38.1	Con	Lab

Greenwich and Lewisham is one of only four Assembly constituencies in which Labour won all the parliamentary seats at the 1997 general election. Indeed Labour's 62% share of the vote then was its highest in any of the 14 areas from which Assembly members will be elected. For a time in the late 1980s Greenwich was a stronghold of the now defunct SDP, but since 1992 it has reverted to its previous Labour loyalties. The Liberal Democrats are not a potent force here, and the Conservatives have significant strength only in parts of the Eltham constituency. A Labour banker.

Votes and seats based on 1992 general election

	Con	Lab	LD	Others
Votes	79,043	112,473	44,009	1,509
% share of vote	33.3	47.5	18.6	0.6
Seat (FPTP)	0	1	0	0

Votes and seats based on 1994 London borough elections

	Con	Lab	LD	Others
Votes	31,051	78,205	22,959	7,190
% share of vote	22.3	56.1	16.5	5.2
Seat (FPTP)	0	1	0	0

Votes and seats based on 1997 general election

	Con	Lab	LD	Others
Votes	46,037	130,522	22,255	11,033
% share of vote	21.9	62.2	10.6	5.3
Seat (FPTP)	0	1	0	0

Votes and seats based on 1998 London borough elections

	Con	Lab	LD	Others
Votes	24,621	56,895	13,127	6,656
% share of vote	24.3	56.2	13.0	6.6
Seat (FPTP)	0	1	0	0

Havering and Redbridge Assembly Constituency

1998 local government electorate   **% of London electorate**
355,131   7.0

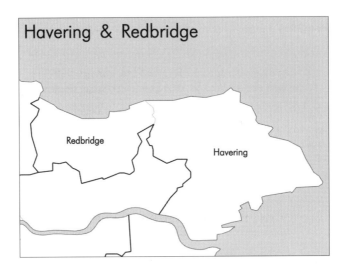

Comprising the boroughs of	Control 1994	Control 1998					
Havering	NOC*	NOC*					
Redbridge	NOC*	NOC*					

and the constituencies of	1992	Won by 1994	1997	% maj.	Second 1997	1998
Chingford and Woodford Green (part)	Con	Con	Con	12.9	Lab	Con
Hornchurch	Con	Lab	Lab	12.9	Con	Lab
Ilford North	Con	Con	Lab	6.6	Con	Con
Ilford South	Con	Lab	Lab	28.4	Con	Lab
Leyton and Wanstead (part)	Lab	Lab	Lab	38.6	Con	Lab
Romford	Con	Lab	Lab	1.5	Con	Con
Upminster	Con	Lab	Lab	6.7	Con	Other

The boroughs of Havering and Redbridge occupy the eastern fringe of the greater London area. Although they contain pockets of originally local authority housing, they are dominated by the owner-occupying and commuting middle-class. The degree to which such groups rebelled against the Conservatives in 1997 can be gauged from the fact that the party won all except one of the parliamentary constituencies in the area in 1992 but *only one* at the last general election following a 16% swing to Labour. There is likely to be a close cross-borough contest between Labour and the Conservatives at the London Assembly elections, but the Conservatives must win here to justify claims about electoral recovery. Residents' Association candidates tend to depress Conservative support in Havering at local elections.

Votes and seats based on 1992 general election

	Con	Lab	LD	Others
Votes	148,322	87,259	34,262	3,179
% share of vote	54.3	32.0	12.5	1.2
Seat (FPTP)	1	0	0	0

Votes and seats based on 1994 London borough elections

	Con	Lab	LD	Others
Votes	51,516	64,083	26,499	15,359
% share of vote	32.7	40.7	16.8	9.8
Seat (FPTP)	0	1	0	0

Votes and seats based on 1997 general election

	Con	Lab	LD	Others
Votes	95,790	119,315	22,380	10,838
% share of vote	38.6	48.0	9.0	4.4
Seat (FPTP)	0	1	0	0

Votes and seats based on 1998 London borough elections

	Con	Lab	LD	Others
Votes	41,031	46,154	15,700	18,710
% share of vote	33.7	38.0	12.9	15.4
Seat (FPTP)	0	1	0	0

Lambeth and Southwark Assembly Constituency

1998 local government electorate
344,001

% of London electorate
6.8

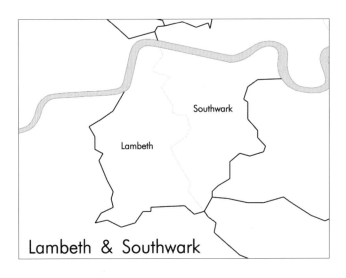

Comprising the boroughs of	Control 1994	Control 1998					
Lambeth	NOC*	Lab					
Southwark	Lab	Lab					

and the constituencies of	1992	Won by 1994	1997	% maj.	Second 1997	1998
Camberwell and Peckham	Lab	Lab	Lab	58.0	Con	Lab
Dulwich and West Norwood	Lab	Lab	Lab	36.8	Con	Lab
Southwark North and Bermondsey	LD	LD	LD	8.3	Lab	LD
Streatham	Lab	Lab	Lab	41.0	Con	Lab
Vauxhall	Lab	LD	Lab	47.8	LD	Lab

Lambeth and Southwark are London's two inner-city boroughs south of the Thames. Four of the five parliamentary seats are held by Labour with massive majorities; the fifth, Southwark North and Bermondsey, was snatched by the Liberal Democrats in a 1983 by-election and is now a Liberal Democrat/Labour marginal. The Liberal Democrats picked up council seats in both boroughs in 1994, but fell back in 1998 and now look to be in little position to challenge Labour's hegemony. Even a low turnout is likely to be insufficient to prevent a Labour victory here.

Votes and seats based on 1992 general election

	Con	Lab	LD	Others
Votes	65,421	107,225	43,343	4,027
% share of vote	29.7	48.7	19.7	1.8
Seat (FPTP)	0	1	0	0

Votes and seats based on 1994 London borough elections

	Con	Lab	LD	Others
Votes	27,233	55,656	49,524	6,513
% share of vote	19.6	40.1	35.6	4.7
Seat (FPTP)	0	1	0	0

Votes and seats based on 1997 general election

	Con	Lab	LD	Others
Votes	32,856	117,086	40,287	8,504
% share of vote	16.5	58.9	20.3	4.3
Seat (FPTP)	0	1	0	0

Votes and seats based on 1998 London borough elections

	Con	Lab	LD	Others
Votes	17,843	49,709	36,322	10,833
% share of vote	15.6	43.3	31.7	9.4
Seat (FPTP)	0	1	0	0

Merton and Wandsworth Assembly Constituency

1998 local government electorate	**% of London electorate**
331,181	6.6

Merton & Wandsworth

Comprising the boroughs of	Control 1994	Control 1998
Merton	Lab	Lab
Wandsworth	Con	Con

and the constituencies of	1992	Won by 1994	1997	% maj.	Second 1997	1998
Battersea	Con	Con	Lab	11.3	Con	Con
Mitcham and Morden	Con	Lab	Lab	28.7	Con	Lab
Putney	Con	Con	Lab	6.8	Con	Con
Tooting	Lab	Lab	Lab	32.6	Con	Con
Wimbledon	Con	Lab	Lab	6.2	Con	Con

The scale of the Conservative defeat in the constituencies of Merton and Wandsworth at the 1997 general election took most commentators by surprise. After all the Tories reigned supreme on Wandsworth council thanks to a low poll tax and the influx of 'yuppies' into the borough. Wimbledon, for its part, was a by-word for affluent Conservatism, with almost 60% of its electors employed in professional or managerial occupations. The Tories did fight back to poll a majority of votes cast in the area at the 1998 local elections and any other result in the Assembly seat contest would be a grievous blow to the party's re-establishment as a competitive electoral force. Labour will not make it easy for them in a battle in which the Liberal Democrats will have only a minor role.

Votes and seats based on 1992 general election

	Con	Lab	LD	Others
Votes	122,213	97,518	27,368	5,526
% share of vote	48.4	38.6	10.8	2.2
Seat (FPTP)	1	0	0	0

Votes and seats based on 1994 London borough elections

	Con	Lab	LD	Others
Votes	65,817	67,605	18,185	11,120
% share of vote	40.4	41.5	11.2	6.8
Seat (FPTP)	0	1	0	0

Votes and seats based on 1997 general election

	Con	Lab	LD	Others
Votes	80,227	120,305	24,187	9,068
% share of vote	34.3	51.5	10.3	3.9
Seat (FPTP)	0	1	0	0

Votes and seats based on 1998 London borough elections

	Con	Lab	LD	Others
Votes	55,798	49,008	15,132	8,744
% share of vote	43.4	38.1	11.8	6.8
Seat (FPTP)	1	0	0	0

North East Assembly Constituency

1998 local government electorate
392,722

% of London electorate
7.8

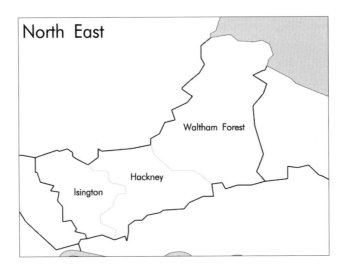

Comprising the boroughs of	Control 1994	Control 1998
Hackney	Lab	NOC*
Islington	Lab	NOC*
Waltham Forest	NOC*	Lab

and the constituencies of	1992	Won by 1994	1997	% maj.	Second 1997	1998
Chingford and Woodford Green (part)	Con	Con	Con	12.9	Lab	Con
Hackney North and Stoke Newington	Lab	Lab	Lab	48.3	Con	Lab
Hackney South and Shoreditch	Lab	Lab	Lab	44.4	LD	Lab
Islington North	Lab	Lab	Lab	55.6	LD	Lab
Islington South and Finsbury	Lab	Lab	Lab	41.2	LD	LD
Leyton and Wanstead (part)	Lab	Lab	Lab	38.6	Con	Lab
Walthamstow	Lab	Lab	Lab	42.8	Con	Lab

The north east London boroughs of Hackney, Islington and Waltham Forest are solidly Labour at general elections, but show split loyalties in local contests. Two of the three councils are currently hung – the Liberal Democrats having outpolled Labour in Islington in 1998 and come a creditable second in the other two. The Conservatives are very much in a minority outside the commuter dormitory of Chingford at the edge of Epping Forest. Labour is almost certain to win the first post the post seat, even allowing for mid-term defections, but votes gained by the Liberal Democrats will make an important contribution to their quest for 'top up' seats across the capital.

Votes and seats based on 1992 general election

	Con	Lab	LD	Others
Votes	84,974	128,056	44,364	6,360
% share of vote	32.2	48.6	16.8	2.4
Seat (FPTP)	0	1	0	0

Votes and seats based on 1994 London borough elections

	Con	Lab	LD	Others
Votes	33,049	79,906	45,007	12,010
% share of vote	19.4	47.0	26.5	7.1
Seat (FPTP)	0	1	0	0

Votes and seats based on 1997 general election

	Con	Lab	LD	Others
Votes	46,611	145,106	35,582	11,771
% share of vote	19.5	60.7	14.9	4.9
Seat (FPTP)	0	1	0	0

Votes and seats based on 1998 London borough elections

	Con	Lab	LD	Others
Votes	23,671	56,484	44,654	12,988
% share of vote	17.2	41.0	32.4	9.4
Seat (FPTP)	0	1	0	0

South West Assembly Constituency

1998 local government electorate
383,579

% of London electorate
7.6

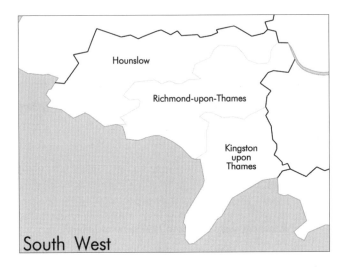

Comprising the boroughs of	Control 1994	Control 1998
Hounslow	Lab	Lab
Kingston upon Thames	LD	NOC*
Richmond upon Thames	LD	LD

and the constituencies of	1992	Won by 1994	1997	% maj.	Second 1997	1998
Isleworth	Con	Lab	Lab	25.7	Con	Lab
Feltham and Heston	Lab	Lab	Lab	32.8	Con	Lab
Kingston and Surbiton	Con	LD	LD	0.1	Con	LD
Richmond Park	Con	LD	LD	5.2	Con	LD
Twickenham	Con	LD	LD	7.4	Con	LD

The Conservatives would have won this seat at all but one of our example elections, but the different patterns of party competition in the three boroughs make for a fascinating three-way race. Labour is strong in Hounslow with the Conservatives in second place, whereas in both Kingston and Richmond the Tories battle for supremacy with the Liberal Democrats. In 1998 the parties were separated by fewer than 4,000 votes. The Conservatives should win this Assembly seat in the mid-term of a Labour government, but will be hard pressed if the Liberal Democrats maximise their local government strength and benefit disproportionately from any fall off in Labour support. This seat looks to be the Liberal Democrats' only real chance of having an Assembly member elected under first past the post.

Votes and seats based on 1992 general election

	Con	Lab	LD	Others
Votes	139,823	72,009	72,417	3,108
% share of vote	48.7	25.1	25.2	1.1
Seat (FPTP)	1	0	0	0

Votes and seats based on 1994 London borough elections

	Con	Lab	LD	Others
Votes	58,144	58,104	62,474	3,855
% share of vote	31.8	31.8	34.2	2.1
Seat (FPTP)	0	0	1	0

Votes and seats based on 1997 general election

	Con	Lab	LD	Others
Votes	95,141	89,133	80,918	8,226
% share of vote	34.8	32.6	29.6	3.0
Seat (FPTP)	1	0	0	0

Votes and seats based on 1998 London borough elections

	Con	Lab	LD	Others
Votes	48,998	46,476	45,508	6,512
% share of vote	33.2	31.5	30.9	4.4
Seat (FPTP)	1	0	0	0

West Central Assembly Constituency

1998 local government electorate   **% of London electorate**
340,000   6.7

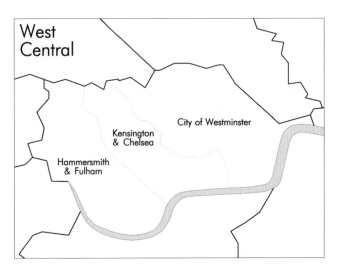

Comprising the boroughs of	Control 1994	Control 1998				
Hammersmith and Fulham	Lab	Lab				
Kensington and Chelsea	Con	Con				
Westminster	Con	Con				

and the constituencies of	1992	Won by 1994	1997	% maj.	Second 1997	1998
Cities of London and Westminster (part)	Con	Con	Con	12.2	Lab	Con
Ealing Acton and Shepherd's Bush (part)	Lab	Lab	Lab	32.6	Con	Lab
Hammersmith and Fulham	Con	Lab	Lab	7.1	Con	Lab
Kensington and Chelsea	Con	Con	Con	25.7	Lab	Con
Regent's Park and Kensington North	Lab	Lab	Lab	31.0	Con	Lab

West Central contains some of the most exclusive, and Conservative, areas of the capital, together with more typically Labour territory with council housing estates and significant ethnic minority populations. The balance of these forces makes the seat quite difficult to call. Labour 'won' quite comfortably in 1997, but then suffered a swing of over 8% to the Tories between then and the 1998 borough elections. The outcome may well depend on turnout – Labour finds it notoriously difficult to persuade many of its heartlands supporters to vote except at general elections – and on whether the Conservatives can take advantage of the 'Westminster factor'. Low council tax levels helped the Conservatives record above average performances in that borough at both the 1994 and 1998 local elections. Their candidate will start as favourite.

Votes and seats based on 1992 general election

	Con	Lab	LD	Others
Votes	106,160	74,545	21,900	5,198
% share of vote	51.1	35.9	10.5	2.5
Seat (FPTP)	1	0	0	0

Votes and seats based on 1994 London borough elections

	Con	Lab	LD	Others
Votes	58,412	51,947	17,164	2,906
% share of vote	44.8	39.8	13.2	2.2
Seat (FPTP)	1	0	0	0

Votes and seats based on 1997 general election

	Con	Lab	LD	Others
Votes	74,335	90,694	20,575	8,057
% share of vote	38.4	46.8	10.6	4.2
Seat (FPTP)	0	1	0	0

Votes and seats based on 1998 London borough elections

	Con	Lab	LD	Others
Votes	50,449	41,270	13,016	1,540
% share of vote	47.5	38.8	12.2	1.4
Seat (FPTP)	1	0	0	0

LONDON

Votes and seats based on 1992 general election

	Con	Lab	LD	Others
Votes	1,630,569	1,332,456	572,432	60,747
% share of vote	45.3	37.1	15.9	1.7
Seats (FPTP)	10	4	0	0
Seats ('Top up')	2	5	4	0
Total	**12**	**9**	**4**	**0**
% share of seats	48	36	16	0.0

Votes and seats based on 1994 London borough elections

	Con	Lab	LD	Green	Others
Votes	697,427	927,557	490,519	48,798	65,267
% share of vote	31.3	41.6	22.0	2.2	2.9
Seats (FPTP)	4	9	1	0	0
Seats ('Top up')	4	2	5	0	0
Total	**8**	**11**	**6**	**0**	**0**
% share of seats	32	44	24	0.0	0.0

Votes and seats based on 1997 general election

	Con	Lab	LD	Ref	Others
Votes	1,036,082	1,643,329	485,511	68,923	87,203
% share of vote	31.2	49.5	14.6	2.1	2.6
Seats (FPTP)	3	11	0	0	0
Seats ('Top up')	5	2	4	0	0
Total	**8**	**13**	**4**	**0**	**0**
% share of seats	32	52	16	0.0	0.0

Votes and seats based on 1998 London borough elections

	Con	Lab	LD	Green	Others
Votes	559,114	707,856	363,428	50,732	62,673
% share of vote	32.1	40.6	20.8	2.9	3.6
Seats (FPTP)	5	9	0	0	0
Seats ('Top up')	4	2	5	0	0
Total	**9**	**11**	**5**	**0**	**0**
% share of seats	36	44	20	0.0	0.0

The Likely Outcome?

It is difficult to comment with any real conviction or authority on the outcome of the Greater London Mayor and Assembly elections. The contests are more than one year away and the main protagonists have yet to be selected. Indeed, the individuals chosen to be each party's mayoral flag-bearer will themselves play a crucial part in determining the visibility of and public interest in the elections.

The statistic which is perhaps most significant at this distance relates to the likelihood of any one candidate or party receiving a majority of the votes cast across London. In only five of the 26 cross-London general and local elections since the capital's boundaries were expanded in 1964 has one or other party secured a share of the vote greater than 50%. The Conservatives have managed this feat on four occasions – the last being the GLC elections of 1977; Labour just once – the 1971 Borough contests. Labour even fell just short in their annus mirabilis of 1997 when they recorded 49.5% of the vote.

Such precedent makes it almost certain that the result of the mayoral contest will hinge on the second preference of voters, and very likely that no one party will have an overall majority in the inaugural Greater London Assembly.

However, such speculation is subject to one great unknown. How will Londoners make use of the three votes they will be entitled to cast? Experience from the United States suggests that electors see no contradiction in voting for a Republican President (or Mayor) and a Democrat legislative candidate – or vice-versa – at the same time. Indeed it is quite possible that one Mayoral candidate may spark off such a bandwagon that the rarity of any one party receiving a majority of the votes of Londoners will become an irrelevance.

The contests for the Assembly members are likely to be more conventional, but here too there could be significant split ticket voting. For example, we have shown that among voters in England who were able to cast local as well as general election votes on 1 May 1997 at least 10% and perhaps as many as one in five chose different parties on the same visit to the polling booth. Similarly, a survey study of how people may cast their vote under different electoral systems found that up to a quarter were prepared to 'vote' for different parties in the constituency and 'top up' ballots of an additional member system election similar to that to be used in London.

The 14 constituency areas for the Assembly are based on combinations of London boroughs. In six cases the same party has 'won' the seat by recording the most votes on each of the last four occasions on which Londoners have voted – twice at general elections and twice in borough contests. In seven cases, reflecting movements in political preference, the Conservatives topped the poll at the 1992 general election but Labour did so at the 1997 general election. Although such individual outcomes will continue to be of interest to party activists in the constituencies, their overall significance is reduced by the fact that 11 Assembly members (44% of the total) will be chosen in a way which ensures that any disparity between votes cast and seats won across the capital is mitigated.

Indeed it was the presence of this corrective mechanism that explains the relatively uncontroversial manner in which the boundaries for the new constituencies were accepted by all parties. In a pure first past the post system the exact way in which electoral areas are drawn has crucial political implications. Where an element of proportionality is added, however, parties can afford to be less concerned about the effective geographical distribution of their support. At the 1992 general election, for example, the Conservatives would have won 10 of the 14 Assembly constituency seats (71.4%) with just 45.3% of the vote. Five years later in 1997 Labour would have won 11 of them (78.6%) with just under half the vote. However, the operation of the 'top up' reduces the 'winner's bonus' under first past the post and compensates which ever of the parties are disadvantaged. The final outcome in 1992, assuming that voters chose the same party in both the constituency and 'top up' contests, would have given the Conservatives 12 of the 25 seats (48% of the total) and in 1997 Labour would have won 13 seats (52% of the total). In both cases a share of seats very much closer to the share of the vote achieved.

Nonetheless any substantial shifts in party support between the constituency and 'top up' votes could be reflected in the final result. Let us assume that constituency votes were cast as in the 1997 general election, resulting in 3 seats for the Conservatives and 11 for Labour. Let us further assume that voters were less inclined to support Labour with their additional, 'top up' vote and instead distributed their preferences 35% Conservative; 40% Labour; 20% Liberal Democrat; and 5% for several disparate 'other' parties. In such a case, and holding the total number of votes cast constant, the Conservatives would receive six 'top up' seats for a total of nine – one more than if there had been no ticket splitting, and the Liberal Democrats five 'top up' seats – also one more. The consequence for Labour of failing to hold on to its constituency level supporters would have been the loss of its two 'top up' seats and, more to the point, an overall majority in the Assembly.

Although the actual division between constituency and 'top up' seats is subject to such changes in the political wind, the overall impact of the system will be to reduce the opportunity for radical shifts in the composition of the Greater London Assembly. In our four examples the number of Conservative seats varies from a high of 12 to a low of eight; Labour seats from 13 to nine: and Liberal Democrat seats from six to four. Under presently conceivable circumstances it is reasonable to assume that the number of Assembly seats won by each party at the May 2000 elections will fall somewhere within those bands and closely reflect its level of support across London.

The concern expressed in some quarters that the system may deliver Assembly representation to a party with scarcely 4% of the vote across London has been addressed in the Greater London Authority Bill by the clause allowing the Secretary of State to impose a formal threshold of not more than 5% of the vote before any group can qualify for a 'top up' seat. Although no single minor party has approached this level of support in past elections in the capital, it will be easier to attract votes for a single London-wide list candidate than it is to organise a campaign in as many constituencies or wards as possible as currently.

Table 5.6: London Votes

Winners of individual constituencies, based on votes in 1992 and 1997 general elections and 1994 and 1998 borough elections

	1992	*1994*	*1997*	*1998*
Barnet and Camden	Con	Lab	Lab	Lab
Bexley and Bromley	Con	Con	Con	Con
Brent and Harrow	Con	Con	Lab	Lab
City and East	Lab	Lab	Lab	Lab
Croydon and Sutton	Con	Con	Con	Con
Ealing and Hillingdon	Con	Lab	Lab	Lab
Enfield and Haringey	Con	Lab	Lab	Lab
Greenwich and Lewisham	Lab	Lab	Lab	Lab
Havering and Redbridge	Con	Lab	Lab	Lab
Lambeth and Southwark	Lab	Lab	Lab	Lab
Merton and Wandsworth	Con	Lab	Lab	Con
North East	Lab	Lab	Lab	Lab
South West	Con	LD	Con	Con
West Central	Con	Con	Lab	Con

Overall result based on 1992 general election

	Con	*Lab*	*LD*	*Others*
% share of vote	45.3	37.1	15.9	1.7
Seats (FPTP)	10	4	0	0
Seats ('Top up')	2	5	4	0
Total	**12**	**9**	**4**	**0**

Overall result based on 1994 London borough elections

	Con	*Lab*	*LD*	*Green*	*Others*
% share of vote	31.3	41.6	22.0	2.2	2.9
Seats (FPTP)	4	9	1	0	0
Seats ('Top up')	4	2	5	0	0
Total	**8**	**11**	**6**	**0**	**0**

Overall result based on 1997 general election

	Con	*Lab*	*LD*	*Ref*	*Others*
% share of vote	31.2	49.5	14.6	2.1	2.6
Seats (FPTP)	3	11	0	0	0
Seats ('Top up')	5	2	4	0	0
Total	**8**	**13**	**4**	**0**	**0**

Overall result based on 1998 London borough elections

	Con	Lab	LD	Green	Others
% share of vote	32.1	40.6	20.8	2.9	3.6
Seats (FPTP)	5	9	0	0	0
Seats ('Top up')	4	2	5	0	0
Total	**9**	**11**	**5**	**0**	**0**

6. Local Elections

Precursors of Change?

Introduction by: **Chris Mead**, *Elections Editor, PA News*

The 6 May council elections will, with the Scottish Parliament and Welsh Assembly polls, amount to the biggest mid-term test a governing party has faced in more than a quarter of a century.

Voting takes place for 362 local authorities across Great Britain – almost everywhere. The few exceptions amount to London, a dozen unitary authorities and wards not up this time in those councils which elect a third of their members each year.

The test is exacerbated for Labour by the fact that most of the councillors up for re-election last faced voters in 1995 – one of the worst years on record for the Tories. It is hard to see how the party can avoid poor morning after headlines as Tories recapture a host of seats they never should have lost in the first place.

Conservatives, who at present control less than 30 councils nationwide, look almost certain to leapfrog Liberal Democrats into second place in the number of powerbases held. But the elections will still be a key test for Tory leader, William Hague – more crucial to his political survival than that of Tony Blair.

A figure of less than 1,000 gains would definitely be bad news for Tories, particularly if it was followed by a poor result in the Commons by-election which would take place at Eddisbury if senior Tory Sir Alastair Goodlad becomes a European Commissioner. Sir Alastair had a majority of just 1,185 at the 1997 general election and a failure substantially to increase that could boost talk of a leadership challenge.

Liberal Democrats are generally on the defensive after making gains in 1995, but recent local by-elections suggest their vote is holding up better than Labour's. If it does so in May it could be a key factor hindering the Tories' recovery of former strongholds in the south of England.

The 1999 polls could be the last such widespread contests before the start of sweeping changes to council electoral structures.

There are strong calls for the Scottish Parliament to introduce proportional representation for local authorities north of the border. In England there are already moves towards a system of United States of America style directly elected, executive mayors. Such a development appears to have personal backing from the Prime Minister.

The mayor of Greater London is due to be elected in May 2000, with Watford Borough council one of a number of authorities seeking to be first in the queue behind London for a referendum on changing to a directly elected mayor.

There was disappointment when moves to allow councils to experiment on this and other issues did not appear in the Queen's Speech outlining the government's programme for this parliamentary session. An earlier backbench measure, introduced by Local Government Association President Lord Hunt of Tamworth, failed in the Commons, but there are hopes that a similar Bill will be taken up by the government later in this session.

The government has also stated its preference for more councils to be elected annually by thirds, particularly in London. The Local Government Commission has started a ward boundaries review in the capital but a Commission spokesman stressed that although 'if councils want to take on board three member wards, they are free to do so', there was no obligation on them.

Another possible development in the pipeline is electronic voting. In October 1998 Warrington council used a by-election to give electors the opportunity, after they had voted conventionally, to try their hand on a voting machine. A survey taken during the demonstration showed a favourable response.

The local government White Paper also suggested a greater use of referendums beyond determining whether there should be an elected mayor. They would be consultative rather than binding, but could be used to seek views on major planning decisions or other matters of public controversy. Legislation on this too is awaited.

Chris Mead

Structure and functions of local government in Great Britain

There are currently 442 principal local authorities in Great Britain. The structure of local government in England, Scotland and Wales has undergone considerable review in recent years, resulting in an overall reduction in the number of councils.

ENGLAND

- **London:** until the establishment of the Greater London Authority in 2000 London is governed by 32 single tier, all-purpose borough councils, plus the Corporation of the City of London. The boroughs elect their entire council every four years, although the number of council seats in each ward varies. The next London borough elections are in 2002.
- **Metropolitan boroughs:** there are 36 metropolitan borough councils covering the areas previously served by the metropolitan counties of Greater Manchester, Merseyside, South Yorkshire, Tyne and Wear, West Midlands and West Yorkshire. They are all-purpose authorities. Elections are held in three years out of four with one-third of the council elected each time. All wards in the metropolitan boroughs have three members, one seat becoming vacant at each election. There will be elections in all the metropolitan boroughs in 1999.
- **Unitary authorities:** 46 new unitary authorities have been created following the Local Government Review of the early 1990s. They have taken over the functions of both district and county councils in their areas and, as such, are all-purpose authorities. One English unitary authority, the Isles of Scilly, has enjoyed that status since 1973. Some unitary councils elect their entire membership every four years; others choose one-third of the council in each of three out of four years. There is similar variability in the number of council seats in each ward. There will be whole council elections in 18 unitary authorities in 1999 and annual elections in a further 17.
- **County councils:** the number of county councils has been reduced following the creation of unitary authorities and there are now 34 of them. The counties of Avon, Berkshire, Cleveland, Hereford and Worcester, Humberside, and the Isle of Wight have been abolished. Parts of Hereford and Worcester have been reconstituted as the county of Worcestershire. The Isle of Wight has become a unitary authority. Each county has a number of constituent district councils and local government functions are divided between them. The major functions of counties include education and social services. All counties have single member wards and elect their entire council every four years. The next county council elections are in 2001.
- **District councils:** there are currently 238 district councils, each forming a second tier authority within a county council area. Districts are responsible for housing, refuse collection, the collection of council tax, and other local services. Some district councils elect their entire membership every four years; others choose one-third of the council in each of three out of four years. There is similar variability in the number of council seats in each ward. There will be whole council elections in 169 unitary authorities in 1999 and annual elections in a further 68. Malvern Hills, alone among the districts, has no elections this year.

SCOTLAND

- **Scottish councils:** a total of 32 Scottish unitary, all-purpose authorities came into full operation in 1996 following inaugural elections in 1995. They replaced the former two tier system comprising nine upper tier regions, 53 lower tier districts and three all-purpose islands councils. Local government structure, electoral arrangements and finance will be among the responsibilities of the new Scottish Parliament. All Scottish councils have single member wards and elect their entire membership at one time. Local elections will be held throughout Scotland in 1999.

WALES

- **Welsh councils:** a total of 22 Welsh unitary, all-purpose authorities came into full operation in 1996 following inaugural elections in 1995. They replaced the former two tier system comprising eight upper tier counties and 37 lower tier districts. All Welsh councils elect their entire membership at one time, although the number of council seats in each ward varies. Local elections will be held throughout Wales in 1999.

Background and likely outcome

The 1999 local elections seem set to mark the first significant reversal in Labour's 10 year march to pre-eminence in British local government. Notwithstanding opinion polls which continue to suggest that the party is even more popular than when it won the general election in 1997, the evidence from local contests presents a rather less upbeat picture.

In May 1998 Labour suffered a net loss of 150 council seats and its national equivalent vote was just 39% – 5% down on the general election and more than 10 points lower than the party's rating in the polls. At the same time the Tories polled 33% – 2% more than in 1997, and the Liberal Democrats 23% – no less than 6% better than their general election performance. Since then Labour has suffered regular defeats in local by-elections and its lead over the Tories appears to have shrunk still further. Our best guess of current national party strengths as measured by local by-election results is:

Conservative	34%
Labour	38%
Liberal Democrat	23%

Two particular factors make 1999 such a dangerous round of elections for Labour. First, it is defending seats won in the record breaking year of 1995. Labour polled a national equivalent 47% of the vote, with the Tories managing no more than a rock-bottom 25%. If those results had been repeated at the general election Tony Blair's majority would have been comfortably in excess of 200! Against that background Labour losses are inevitable. Indeed our estimate above suggests a 9% swing from Labour to the Conservatives since 1995.

Second, this point in the electoral cycle sees by far the largest number of council seats falling vacant and whole councils having to stand for re-election. On 6 May 1999 some 13,000 councillors will be elected and 187 English unitary and district authorities, as well as 54 councils in Scotland and Wales, will have 'all out' elections. Such an extensive range of contests gives scope for any party's gains or losses to run into four figures and for tens of councils to change hands.

It will be difficult, however, precisely to measure the parties' performances this year because of two important alterations to the architecture of local government since 1995. Many district councils which had elections then subsequently became unitary authorities and held new elections to signal that event. For these authorities the benchmarks of electoral change now date from 1996 or 1997 and not 1995.

The second alteration is that other authorities, both districts and unitaries, have been re-warded by the Local Government Commission for England. In such cases no comparison can be made with previous results in individual wards and, hence, no calculation of the swing required for the council to change party control. The Local Government Commissions in both Scotland and Wales have been similarly engaged and extensive changes in ward boundaries will be implemented in both countries.

The upshot is that only the 36 metropolitan boroughs and 207 of the 342 other authorities which had elections in 1995 are wholly unchanged from four years ago – see Table 6.1. Strictly speaking this means that gains and losses can only be tallied with reference to those councils. The rest, which account for four in ten of all seats being contested on 6 May, are assumed to start with a clean sheet.

This is by no means an isolated example of the complexities and confusions of the British local electoral system, but it is one that has been seized on with alacrity by the party spin doctors. Labour allowed it to leak from its conference in October that it was bracing itself to lose 2,000 seats at the 1999 local elections, which were then still some seven months away! The argument appeared to be that the party had made that many gains in 1995 and must expect to suffer a reaction now that it was in government.

However, even if Labour's popularity slumps as badly as it is claiming to fear, the reduction in the number of like-with-like contests brought about by the changes described above make it virtually impossible that seat losses will be of that scale. Labour won over 6,200 seats in 1995, but only half that number are being fought again unchanged. A triumph, Labour will trumpet, when its seat losses – strictly calculated against equivalent contests in 1995 – fall far below the 'predicted' level.

The Conservatives face their own problem in trying to maximise the publicity spin-off from likely seat gains. If structures and boundaries had remained unchanged, even 1,000 seat gains in 1999 would mean little more than a recovery from the nadir of 1995 to the same level of support achieved in their disastrous general election campaign. In the new situation they must set their expectations lower so that they can be confident of exceeding them in any conventional calculation of gains and losses. The Tories say they hope for 500 gains knowing, quite as clearly as Labour, that the truth is rather different.

Fortunately it does seem possible to provide a rough and ready means of cutting through the spin. We propose to make conventional calculations for likely gains and losses in those seats unaffected by structural or boundary changes using as our base the current share of the vote figures derived from local by-elections and set out above. For the rest we will total up the number of seats the parties are defending from the previous elections and make the assumption that they will lose or gain in the same ratio. For example, if we predict that Labour will lose one in six of its like-with-like contests, we will assume that a similar proportion of its current seats will be lost in those councils having 'clean sheet' elections and add this to the total.

On this basis, the Conservatives might expect to gain about 1,300 seats in England alone; Labour to lose about 1,100; and the Liberal Democrats to lose about 200.

Several councils will also change hands. Among the metropolitan boroughs Labour could lose control of Calderdale, Kirklees, Sheffield – where the Liberal Democrats will hope to repeat their advances of 1998 – and Trafford. The party's overall majority is also vulnerable in the unitary authorities of Milton Keynes, North East Lincolnshire and York.

In the districts several councils hold out the prospect of gains for the Conservatives. Bromsgrove, Gedling and South Ribble could be taken straight from Labour, whereas Ashford, Chichester, East Hampshire, Mid Bedfordshire, Ribble Valley, Rushcliffe, South Buckinghamshire, and Wellingborough currently have no one party with a majority.

In some ways the 'cockpit' of this year's local council contests is Hertfordshire. Labour controls 6 of the 10 districts within the county, but looks vulnerable in all of them except Stevenage. There will be no clearer test of the strength of the Tory recovery than its ability to win back voters in its former home counties heartlands.

One outcome does, however, look clear. Labour's overall majority on the Local Government Association is unlikely to survive these elections. No single party will command a majority on its committees. Will the level of co-operation between Labour and Liberal Democrats now displayed in parliament and Cabinet committee then materialise in the more disputatious world of the Association?

Table 6.1: The pattern of local government elections, May 1999

Elections for one-third of authority – no boundary changes

Type of authority	Number of councils	Previous election for comparison
Metropolitan boroughs	36	1995
Unitary authorities	2	1995
Unitary authorities	6	1996
Unitary authorities	9	1997
District councils	68	1995

Elections for whole authority – no boundary changes

Type of authority	Number of councils	Previous election for comparison
Unitary authorities	7	1995
Unitary authorities	7	1996
District councils	120	1995
Welsh councils	10	1995

Elections for whole authority – with boundary changes

Type of authority	Number of councils	Previous election for comparison
Unitary authorities	4	n/a
District councils	49	n/a
Scottish councils	32	n/a
Welsh councils	12	n/a
Total councils with elections	**362**	

Election statistics and prospects by authority*

In the text that follows, NOC = no overall control. That is, no single party has a majority of seats on the council.

Metropolitan Boroughs

Elections will take place in all 827 wards in the 36 metropolitan boroughs. The seat falling vacant in each ward is that last contested in 1995 and there have been no boundary changes. In some wards the opportunity will be taken to hold by-elections at the same time as the annual elections and, where this happens, more than one seat will be contested. In the summary statistics that follow the share of the vote is that achieved by the parties at the 1995 local elections. The number of seats and council control reflects the situation following the 1998 local elections. The swing calculations in the comments on each council are done with reference to the 1995 results and thus to the actual vacancies occurring this year.

Table 6.2: 1995 Metropolitan borough election results

	Total votes	% share of vote	% change on 1991	Wards contested	Seats won
Con	545,339	19.9	−11.9	728	49
Lab	1,565,315	57.1	12.0	826	682
LDem	523,629	19.1	0.3	638	101
Ind	22,005	0.8		62	1
Green	25,064	0.9	−0.9	137	0
Other	58,774	2.1		145	9
Total	2,740,126			827	842

Greater Manchester

	Con	Lab	LDem	Other	Control

Bolton

| 1995 % share | 24.0 | 54.3 | 19.3 | 2.3 | Lab |
| Total Seats | 8 | 47 | 5 | 0 | |

No change in control possible. Lab vulnerable to Con in Astley Bridge and Bradshaw; to LDs in Horwich and Westhoughton.

Bury

| 1995 % share | 28.5 | 62.8 | 8.4 | 0.2 | Lab |
| Total Seats | 6 | 39 | 3 | 0 | |

No change in control possible. Con win two seats from Lab on 9% swing since 1995.

Manchester

| 1995 % share | 11.9 | 63.3 | 20.7 | 4.1 | Lab |
| Total Seats | 0 | 84 | 15 | 0 | |

No change in control possible. Big swing from Lab to LD in autumn 1998 by-election could herald LD gains.

Oldham

| 1995 % share | 13.8 | 48.6 | 35.5 | 2.1 | Lab |
| Total Seats | 0 | 36 | 23 | 1 | |

Change in control unlikely. Con could gain Chadderton North and LD both Hollinwood and Lees – all from Lab.

	Con	Lab	LDem	Other	Control
Rochdale					
1995 % share	14.4	51.5	33.4	0.7	Lab
Total Seats	6	36	18	0	

Change in control unlikely. Lab vulnerable to 6% swing to LD in 2 seats; LD at risk from same swing to Lab in three others.

Salford					
1995 % share	13.5	71.5	14.5	0.5	Lab
Total Seats	0	57	3	0	

No change in control possible. Lab won 19 out of 20 seats in 1995 and 1998. LD held Worsley is a three-way marginal.

Stockport					
1995 % share	23.3	39.6	33.7	3.4	NOC
Total Seats	3	27	30	3	

LDs need two seats for control. Cheadle (Con 5% maj.) and East Bramhall (Con 6% maj.) will be their prime targets.

Tameside					
1995 % share	21.5	65.8	8.9	3.8	Lab
Total Seats	2	49	2	4	

No change in control possible. Best Tories can hope for is to double their representation from two to four!

Trafford					
1995 % share	38.3	46.9	13.3	1.6	Lab
Total Seats	23	36	4	0	

Lab overall control vulnerable to 8% swing to Con. The last Tory Metropolitan Borough to fall and their top target.

Wigan					
1995 % share	10.2	72.8	14.7	2.2	Lab
Total Seats	0	70	1	1	

No change in control possible – Lab won 24 out of 24 in 1995. Con likely still to have no seats on the council.

Merseyside

Knowsley					
1995 % share	8.8	82.0	3.9	5.4	Lab
Total Seats	0	65	1	0	

No change in control possible. Lab won everything in 1995, with seven councillors returned unopposed.

Liverpool					
1995 % share	5.6	48.0	38.3	8.2	LD
Total Seats	0	39	52	8	

LDs have the scope to make a further half-dozen gains from Lab this year.

St Helens					
1995 % share	12.1	63.6	21.9	2.4	Lab
Total Seats	2	42	10	0	

No change in control possible. Con and LD could each gain an extra seat.

Sefton					
1995 % share	22.5	44.9	29.6	3.0	NOC
Total Seats	14	31	23	1	

Some Con/LD marginals in Southport; Lab safe in Bootle. Will stay hung.

	Con	**Lab**	**LDem**	**Other**	**Control**
Wirral					
1995 % share	25.8	53.6	20.1	0.6	Lab
Total Seats	16	41	8	1	

Change in control unlikely. Con should gain Clatterbridge and Wallasey (3% swing from Lab) and perhaps Bebington (6% swing).

South Yorkshire

Barnsley					
1995 % share	6.9	71.9	0.0	21.2	Lab
Total Seats	1	63	0	2	

No change in control possible. Lab won 13 out of 22 unopposed in 1995. Con could win Penistone East in a very good year.

Doncaster					
1995 % share	15.9	69.5	8.9	5.7	Lab
Total Seats	3	47	6	7	

Change in control unlikely. Lab rocked by local council scandals – won 20 out of 21 in 1995 but only 12 out of 21 last year.

Rotherham					
1995 % share	13.1	82.5	4.4	0.0	Lab
Total Seats	1	65	0	0	

No change in control possible. Con won Broom in 1998 and should do so again. Little LD strength here.

Sheffield					
1995 % share	11.4	47.4	39.0	2.3	Lab
Total Seats	1	50	36	0	

Lab could lose Sheffield for first time since 1968. 6% swing will give LD seven gains and tie the council!

Tyne & Wear

Gateshead					
1995 % share	5.9	65.4	23.5	5.2	Lab
Total Seats	0	51	15	0	

No change in control possible. LD could win Crawcrook and Greenside on 2% swing, but other seats look safe.

Newcastle upon Tyne					
1995 % share	12.9	62.0	23.4	1.7	Lab
Total Seats	0	65	13	0	

No change in control possible. Lab only vulnerable in Blakelaw and in Dene – both to LD.

North Tyneside					
1995 % share	21.3	65.6	10.5	2.7	Lab
Total Seats	8	43	7	2	

Change in control unlikely. Con did well here in 1998 and would collect three seats from Lab on 9% swing.

South Tyneside					
1995 % share	6.3	64.9	20.4	8.4	Lab
Total Seats	0	51	6	3	

No change in control possible. Most seats are safe and none may change hands.

	Con	Lab	LDem	Other	Control
Sunderland					
1995 % share	17.6	74.3	5.6	2.5	Lab
Total Seats	4	68	2	1	

No change in control possible. Con should gain Fulwell and St Michaels as they did in 1998.

West Midlands

Birmingham

1995 % share	25.7	53.6	18.2	2.5	Lab
Total Seats	17	83	16	1	

Change in control unlikely. Con win four seats from Lab on 6% swing and become the clear second party.

Coventry

1995 % share	23.2	62.4	11.4	3.1	Lab
Total Seats	7	45	0	2	

No change in control possible. Con should win Bablake and Earlsdon from Lab. LDs are weak.

Dudley

1995 % share	25.4	62.5	9.5	2.7	Lab
Total Seats	7	58	7	0	

No change in control possible. LDs have made a recent push in the two Lab held Kingswinford wards.

Sandwell

1995 % share	22.3	63.2	11.2	3.3	Lab
Total Seats	2	60	9	1	

No change in control possible. Little scope either for gains and losses in seats.

Solihull

1995 % share	32.4	30.4	28.0	9.3	NOC
Total Seats	20	17	11	3	

Change in control unlikely. Most seats are safe and the parties well-prepared to repel boarders!

Walsall

1995 % share	28.1	54.9	10.4	6.6	NOC
Total Seats	16	30	6	8	

Change in control unlikely. The most marginal seats are Lab held. Little chance of Lab gaining control.

Wolverhampton

1995 % share	30.4	56.7	11.5	1.4	Lab
Total Seats	14	44	2	0	

No change in control possible. Con win three seats on 5% swing from Lab.

West Yorkshire

Bradford

1995 % share	28.5	54.4	13.8	3.2	Lab
Total Seats	18	65	7	0	

Change in control unlikely. Nine Lab seats look vulnerable – 7 to Con and two to LD.

Calderdale

1995 % share	25.5	50.8	15.3	8.4	Lab
Total Seats	13	28	12	1	

Labour lose control on swing of just 2% to Con. Both Hipperholme & Lightcliffe and Warley would fall.

	Con	Lab	LDem	Other	Control
Kirklees					
1995 % share	22.8	47.6	23.3	6.3	Lab
Total Seats	7	43	20	2	

Lab will remain largest party, but may struggle to retain majority. Watch for a Green gain in Newsome.

	Con	Lab	LDem	Other	Control
Leeds					
1995 % share	19.5	59.0	18.4	3.1	Lab
Total Seats	9	80	9	1	

No change in control possible. Con should make at least four gains.

	Con	Lab	LDem	Other	Control
Wakefield					
1995 % share	13.3	74.8	6.6	5.3	Lab
Total Seats	2	60	0	1	

No change in control possible. Lab won 21 out of 21 seats in 1995 – all bar one with majority in excess of 25%.

District Councils

The pattern of elections for the English district councils is being complicated this year by changes which have occurred since the comparable contests in 1995. New unitary councils have replaced districts in several parts of the country (and are considered under a separate heading) and 49 districts have recently undergone the revision of ward boundaries. Indeed only 188 of the 276 districts which had elections in 1995 have emerged unscathed from these processes. The summary results for 1995 include only the 4,169 wards in those districts, compared with a total of 5,907 wards in 1995.

Table 6.3: 1995 District council election results

	Total Votes	% share of vote	Wards contested	Seats won
Con	1,397,091	26.6	3,086	1,400
Lab	1,813,230	34.6	3,159	2,412
LDem	1,387,937	26.5	2,764	1,734
Ind	498,435	9.5	1,090	816
Green	39,252	0.7	268	6
Other	109,636	2.1	303	133
Total	5,245,581		4,169	6,501

In the descriptions that follow we distinguish between councils which are having elections on a like-with-like basis compared with 1995 and those which have undergone boundary changes, and between authorities which have whole council elections and those which have annual elections for a third of the council in the same way as the metropolitan boroughs.

For councils without boundary changes the share of the vote is that achieved by the parties at the previous round of elections in 1995. In authorities with whole council elections the number of seats reflects the situation following those elections, but 'Control' takes account of any by-election gains or losses since 1995. In councils with annual elections the number of seats and council control affects the situation following the most recent contests. The swing calculations in the comments on each council are done with reference to the individual ward results in 1995.

For districts which have had boundary changes the share of the vote is that achieved by the parties at the previous round of elections in 1995. It is not reported for those authorities which elected only part of the council in 1995 but will be electing an entire new council this year. The seat total for each party in an authority is based on an estimate of what the results might have been in 1995 if the new ward boundaries had then been in place. It is not possible to make 'swing to win' calculations in either case. 'Control' is the current control of the council.

Districts without boundary changes

Whole Council Elections – 1995 Base

	Con	Lab	LDem	Other	Control

Arun (West Sussex)

| 1995 % share | 37.3 | 23.6 | 30.7 | 8.5 | Con |
| Total Seats | 29 | 10 | 14 | 3 | |

Con could lose control or increase majority in three currently split wards – Barnham, Littlehampton Beach, Marine.

Ashfield (Nottinghamshire)

| 1995 % share | 16.2 | 72.7 | 3.1 | 8.0 | Lab |
| Total Seats | 0 | 33 | 0 | 0 | |

Will stay Lab. The most marginal ward has a 25% Lab majority. In 11 out of 15 wards the margin is more than 50%.

Ashford (Kent)

| 1995 % share | 32.2 | 26.3 | 33.8 | 7.7 | NOC |
| Total Seats | 18 | 13 | 15 | 3 | |

Con need seven seats and 6% swing for majority control. Ashford has 45 wards, most with electorates of less than 2,000.

Aylesbury Vale (Buckinghamshire)

| 1995 % share | 29.9 | 18.4 | 39.2 | 12.5 | LD |
| Total Seats | 12 | 5 | 33 | 8 | |

LD majority has been cut at by-elections since 1995. A 3% swing to Con will wipe it out.

Babergh (Suffolk)

| 1995 % share | 23.3 | 29.2 | 21.2 | 26.2 | NOC |
| Total Seats | 9 | 12 | 7 | 14 | |

Will stay NOC. Each party has areas of strength; several Inds unopposed in 1995.

Blaby (Leicestershire)

| 1995 % share | 36.6 | 39.0 | 17.2 | 7.2 | NOC |
| Total Seats | 12 | 17 | 9 | 1 | |

Con can win the eight seats needed simply by sweeping up in wards split with Lab in 1995.

Bolsover (Derbyshire)

| 1995 % share | 4.8 | 63.2 | 12.1 | 19.9 | Lab |
| Total Seats | 0 | 35 | 0 | 2 | |

Will stay Lab. Lab returned unopposed in 11 out of 24 wards in 1995.

Braintree (Essex)

| 1995 % share | 26.1 | 47.0 | 14.9 | 12.0 | Lab |
| Total Seats | 10 | 37 | 6 | 7 | |

Some solid Lab wards. Con need to repeat 1991 performance on 7% swing to deprive Lab of control.

Breckland (Norfolk)

| 1995 % share | 31.8 | 40.7 | 11.8 | 15.6 | NOC |
| Total Seats | 18 | 25 | 2 | 8 | |

Con have eaten into Lab support at by-elections. Con require 8% swing for control.

Bridgnorth (Shropshire)

| 1995 % share | 11.0 | 21.2 | 25.1 | 42.7 | Ind |
| Total Seats | 3 | 6 | 4 | 20 | |

Several former Con stood and won as Ind Con in 1995. Likely to become NOC.

	Con	Lab	LDem	Other	Control
Bromsgrove (Worcestershire)					
1995 % share	39.1	48.8	10.6	1.6	Lab
Total Seats	12	24	3	0	

Con need 7% swing from Lab to take control. Con recorded good result here at 1997 general election.

	Con	Lab	LDem	Other	Control
Broxtowe (Nottinghamshire)					
1995 % share	27.2	46.0	20.9	6.0	Lab
Total Seats	7	36	5	1	

Lab's stunning 1995 victory vulnerable to 5% swing. Con held from 1973-95 – need 9% swing to regain.

	Con	Lab	LDem	Other	Control
Canterbury (Kent)					
1995 % share	29.3	32.2	33.9	4.6	NOC
Total Seats	10	15	24	0	

LD very close to control, but may suffer from swing back to Con. Tankerton, split with Con in 1995, is key.

	Con	Lab	LDem	Other	Control
Caradon (Cornwall)					
1995 % share	5.0	9.8	42.2	43.0	NOC
Total Seats	0	2	19	20	

LD need two gains to take one of their Cornish parliamentary heartlands. Their fate rests on how well surviving Inds perform.

	Con	Lab	LDem	Other	Control
Carrick (Cornwall)					
1995 % share	18.2	19.2	38.4	24.2	NOC
Total Seats	7	8	21	9	

Some marginal wards, many involving Inds. Likely to stay NOC.

	Con	Lab	LDem	Other	Control
Castle Point (Essex)					
1995 % share	28.0	53.2	17.9	0.9	Lab
Total Seats	5	34	0	0	

Lab did so well here in 1995 that Con need 12% swing for control. Lab also won parliamentary seat.

	Con	Lab	LDem	Other	Control
Charnwood (Leicestershire)					
1995 % share	32.5	47.4	14.5	5.7	Lab
Total Seats	15	30	5	2	

Some safe looking Lab wards, but council goes NOC on 5% swing Lab to Con.

	Con	Lab	LDem	Other	Control
Chelmsford (Essex)					
1995 % share	28.4	25.0	38.2	8.4	LD
Total Seats	13	7	32	4	

LD have long-standing record of local success here. However, control now vulnerable to 4% swing to Con.

	Con	Lab	LDem	Other	Control
Chester Le Street (Durham)					
1995 % share	6.1	58.3	15.0	20.6	Lab
Total Seats	1	30	1	1	

Will stay Lab. Con fielded just three and LD seven candidates in 1995.

	Con	Lab	LDem	Other	Control
Chesterfield (Derbyshire)					
1995 % share	7.6	56.8	35.3	0.4	Lab
Total Seats	0	37	10	0	

LD have eaten into Lab vote at local and parliamentary level. Now need 7% swing to deprive Lab of control.

	Con	Lab	LDem	Other	Control
Chichester (West Sussex)					
1995 % share	41.4	12.2	37.2	9.2	NOC
Total Seats	20	1	25	4	

Con have made by-election gains since 1995. Need 3% swing overall from LD to take control.

	Con	Lab	LDem	Other	Control
Chiltern (Buckinghamshire)					
1995 % share	42.2	11.9	40.2	5.7	NOC
Total Seats	22	1	24	3	

Con controlled from 1973-95 – need 4% swing from LD to win it back. LD gain control by taking seats in split wards.

	Con	Lab	LDem	Other	Control
Christchurch (Dorset)					
1995 % share	31.3	1.8	36.6	30.3	NOC
Total Seats	8	0	10	7	

LD need three seats in split wards (Chewton, Nea) for control. Con would take over with 2.5% swing from LD.

	Con	Lab	LDem	Other	Control
Cotswold (Gloucestershire)					
1995 % share	0.9	17.3	26.6	55.3	Ind
Total Seats	3	5	8	29	

Increased party competition threatens Ind control. Likely to become NOC.

	Con	Lab	LDem	Other	Control
Dartford (Kent)					
1995 % share	30.7	57.6	1.1	10.7	Lab
Total Seats	10	35	0	2	

Most Lab wards have substantial majorities. 13% swing to Con required for Lab to lose control.

	Con	Lab	LDem	Other	Control
Derbyshire Dales (Derbyshire)					
1995 % share	38.8	21.3	38.4	1.5	NOC
Total Seats	15	8	16	0	

Individuals often out-perform their party here. Con need 4% swing from LD; LD can win in split wards.

	Con	Lab	LDem	Other	Control
Derwentside (Durham)					
1995 % share	3.7	63.9	1.8	30.6	Lab
Total Seats	0	50	0	5	

Lab looks impregnable. Only marginals in 1995 were in Lab/Ind seats.

	Con	Lab	LDem	Other	Control
Dover (Kent)					
1995 % share	29.2	57.4	11.0	2.3	Lab
Total Seats	15	37	4	0	

Lab lose control on 8.5% swing to Con.

	Con	Lab	LDem	Other	Control
Durham (Durham)					
1995 % share	3.8	56.3	24.5	15.4	Lab
Total Seats	0	38	7	4	

LD have made some inroads, but in most wards remain too far behind to threaten Lab control.

	Con	Lab	LDem	Other	Control
Easington (Durham)					
1995 % share	1.1	60.4	0.0	38.5	Lab
Total Seats	0	44	3	4	

Lab a certain bet. Con fielded only two candidates in 1995. Continuing Liberal party carried 'centrist' flag.

	Con	Lab	LDem	Other	Control
East Cambridgeshire (Cambridgeshire)					
1995 % share	15.4	17.7	29.2	37.8	Ind
Total Seats	1	3	12	21	

District contains unusual four- and five-member wards. The intervention of more party candidates makes NOC likely.

	Con	Lab	LDem	Other	Control

East Devon (Devon)

	Con	Lab	LDem	Other	Control
1995 % share	37.4	17.1	27.0	18.5	Con
Total Seats	31	0	20	9	

By-election changes have put this in and out of Con control since 1995. Con need 1% swing to make it safe.

East Dorset (Dorset)

	Con	Lab	LDem	Other	Control
1995 % share	36.7	10.3	47.1	5.9	LD
Total Seats	13	0	23	0	

6% LD to Con swing ties the council. Con need 9% swing for overall control.

East Hampshire (Hampshire)

	Con	Lab	LDem	Other	Control
1995 % share	31.1	16.3	39.0	13.6	LD
Total Seats	12	0	26	4	

LD control vulnerable to combination of 2% swing to Lab plus 3% to Con. To win outright Con need 7.5%.

East Staffordshire (Staffordshire)

	Con	Lab	LDem	Other	Control
1995 % share	26.5	52.0	8.1	13.4	Lab
Total Seats	4	36	3	3	

Usually a tight Con/Lab battle – until 1995. A swing against Lab in excess of 11% is required for NOC.

Epsom & Ewell (Surrey)

	Con	Lab	LDem	Other	Control
1995 % share	0.0	17.1	25.5	57.4	Ind
Total Seats	0	3	3	33	

Council dominated by non-party residents groups ever since 1973. Votes Con at general elections though.

Erewash (Derbyshire)

	Con	Lab	LDem	Other	Control
1995 % share	29.7	51.0	10.5	8.8	Lab
Total Seats	8	40	2	2	

Lab lose control on 10% swing to Con. Con make 12 gains with 6% swing.

Fenland (Cambridgeshire)

	Con	Lab	LDem	Other	Control
1995 % share	35.8	42.0	14.1	8.1	NOC
Total Seats	14	21	2	3	

Lab have lost control through by-elections since 1995. A 6% swing from Lab will put Con back in charge.

Forest Heath (Suffolk)

	Con	Lab	LDem	Other	Control
1995 % share	36.5	29.1	19.2	15.3	NOC
Total Seats	10	4	6	5	

Con need 3% swing from Lab to take control. Presence of Inds makes it difficult to compile a majority.

Forest Of Dean (Gloucestershire)

	Con	Lab	LDem	Other	Control
1995 % share	1.5	48.5	17.2	32.9	Lab
Total Seats	1	30	5	13	

Likely to stay Lab – Inds pose biggest threat. Five-member Cinderford and Lydney wards are Lab strongholds.

Fylde (Lancashire)

	Con	Lab	LDem	Other	Control
1995 % share	26.6	22.2	13.4	37.9	NOC
Total Seats	17	6	4	22	

Strong Ratepayers group likely to frustrate Con hopes of winning for first time since 1987.

	Con	Lab	LDem	Other	Control
Gedling (Nottinghamshire)					
1995 % share	36.3	46.0	13.3	4.5	Lab
Total Seats	20	29	7	1	

One Lab seat lost in one of three split wards and the council becomes NOC. Con need nine gains (4.5% swing) to win.

Gravesham (Kent)					
1995 % share	29.7	61.6	8.7	0.0	Lab
Total Seats	10	34	0	0	

Lab holds 25 of its seats with majorities of 35% or more. 12% swing to Con yields only six gains.

Guildford (Surrey)					
1995 % share	35.1	16.5	42.9	5.5	NOC
Total Seats	13	6	23	3	

LD have lost control at by-elections. Con can make four gains in split wards. Likely to remain NOC.

Hambleton (North Yorkshire)					
1995 % share	35.0	23.1	15.1	26.9	NOC
Total Seats	19	4	3	21	

Con claim control because of alliance with Inds. Victory is within Con grasp – 2% swing from Ind.

Harborough (Leicestershire)					
1995 % share	31.5	29.9	24.9	13.6	NOC
Total Seats	12	8	13	4	

Will remain hung – few marginal opportunities for Con or LD to make gains required for control.

High Peak (Derbyshire)					
1995 % share	20.5	48.7	23.2	7.6	Lab
Total Seats	5	30	5	4	

Lab control vulnerable to 5% swing against party. Lab will remain largest party.

Hinckley & Bosworth (Leicestershire)					
1995 % share	29.3	37.7	32.6	0.4	NOC
Total Seats	5	13	16	0	

Con largest party following 4% swing from Lab, 5% from LD. LD gain control by winning split wards.

Horsham (West Sussex)					
1995 % share	42.3	7.7	41.9	8.1	LD
Total Seats	17	0	24	2	

LD lose control on 3% swing to Con. Con comfortably take over with 7% swing.

Kennet (Wiltshire)					
1995 % share	24.3	32.0	20.0	23.7	NOC
Total Seats	9	8	8	14	

No group likely to get 20 seats needed for overall majority. Con become largest party on 4.5% swing.

Kerrier (Cornwall)					
1995 % share	6.1	29.5	33.6	30.8	NOC
Total Seats	1	14	13	16	

Variable patterns of party strength and contestation make continuing NOC likeliest outcome.

Kings Lynn & W Norfolk (Norfolk)					
1995 % share	24.1	43.4	14.7	17.9	Lab
Total Seats	7	37	6	3	

Con have claimed many of the Inds since 1995. Lab lose 10 seats and control on 6% swing to Con/Ind.

	Con	Lab	LDem	Other	Control
Lancaster (Lancashire)					
1995 % share	19.9	42.8	12.8	24.5	Lab
Total Seats	11	34	5	10	

Most Lab wards safe, but control goes on 4.5% swing to LD/Ind in Heysham North and Scotforth East.

	Con	Lab	LDem	Other	Control
Lewes (East Sussex)					
1995 % share	32.5	13.7	43.0	10.8	LD
Total Seats	16	2	28	2	

LD took seat at general election. Need that boost to counter 4% swing which would see LD lose control.

	Con	Lab	LDem	Other	Control
Lichfield (Staffordshire)					
1995 % share	35.2	47.1	5.8	11.9	Lab
Total Seats	17	33	2	4	

Con controlled from 1976-95. Con need 7% swing to oust Lab, but 12.5% from Lab and 5% from LD to win themselves.

	Con	Lab	LDem	Other	Control
Maldon (Essex)					
1995 % share	33.4	27.4	7.6	31.6	NOC
Total Seats	12	7	1	10	

3.5% Con swing from Lab would produce five gains and control. Inds complicate predictions.

	Con	Lab	LDem	Other	Control
Mansfield (Nottinghamshire)					
1995 % share	11.2	67.9	18.8	2.1	Lab
Total Seats	1	45	0	0	

Will stay Lab. Con ought to gain four seats in Berry Hill and Oakham wards. Leeming is Lab/LD marginal.

	Con	Lab	LDem	Other	Control
Melton (Leicestershire)					
1995 % share	32.9	30.7	26.4	10.0	NOC
Total Seats	9	5	9	3	

Con could gain control if they field full slate of candidates. Likely to stay NOC.

	Con	Lab	LDem	Other	Control
Mid Bedfordshire (Bedfordshire)					
1995 % share	35.6	37.2	16.8	10.4	NOC
Total Seats	21	20	5	7	

Tight outcome in 1995, but Con usually win well. To take control Con need 3% swing and to win seats in split wards.

	Con	Lab	LDem	Other	Control
Mid Devon (Devon)					
1995 % share	2.8	17.5	40.2	39.5	LD
Total Seats	0	1	21	18	

Biggest threat to LD posed by Inds. Local reputations still count for a good deal in places like this.

	Con	Lab	LDem	Other	Control
Mid Suffolk (Suffolk)					
1995 % share	23.5	37.0	27.2	12.3	NOC
Total Seats	6	17	12	5	

Con gain four seats on 5% swing from Lab. Will remain NOC.

	Con	Lab	LDem	Other	Control
Mid Sussex (West Sussex)					
1995 % share	33.4	19.5	40.2	6.8	NOC
Total Seats	18	4	28	4	

LD control lost at by-elections since 1995. Con take over with 7.5% swing from LD.

	Con	Lab	LDem	Other	Control
New Forest (Hampshire)					
1995 % share	40.0	6.0	48.0	6.0	LD
Total Seats	23	0	32	3	

Another LD council vulnerable to swing back to Con. Control lost on 6% swing to Con; Con need 8% swing to take over.

	Con	Lab	LDem	Other	Control
Newark & Sherwood (Nottinghamshire)					
1995 % share	26.0	41.7	19.0	13.3	Lab
Total Seats	10	37	5	2	

Lab lose five seats on 6% swing to Con, but should hold on to council majority.

	Con	Lab	LDem	Other	Control
North Cornwall (Cornwall)					
1995 % share	4.2	7.5	34.1	54.2	Ind
Total Seats	1	0	12	25	

LD likely to mount further partisan attack on Inds. Pattern of contestation will be the key to outcome.

	Con	Lab	LDem	Other	Control
North Devon (Devon)					
1995 % share	16.6	12.0	45.8	25.7	LD
Total Seats	1	0	28	15	

LD have made by-election gains from Ind and will hope to consolidate. Generally weak Con and Lab challenge.

	Con	Lab	LDem	Other	Control
North Dorset (Dorset)					
1995 % share	19.4	12.5	34.9	33.1	LD
Total Seats	1	1	18	13	

Classic council politics in the rural south west. LD win seats from Ind; Con and Lab yet fully to respond.

	Con	Lab	LDem	Other	Control
North East Derbyshire (Derbyshire)					
1995 % share	24.2	52.4	9.6	13.8	Lab
Total Seats	4	44	3	2	

Safe Lab territory. A 10% swing and repeat of 1991 would put Con in double figures.

	Con	Lab	LDem	Other	Control
North Norfolk (Norfolk)					
1995 % share	16.9	33.3	27.1	22.6	NOC
Total Seats	4	19	12	11	

A parliamentary three-way marginal. Con only contested 16 out of 46 seats in 1995. Likely to remain NOC.

	Con	Lab	LDem	Other	Control
North Shropshire (Shropshire)					
1995 % share	7.7	13.5	4.7	74.2	Ind
Total Seats	2	6	0	31	

14 out of 26 wards uncontested in 1995, and further nine featuring just Inds. Will stay Ind.

	Con	Lab	LDem	Other	Control
North Warwickshire (Warwickshire)					
1995 % share	29.2	63.9	3.8	3.1	Lab
Total Seats	4	29	0	1	

Will stay Lab. Only nine seats would change hands even on a 15% swing from Lab to Con.

	Con	Lab	LDem	Other	Control
North West Leicestershire (Leicestershire)					
1995 % share	19.7	58.2	4.1	18.0	Lab
Total Seats	3	35	0	2	

Will stay Lab. Twelve Lab councillors elected unopposed in 1995; others fought only Inds.

	Con	Lab	LDem	Other	Control
North Wiltshire (Wiltshire)					
1995 % share	24.1	23.3	45.6	7.1	LD
Total Seats	12	7	29	4	

District contains 42 generally small, single member wards. LD lose control on 5% swing to Con.

	Con	Lab	LDem	Other	Control
Oadby & Wigston (Leicestershire)					
1995 % share	23.3	18.8	56.6	1.3	LD
Total Seats	1	0	25	0	

Gained by LD in 1991. Con need 12.5% swing both to oust LD and take over themselves.

	Con	Lab	LDem	Other	Control

Oswestry (Shropshire)

	Con	Lab	LDem	Other	Control
1995 % share	4.6	26.6	25.4	43.4	Ind
Total Seats	3	8	4	14	

Will remain NOC. Retains rural pattern of uncontested seats and patchy party contestation.

Restormel (Cornwall)

	Con	Lab	LDem	Other	Control
1995 % share	13.6	13.4	42.8	30.2	LD
Total Seats	2	3	30	9	

LD by-election losses since 1995. Control vulnerable to 4% swing – if other parties field full slates.

Ribble Valley (Lancashire)

	Con	Lab	LDem	Other	Control
1995 % share	40.4	8.5	48.9	2.2	NOC
Total Seats	19	1	19	0	

Finely balanced in 1995, but Con can win back with 5% swing in either Ribchester or Whalley wards.

Richmondshire (North Yorkshire)

	Con	Lab	LDem	Other	Control
1995 % share	12.7	15.8	31.3	40.2	Ind
Total Seats	1	0	8	25	

Some 1995 Inds now claimed by Con – like neighbouring Hambleton. Ind should retain formal control.

Rother (East Sussex)

	Con	Lab	LDem	Other	Control
1995 % share	30.3	18.4	39.0	12.4	NOC
Total Seats	13	7	20	5	

LD numbers whittled away by Con in post-1995 by-elections. Con need 10% swing for control/LD need 5%.

Rushcliffe (Nottinghamshire)

	Con	Lab	LDem	Other	Control
1995 % share	38.8	36.3	19.2	5.7	NOC
Total Seats	26	17	10	1	

Large Con majorities 1973-95. Four split wards – Bingham, Leake, Malkin and Melton – offer Con easy victory.

Ryedale (North Yorkshire)

	Con	Lab	LDem	Other	Control
1995 % share	24.3	15.6	31.9	28.2	NOC
Total Seats	4	1	9	7	

Comparisons complicated by expansion of York boundaries in 1996. Likely to stay NOC.

Salisbury (Wiltshire)

	Con	Lab	LDem	Other	Control
1995 % share	27.8	23.4	32.4	16.5	NOC
Total Seats	8	11	29	10	

LD could gain control by winning a seat in several split wards – or just as easily slip back.

Scarborough (North Yorkshire)

	Con	Lab	LDem	Other	Control
1995 % share	21.9	35.6	19.6	22.9	NOC
Total Seats	13	24	4	8	

Lab came close in 1995 and won the parliamentary seat in 1997. Likely to stay NOC.

Sedgefield (Durham)

	Con	Lab	LDem	Other	Control
1995 % share	3.1	63.3	15.3	18.3	Lab
Total Seats	0	47	0	2	

No threat to Lab in council covering much of Blair's own constituency.

Selby (North Yorkshire)

	Con	Lab	LDem	Other	Control
1995 % share	27.1	48.2	8.3	16.5	Lab
Total Seats	9	26	1	5	

Comparisons complicated by expansion of York boundaries in 1996. Likely to stay Lab.

	Con	Lab	LDem	Other	Control
Sevenoaks (Kent)					
1995 % share	33.2	16.2	34.7	15.9	NOC
Total Seats	17	11	20	5	

Con need 4% swing from both Lab and LD to gain.

Shepway (Kent)					
1995 % share	29.1	27.4	24.1	19.5	NOC
Total Seats	19	13	18	6	

Con could get close on 6% swing from Lab, but pattern of party strengths makes NOC more likely.

South Buckinghamshire (Buckinghamshire)					
1995 % share	41.1	10.3	20.7	28.0	NOC
Total Seats	19	0	4	17	

A clean sweep in currently split wards would see Con home and dry.

South Derbyshire (Derbyshire)					
1995 % share	26.2	53.8	1.7	18.3	Lab
Total Seats	6	27	0	1	

Will stay Lab. Few true Lab/Con marginals and plenty of Inds to complicate matters.

South Norfolk (Norfolk)					
1995 % share	28.3	21.7	44.8	5.3	LD
Total Seats	12	3	30	2	

Forty mostly small wards. LD lose control on 9% swing to Con.

South Oxfordshire (Oxfordshire)					
1995 % share	31.1	20.3	35.9	12.8	NOC
Total Seats	9	13	21	7	

Con enjoyed substantial majority 1976-95. Swing of 10% from both Lab and LD required to win back.

South Ribble (Lancashire)					
1995 % share	33.9	46.1	19.3	0.7	Lab
Total Seats	16	29	9	0	

Con win 15 seats and control on 7.5% swing from Lab. Con won all of them at the 1991 elections.

South Shropshire (Shropshire)					
1995 % share	6.0	17.0	24.8	52.2	Ind
Total Seats	0	1	8	31	

Few parties and few contests outside Ludlow. Likely to remain one of dozen English districts in Ind hands.

South Staffordshire (Staffordshire)					
1995 % share	38.3	30.2	14.6	16.9	Con
Total Seats	26	12	4	7	

A rare Con hold in 1995. Con unlikely to fall back this year.

Spelthorne (Surrey)					
1995 % share	38.5	39.0	21.8	0.6	Con
Total Seats	22	15	3	0	

Con only just held on in 1995. A 2% swing from Lab will net them seven seats and a comfortable majority.

St Edmundsbury (Suffolk)					
1995 % share	35.7	46.5	8.9	8.9	NOC
Total Seats	14	23	4	3	

Lab has lost control in post-1995 by-elections. Con need 5% swing from Lab and to displace some Inds.

	Con	Lab	LDem	Other	Control

Stafford (Staffordshire)

| 1995 % share | 29.7 | 41.6 | 23.0 | 5.7 | Lab |
| Total Seats | 16 | 33 | 10 | 1 | |

Lab vulnerable to attack from Con and LD in four split wards – Baswich, Haywood, Seighford and Swynnerton.

Staffordshire Moorlands (Staffordshire)

| 1995 % share | 16.7 | 31.6 | 13.8 | 37.9 | NOC |
| Total Seats | 8 | 27 | 7 | 14 | |

Lab could clean up in split wards and take control, but more likely to stay NOC.

Suffolk Coastal (Suffolk)

| 1995 % share | 33.8 | 33.3 | 26.2 | 6.7 | NOC |
| Total Seats | 18 | 17 | 15 | 5 | |

Con have shown evidence of recovery in by-elections, and need 5% swing from both Lab and LD to win.

Surrey Heath (Surrey)

| 1995 % share | 51.2 | 19.4 | 28.4 | 1.0 | Con |
| Total Seats | 23 | 5 | 8 | 0 | |

Con won here in 1995 as everywhere else was turning to dust. Scope for a handful of Con gains.

Teesdale (Durham)

| 1995 % share | 5.8 | 35.6 | 0.0 | 58.6 | Ind |
| Total Seats | 2 | 11 | 0 | 18 | |

Lab has made some inroads into previously uncontested Ind territory. Could become NOC this year.

Teignbridge (Devon)

| 1995 % share | 14.9 | 21.0 | 33.7 | 30.4 | NOC |
| Total Seats | 5 | 7 | 25 | 21 | |

LD could take control by fielding a full slate and winning seats in wards split in 1995.

Tendring (Essex)

| 1995 % share | 22.9 | 42.8 | 19.0 | 15.3 | Lab |
| Total Seats | 8 | 37 | 7 | 8 | |

Another Lab council victory heralding general election success in 1997. Lab lose on 4% swing to Con and LD.

Test Valley (Hampshire)

| 1995 % share | 36.6 | 12.4 | 46.9 | 4.2 | Con |
| Total Seats | 22 | 0 | 22 | 0 | |

LD took this in 1995, but then lost two by-elections. Con get home comfortably by winning in split wards.

Tewkesbury (Gloucestershire)

| 1995 % share | 13.6 | 25.3 | 19.0 | 42.1 | Ind |
| Total Seats | 3 | 4 | 8 | 21 | |

Political party candidates in most wards in 1995, but Inds proving hard to remove. Could go NOC.

Thanet (Kent)

| 1995 % share | 24.2 | 47.4 | 9.1 | 19.4 | Lab |
| Total Seats | 3 | 45 | 4 | 2 | |

Lab won seven wards here in 1991 but 23 in 1995. Swing of 9% across the board now needed to dislodge them.

	Con	Lab	LDem	Other	Control
Tonbridge & Malling (Kent)					
1995 % share	35.5	28.3	34.2	2.0	NOC
Total Seats	23	11	21	0	

Con held from 1973-95. They can win it back with a 5% swing from LD.

Torridge (Devon)					
1995 % share	6.1	19.5	37.2	37.2	NOC
Total Seats	2	5	11	18	

Some pockets of party strength, but likely to remain NOC with several Inds returned unopposed.

Uttlesford (Essex)					
1995 % share	35.8	15.9	40.1	8.3	NOC
Total Seats	12	4	19	7	

LD gain three seats and control on swing of just 2%. A 3% swing from LD to Con makes Con largest party.

Vale Of White Horse (Wiltshire)					
1995 % share	32.5	19.1	44.9	3.6	LD
Total Seats	11	5	34	1	

Gained by LD from Con in 1995. LD lose control on 5% swing from Con.

Warwick (Warwickshire)					
1995 % share	30.8	39.5	20.0	9.7	NOC
Total Seats	13	17	11	4	

Con should become largest party, but will remain NOC.

Waverley (Surrey)					
1995 % share	36.9	9.3	48.5	5.3	LD
Total Seats	17	2	37	1	

LD now have a small cushion in affluent south west Surrey. A 5.5% swing to Con would undo them.

Wealden (East Sussex)					
1995 % share	36.2	13.4	37.0	13.4	Con
Total Seats	29	0	24	5	

By-election victories since 1995 have given Con control. Swing of 5% from LD gives Con 11 seats.

Wear Valley (Durham)					
1995 % share	0.0	53.6	27.3	19.1	Lab
Total Seats	0	32	3	5	

Lab enjoys smaller ward majorities than in other of its North East strongholds, but will retain control.

West Devon (Devon)					
1995 % share	5.5	16.7	39.1	38.7	NOC
Total Seats	0	1	14	15	

On paper LD are 1% swing away from control, but who you are still counts as much your party label here.

West Dorset (Dorset)					
1995 % share	29.4	20.4	29.0	21.2	NOC
Total Seats	18	5	13	19	

Plenty of unopposed seats and unusual patterns of party contestation in 1995. Likely to stay NOC.

West Wiltshire (Wiltshire)					
1995 % share	27.4	20.0	42.3	10.3	LD
Total Seats	8	4	28	3	

LD control more vulnerable to swing to Lab than to Con, which may be enough to save them.

	Con	Lab	LDem	Other	Control
Wychavon (Worcestershire)					
1995 % share	28.4	20.2	30.2	21.3	NOC
Total Seats	13	10	15	11	

Plenty of marginal wards, but an even spread among the parties suggests this will stay NOC.

	Con	Lab	LDem	Other	Control
Wycombe (Buckinghamshire)					
1995 % share	37.0	30.2	27.3	5.5	NOC
Total Seats	24	15	18	3	

Con lost for the first time ever in 1995. Seven gains on a swing of just over 2% will see Con returned to power.

	Con	Lab	LDem	Other	Control
Wyre (Lancashire)					
1995 % share	40.6	43.1	8.0	8.3	Lab
Total Seats	19	31	4	2	

Lab lose control on 1% swing to Con; Con can take over with 5% from Lab and a full slate of candidates.

Annual Elections – 1995 base

	Con	Lab	LDem	Other	Control
Adur (West Sussex)					
1995 % share	24.0	28.6	46.8	0.7	LD
Total Seats	5	10	22	2	

LD lose two seats to Con on 5% swing, but would retain control. LD vulnerable from 4% swing to Lab as well.

	Con	Lab	LDem	Other	Control
Amber Valley (Derbyshire)					
1995 % share	26.5	62.1	6.0	5.3	Lab
Total Seats	6	37	0	0	

No change in control possible. Con win Shipley Park and Wingfield on 6% swing.

	Con	Lab	LDem	Other	Control
Basildon (Essex)					
1995 % share	28.0	48.3	23.5	0.2	Lab
Total Seats	6	23	13	0	

Lab and LD cleaned up in 1995. Most marginal seats are LD/Con. 12% swing to Con required for Lab to lose.

	Con	Lab	LDem	Other	Control
Basingstoke & Deane (Hampshire)					
1995 % share	33.6	32.4	31.6	2.5	NOC
Total Seats	25	15	13	4	

A difficult target for Con. They need four seats, but winning more than three will need a swing in excess of 15%.

	Con	Lab	LDem	Other	Control
Bassetlaw (Nottinghamshire)					
1995 % share	25.1	62.1	6.4	6.4	Lab
Total Seats	8	35	3	4	

Very safe for Lab. In theory they could lose control, but only by failing in wards with 50%+ majorities.

	Con	Lab	LDem	Other	Control
Bedford (Bedfordshire)					
1995 % share	25.7	44.0	27.2	3.2	NOC
Total Seats	9	22	15	7	

Lab has little scope for further gains. Will remain hung.

	Con	Lab	LDem	Other	Control
Brentwood (Essex)					
1995 % share	30.4	19.3	48.8	1.6	LD
Total Seats	11	2	25	1	

LD since 1992. Should remain safe this year, though LD have little to spare over Lab in Brentwood South.

	Con	Lab	LDem	Other	Control
Broadland (Norfolk)					
1995 % share	27.5	40.4	26.9	5.1	NOC
Total Seats	21	16	8	4	

Con can gain a couple on 5% swing from Lab; the necessary four extra seats look a more difficult task.

	Con	Lab	LDem	Other	Control
Burnley (Lancashire)					
1995 % share	11.2	59.7	25.4	3.7	Lab
Total Seats	2	31	9	6	

Large Lab majorities make continuing control a near certainty.

	Con	Lab	LDem	Other	Control
Cambridge (Cambridgeshire)					
1995 % share	15.6	45.4	37.0	2.0	NOC
Total Seats	3	21	18	0	

Always a tight Lab/LD battle at local level. Lab need to win East Chesterton from LD (6% maj.) for control.

	Con	Lab	LDem	Other	Control
Cannock Chase (Staffordshire)					
1995 % share	14.7	65.4	14.1	5.8	Lab
Total Seats	0	39	3	0	

No change in control possible. Con can get back on council by winning Parkside from Lab on 7% swing.

	Con	Lab	LDem	Other	Control
Cheltenham (Gloucestershire)					
1995 % share	28.0	14.5	48.7	8.8	LD
Total Seats	9	0	27	5	

LD won 12 out of 14 seats in 1995. Four go to Con on 5% swing, but it will take seven LD losses for council to be NOC.

	Con	Lab	LDem	Other	Control
Cherwell (Oxfordshire)					
1995 % share	30.7	51.8	17.3	0.2	NOC
Total Seats	17	24	7	4	

Lab won here in 1996, but lost seats at by-elections and in 1998. Likely to remain hung.

	Con	Lab	LDem	Other	Control
Chorley (Lancashire)					
1995 % share	21.7	56.8	17.9	3.6	Lab
Total Seats	6	33	7	2	

Lab has enough very safe seats to guarantee continuing control this year.

	Con	Lab	LDem	Other	Control
Colchester (Essex)					
1995 % share	25.3	36.1	37.8	0.8	NOC
Total Seats	15	17	27	1	

LD lost control in 1998. Could lose further seats to both Con and Lab this year.

	Con	Lab	LDem	Other	Control
Craven (North Yorkshire)					
1995 % share	30.5	22.9	33.3	13.3	NOC
Total Seats	13	4	13	4	

Con could win control on a 7% swing from LD. Much will depend on patterns of contestation.

	Con	Lab	LDem	Other	Control
Crawley (West Sussex)					
1995 % share	19.4	64.3	15.7	0.5	Lab
Total Seats	3	27	2	0	

No change in control possible. Con could win the two Pound Hill wards on 10% swing from Lab.

	Con	Lab	LDem	Other	Control
Eastbourne (East Sussex)					
1995 % share	33.8	14.9	50.5	0.9	LD
Total Seats	12	0	18	0	

A repeat of the 1998 results will put Con in control. Four seats change hands on a 6% LD to Con swing.

Eastleigh (Hampshire)					
1995 % share	24.0	28.2	46.4	1.4	LD
Total Seats	7	8	29	0	

LD should just hold on – helped by being under threat from Lab rather than Con in most marginal wards.

Elmbridge (Surrey)					
1995 % share	30.8	18.7	20.4	30.0	NOC
Total Seats	23	7	8	22	

Will remain NOC. Most seats have big majorities and the residents' groups are well dug in.

Epping Forest (Essex)					
1995 % share	28.8	37.1	20.1	14.0	NOC
Total Seats	15	17	15	12	

A remarkably even four-way split. No party has the scope to win overall control.

Exeter (Devon)					
1995 % share	17.9	52.0	21.2	9.0	Lab
Total Seats	3	22	8	3	

Likely to stay Lab. Con should win back Countess Wear. Liberal Party still represented in St Loye's ward.

Fareham (Hampshire)					
1995 % share	35.7	26.8	34.2	3.4	NOC
Total Seats	14	8	16	4	

Will remain NOC. Con become largest party on 1% swing from LD – they won the relevant wards in 1998.

Gloucester (Gloucestershire)					
1995 % share	22.4	53.6	24.0	0.0	Lab
Total Seats	6	25	8	0	

Some wards in Gloucester do not have elections this year following boundary changes. Likely to remain Lab.

Gosport (Hampshire)					
1995 % share	28.8	26.9	32.9	11.4	NOC
Total Seats	9	10	3	8	

Internal disputes have harmed the LD cause here. Will stay NOC.

Great Yarmouth (Norfolk)					
1995 % share	32.3	59.5	8.2	0.0	Lab
Total Seats	12	36	0	0	

Lab is currently well-entrenched. Con could pick up five seats simply by matching 1998 performance.

Harlow (Essex)					
1995 % share	20.3	65.7	13.8	0.2	Lab
Total Seats	1	38	3	0	

No change in control possible. Lab has 50%+ majorities in eight of the 13 seats it is defending.

	Con	Lab	LDem	Other	Control
Harrogate (North Yorkshire)					
1995 % share	26.3	19.7	52.5	1.5	LD
Total Seats	14	4	40	1	

Likely to remain LD. LD won 17 out of 20 wards in 1995 – most by comfortable majorities.

	Con	Lab	LDem	Other	Control
Hart (Hampshire)					
1995 % share	33.6	10.7	40.9	14.9	NOC
Total Seats	14	0	15	6	

Will remain NOC. In most cases the parties – and Inds – look secure in their own territory.

	Con	Lab	LDem	Other	Control
Hastings (East Sussex)					
1995 % share	19.1	43.4	37.5	0.0	Lab
Total Seats	1	18	13	0	

Lab ousted LD here in 1998. Lab defend five seats, but only Central St Leonards is marginal. Should stay Lab.

	Con	Lab	LDem	Other	Control
Havant (Hampshire)					
1995 % share	29.9	30.4	32.7	7.0	NOC
Total Seats	14	8	14	6	

Con become largest party by winning three seats on 3% swing from LD. Control beyond Con this year.

	Con	Lab	LDem	Other	Control
Huntingdon (Cambridgeshire)					
1995 % share	38.0	28.8	30.8	2.4	Con
Total Seats	34	3	14	2	

One of a handful of councils that has stayed faithful to Con throughout. They will not lose it this year.

	Con	Lab	LDem	Other	Control
Hyndburn (Lancashire)					
1995 % share	29.2	64.3	1.7	4.9	Lab
Total Seats	12	35	0	0	

Lab won all 16 seats in 1995. Con posted some large swings in 1998, but Labour control not threatened.

	Con	Lab	LDem	Other	Control
Ipswich (Suffolk)					
1995 % share	23.9	63.0	12.9	0.2	Lab
Total Seats	8	40	0	0	

No change in control possible. LD came third in every ward in 1995.

	Con	Lab	LDem	Other	Control
Maidstone (Kent)					
1995 % share	26.0	36.0	31.6	6.4	NOC
Total Seats	13	16	21	5	

LD look to have hit their ceiling in terms of seats. Will stay NOC.

	Con	Lab	LDem	Other	Control
Mole Valley (Surrey)					
1995 % share	30.8	7.7	42.2	19.3	NOC
Total Seats	14	2	16	9	

With only a third of the seats up for grabs, neither Con nor LD can make sufficient progress to win outright.

	Con	Lab	LDem	Other	Control
Newcastle-Under-Lyme (Staffordshire)					
1995 % share	14.8	55.0	29.3	0.9	Lab
Total Seats	5	42	9	0	

No change in control possible. LD have a bridgehead in parts of the area, but this is Lab territory.

	Con	Lab	LDem	Other	Control
Norwich (Norfolk)					
1995 % share	14.4	57.2	26.5	1.9	Lab
Total Seats	0	35	13	0	

Lab all but mathematically safe. LD should gain University ward; Eaton – 4% swing from LD – is best Con bet.

	Con	Lab	LDem	Other	Control
Nuneaton & Bedworth (Warwickshire)					
1995 % share	25.1	70.1	2.4	2.5	Lab
Total Seats	4	41	0	0	

No change in control possible. Con could make two gains on 11% swing from Lab.

	Con	Lab	LDem	Other	Control
Oxford (Oxfordshire)					
1995 % share	17.9	52.5	16.6	13.0	Lab
Total Seats	0	33	14	4	

Likely to stay Lab. Greens do well here – party could make three gains in Central, East and St Clements.

	Con	Lab	LDem	Other	Control
Pendle (Lancashire)					
1995 % share	14.4	42.4	42.6	0.6	LD
Total Seats	3	18	29	1	

LD face a tough fight to hold on to power. Three seats vulnerable to 2% swing to Lab.

	Con	Lab	LDem	Other	Control
Penwith (Cornwall)					
1995 % share	23.1	33.3	26.3	17.4	NOC
Total Seats	7	6	12	9	

Will remain NOC. A personal vote is still important here and can make a nonsense of swing predictions.

	Con	Lab	LDem	Other	Control
Preston (Lancashire)					
1995 % share	28.5	43.5	28.0	0.0	Lab
Total Seats	13	30	13	1	

Lab has majority of just three, but 10 of the 11 seats being defended have majorities in excess of 28%.

	Con	Lab	LDem	Other	Control
Redditch (Worcestershire)					
1995 % share	19.4	59.5	19.8	1.3	Lab
Total Seats	4	23	2	0	

Lab won 10 out of 10 in 1995. Abbey vulnerable to 1.5% swing to LD, and West to similar shift to Con.

	Con	Lab	LDem	Other	Control
Reigate & Banstead (Surrey)					
1995 % share	30.7	32.6	28.4	8.2	NOC
Total Seats	19	13	11	6	

A repeat of 1998 would see Con gain three seats, but they need six to take control.

	Con	Lab	LDem	Other	Control
Rochford (Essex)					
1995 % share	25.4	28.7	42.6	3.3	NOC
Total Seats	6	12	18	4	

LD have lost ground since 1996 high point. Two seats will be lost to Con and one to Lab on 5% swing against LD.

	Con	Lab	LDem	Other	Control
Rossendale (Lancashire)					
1995 % share	39.3	59.1	0.0	1.5	Lab
Total Seats	11	25	0	0	

Lab should be safe, though three seats fall on 7% Lab to Con swing.

	Con	Lab	LDem	Other	Control
Rugby (Warwickshire)					
1995 % share	25.0	49.3	13.9	11.9	NOC
Total Seats	12	22	5	9	

Will remain NOC. Lab look to have missed chance to take Rugby – this year could lose a couple of seats.

	Con	Lab	LDem	Other	Control
Runnymede (Surrey)					
1995 % share	41.4	34.7	13.5	10.4	Con
Total Seats	23	12	1	6	

Con won back in 1998 and will look to consolidate. A 7% swing from Lab gives Con three gains.

	Con	**Lab**	**LDem**	**Other**	**Control**
Rushmoor (Hampshire)					
1995 % share	34.0	32.7	32.1	1.2	NOC
Total Seats	17	14	14	0	

Con should gain ground, and can take control with 10% swing from Lab and LD.

Shrewsbury & Atcham (Shropshire)					
1995 % share	21.2	43.9	33.5	1.4	NOC
Total Seats	11	21	12	4	

Will stay hung. Con likely to win Copthorne from LD and Sutton from Lab.

South Bedfordshire (Bedfordshire)					
1995 % share	27.3	46.7	22.2	3.8	NOC
Total Seats	13	21	16	3	

Lab effectively has no chance of gaining the six seats required for control. Will remain hung.

South Cambridgeshire (Cambridgeshire)					
1995 % share	28.0	33.8	19.6	18.6	NOC
Total Seats	15	9	13	18	

Very patchy contestation for council with annual elections – 9 out of 19 wards unopposed in 1995. No change possible.

Stratford On Avon (Warwickshire)					
1995 % share	25.6	21.7	38.5	14.2	NOC
Total Seats	18	5	24	8	

Some previous Con councillors stood and were re-elected as Ind in 1995. Con need to recover that ground.

Stroud (Gloucestershire)					
1995 % share	20.9	40.3	22.7	16.1	NOC
Total Seats	10	26	9	10	

Likely to stay NOC, Lab having lost control in 1998. Greens defending seat in Trinity ward.

Swale (Kent)					
1995 % share	22.1	42.7	33.8	1.5	NOC
Total Seats	7	19	22	1	

LD have always fallen just short of a majority here and are unlikely to get any closer this year. Will stay NOC.

Tamworth (Staffordshire)					
1995 % share	16.8	64.1	5.6	13.5	Lab
Total Seats	1	28	0	1	

No change in control possible. Spital ward is a Lab/Con marginal; Con could also win Trinity in a good year.

Tandridge (Surrey)					
1995 % share	38.7	14.3	47.0	0.0	NOC
Total Seats	17	7	18	0	

Con need to gain five on a 9% swing from LD for control. 1998 results give Con some cause for optimism.

Tunbridge Wells (Kent)					
1995 % share	31.7	19.6	42.6	6.2	Con
Total Seats	27	7	12	2	

Con beat LD at their own 'pavement politics' game here in 1998. Con could gain another four or five seats.

	Con	Lab	LDem	Other	Control
Waveney (Suffolk)					
1995 % share	23.8	61.9	14.3	0.0	Lab
Total Seats	3	41	2	2	

No change in control possible. Lab won all 16 seats here in 1995. Three now vulnerable to 5% swing to Con.

	Con	Lab	LDem	Other	Control
West Lancashire (Lancashire)					
1995 % share	36.1	60.9	0.0	3.1	Lab
Total Seats	20	32	0	3	

Con and Lab each have safe territory here. Lab can lose three seats to Con on 6% swing, but still retain power.

	Con	Lab	LDem	Other	Control
West Oxfordshire (Oxfordshire)					
1995 % share	16.7	39.4	18.8	25.2	NOC
Total Seats	14	10	12	13	

An even spread across four political groups. An overall majority for any one is inconceivable at present.

	Con	Lab	LDem	Other	Control
Weymouth & Portland (Dorset)					
1995 % share	9.8	39.0	32.7	18.5	NOC
Total Seats	0	16	13	6	

Lab unlikely to make two gains required. Con have not won a seat since 1992 – best bet is Wyke Regis.

	Con	Lab	LDem	Other	Control
Winchester (Hampshire)					
1995 % share	29.7	21.5	45.0	3.8	LD
Total Seats	10	4	37	4	

Parliamentary success has boosted LD prospects here. Will survive loss of four seats to Con on 4.5% swing.

	Con	Lab	LDem	Other	Control
Woking (Surrey)					
1995 % share	32.9	23.9	43.2	0.0	NOC
Total Seats	11	7	16	1	

LD lost control in 1998. LD are well-entrenched in most wards so should remain largest party.

	Con	Lab	LDem	Other	Control
Worcester (Worcestershire)					
1995 % share	27.6	50.6	16.5	5.4	Lab
Total Seats	10	22	2	2	

Should stay Lab. Six of the seven seats Lab is defending are very safe.

	Con	Lab	LDem	Other	Control
Worthing (West Sussex)					
1995 % share	34.1	13.1	52.0	0.8	LD
Total Seats	15	0	21	0	

Con gained five seats from LD in 1998. A repeat this year – on a 16% swing! – would give them a majority.

	Con	Lab	LDem	Other	Control
Wyre Forest (Worcestershire)					
1995 % share	17.2	51.6	29.4	1.9	Lab
Total Seats	4	28	6	4	

Lab defending nine seats and needs to hold only three to retain control. Will only be unseated by a 20% swing.

Districts with whole council elections following boundary changes

Total number of seats 'notionally' to be defended by each party

Con	517
Lab	966
LD	436
Other	264
Total	2,183

Councils which also had whole council elections in 1995

	Con	Lab	LDem	Other	Control
Allerdale (Cumbria)					
1995 % share	14.3	47.3	19.4	19.0	Lab
Total Seats	8	37	4	7	
Alnwick (Northumberland)					
1995 % share	15.6	28.3	37.7	18.5	NOC
Total Seats	4	7	13	6	
Berwick Upon Tweed (Northumberland)					
1995 % share	17.2	9.7	38.2	34.9	NOC
Total Seats	1	2	14	12	
Blyth Valley (Northumberland)					
1995 % share	4.0	63.9	29.1	3.0	Lab
Total Seats	0	43	7	0	
Boston (Lincolnshire)					
1995 % share	24.5	32.6	26.0	16.9	NOC
Total Seats	6	13	7	6	
Castle Morpeth (Northumberland)					
1995 % share	16.4	29.2	24.0	30.5	NOC
Total Seats	6	14	6	7	
Copeland (Cumbria)					
1995 % share	31.0	59.4	2.6	7.0	Lab
Total Seats	11	37	0	3	
Corby (Northamptonshire)					
1995 % share	15.5	67.4	5.1	12.0	Lab
Total Seats	2	25	2	0	
Dacorum (Hertfordshire)					
1995 % share	32.1	43.3	18.9	5.7	Lab
Total Seats	16	31	3	2	
East Hertfordshire (Hertfordshire)					
1995 % share	37.1	31.9	24.2	6.9	NOC
Total Seats	24	8	16	2	

	Con	Lab	LDem	Other	Control
East Lindsey (Lincolnshire)					
1995 % share	4.9	28.8	13.8	52.5	Ind
Total Seats	2	13	3	42	
East Northamptonshire (Northamptonshire)					
1995 % share	37.6	46.4	7.2	8.8	Lab
Total Seats	9	26	1	0	
Eden (Cumbria)					
1995 % share	0.0	11.8	10.2	78.0	Ind
Total Seats	0	3	3	32	
Kettering (Northamptonshire)					
1995 % share	25.7	52.2	16.1	6.0	Lab
Total Seats	7	33	2	3	
Mendip (Somerset)					
1995 % share	23.5	21.4	43.0	12.2	NOC
Total Seats	8	10	24	4	
North Kesteven (Lincolnshire)					
1995 % share	14.4	37.0	20.6	28.0	NOC
Total Seats	2	18	6	14	
Northampton (Northamptonshire)					
1995 % share	24.1	56.0	17.6	2.3	Lab
Total Seats	4	35	8	0	
Sedgemoor (Somerset)					
1995 % share	36.3	25.3	31.6	6.7	NOC
Total Seats	21	15	12	2	
South Hams (Devon)					
1995 % share	30.9	17.5	30.0	21.7	NOC
Total Seats	15	3	10	12	
South Holland (Lincolnshire)					
1995 % share	23.0	32.2	3.0	41.9	NOC
Total Seats	6	13	0	19	
South Kesteven (Lincolnshire)					
1995 % share	25.7	30.2	12.8	31.4	NOC
Total Seats	14	18	7	19	
South Northamptonshire (Northamptonshire)					
1995 % share	35.6	31.3	17.1	16.1	NOC
Total Seats	15	10	8	9	
South Somerset (Somerset)					
1995 % share	24.9	11.6	50.3	13.3	LD
Total Seats	6	1	47	6	
Taunton Deane (Somerset)					
1995 % share	30.2	23.0	41.6	5.2	LD
Total Seats	15	9	28	2	

	Con	Lab	LDem	Other	Control
Tynedale (Northumberland)					
1995 % share	26.9	35.4	18.2	19.4	NOC
Total Seats	12	20	12	8	
Vale Royal (Cheshire)					
1995 % share	26.9	49.0	18.4	5.8	Lab
Total Seats	16	40	1	0	
Wansbeck (Northumberland)					
1995 % share	1.8	65.6	32.7	0.0	Lab
Total Seats	0	45	0	0	
Wellingborough (Northamptonshire)					
1995 % share	45.4	44.7	4.4	5.6	NOC
Total Seats	17	16	0	3	
West Somerset (Somerset)					
1995 % share	20.9	27.4	20.6	31.2	NOC
Total Seats	10	9	2	10	

Councils which had elections by thirds in 1995

	Con	Lab	LDem	Other	Control
Barrow In Furness (Cumbria)					
Total Seats	10	26	0	2	Lab
Broxbourne (Hertfordshire)					
Total Seats	25	12	1	0	Con
Carlisle (Cumbria)					
Total Seats	15	33	3	1	Lab
Chester (Cheshire)					
Total Seats	20	24	16	0	NOC
Congleton (Cheshire)					
Total Seats	7	12	29	0	LD
Crewe & Nantwich (Cheshire)					
Total Seats	16	36	3	1	Lab
Daventry (Northamptonshire)					
Total Seats	18	15	3	2	NOC
Ellesmere Port & Neston (Cheshire)					
Total Seats	8	35	0	0	Lab
Hertsmere (Hertfordshire)					
Total Seats	12	21	6	0	Lab
Lincoln (Lincolnshire)					
Total Seats	1	32	0	0	Lab
Macclesfield (Cheshire)					
Total Seats	38	12	7	3	Con

	Con	Lab	LDem	Other	Control
North Hertfordshire (Hertfordshire)					
Total Seats	17	26	5	1	Lab
Purbeck (Dorset)					
Total Seats	7	3	8	6	NOC
South Lakeland (Cumbria)					
Total Seats	11	10	22	9	NOC
St Albans (Hertfordshire)					
Total Seats	11	15	32	0	LD
Stevenage (Hertfordshire)					
Total Seats	0	38	1	0	Lab
Three Rivers (Hertfordshire)					
Total Seats	17	7	24	0	NOC
Watford (Hertfordshire)					
Total Seats	6	21	9	0	Lab
Welwyn Hatfield (Hertfordshire)					
Total Seats	18	30	0	0	Lab
West Lindsey (Lincolnshire)					
Total Seats	3	4	21	9	NOC

Unitary Authorities

Unitary authorities have been established in 46 areas in England following the Local Government Review of the early 1990s. Some of these authorities had their inaugural elections in 1995 and some in 1996, with the final tranche coming in 1997. They were allowed discretion over whether subsequent elections should be for the whole council or for part of the council on an annual basis. The result was to render the electoral cycle for unitary authorities quite complex.

In the information that follows we divide councils in terms of both the year with which the 1999 contests should be compared and whether the whole or just a part of the council was elected. The summary of the previous result includes only those authorities and wards which have elections again on unchanged boundaries in 1999. The share of the vote is that achieved by the parties at the previous round of elections (1995, 1996 or 1997) and is only given for those authorities which will be electing the entire council. The number of seats and council control reflects the situation following the most recent elections in the authority. The swing calculations in the comments on each council are done with reference to the individual ward results in the appropriate base year.

Unitary authorities – 1995 base

Table 6.4: 1995 Unitary authority election results

	Total votes	% share of vote	Wards contested	Seats won
Con	101,438	21.2	172	41
Lab	233,558	48.7	198	291
LDem	96,954	20.2	156	59
Ind	34,450	7.2	43	11
Green	426	0.1	1	0
Other	12,563	2.6	15	5
Total	479,389		197	407

Whole Council Elections

	Con	Lab	LDem	Other	Control
East Riding of Yorkshire					
1995 % share	27.9	29.1	27.5	15.5	NOC
Total Seats	19	23	18	7	

Likely to stay NOC, but Con should make enough gains to become the largest party. Some fascinating three-way marginals.

	Con	Lab	LDem	Other	Control
Middlesbrough					
1995 % share	21.8	64.0	9.5	4.7	Lab
Total Seats	2	46	4	1	

Will stay Lab – most of its wards very safe. Con and LD could pick up a handful of seats between them.

	Con	Lab	LDem	Other	Control
North East Lincolnshire					
1995 % share	18.8	44.9	24.2	12.1	Lab
Total Seats	2	32	7	1	

Labour ought just to hold on. Seven Lab seats vulnerable to a 4% swing to Con; a couple of others could fall to LD.

	Con	Lab	LDem	Other	Control
North Lincolnshire					
1995 % share	26.8	50.8	2.5	19.8	Lab
Total Seats	6	35	0	1	

Unlikely to change hands. Con need 10% swing from Lab for council to be hung. LD make little impact here.

	Con	Lab	LDem	Other	Control
Redcar & Cleveland					
1995 % share	19.2	57.2	16.7	6.9	Lab
Total Seats	1	49	7	2	

Will stay Lab, though scope for up to 10 Con gains outside Redcar itself.

	Con	Lab	LDem	Other	Control
Stockton-on-Tees					
1995 % share	23.1	55.5	21.0	0.4	Lab
Total Seats	7	44	4	0	

Will stay Lab. A 9% swing would produce seven Con and two LD gains. Beyond that most wards look very safe.

	Con	Lab	LDem	Other	Control
York					
1995 % share	17.0	45.9	28.0	9.1	Lab
Total Seats	3	30	17	3	

A 'new model' council though Labour did very well in York at the general election. A 6.5% swing against Labour needed for NOC

New boundaries

In the following four authorities the seat total for each party is based on an estimate of what the results might have been in 1995 if the new ward boundaries had then been in place. The share of the vote is that achieved by the parties at the previous round of elections in 1995.

	Con	Lab	LDem	Other	Control
Bath & NE Somerset					
1995 % share	28.9	34.1	34.7	2.4	NOC
Total Seats	19	21	25	0	
Bristol					
1995 % share	24.7	51.4	19.9	4.1	Lab
Total Seats	7	52	9	0	
North Somerset					
1995 % share	29.7	19.9	35.8	14.6	LD
Total Seats	21	5	31	4	
South Gloucestershire					
1995 % share	25.2	38.4	32.2	4.2	NOC
Total Seats	9	33	26	2	

Annual elections

	Con	Lab	LDem	Other	Control
Hartlepool					
Total Seats	5	33	8	1	Lab

Change in control unlikely. Con and LD should each gain a couple, but partial election eases Lab task.

	Con	Lab	LDem	Other	Control
Kingston upon Hull					
Total Seats	1	53	4	2	Lab

No change in control possible. LD have given Lab a fright in some wards, and some intra-Lab battles likely.

Unitary authorities – 1996 base

Table 6.5: 1996 Unitary authority election results

	Total votes	% share of vote	Wards contested	Seats won
Con	169,616	26.2	226	68
Lab	298,512	46.0	236	249
LDem	141,156	21.8	203	106
Ind	18,010	2.8	37	26
Green	13,697	2.1	61	1
Other	7,430	1.1	30	0
Total	648,421		241	450

Whole Council Elections

	Con	Lab	LDem	Other	Control
Bournemouth					
1996 % share	33.6	21.6	35.7	9.1	NOC
Total Seats	19	6	28	4	

LD could win control by taking all seats in currently split wards. Outright win probably beyond Tories this year.

	Con	Lab	LDem	Other	Control
Brighton & Hove					
1996 % share	32.6	46.7	9.1	11.6	Lab
Total Seats	22	54	0	2	

Likely to stay Lab, but 16 seats vulnerable to 7.5% swing to Con. LD close only in one ward (Brunswick) in 1996.

	Con	Lab	LDem	Other	Control
Darlington					
1996 % share	32.4	59.2	6.9	1.5	Lab
Total Seats	13	36	2	1	

Will stay Lab. Most of marginal wards from 1996 are Con held. 10% swing from Lab would yield only 5 gains.

	Con	Lab	LDem	Other	Control
Leicester					
1996 % share	20.9	55.1	19.3	4.8	Lab
Total Seats	7	41	8	0	

Likely to stay Lab. LD by-election inroads since 1996, but large majorities will hamper chance of significant gains.

	Con	Lab	LDem	Other	Control
Luton					
1996 % share	23.7	48.9	24.2	3.2	Lab
Total Seats	3	36	9	0	

Likely to stay Lab. Only three Lab held wards (nine seats) have majorities of less than 25%.

	Con	Lab	LDem	Other	Control
Poole					
1996 % share	35.9	21.8	39.7	2.6	LD
Total Seats	13	3	23	0	

LD more vulnerable to Lab than Con, which may help them keep control. Canford Cliffs one of safest Con wards in Britain.

	Con	Lab	LDem	Other	Control
Rutland					
1996 % share	12.3	19.8	24.0	43.9	NOC
Total Seats	2	2	5	11	

Will remain NOC. LD likely to further politicisation which has given them two by-election gains from Ind since 1996.

Annual elections

	Con	Lab	LDem	Other	Control
Derby					
Total Seats	4	37	3	0	Lab

No change in control possible. Con could win four from Lab on 10% swing. LD likely to gain Blagreaves as in 1998.

Milton Keynes

Total Seats	4	27	19	1	Lab

Lab will lose control if Con gain two seats on 3.5% swing from 1996 and Lab do not compensate in LD/Lab marginals.

Portsmouth

Total Seats	8	21	10	0	Lab

Most marginal seats are Con/LD. Lab control vulnerable to losses in Copnor and Cosham – swings of over 10% needed.

Southampton

Total Seats	3	28	14	0	Lab

Likely to stay Lab. Con should pick up seats in Harefield and Sholing (6% swing) and Lab could also suffer LD ambushes.

Stoke On Trent

Total Seats	1	54	3	2	Lab

No change in control possible. LD will continue to pick away at Lab; Con will win another Trentham Park seat.

Swindon

Total Seats	5	40	9	0	Lab

Will stay Lab. Some very tight contests in 1998 – Con won Highworth by one vote; LD took Lawns by five votes over Con.

Unitary authorities – 1997 base

Table 6.6: 1997 Unitary authority election results

	Total votes	% share of vote	Wards contested	Seats won
Con	206,808	31.6	138	36
Lab	275,874	42.2	147	94
LDem	147,347	22.5	111	19
Ind	7,977	1.2	21	2
Green	2,040	0.3	5	0
Other	13,645	2.1	20	1
Total	653,691		152	152

Annual elections

	Con	Lab	LDem	Other	Control

Blackburn with Darwen
Total Seats — Con 12, Lab 46, LDem 4, Other 0, Control Lab
Will stay Lab. Earcroft and Meadowfield, both requiring 5% swings, good tests of Con recovery since general election.

Halton
Total Seats — Con 1, Lab 47, LDem 8, Other 0, Control Lab
No change in control possible. Most seats safe, but tight between LD and Lab in Heath and Norton wards.

Peterborough
Total Seats — Con 24, Lab 27, LDem 2, Other 4, Control NOC
Likely to stay hung. No elections in two of the most marginal Lab/Con wards. Con largest party on 6% swing.

Reading
Total Seats — Con 3, Lab 36, LDem 6, Other 0, Control Lab
No change in control possible. Con gain five seats on 6% swing from Lab.

Slough
Total Seats — Con 4, Lab 34, LDem 0, Other 3, Control Lab
No change in control possible. The continuing Liberal party does well in a handful of wards.

Southend On Sea
Total Seats — Con 19, Lab 7, LDem 13, Other 0, Control NOC
Con need 5% swing from LD for control. It could have been even easier with different seats in split wards falling vacant.

Thurrock
Total Seats — Con 3, Lab 36, LDem 0, Other 0, Control Lab
Will stay Lab. Con should double their seats (5% swing), but most parts of Thames-side Essex will remain loyal to Lab.

Warrington
Total Seats — Con 4, Lab 45, LDem 11, Other 0, Control Lab
No change in control possible. Lab enjoys comfortable majorities. Most marginal Lab/Con seat is Westbrook (17.2%).

Wokingham
Total Seats — Con 31, Lab 0, LDem 23, Other 0, Control CON
The co-incident general election helped Con here in 1997. A 4% swing to LD in the locals means Con lose overall control.

Scottish Local Authorities

All local authorities in Scotland have undergone extensive revisions of the boundaries of individual wards. In some cases this has led to many more or many fewer council seats being created. It has proved impossible to make a robust judgement about what the results in the new wards might have been if they had been in existence in 1995. We therefore list here the actual results for each of the 29 mainland Scottish local authorities in 1995 together with an indication of any change in the size of council. All councillors in Scotland are elected in single member wards.

Table 6.7: 1995 Scottish local election results

	Total votes	% share of vote	% change on 1992	Wards contested	Seats won
Con	191,760	11.4	−11.8	578	82
Lab	744,485	44.4	10.4	935	615
LDem	165,600	9.9	0.4	528	121
SNP	451,505	26.9	2.6	999	183
Ind	112,031	6.7	−0.6	288	154
Green	2,080	0.1	−0.4	24	0
Other	10,667	0.6	−0.7	46	6
Total	1,678,128			1,161	1,161

1995 Scottish local election results by authority

	Con	Lab	LDem	SNP	Other	Control	New Council
Aberdeen							
1995 % share	14.4	42.0	23.9	18.1	1.6	Lab	43
Total Seats	9	30	10	1	0		
Aberdeenshire							
1995 % share	10.8	6.3	24.0	33.1	25.9	NOC	68
Total Seats	4	0	15	15	13		
Angus							
1995 % share	18.6	15.5	6.9	53.4	5.6	SNP	29
Total Seats	2	0	2	21	1		
Argyll & Bute							
1995 % share	13	10	14	12.5	50.5	Ind	36
Total Seats	3	2	3	4	21		
Clackmannan							
1995 % share	3.0	54.1	3.9	38.5	0.6	Lab	18
Total Seats	1	8	0	3	0		
Dumfries & Galloway							
1995 % share	10.2	25.2	10.9	14.7	39.1	NOC	47
Total Seats	2	21	10	9	28		

	Con	Lab	LDem	SNP	Other	Control	New Council
Dundee							
1995 % share	13.8	53.7	2.5	25.2	4.8	Lab	29
Total Seats	4	28	0	3	1		
East Ayrshire							
1995 % share	6.9	56.4	0.3	36.1	0.2	Lab	32
Total Seats	0	22	0	8	0		
East Dunbartonshire							
1995 % share	19.3	40.9	23.8	16.1	0.0	Lab	24
Total Seats	2	15	9	0	0		
East Lothian							
1995 % share	18.9	56.0	6.6	16.9	1.6	Lab	23
Total Seats	3	15	0	0	0		
East Renfrewshire							
1995 % share	29.2	31.4	14.9	17.7	6.9	NOC	20
Total Seats	9	8	2	0	1		
Edinburgh							
1995 % share	23.3	40.7	18.1	17.3	0.7	Lab	58
Total Seats	14	34	10	0	0		
Falkirk							
1995 % share	3.6	52.0	0.1	36.6	7.6	Lab	32
Total Seats	2	23	0	8	3		
Fife							
1995 % share	5.8	46.5	20.1	21.2	6.3	Lab	78
Total Seats	0	54	25	10	3		
Glasgow							
1995 % share	6.6	61.5	3.4	22.8	5.7	Lab	79
Total Seats	3	77	1	1	1		
Highland							
1995 % share	0.9	12.2	6.7	17.4	62.8	Ind	80
Total Seats	1	7	4	9	51		
Inverclyde							
1995 % share	3.7	49.6	29.6	16.2	0.9	Lab	20
Total Seats	1	14	5	0	0		
Midlothian							
1995 % share	4.2	57.4	3.5	34.5	0.3	Lab	18
Total Seats	0	13	0	2	0		
Moray							
1995 % share	2.2	19.7	8.1	50.2	19.8	SNP	26
Total Seats	0	3	0	13	2		
North Ayrshire							
1995 % share	11.8	55.9	2.8	24.8	4.7	Lab	30
Total Seats	1	27	0	1	1		

	Con	Lab	LDem	SNP	Other	Control	New Council
North Lanarkshire							
1995 % share	3.9	62.3	0.2	30.2	3.4	Lab	70
Total Seats	0	59	0	8	2		
Perth & Kinross							
1995 % share	24.8	14.3	13	41	6.8	SNP	41
Total Seats	2	6	5	18	1		
Renfrewshire							
1995 % share	7.8	46.3	5.9	38.6	1.4	Lab	40
Total Seats	2	22	3	13	0		
Scottish Borders							
1995 % share	14.8	3.3	24.0	18.9	39	Ind	34
Total Seats	3	2	15	8	30		
South Ayrshire							
1995 % share	28.3	56	0	12	3.7	Lab	30
Total Seats	4	21	0	0	0		
South Lanarkshire							
1995 % share	6.9	57.1	7.1	26.9	2	Lab	67
Total Seats	2	62	2	8	0		
Stirling							
1995 % share	25.4	49.1	4.6	18.9	1.9	Lab	22
Total Seats	7	13	0	2	0		
West Dunbartonshire							
1995 % share	1.2	50.5	0.3	42.6	5.5	Lab	22
Total Seats	0	14	0	7	1		
West Lothian							
1995 % share	4.2	46.9	2.0	44.6	2.4	Lab	32
Total Seats	1	15	0	11	0		

Welsh Local Authorities

Fourteen local authorities in Wales have undergone reviews of the boundaries of individual wards since the last local elections in 1995. In some cases this has led to more or fewer council seats being created. In two authorities reviewed, Merthyr Tydfil and Neath & Port Talbot, no changes were recommended. In the 12 other cases change was relatively modest and it has proved possible to make a fairly robust judgement about what the results in the new wards might have been if they had been in existence in 1995. In authorities where there has been no change we list here the actual results and comment on the scope for change in 1999 compared with 1995. Where boundaries have been changed we show the share of the vote for each party in 1995 and provide an estimate of how the new seats might have been distributed.

Table 6.8: 1995 Welsh local election results

	Total votes	% share of vote	% change on 1991	Wards contested	Seats won	Wards won
Con	75,448	8.3	−4.2	180	42	29
Lab	404,013	44.7	9.7	598	726	426
LDem	95,376	10.5	1.8	249	79	52
PC	115,900	12.8	2.1	303	113	89
Ind	168,074	18.6	−5.6	446	292	254
Green	10,161	1.1	−0.1	57	0	0
Other	36,652	4.1	−3.6	358	20	11
Total	904,624			865	1,272	

Table 6.9: Actual and notional seats being defended in Wales in 1999

	Actual	Notional	Total
Con	21	21	42
Lab	278	460	738
LD	18	58	76
PC	67	47	114
Ind/Other	102	197	299
Total	486	783	1,269

Authorities without boundary changes

	Con	Lab	LDem	PC	Other	Control
Anglesey						
1995 % share	4.4	10.2	0.0	31.8	53.6	Ind
Total Seats	1	6	0	7	26	

Twenty-one of 40 councillors were returned unopposed in 1995. Ind control could be threatened by more party contestation

	Con	Lab	LDem	PC	Other	Control
Blaenau Gwent						
1995 % share	5.6	54.0	0.6	9.3	30.5	Lab
Total Seats	1	33	0	1	7	

Change in control very unlikely. Lab candidates sometimes opposed by disaffected former party members

	Con	Lab	LDem	PC	Other	Control
Gwynedd						
1995 % share	0.0	14.6	2.1	44.5	39.6	PC
Total Seats	0	9	3	45	26	

PC should retain control in an area taking in two of their Westminster seats. Twenty-one PC candidates unopposed in 1995.

	Con	Lab	LDem	PC	Other	Control
Ceredigion						
1995 % share	0.0	1.8	27.8	30.9	44.5	Ind
Total Seats	0	1	11	6	26	

Both PC and LD could field more candidates in 1999 and threaten Ind control. Constituency of the same name is PC held.

	Con	Lab	LDem	PC	Other	Control
Monmouthshire						
1995 % share	29.0	45.2	11.8	0.0	14.0	Lab
Total Seats	11	26	1	0	4	

A 5% Lab to Con swing deprives Lab of power. Con need swing well into double figures to take over themselves.

	Con	Lab	LDem	PC	Other	Control
Merthyr Tydfil*						
1995 % share	0.0	51.1	0.0	5.0	45.5	Lab
Total Seats	0	29	0	0	4	

Will stay Lab. In 1995 PC was the only other major party to contest – a single candidate in a 4-seat ward!

	Con	Lab	LDem	PC	Other	Control
Neath & Port Talbot*						
1995 % share	0.2	55.4	6.6	15.1	22.7	Lab
Total Seats	0	51	2	3	8	

Another Lab bastion with many unopposed returns and few opposition party candidates.

	Con	Lab	LDem	PC	Other	Control
Newport						
1995 % share	20.7	64.3	10.3	0.0	4.8	Lab
Total Seats	1	46	0	0	0	

Will stay Lab, but a 7% swing would allow Con to capture five Lab seats.

	Con	Lab	LDem	PC	Other	Control
Torfaen						
1995 % share	2.9	54.4	11.7	0.0	33.5	Lab
Total Seats	1	41	1	0	1	

Very safe for Lab. Con wards are an endangered species in the valleys, but marginal Llanyrafon South is one of them.

	Con	Lab	LDem	PC	Other	Control
Vale of Glamorgan						
1995 % share	26.8	46.1	6.5	13.3	8.5	Lab
Total Seats	6	36	0	5	0	

Likely to stay Lab, though Con could win all five seats in Alexandra ward and seven others on a 6% swing.

Authorities which have had their boundaries reviewed, but where no changes were made.

Authorities with boundary changes

	Con	Lab	LDem	PC	Other	Control
Bridgend						
1995 % share	18.5	57.4	5.5	4.5	14.5	Lab
Total Seats	2	50	0	0	2	
Caerphilly						
1995 % share	3.1	58.7	3.5	27.1	7.7	Lab
Total Seats	0	61	0	9	3	
Cardiff						
1995 % share	15.6	51.6	18.0	7.4	11.3	Lab
Total Seats	2	62	9	1	0	
Carmarthenshire						
1995 % share	1.9	40.7	8.4	16.0	33.3	NOC
Total Seats	0	36	3	7	28	
Conwy						
1995 % share	13.8	31.9	31.4	8.3	14.6	NOC
Total Seats	8	19	17	2	13	
Denbighshire						
1995 % share	5.6	27.9	8.0	16.1	42.8	NOC
Total Seats	0	19	3	7	18	
Flintshire						
1995 % share	4.9	48.3	12.1	2.5	32.1	Lab
Total Seats	3	46	4	1	16	
Pembrokeshire						
1995 % share	0.6	28.8	6.5	3.1	61.3	Ind
Total Seats	0	13	3	3	41	
Powys						
1995 % share	3.8	14.6	16.0	2.3	66.5	Ind
Total Seats	2	8	8	1	54	
Rhondda/Cynon/Taff						
1995 % share	0.0	52.8	0.0	32.8	15.9	Lab
Total Seats	0	56	0	15	4	
Swansea						
1995 % share	10.4	50.1	20.7	3.3	17.2	Lab
Total Seats	1	56	7	1	7	
Wrexham						
1995 % share	7.7	48.2	12.7	4.5	26.9	Lab
Total Seats	3	34	4	0	11	

7. The Jenkins Commission and the Next General Election

Heaven Can Wait?

Introduction by: **Michael Brunson**, *Political Editor, ITN*

For those advocating electoral reform, the coming year will be as close as it gets to heaven. Actual heaven – the holding of all elections in the United Kingdom using a voting system that is fully proportional – is still some way off. However, three elections which will involve, to a greater or lesser degree, the use of proportional systems for the first time, are to be held in Great Britain in 1999. Notice, though, the deliberate use of the term 'Great Britain'. In recent years, that other constituent part of the United Kingdom, Northern Ireland, has become increasingly accustomed to the use of PR.

Now, voters in England, Scotland and Wales are to have their first serious taste of it. In the European elections, and in the elections for the new Scottish Parliament and Welsh Assembly, the final number of candidates elected will depend on the total numbers of votes cast in the election as a whole, and not just on the aggregation of the results in single-member constituencies.

For the supporters of PR, that is a huge step forward. Just how huge is best summed up by the Leader of the Liberal Democrats, Paddy Ashdown. When I asked him for his thoughts as he approached the coming campaigns, his answer was forthright. 'For everybody else,' he said, 'polling day in these elections will mark the end of a few weeks of campaigning. For us, it will be the culmination of a struggle that has lasted the best part of a century.'

Overstating the case? I think not, for although the arrangements are slightly different for each of the polls, the key factor is that none of the three elections, which could all, in theory, have used undiluted first past the post systems, will do so. That is a very big change.

Ever since the European Parliament switched from being a nominated to an elected body, Britain has been under pressure to elect its MEPs in the same way as all other members of the European Union. This year, for the first time, all MEPs from the United Kingdom will be picked under a proportional system – though only, of course, after an epic battle between the House of Lords and the House of Commons. Even there, the question was not first past the post versus PR, but what kind of PR to have. In addition, polling for the new Scottish and Welsh legislatures will involve a hybrid system – a mixture of conventional first past the post constituency-based elections, together with additional members elected from across individual regions to mitigate any disparities between votes gained and seats won.

So, for those who have long argued for what they would regard as a fairer voting system, all that is a huge step forward. What happens in these three elections will provide them with the best evidence yet, they hope, to support their case for that ultimate goal – extending PR to the election of MPs to Westminster.

That, of course, remains the biggest and greatest prize – the Holy Grail at the end of the long journey towards pure electoral heaven. Last year, supporters of PR at Westminster received an enormous boost in the shape of the report of the Jenkins Commission. It recommended that there should be reform, albeit in the shape of a reasonably mild form of PR known as 'Alternative Vote Plus'

But will it happen? Tony Blair welcomed the Jenkins Report, by saying that it made a 'powerful case' for a new voting system, yet his Home Secretary, Jack Straw, could barely conceal his disgust at the idea. Mr Straw, who has ministerial responsibility for electoral matters, appeared to dismiss the Jenkins formula, when he told MPs that he found it 'ingenious'. The Labour Party is clearly split on the issue, and most Conservatives are as instinctively opposed to any change to the Westminster voting system, as the Liberal Democrats are instinctively in favour of it.

So, on PR for Westminster, there is a battle ahead, and it is one that Tony Blair is clearly minded to postpone until after the next General Election. For the moment, he is relying on the formula that holding the promised referendum on the issue before then 'is not ruled out', but he points, in the same breath, to the welter of other constitutional change which is under way. The case can certainly be made, and the Prime Minister seems implicitly to be making it, that, before moving further along the PR road, it would be wise to see how things work out this year, especially in Scotland where a ruling coalition in the new Parliament seems a certainty. Heaven, Mr Blair is signalling, can wait.

Michael Brunson

Jenkins in brief

- Appointed December 1997; reported October 1998
- Recommended electing MPs by 'Alternative Vote Plus' system
- Electors would have two votes:
  one for a single member constituency with candidates to be ranked in order of preference;
  one for a wider city or county 'top up' area with a single vote cast for a candidate or party
- Between 80-85% of MPs would be elected in constituencies. The winning candidate would be the first to receive, if necessary after the distribution of preferences, 50% plus one of the votes cast
- The remaining 15-20% of MPs would be elected for 'top up' areas. Seats would be allocated in such a way as to mitigate any disparities between votes cast and seats won in the individual constituencies within the area
- No change to the electoral system unless supported by the people at a referendum

A short history of electoral reform

Electoral reform has made periodic appearances on the British political agenda for more than a century. Towards the end of the nineteenth century there were calls for the Single Transferable Vote (STV), invented by the English lawyer, Thomas Hare, to replace the existing first past the post (FPTP) system. Under STV, voters would be asked to list candidates in order of preference, placing a '1' next to their favourite candidate followed by a '2' against their next favoured candidate and so on. Voters would be free to express as many preferences as they chose. It was claimed the system would empower voters and reduce the scope of parties to impose their own choice of candidates upon the electorate. Although STV was championed by, amongst others, the MP and philosopher John Stuart Mill, the scheme found no support among party leaders. It was left to the Proportional Representation Society, founded in 1884 and now known as the Electoral Reform Society, to lead the campaign in favour of STV.

In 1910 a Royal Commission on Electoral Systems recommended use of the Alternative Vote (AV). This system, which now forms a part of the recommendations of the Jenkins Commission, retains single member parliamentary constituencies but instead of marking a single 'X' voters are asked to rank candidates in order of preference, marking a '1' against the most preferred, '2' against the next and so on. Any candidate with an absolute majority (50% plus 1) of first preferences is automatically elected. If no-one wins a majority then the bottom-placed candidate is eliminated and his or her second preference votes are redistributed among the remaining candidates. This process of elimination and redistribution continues until one of the candidates achieves an overall majority.

During the First World War a Speaker's Conference addressed the issue of a new voting system. In 1917 it recommended using STV in urban constituencies with AV to be adopted elsewhere. Later that year the Commons clashed with the Lords over electoral reform. The Commons favoured AV; the Lords preferred STV. The compromise saw plans for AV abandoned while STV would be used for the election of just 100 MPs. This agreement proved unsatisfactory and the 1918 election was conducted under the existing rules. While much of the rest of Europe adopted some form of proportional representation (PR) the reform opportunity in Britain had passed. Had the supporters of AV and STV managed to unite behind a common scheme then FPTP might have been replaced.

By the late 1920s party opinion had hardened. The Conservative party disliked AV because it believed that Labour voters' second preferences would favour Liberal candidates. Once in office Labour was less inclined towards reform but, if pushed, supported AV. The Liberals, now threatened with parliamentary extinction, preferred STV. During the minority Labour administration of 1929-1931 another reform measure was introduced. Labour, requiring Liberal support, reluctantly plumped for AV. The Bill passed through the Commons but was subsequently defeated in the House of Lords. The economic crisis that erupted in 1931 prevented any further progress.

In the 1970s, however, interest in electoral reform was reawakened. First, STV was introduced for elections in Northern Ireland. Second, the Royal Commission on the Constitution, chaired by Lord Kilbrandon, came down in favour of STV for national and regional assembly elections. Third, the influential Hansard Society published a report which recommended that FPTP be replaced by a version of the Additional Member System (AMS). In 1977, James Callaghan's Labour government, by then in a parliamentary pact with the Liberals, officially supported a regionally-based open party list system for use in European elections. A free vote of the House of Commons saw many Labour MPs vote against and the proposal was rejected.

In 1990, following a third successive general election defeat, Labour's National Executive Committee, asked Raymond (later Lord) Plant to chair a working party to examine alternative electoral procedures. Its initial remit included the European parliament, a revised second chamber as well as national and regional assemblies. Later, the committee was asked to consider parliamentary elections. During the 1992 general election campaign Labour's leader, Neil Kinnock, refused to commit the party to electoral reform, preferring instead to wait for the Plant committee report. In April 1993 a majority of the committee backed the Supplementary Vote (SV) system. MPs would still be elected in single member constituencies but, as with AV, the system requires that winners receive an overall majority. The ballot paper would present voters with two columns alongside the list of candidates. An 'X' vote for their favoured candidate is entered in the first column in the usual way while the second column can be used to indicate a second choice. Candidates with an absolute majority of first preferences are elected. If no-one receives a majority, all except the two candidates with the largest number of first preference votes are eliminated. The second choice votes of the excluded candidates are then re-distributed. The winner is the candidate in the now two-horse race who has the greater total number of preference votes. Labour's leader, by then John Smith, committed the party to a referendum on electoral reform. Tony Blair was happy to endorse this commitment during his battle for the party leadership in 1994. The 1997 manifesto formally endorsed the holding of a referendum and added that an independent commission would be appointed to seek a proportional alternative to FPTP to put before the people.

The Independent Commission on the Voting System

In December 1997 the government appointed the promised independent Commission on the voting system. It was to be chaired by Lord Jenkins of Hillhead. Roy Jenkins served as Labour's Chancellor of the Exchequer between 1967-1970, Deputy Leader of the party between 1970-1972, later becoming Home Secretary. As Home Secretary he presented a paper in favour of PR to the Cabinet but it was rejected. In 1977 he was appointed President of the European Commission and while in Brussels he was active in helping to form the Social Democratic Party (SDP) which broke away from the Labour party. There were four other members of the Commission. Baroness Gould was a member of Labour's Plant committee which supported SV. David Lipsey, Political Editor of the Economist and a former Chairman of the Fabian Society, was a known advocate of AV. Sir John Chilcot, as a former Permanent Secretary at the Northern Ireland Office, would have been familiar with the pros and cons of STV. The final member, Lord Alexander, Chairman of National Westminster Bank, was a Conservative who had advocated PR in his *Voice for the People: A Constitution for Tomorrow*, published in 1997. Critics argued that none of the Commission members would present the objective case for the current system.

The government specified four requirements for any alternative electoral system in the Commission's terms of reference. First, was the need for 'broad proportionality'. FPTP often creates an imbalance between vote and seat shares. Generally speaking, larger parties tend to be over-rewarded with seats while smaller parties win votes but very few, if any, seats. A pure PR system would be one where each party's share of seats matched exactly its share of the vote. The inclusion of the word 'broad' gave the Commission scope to find a system that simply promised better proportionality than the current system. Second, was the need to maintain stable government. Some interpreted this to mean that any scheme would have to ensure that popular parties would be able to win parliamentary majorities and that coalition government be minimised. The third requirement dealt with the desirability of extending voter choice. Unlike FPTP, systems such as AV, SV and STV, as well as mixed systems such as AMS, all permit more expressive voting, with voters signalling preferences among candidates and/or parties. Finally, although by no means least in the minds of MPs, the Commission was required to ensure that any alternative voting system should recognise the importance of a link between the elected member and a geographical constituency. But, as the Commission itself pointed out, this term of reference merely stated that 'a link' between MP and constituency had to be respected. How that relationship was to be operationalised was open to interpretation.

The Commission invited, through a series of national advertisements, written evidence from the general public, as well as academics, political parties, pressure groups and other organisations. More than 1500 written submissions were received, some of which were published as Volume 2 of the official report. These may be viewed at the website, http://www.official-documents.co.uk/document/cm40/4090/4090.htm. All of the main political parties submitted evidence. A total of 24 individual MPs wrote to the Commission. Dr. David Butler of Oxford University convened a small group of academics to provide technical assistance regarding particular issues. Other academics and commentators with a special interest in electoral systems also submitted evidence. Additionally, organisations such as the Association of Electoral Administrators, Centre for Policy Studies, Charter 88, Democratic Audit, Electoral Reform Society and the Fawcett Society all made contributions. The Commission also held a number of public meetings between March and July 1998. Approximately 1,000 people attended these meetings with around one third contributing to discussions. National Opinion Polls (NOP) were asked to test public responses to various aspects of the operation of alternative electoral systems. Commission members visited Australia, Germany, Ireland and New Zealand to examine the operation of electoral procedures in those countries.

Strengths and Weaknesses of First Past the Post

Understanding the reasoning behind the Commission's final choice of AV plus is helped by its analysis of the strengths and weaknesses of the current system. FPTP is not without its qualities. The general public are familiar with it, it is easily understood, and voters find no difficulty in casting a ballot. Elections nearly always produce a clear winner and so the system can be regarded as decisive. Although voting took place in constituencies voters could, indirectly, play a part in electing a government since FPTP invariably resulted in single party administrations. The report identifies the relationship between MPs and their geographical base as a crucial feature of the current system. The direct relationship between MP and constituency encouraged elected members to act on behalf of all constituents, and gave a degree of independence from excessive party control, particularly to 'unorthodox' MPs.

However, the defects of winner takes all elections were believed by the Commission to outweigh such strengths, necessitating the search for an alternative. FPTP exaggerates movements of electoral opinion, leading to parliamentary landslides such as that which occurred in 1997. Research conducted by NOP indicated that the public were deeply suspicious of a system that permitted parties to win large parliamentary majorities with less than a majority of votes. The treatment of minor parties also gave cause for concern. The Liberal Democrats, with a national vote of 17%, captured just 7% of seats while geographically concentrated parties such as Plaid Cymru fared rather better. It was perverse that the system should disadvantage a party with a broader appeal since that was better for national cohesion. The electoral system had driven the two main parties into 'electoral deserts'. Conservatives were entirely unrepresented in Scotland and Wales and absent from most of the major cities. Labour, despite its landslide, had relatively few MPs in some other parts of the country, particularly southern England. FPTP elections were won and lost in the marginals, causing parties to concentrate campaign resources in 150 or so constituencies. Minority party voters in safe seats may never see their choice of candidate elected. In such circumstances it is, perhaps, remarkable not that turnout is falling but that it has remained as high. Because Britain no longer had a two party system an increasing number of MPs were elected with less than a majority of votes. Or, to put it another way, more people voted against than for the successful candidate. Finally, the Commission noted how electoral bias had developed, favouring one or other of the main parties. For much of the post-war period the system had benefited the Conservatives but the last two general elections had seen the bias move decisively in Labour's favour.

The search for an alternative

Were there any alternatives that would not involve wholesale constituency boundary changes? Majoritarian systems, including AV, which could operate with current boundaries were rejected as a solution because they would produce a less proportional result than even FPTP. STV, the favoured choice of the Liberal Democrats and the Electoral Reform Society, was rejected because of the perception that it would be difficult for the public to adapt to such a system and that it would require unacceptably large constituencies in rural areas.

That thinking lead the Commission to favour a mixed system. A proportion of MPs could be elected in single member constituencies with the remainder elected following a 'top up' procedure designed to redress any disproportionality. The principal advantage of such a mixture would be the flexibility in reconciling the apparently contradictory requirements for broad proportionality whilst maintaining the MP-constituency link. The new system would give electors two votes which could, if desired, be cast for different parties. One vote in a single member constituency, the second in a 'top up' area consisting of a small cluster of constituencies. The second vote would ideally be cast for an open party list with candidates arranged in order of nomination by the different parties.

Three critical issues had still to be resolved. First, the proportion of constituency-based MPs to those elected in 'top up' areas. Second, the size of those 'top up' areas and, by definition, the number of MPs to be elected for each. Third, whether MPs elected in the single-member constituencies should continue to be chosen by FPTP or some other method.

On the first issue the Commission believed that the German system, with a 50:50 split between the two types of seat, represented an 'extreme form'. Too many list MPs were undesirable, having all of the advantages of being a constituency MP but with a smaller range of responsibilities. Furthermore, halving the number of constituencies would mean geographically much larger seats in rural Britain thereby weakening the MP-constituency link. In the Commission's view, between 15-20% of MPs should be drawn from party lists. Only parties which had contested half or more of the constituencies in a 'top up' area would be allowed candidates on the party list. The report maintained, citing research conducted on its behalf, that despite having only a fifth or less of MPs elected by PR this arrangement would both comply with 'broad proportionality' and allow a popular party to win a majority of seats with less than a majority of votes. As the Commission itself put it, 'we would not wish to propound a system which would involve permanent coalition' (para 122).

The second issue concerned the geography and representation of the 'top up' areas. It was, for example, possible to use national or regional boundaries as the building blocks. Alternatively, clusters of constituencies could be based on county areas or large cities. Choosing between those options helps illustrate the tension between maintaining an MP's geographical link and the need for broad proportionality. Complying with the requirement for proportionality is easier if the number of seats in each 'top up' area is relatively large. Such areas, however, run counter to the need to allow MPs to represent a reasonably tightly defined geographical area. Instead, the Commission chose to base 'top up' seats on counties and cities with an average of approximately 500,000 electors in each area. In Devon, for example, there would be nine single member constituencies and two 'top up' seats. The city of Birmingham would have a similar arrangement. Basing 'top up' areas on a relatively small constituency clustering would not only 'restore some cohesion of representation to the recently weakened traditional localities of Britain', but would also prove better than the alternative of large areas with 'top up' MPs appearing as 'a flock of unattached birds clouding the sky and wheeling under central party directions' (para 134).

The remaining issue was the choice of method for electing MPs in constituencies. The Commission believed that AV was to be preferred over FPTP. A majoritarian system such as AV would overcome the problem that an increasing number of MPs were elected on a minority of votes. Moreover, fewer votes would be 'wasted' since small party supporters could still influence the outcome. That would prove beneficial to levels of electoral participation. Candidates, requiring the support of a majority of voters to be elected, would broaden their appeal rather than rely on a hard core of party faithful. Candidates would not constantly attack one another for fear of alienating voters whose second preferences might determine the outcome. Party politics might become less confrontational and more consensual. The clinching argument appears to have been that under a winner takes all system parties have a vested interest in attacking opponents before the election takes place. Once the election is over, however, if the parliamentary arithmetic requires a coalition, then deals are struck with former enemies. Because AV elections would need to be fought in a less confrontational manner the process of post-election bargaining would not appear to the public as such a cynical 'U-turn'.

One Commission member, Lord Alexander, objected to AV and wrote a note of reservation to the main report. In his view, under AV the lower preferences of supporters of the strongest candidates would be ignored while those of the weaker candidates would count. Such an approach was illogical, he argued, quoting in support Winston Churchill's description of AV that it only takes account of 'the most worthless votes of the most worthless candidates'. Much would depend on the finishing order of candidates according to first preference votes. AV was unacceptable because there is too much scope for the outcome to be random. In an election where one party was particularly unpopular, for example Labour in 1983 or the Conservatives in 1997, then that party could be punished disproportionately. For these reasons, Lord Alexander backed continuation of FPTP for single member constituencies whilst supporting the rest of the Commission's recommendations.

The system proposed by Jenkins

The Commission's recommendation was that Alternative Vote Plus, or Alternative Vote Top Up, was the best alternative to First Past the Post for the election of the House of Commons. The system is a combination of the Alternative Vote and Additional Member systems and would involve electors casting two ballots.

The Commission envisages that some 80-85% of MPs would continue to be elected on an individual constituency basis, but the Alternative Vote system would be used to choose them. For this election, the first vote, voters would mark their ballot papers in order of preference for the various candidates. If no candidate received an absolute majority of first preference votes at the initial count, the candidate with the fewest votes would be eliminated and his/her second preference votes distributed between the other candidates. This process continues until one candidate has an overall majority of the votes.

The remaining 15-20% of MPs would be chosen in a way designed to correct any disparities between votes cast and seats won produced by the first stage. Electors would cast a single 'X', the second vote, for a party or individual candidate to represent a pre-defined geographical area. Within each area the process of allocating the available additional seats would begin by dividing the total number of second votes cast for each party by the number of individual constituencies it has won **plus one**. The first seat is then allocated to the party with the highest remaining vote and to the candidate in first place on that party's list. Each time a party gains a seat the number by which its total vote is to be divided increases by one. The party with the largest remaining vote after each calculation is awarded the next seat, and so on until all the vacancies have been filled.

The electoral impact

What impact would the Jenkins proposals have on the electoral future of Britain? The report contains projections of how 'AV plus' might have performed at the last two general elections. Table 7.1 summarises these figures which assume either 15% or 20% 'top up' seats. A number of interesting effects could accompany the change from FPTP to a new system. The number of seats captured by the largest party, the so-called 'winner's bonus', would be reduced. Instead of winning 419 seats in 1997, Labour could have won 59 fewer with a 20% 'top up'. Blair's parliamentary majority would have fallen from 179 to 61. In 1992 the Conservatives might have won just 309 seats compared with the notional result of 336 seats. Instead of having a majority of 27 the Conservatives would have been merely the largest party in a hung parliament. The Liberal Democrats appear to be the principal beneficiary of a different system. The potential increase in representation for the Liberal Democrats could be dramatic. The projections show that the party would have doubled its number of seats in 1994 and quadrupled the number it won in 1992.

CONSTITUENCY VOTE

This vote will help to decide who is the constituency MP for Westbury. Rank the candidates in order of preference (1 for your preferred candidate, then 2, 3 etc). Rank as many candidates as you wish.

Place the candidates in order of preference (1,2,3 etc)

Stephen Collins
Conservative

Candice Crosby
Liberal Democrat

Dennis Graham
Referendum Party

Stephanie Mills
Natural Law Party

Amina Mir
Independent

Diane Morgan
Labour

Martin Newman
Green Party

Peter Quine
Independent

Robert Russell
UK Independence Party

SECOND VOTE

This vote will help to decide the total number of seats for each party in the county of Purfordshire. You may vote either for one party, or if you wish, for one of the listed candidates. A vote for a listed candidate will also be counted as a vote for that candidates party.

EITHER	OR
Put an "X" against the party of your choice	Put an "X" against the candidate of your choice
☐ **Conservative**	☐ Giles Anderson ☐ John Coleman ☐ Julia Smith
☐ **Labour**	☐ Helen Baxter ☐ Tom Franklyn ☐ Donna Jones
☐ **Liberal Democrat**	☐ Carol Newton ☐ Fazal Hussain ☐ Julian Morison
☐ **Natural Law**	☐ Paul Delaney ☐ Nasian Shah
☐ **Referendum**	☐ Anthony Barber ☐ Denise Doherty

Table 7.1 Estimated outcomes of the 1992 and 1997 general elections under 'AV Plus'

	Con	Lab	LibDem	Others	Outcome
1997 g.e.	165	419	46	29	Lab. majority 179
20% 'top up'	175	360	90	34	Lab. majority 61
15% 'top up'	160	378	88	23	Lab majority 97
1992 g.e.*	343	273	18	25	Con. majority 27
20% 'top up'	309	240	81	29	No overall majority
15% 'top up'	315	244	71	29	No overall majority

* Between 1992 and 1997 boundary changes took place which increased the size of the House of Commons from 651 to 659 seats. The projections for 1992 assume a 659 member House of Commons.

These projections are not wholly uncontentious. The calculations were undertaken for the Commission by Professor Patrick Dunleavy of the London School of Economics and Dr Helen Margetts of Birkbeck College. They arrived at the voting figures for the 'top up' areas simply by aggregating votes cast at the 1997 general election in parliamentary constituencies. That method assumes that electors with two votes would not engage in 'split-ticket' voting, supporting one party in the constituency, another in the 'top up' area. As Dunleavy and Margetts themselves acknowledge, however, vote splitting on a significant scale could affect their seat projections. In 1997, for example, at least 10%, and possibly as many as 20%, of voters with two ballots, one parliamentary the other local, cast them for different parties. That proportion would almost certainly have been much larger had the Jenkins system been in place at the last general election. It would have lead to a different outcome from that described in Table 7.1. Greater reservations apply to the seat projections for 1992. The voting figures used by Dunleavy and Margetts are estimates of what the results of the 1992 election would have been had the 1997 boundaries been in place. The authors note 'reservations about the accuracy of the . . . recalculated data' but proceed nevertheless to make their projections on that basis. Moreover, such projections cannot be 'scientific' since voters will respond differently in new contexts. The estimates provided in the Jenkins report might have been the best available but they should be regarded as indicative, not definitive.

Reactions to Jenkins

Reactions to the Jenkins Commission proposals ranged from those implacably opposed to those believing the recommendations provided the best of all possible worlds. Crucially, Prime Minister Blair accepted that the report had made a powerful case for reform, though adding that there was no need to rush into legislation. His Cabinet, however, is divided, with a majority appearing to favour retention of the current system. Two crucial players in any reform process would be Jack Straw, the Home Secretary and Margaret Beckett, Leader of the House of Commons and responsible for timetabling the government's parliamentary business. Straw claimed the report was 'ingenious', that the recommended alternative looked complicated and that it might be appropriate to let other constitutional changes settle down before any further upheaval took place. Lord Jenkins found the Home Secretary's viewpoint 'absolute nonsense'. Beckett, a long-standing opponent of PR, remained 'sceptical'. Most prominent among the pro-reform Cabinet members was Foreign Secretary, Robin Cook. He argued that Labour's manifesto committed the party to a referendum before the next general election, a view not shared by many of his colleagues.

As expected the Conservative party loudly proclaimed its opposition to change with William Hague declaring it would be 'a great mistake to move to this ridiculous dog's breakfast'. The Liberal Democrats, despite the party's long-standing support for STV, welcomed 'AV plus' and looked forward to an early referendum. Backbenchers from all parties are mobilising rival campaigns. Labour's FPTP group has claimed the backing of more than a 100 of the party's MPs, while a pro-reform group, Make Votes Count, claims substantial cross-bench support. With opinion deeply divided the outcome of any referendum vote, held before or after the next general election, would be in the balance. However, even the Jenkins Commission recognised that the next election would be fought under the current rules. The composition of the House of Commons after that election could be a crucial factor in determining whether Britain changes its electoral system.

The battleground for the next general election

The general election to be called by May 2002 will be fought under an electoral system that is heavily biased against the Conservative party. In 1997, Labour polled 43% of the vote but won 64% of seats; the Conservatives with 31% of votes captured only 25% of seats. On average, it took only 32,318 votes to elect each Labour MP but 58,127 votes to elect each Conservative. If the two main parties were to win an equal share of the vote at the next general election, say 38%, a uniform swing would produce an overall Labour majority of about 20 seats. In order to finish with more seats than Labour at the next election the Conservatives will need a lead of more than 6% in the popular vote. A Conservative lead over Labour of some 10% would be necessary to give the Tories a bare majority in the House of Commons. Table 7.3 reveals the real extent of electoral bias against the Conservative party.

Table 7.2: The 1997 General Election Result

	Votes	% vote	% change 1992/97	Candidates	Seats
Con	9,600,943	30.7	−11.2	648	165
Lab	13,518,167	43.2	+8.8	639	418
Lib Dem	5,242,947	16.8	−1.1	639	46
SNP/PC	782,580	2.5	+0.2	112	10
Green	63,991	0.2	−0.3	95	–
NLP	30,604	0.1	−0.1	197	–
Referendum	811,849	2.6	–	547	–
UKInd	105,722	0.3	–	193	–
Others	1,129,481	3.6	+0.8	654	20
Total Vote	31,286,284			3724	659
Electorate	43,846,152	71.4% turnout			

Table 7.3. Electoral system bias at the next general election

Distribution of vote	Likely outcome
10% Lab lead over Con	Lab overall majority 160
5% Lab lead over Con	Lab overall majority 90
2% Lab lead over Con	Lab overall majority 40
Equal vote share (38%)	Lab overall majority 20
2% Con lead over Lab	Lab largest party (50 more seats than Con)
5% Con lead over Lab	Lab largest party (20 more seats than Con)
10% Con lead over Lab	Con overall majority 1.

The cliché happens to be true – the Conservatives have a mountain to climb. The nature of that task can be summarised according to the size of swing required for different electoral outcomes.

- A swing of 8% from Labour to Conservative at the next general election would cost Tony Blair his majority.
- A swing of 10% would see the Conservatives overtake Labour as the largest party in a hung parliament.
- A swing of 12% is required for the Conservatives to win an overall majority.

For the record, the swing in 1997 was 10.5% – twice as large as at any post-war election.

Opinion polls conducted since the election suggest the Conservatives are struggling to stay in touch with Labour. Exit polls conducted at that election showed the Conservatives received a plurality of votes only from those in professional or managerial occupations and from those who owned their own home outright. Young voters were overwhelmingly behind New Labour. Conservative support did hold up among the over 65s but a significant number of those voters will have died before the next election. Nevertheless, recent elections have shown that the electorate's ties with the political parties have weakened. Electoral volatility has increased, making election outcomes far from certain. Those Conservative voters that deserted to the other parties in 1997, including the Referendum party, may return. Labour's reputation amongst voters cannot be guaranteed between now and the next general election. The battleground for that election is described in Table 7.4.

Table 7.4 : The Electoral Battleground

Seats are listed in rank order of marginality. Following the constituency name is the percentage majority of the winning party, its lead in votes and the party which finished in second place. The results are those at the last general election and take no account of any by-election changes or changes in an MP's party allegiance. The Speaker's seat of West Bromwich West is omitted from this list.

Labour seats

		%maj	*votes*	*2nd*
1	Kettering	0.33	189	Con
2	Wellingborough	0.33	187	Con
3	Milton Keynes North E.	0.47	240	Con
4	Rugby & Kenilworth	0.81	495	Con
5	Northampton South	1.30	744	Con
6	Romford	1.54	649	Con
7	Lancaster & Wyre	2.20	1,295	Con
8	Harwich	2.27	1,216	Con
9	Norfolk North West	2.32	1,339	Con
10	Castle Point	2.35	1,143	Con
11	Harrow West	2.36	1,240	Con
12	Bristol West	2.38	1,493	Con
13	Braintree	2.61	1,451	Con
14	Shrewsbury & Atcham	3.02	1,670	Con
15	Enfield Southgate	3.08	1,433	Con
16	Conwy	3.84	1,596	LD
17	Gillingham	3.91	1,980	Con
18	Sittingbourne & Sheppey	4.18	1,929	Con
19	Clwyd West	4.59	1,848	Con
20	Stroud	4.74	2,910	Con
21	Inverness East, Nairn & Lochaber	4.90	2,339	SNP
22	Falmouth & Camborne	5.01	2,688	Con
23	Hastings & Rye	5.22	2,560	Con
24	Warwick & Leamington	5.65	3,398	Con
25	Shipley	5.67	2,996	Con
26	Chatham & Aylesford	5.68	2,790	Con
27	Newark	5.80	3,016	Con
28	Wirral West	5.84	2,738	Con
29	Wimbledon	6.18	2,990	Con
30	Eastwood	6.19	3,236	Con
31	Reading West	6.19	2,997	Con
32	Oldham East & Saddleworth	6.26	3,389	LD
33	Finchley & Golders Green	6.34	3,189	Con
34	Thanet South	6.40	2,878	Con
35	Ilford North	6.60	3,224	Con
36	Hemel Hempstead	6.60	3,636	Con
37	The Wrekin	6.68	3,025	Con
38	Upminster	6.70	2,770	Con
39	Putney	6.76	2,976	Con
40	Selby	6.81	3,836	Con
41	Croydon Central	6.98	3,897	Con

Labour seats

		%maj	votes	2nd
42	Bexleyheath & Crayford	7.08	3,415	Con
43	Hammersmith & Fulham	7.11	3,842	Con
44	Gedling	7.29	3,802	Con
45	Reading East	7.56	3,795	Con
46	Aberdeen South	7.64	3,365	LD
47	Brighton Kemptown	7.66	3,534	Con
48	Leeds North West	7.79	3,844	Con
49	Hove	8.23	3,959	Con
50	Carmarthen East & Dinefwr	8.27	3,450	PC
51	Dartford	8.32	4,328	Con
52	Stafford	8.33	4,314	Con
53	Bradford West	8.51	3,877	Con
54	Monmouth	8.52	4,178	Con
55	Colne Valley	8.58	4,840	Con
56	Wansdyke	8.77	4,799	Con
57	St Albans	8.78	4,459	Con
58	Glasgow Govan	9.04	2,914	SNP
59	Ribble South	9.20	5,084	Con
60	Scarborough & Whitby	9.43	5,124	Con
61	Rochdale	9.45	4,545	LD
62	Portsmouth North	9.55	4,323	Con
63	Broxtowe	9.59	5,575	Con
64	Birmingham Edgbaston	9.99	4,842	Con
65	Wolverhampton S. W.	10.46	5,118	Con
66	Watford	10.49	5,792	Con
67	Brent North	10.53	4,019	Con
68	Welwyn Hatfield	10.56	5,595	Con
69	Ochil	10.62	4,652	SNP
70	Edinburgh Pentlands	10.63	4,862	Con
71	Gravesham	10.85	5,779	Con
72	Loughborough	10.91	5,712	Con
73	Swindon South	11.03	5,645	Con
74	Calder Valley	11.08	6,255	Con
75	Chesterfield	11.24	5,775	LD
76	Battersea	11.31	5,360	Con
77	Stourbridge	11.36	5,645	Con
78	Burton	11.61	6,330	Con
79	Pudsey	11.77	6,207	Con
80	Medway	11.97	5,354	Con
81	Morecambe & Lunesdale	12.11	5,965	Con
82	Hendon	12.30	6,155	Con
83	Wyre Forest	12.62	6,946	Con
84	Forest of Dean	12.64	6,343	Con
85	Hornchurch	12.93	5,680	Con
86	Batley & Spen	13.08	6,141	Con
87	Brigg & Goole	13.65	6,389	Con
88	Redditch	13.69	6,125	Con
89	Keighley	13.85	7,132	Con
90	Birmingham Yardley	14.07	5,315	LD
91	Gloucester	14.26	8,259	Con

Labour seats

		%maj	votes	2nd
92	Bury North	14.29	7,866	Con
93	Enfield North	14.31	6,822	Con
94	Worcester	14.38	7,425	Con
95	Bolton West	14.39	7,072	Con
96	Wirral South	14.56	7,004	Con
97	Ayr	14.62	6,543	Con
98	Stirling	14.92	6,411	Con
99	Tamworth	15.04	7,496	Con
100	Peterborough	15.12	7,323	Con
101	Erewash	15.14	9,135	Con
102	Leeds North East	15.29	6,959	Con
103	Kilmarnock & Loudoun	15.31	7,256	SNP
104	High Peak	15.38	8,791	Con
105	Swindon North	15.93	7,688	Con

Labour loses its overall majority

106	Elmet	16.23	8,779	Con
107	Crosby	16.27	7,182	Con
108	Ealing North	16.44	9,160	Con
109	Blackpool N. & Fleetwood	16.64	8,946	Con
110	Cardiff North	16.76	8,126	Con
111	Bedford	16.96	8,300	Con
112	Harrow East	17.08	9,734	Con
113	Chorley	17.10	9,870	Con
114	Norwich North	17.20	9,470	Con
115	Great Yarmouth	17.73	8,668	Con
116	Cleethorpes	18.18	9,176	Con
117	Cardiff Central	18.75	7,923	LD
118	City of Chester	18.76	10,553	Con
119	Derby North	18.91	10,615	Con
120	Exeter	18.92	11,705	Con
121	Dewsbury	19.32	8,323	Con
122	Northampton North	19.34	10,000	Con
123	Dumfries	19.47	9,643	Con
124	Vale of Glamorgan	19.53	10,532	Con
125	Warrington South	19.62	10,807	Con
126	Staffordshire Moorlands	19.66	10,049	Con
127	Dudley North	19.78	9,457	Con
128	Middlesbrough S. & Cleveland E.	19.79	10,607	Con
129	Plymouth Sutton	19.81	9,440	Con

Conservatives overtake Labour as largest party

130	Renfrewshire West	20.05	7,979	SNP
131	Birmingham Hall Green	20.13	8,420	Con
132	Milton Keynes S. W.	20.28	10,292	Con
133	Luton North	20.34	9,626	Con
134	Preseli Pembrokeshire	20.60	8,736	Con
135	Bristol North West	20.60	11,382	Con

Labour Seats

		% maj	votes	2nd
136	Halesowen & Rowley Regis	21.20	10,337	Con
137	Amber Valley	21.20	11,613	Con
138	Rossendale & Darwen	21.38	10,949	Con
139	Waveney	21.50	12,093	Con
140	Ipswich	21.58	10,436	Con
141	Dover	21.66	11,739	Con
142	Coventry South	21.85	10,953	Con
143	Corby	21.98	11,860	Con
144	Harlow	21.99	10,514	Con
145	Tynemouth	22.04	11,273	Con
146	Halifax	22.18	11,212	Con
147	Western Isles	22.20	3,576	SNP
148	Stockton South	22.23	11,585	Con
149	Stevenage	22.54	11,582	Con
150	Carmarthen W. & Pembrokeshire S.	22.56	9,621	Con
151	Blackpool South	22.63	11,616	Con
152	Vale of Clwyd	22.88	8,955	Con
153	Pendle	23.01	10,824	Con
154	Crawley	23.22	11,707	Con
155	Derbyshire South	23.29	13,967	Con
156	Eltham	23.45	10,182	Con
157	Luton South	23.49	11,319	Con
158	Hyndburn	23.72	11,448	Con
159	Kingswood	23.80	14,253	Con
160	Lincoln	23.91	11,130	Con

Conservatives win an overall majority

161	Bury South	24.58	12,381	Con
162	Dundee East	24.58	9,961	SNP
163	Basildon	25.02	13,280	Con
164	Bethnal Green & Bow	25.26	11,285	Con
165	Nuneaton	25.30	13,540	Con
166	Leicestershire N. W.	25.41	13,219	Con
167	Edinburgh South	25.54	11,452	Con
168	Brentford & Isleworth	25.70	14,424	Con
169	Bolton North East	25.75	12,669	Con
170	Edinburgh Central	25.90	11,070	Con
171	Aberdeen North	26.06	10,010	SNP
172	Southampton Test	26.09	13,684	Con
173	Walsall South	26.16	11,312	Con
174	Dumbarton	26.37	10,883	SNP
175	Southampton Itchen	26.43	14,229	Con
176	Edinburgh North & Leith	26.81	10,978	SNP
177	Cunninghame North	26.84	11,039	Con
178	Brighton Pavilion	26.93	13,181	Con
179	Dudley South	27.20	13,027	Con
180	Warwickshire North	27.23	14,767	Con
181	Linlithgow	27.33	10,838	SNP

Labour Seats

		% maj	votes	2nd
182	Slough	27.38	13,071	Con
183	Livingston	27.42	11,747	SNP
184	Cambridge	27.54	14,137	Con
185	Nottingham South	27.54	13,364	Con
186	Cannock Chase	27.65	14,478	Con
187	Weaver Vale	27.84	13,448	Con
188	Birmingham Selly Oak	27.87	14,088	Con
189	Midlothian	28.00	9,870	SNP
190	Stretford & Urmston	28.01	13,640	Con
191	Norwich South	28.03	14,239	Con
192	Ilford South	28.39	14,200	Con
193	Carlisle	28.41	12,390	Con
194	Mitcham & Morden	28.66	13,741	Con
195	Bradford South	28.71	12,936	Con
196	Wakefield	28.93	14,604	Con
197	Copeland	28.98	11,996	Con
198	Walsall North	29.07	12,588	Con
199	Birmingham Northfield	29.46	11,443	Con
200	Glasgow Kelvin	29.60	9,665	SNP
201	Sherwood	29.74	16,812	Con
202	Gower	30.01	13,007	Con
203	Edmonton	30.05	13,472	Con
204	Barrow & Furness	30.06	14,497	Con
205	Hampstead & Highgate	30.17	13,284	Con
206	Aberdeen Central	30.33	10,801	Con
207	Clydesdale	30.41	13,809	SNP
208	Telford	30.42	11,290	Con
209	Blackburn	30.43	14,451	Con
210	Bradford North	30.48	12,770	Con
211	Ellesmere Port & Neston	30.51	16,035	Con
212	Dundee West	30.56	11,859	SNP
213	Coventry North West	30.56	16,601	Con
214	Kirkcaldy	30.62	10,710	SNP
215	Cumbernauld & Kilsyth	30.89	11,128	SNP
216	Regent's Park & Kensington N.	30.96	14,657	Con
217	Sheffield Hillsborough	31.03	16,451	LD
218	Derby South	31.08	16,106	Con
219	Delyn	31.15	12,693	Con
220	Crewe & Nantwich	31.22	15,798	Con
221	Lancashire West	31.28	17,119	Con
222	Birmingham Erdington	31.32	12,657	Con
223	Wolverhampton N. E.	31.37	12,987	Con
224	Leicester West	31.44	12,864	Con
225	Morley & Rothwell	32.14	14,750	Con
226	Falkirk East	32.18	13,385	SNP
227	Wrexham	32.29	11,762	Con
228	Lewisham East	32.42	12,127	Con
229	Tooting	32.56	15,011	Con
230	Ealing Acton & Shepherd's Bush	32.56	15,650	Con

Labour Seats

		% maj	votes	2nd
231	Cardiff South & Penarth	32.68	13,861	Con
232	West Bromwich East	32.74	13,584	Con
233	East Lothian	32.74	14,221	Con
234	Feltham & Heston	32.76	15,273	Con
235	Strathkelvin & Bearsden	32.77	16,292	Con
236	Wythenshawe & Sale E.	32.98	15,019	Con
237	Darlington	33.27	16,025	Con
238	Bristol East	33.52	16,159	Con
239	Fife Central	33.64	13,713	SNP
240	Don Valley	33.65	14,659	Con
241	Dunfermline West	33.91	12,354	SNP
242	Clydebank & Milngavie	34.08	13,320	SNP
243	Scunthorpe	34.09	14,173	Con
244	Paisley South	34.14	12,750	SNP
245	Leicester South	34.28	16,493	Con
246	Stalybridge & Hyde	34.37	14,806	Con
247	Edinburgh E. & Musselburgh	34.50	14,530	SNP
248	Heywood & Middleton	34.70	17,542	Con
249	Hayes & Harlington	34.78	14,291	Con
250	Oxford East	34.81	16,665	Con
251	Motherwell & Wishaw	34.93	12,791	SNP
252	Croydon North	35.00	18,398	Con
253	Newcastle-under-Lyme	35.02	17,206	Con
254	Clwyd South	35.07	13,810	Con
255	York	35.18	20,523	Con
256	Bridgend	35.25	15,248	Con
257	Derbyshire North E.	35.25	18,321	Con
258	Oldham West & Royton	35.42	16,201	Con
259	Huddersfield	35.57	15,848	Con
260	East Kilbride	35.63	17,384	SNP
261	Swansea West	35.73	14,459	Con
262	Newcastle upon Tyne Central	35.76	16,480	Con
263	Falkirk West	35.92	13,783	SNP
264	Bassetlaw	36.14	17,348	Con
265	Blaydon	36.16	16,605	LD
266	Newport West	36.16	14,537	Con
267	Newport East	36.30	13,523	Con
268	Thurrock	36.55	17,256	Con
269	Plymouth Devonport	36.69	19,067	Con
270	Dulwich & West Norwood	36.76	16,769	Con
271	Normanton	36.96	15,893	Con
272	Airdrie & Shotts	37.43	15,412	SNP
273	Paisley North	37.54	12,814	SNP
274	Greenock & Inverclyde	37.59	13,040	SNP
275	Great Grimsby	37.69	16,244	Con
276	Burnley	37.71	17,062	Con
277	Worsley	37.92	17,741	Con
278	Warrington North	38.10	19,527	Con
279	Lewisham West	38.11	14,317	Con
280	Leyton & Wanstead	38.62	15,186	Con

Labour Seats

		% maj	votes	2nd
281	Bristol South	38.77	19,328	Con
282	Nottingham East	38.80	15,419	Con
283	Cardiff West	38.80	15,628	Con
284	Glasgow Cathcart	38.83	12,965	SNP
285	Preston	38.86	18,680	Con
286	Llanelli	38.92	16,039	PC
287	Alyn & Deeside	39.10	16,403	Con
288	Ealing Southall	39.21	21,423	Con
289	Hartlepool	39.39	17,508	Con
290	Sheffield Heeley	39.47	17,078	LD
291	Stoke-on-Trent S.	39.59	18,303	Con
292	Warley	39.73	15,451	Con
293	Workington	39.81	19,656	Con
294	Hornsey & Wood Green	39.81	20,499	Con
295	Hull West & Hessle	40.48	15,525	LD
296	Stockport	40.52	18,912	Con
297	Wallasey	40.72	19,074	Con
298	Barnsley West & Penistone	40.91	17,267	Con
299	Streatham	41.04	18,423	Con
300	Doncaster Central	41.10	17,856	Con
301	Islington South & Finsbury	41.24	14,563	LD
302	Birmingham Perry Barr	41.31	18,957	Con
303	Leicester East	41.49	18,422	Con
304	Birmingham Hodge Hill	41.58	14,200	Con
305	Blyth Valley	41.75	17,736	LD
306	Erith & Thamesmead	41.90	17,424	Con
307	Cunninghame South	41.95	14,869	SNP
308	Glasgow Pollok	42.04	13,791	SNP
309	Manchester Withington	42.20	18,581	Con
310	Glasgow Rutherglen	42.25	15,007	SNP
311	Liverpool Garston	42.36	18,417	LD
312	Newcastle upon Tyne N.	42.74	19,332	Con
313	Walthamstow	42.81	17,149	Con
314	Carrick, Cumnock & Doon, Valley	42.83	21,062	Con
315	Liverpool Wavertree	42.90	19,701	LD
316	Mansfield	43.26	20,518	Con
317	Wolverhampton S. E.	43.59	15,182	Con
318	Denton & Reddish	44.07	20,311	Con
319	Redcar	44.25	21,667	Con
320	Hackney South & Shoreditch	44.40	14,990	LD
321	Glasgow Anniesland	44.73	15,154	SNP
322	Greenwich & Woolwich	44.87	18,128	Con
323	Ashfield	44.91	22,728	Con
324	Hamilton North & Bellshill	44.91	17,067	SNP
325	Stoke-on-Trent N.	44.98	17,392	Con
326	Brent East	45.03	15,882	Con
327	Nottingham North	45.41	18,801	Con
328	Bishop Auckland	45.74	21,064	Con
329	City of Durham	45.80	22,504	Con

Labour Seats

		% maj	votes	2nd
330	Sheffield Central	46.42	16,906	LD
331	Glasgow Baillieston	46.59	14,840	SNP
332	Birmingham Sparkbrook & Small Heath	46.75	19,526	Con
333	Coventry North East	46.94	22,569	Con
334	Holborn & St Pancras	47.11	17,903	Con
335	Dagenham	47.16	17,054	Con
336	St Helens North	47.57	23,417	Con
337	Manchester Gorton	47.76	17,342	LD
338	Vauxhall	47.77	18,660	LD
339	Eccles	47.97	21,916	Con
340	Hamilton South	47.98	15,878	SNP
341	Glasgow Maryhill	47.99	14,264	SNP
342	Stockton North	48.02	21,357	Con
343	Poplar & Canning Town	48.17	18,915	Con
344	Barking	48.22	15,896	Con
345	Hackney N. & Stoke Newington	48.26	15,627	Con
346	East Ham	48.53	19,358	Con
347	Ashton under Lyne	48.57	22,965	Con
348	Leeds East	48.80	17,466	Con
349	Leeds West	49.16	19,771	Con
350	Bolton South East	49.16	21,311	Con
351	Sunderland South	49.19	19,638	Con
352	Sheffield Attercliffe	49.23	21,818	Con
353	Stoke-on-Trent C.	49.51	19,924	Con
354	Wansbeck	49.52	22,367	LD
355	Jarrow	49.91	21,933	Con
356	Pontypridd	50.44	23,129	LD
357	Hull North	50.79	19,705	Con
358	Rother Valley	50.88	23,485	Con
359	Dunfermline East	51.26	18,751	SNP
360	Coatbridge & Chryston	51.30	19,292	SNP
361	Salford	51.53	17,069	Con
362	Sunderland North	51.55	19,697	Con
363	Wigan	51.67	22,643	Con
364	Knowsley N. & Sefton E.	52.61	26,147	Con
365	Hemsworth	52.76	23,992	Con
366	Halton	53.22	23,650	Con
367	Leigh	53.34	24,496	Con
368	Sedgefield	53.36	25,143	Con
369	Durham North West	53.44	24,754	Con
370	Tottenham	53.58	20,200	Con
371	St Helens South	53.64	23,739	Con
372	Middlesbrough	54.27	25,018	Con
373	Manchester Blackley	54.78	19,588	Con
374	Glasgow Springburn	54.87	17,326	SNP
375	Doncaster North	55.00	21,937	Con
376	Birkenhead	55.55	21,843	Con
377	Islington North	55.65	19,955	LD
378	Durham North	55.76	26,299	Con

Labour Seats

		% maj	votes	2nd
379	Leeds Central	55.90	20,689	Con
380	Lewisham Deptford	56.11	18,878	Con
381	Torfaen	56.74	24,536	Con
382	South Shields	56.83	22,153	Con
383	Rotherham	57.02	21,469	Con
384	Brent South	57.08	19,691	Con
385	Caerphilly	57.08	25,839	Con
386	Liverpool Riverside	57.16	21,799	LD
387	Newcastle upon Tyne E. & Wallsend	57.25	23,811	Con
388	Bolsover	57.26	27,149	Con
389	Wentworth	57.34	23,959	Con
390	Hull East	57.60	23,318	Con
391	West Ham	57.91	19,494	Con
392	Gateshead E. & Washington W.	57.91	24,950	Con
393	Camberwell & Peckham	57.98	16,451	Con
394	Makerfield	58.15	26,177	Con
395	Manchester Central	58.69	19,682	LD
396	Sheffield Brightside	58.92	19,954	LD
397	Tyneside North	59.05	26,643	Con
398	Cynon Valley	59.11	19,755	PC
399	Glasgow Shettleston	59.18	15,868	SNP
400	Aberavon	59.98	21,571	LD
401	Birmingham Ladywood	60.78	23,082	Con
402	Rhondda	61.09	24,931	PC
403	Barnsley E. & Mexborough	61.76	26,763	Con
404	Liverpool West Derby	62.14	26,197	LD
405	Pontefract & Castleford	62.14	25,725	Con
406	Houghton & Washington E.	63.49	26,555	Con
407	Ogmore	64.22	24,447	Con
408	Knowsley South	64.53	30,708	Con
409	Neath	64.84	26,741	Con
410	Tyne Bridge	65.73	22,906	Con
411	Islwyn	65.74	23,931	LD
412	Swansea East	66.11	25,569	Con
413	Barnsley Central	67.15	24,501	Con
414	Liverpool Walton	67.25	27,038	LD
415	Merthyr Tydfil & Rhymney	69.20	27,086	LD
416	Blaenau Gwent	70.74	28,035	LD
417	Easington	71.64	30,012	Con
418	Bootle	74.36	28,421	Con

Conservative seats

		% maj	votes	2nd
1	Dorset South	0.16	77	Lab
2	Bedfordshire South West	0.25	132	Lab
3	Teignbridge	0.45	281	LD
4	Hexham	0.49	222	Lab
5	Lichfield	0.49	238	Lab
6	Bury St Edmunds	0.66	368	Lab
7	Wells	0.94	528	LD
8	Meriden	1.06	582	Lab
9	Dorset Mid & Poole North	1.34	681	LD
10	Boston & Skegness	1.39	647	Lab
11	Totnes	1.63	877	LD
12	Uxbridge	1.74	724	Lab
13	Bosworth	1.97	1,027	Lab
14	Chipping Barnet	2.09	1,035	Lab
15	Norfolk North	2.20	1,293	LD
16	Beverley & Holderness	2.30	1,211	Lab
17	Norfolk Mid	2.33	1,336	Lab
18	Eddisbury	2.40	1,185	Lab
19	Billericay	2.45	1,356	Lab
20	Tiverton & Honiton	2.80	1,653	LD
21	Altrincham & Sale West	2.91	1,505	Lab
22	Bridgwater	3.29	1,796	LD
23	Dorset West	3.44	1,840	LD
24	Eastbourne	3.79	1,994	LD
25	Suffolk West	3.80	1,867	Lab
26	Christchurch	3.85	2,165	LD
27	Norfolk South West	4.19	2,464	Lab
28	Basingstoke	4.20	2,397	Lab
29	Shropshire North	4.26	2,195	Lab
30	Wycombe	4.53	2,370	Lab
31	Surrey South West	4.77	2,694	LD
32	Orpington	4.91	2,952	LD
33	Grantham & Stamford	5.08	2,692	Lab
34	Dorset North	5.22	2,746	LD
35	Aldridge-Brownhills	5.45	2,526	Lab
36	Southend West	5.62	2,615	LD
37	Thanet North	5.65	2,766	Lab
38	Suffolk Coastal	5.78	3,254	Lab
39	Hertfordshire North East	5.94	3,088	Lab
40	Wiltshire North	5.99	3,475	LD
41	Cheadle	6.08	3,189	LD
42	Hertsmere	6.11	3,075	Lab
43	Spelthorne	6.69	3,473	Lab
44	Suffolk Central & Ipswich N.	6.70	3,538	Lab
45	Yorkshire East	6.81	3,337	Lab
46	Old Bexley & Sidcup	6.94	3,569	Lab
47	Stone	7.19	3,818	Lab
48	Canterbury	7.33	3,964	Lab
49	Havant	7.72	3,729	Lab

Conservative seats

		% maj	votes	2nd
50	Worcestershire West	7.79	3,846	LD
51	Suffolk South	8.03	4,175	Lab
52	Banbury	8.10	4,737	Lab
53	Rushcliffe	8.14	5,055	Lab
54	Guildford	8.41	4,791	LD
55	Faversham & Kent Mid	8.41	4,173	Lab
56	Derbyshire West	8.59	4,885	Lab
57	Westmorland & Lonsdale	8.90	4,521	LD
58	Rochford & Southend E.	9.08	4,225	Lab
59	Beckenham	9.11	4,953	Lab
60	Cambridgeshire North E.	9.20	5,101	Lab
61	Bromsgrove	9.27	4,845	Lab
62	Sleaford & North Hykeham	9.63	5,123	Lab
63	Ashford	9.68	5,355	Lab
64	Worthing E. & Shoreham	9.89	5,098	LD
65	Epping Forest	9.91	5,252	Lab
66	Bournemouth East	10.00	4,342	LD
67	Ryedale	10.37	5,058	LD
68	Charnwood	10.50	5,900	Lab
69	New Forest East	10.63	5,215	LD
70	Essex North	10.69	5,476	Lab
71	Westbury	10.73	6,088	LD
72	Salisbury	10.78	6,276	LD
73	Wantage	10.86	6,089	Lab
74	Woking	11.15	5,678	LD
75	Poole	11.32	5,298	LD
76	Chelmsford West	11.42	6,691	LD
77	Congleton	11.48	6,130	LD
78	Ribble Valley	11.60	6,640	LD
79	Bedfordshire N. E.	11.68	5,883	Lab
80	Norfolk South	11.88	7,378	LD
81	Daventry	11.95	7,378	Lab
82	Blaby	12.08	6,474	Lab
83	Cities of London & Westminster	12.16	4,881	Lab
84	Folkestone & Hythe	12.17	6,332	LD
85	Aldershot	12.23	6,621	LD
86	Harborough	12.31	6,524	LD
87	Witney	12.46	7,028	Lab
88	Hertford & Stortford	12.62	6,885	Lab
89	Hitchin & Harpenden	12.72	6,671	Lab
90	Ludlow	12.77	5,909	LD
91	Sussex Mid	12.82	6,854	LD
92	Chingford & Woodford Green	12.86	5,714	Lab
93	Gosport	12.94	6,258	Lab
94	Bedfordshire Mid	13.50	7,090	Lab
95	Louth & Horncastle	13.81	6,900	Lab
96	Bournemouth West	13.90	5,710	LD
97	Devon South West	14.01	7,397	Lab
98	Woodspring	14.07	7,734	LD

Conservative seats

		% maj	votes	2nd
99	Broxbourne	14.16	6,653	Lab
100	Devon East	14.26	7,494	LD
101	Gainsborough	14.28	6,826	Lab
102	Aylesbury	14.63	8,419	LD
103	Worthing West	14.99	7,713	LD
104	Haltemprice & Howden	15.16	7,514	LD
105	Staffordshire South	15.30	7,821	Lab
106	Tunbridge Wells	15.52	7,506	LD
107	Bognor Regis & Littlehampton	15.76	7,321	Lab
108	Cambridgeshire N. W.	15.88	7,754	Lab
109	South Holland & The Deepings	15.94	7,991	Lab
110	Macclesfield	15.97	8,654	Lab
111	Reigate	16.07	7,741	Lab
112	Cambridgeshire South	16.23	8,712	LD
113	Devizes	16.29	9,782	LD
114	Cambridgeshire S. E.	16.46	9,349	Lab
115	Romsey	16.57	8,585	LD
116	Rutland & Melton	16.79	8,836	Lab
117	Fylde	17.21	8,963	Lab
118	Ruislip Northwood	17.38	7,794	Lab
119	Chichester	17.45	9,734	LD
120	Leominster	17.48	8,835	LD
121	Bracknell	17.58	10,387	Lab
122	Tewkesbury	17.71	9,234	LD
123	Maidstone & The Weald	17.91	9,603	Lab
124	Hertfordshire S. W.	18.08	10,021	Lab
125	Vale of York	18.25	9,721	Lab
126	Worcestershire Mid	18.52	9,412	Lab
127	Saffron Walden	18.53	10,573	LD
128	Wokingham	18.69	9,365	LD
129	Mole Valley	18.75	10,221	LD
130	Brentwood & Ongar	19.10	9,690	LD
131	Runnymede & Weybridge	19.15	9,875	Lab
132	Solihull	19.35	11,397	LD
133	Windsor	19.53	9,917	LD
134	Fareham	19.85	10,358	Lab
135	Maldon & Chelmsford E.	19.92	10,039	Lab
136	Hampshire East	19.94	11,590	LD
137	Tonbridge & Malling	20.78	10,230	Lab
138	Rayleigh	20.82	10,684	Lab
139	Sevenoaks	20.86	10,461	Lab
140	Penrith & The Border	20.90	10,233	LD
141	Richmond (Yorks)	21.05	10,051	Lab
142	Bromley & Chislehurst	21.08	11,118	Lab
143	Hampshire North W.	21.13	11,551	LD
144	Epsom & Ewell	21.27	11,525	Lab
145	Skipton & Ripon	21.38	11,620	LD
146	Henley	21.67	11,167	LD
147	Croydon South	22.01	11,930	Lab

Conservative seats

		% maj	votes	2nd
148	Bexhill & Battle	22.66	11,100	LD
149	Stratford-on-Avon	22.72	14,106	LD
150	New Forest West	22.78	11,332	LD
151	Cotswold	23.41	11,965	LD
152	Maidenhead	23.54	11,981	LD
153	Wealden	24.03	14,204	LD
154	Buckingham	25.07	12,386	Lab
155	Kensington & Chelsea	25.67	9,519	Lab
156	Horsham	26.00	14,862	LD
157	Chesham & Amersham	26.55	13,859	LD
158	Esher & Walton	27.07	14,528	Lab
159	Arundel & South Downs	27.34	14,035	LD
160	Surrey East	27.61	15,093	LD
161	Beaconsfield	27.86	13,987	LD
162	Hampshire North E.	28.17	14,398	LD
163	Sutton Coldfield	28.41	14,885	Lab
164	Surrey Heath	29.76	16,287	LD
165	Huntingdon	31.85	18,140	Lab

Liberal Democrat seats

		%maj	votes	2nd
1	Winchester	0.00	2	Con
2	Torbay	0.02	12	Con
3	Kingston & Surbiton	0.10	56	Con
4	Somerton & Frome	0.23	130	Con
5	Eastleigh	1.36	754	Con
6	Weston-Super-Mare	2.39	1,274	Con
7	Lewes	2.64	1,300	Con
8	Colchester	3.04	1,581	Con
9	Devon West & Torridge	3.31	1,957	Con
10	Northavon	3.42	2,137	Con
11	Tweeddale, Ettrick & Lauderdale	3.82	1,489	Lab
12	Taunton	4.00	2,443	Con
13	Sutton & Cheam	4.45	2,097	Con
14	Carshalton & Wallington	4.68	2,267	Con
15	Richmond Park	5.19	2,951	Con
16	Aberdeenshire W & Kincardine	6.16	2,662	Con
17	Twickenham	7.36	4,281	Con
18	Caithness, Sutherland & Easter Ross	7.74	2,259	Lab
19	Southwark N. & Bermondsey	8.30	3,387	Lab
20	Portsmouth South	8.37	4,327	Con
21	Isle of Wight	8.76	6,406	Con
22	Ross, Skye & Inverness W.	10.06	4,019	Lab
23	Oxford West & Abingdon	10.27	6,285	Con
24	Devon North	11.28	6,181	Con

Liberal Democrat seats

		%maj	votes	2nd
25	Cornwall South East	11.28	6,480	Con
26	Brecon & Radnorshire	11.89	5,097	Con
27	Southport	12.17	6,160	Con
28	Hereford	12.65	6,648	Con
29	Harrogate & Knaresborough	13.09	6,236	Con
30	Cheltenham	13.21	6,645	Con
31	St Ives	13.30	7,170	Con
32	Newbury	15.08	8,517	Con
33	Edinburgh West	15.23	7,253	Con
34	Gordon	16.56	6,997	Con
35	Argyll & Bute	17.02	6,081	SNP
36	Bath	17.26	9,319	Con
37	Sheffield Hallam	18.19	8,271	Con
38	Berwick-upon-Tweed	19.24	8,042	Lab
39	Montgomeryshire	19.74	6,303	Con
40	Yeovil	21.10	11,403	Con
41	Truro & St Austell	22.03	12,501	Con
42	Roxburgh & Berwickshire	22.63	7,906	Con
43	Cornwall North	23.67	13,847	Con
44	Hazel Grove	23.94	11,814	Con
45	Fife North East	24.75	10,356	Con
46	Orkney & Shetland	33.72	6,968	Lab

Scottish Nationalist seats

		%maj	votes	2nd
1	Perth	7.05	3,141	Con
2	Tayside North	9.12	4,160	Con
3	Galloway & Upper Nithsdale	13.38	5,624	Con
4	Moray	14.00	5,566	Con
5	Angus	23.65	10,189	Con
6	Banff & Buchan	31.97	12,845	Con

Plaid Cymru seats

		%maj	votes	2nd
1	Ynys Mon	6.21	2,481	Lab
2	Ceredigion	17.32	6,961	Lab
3	Caernarfon	21.59	7,449	Lab
4	Meirionnydd Nant Conwy	27.69	6,805	Lab

Independent seat

	%maj	votes	2nd
Tatton	22.70	11,077	Con

Ulster Unionist seats

		%maj	votes	2nd
1	Tyrone West	2.51	1,161	SDLP
2	Londonderry East	9.96	3,794	DUP
3	Belfast South	11.65	4,600	SDLP
4	Strangford	14.06	5,852	DUP
5	Antrim East	18.60	6,389	APNI
6	Upper Bann	19.36	9,252	SDLP
7	Fermanagh & South Tyrone	28.35	13,688	SF
8	Belfast North	31.42	13,024	SDLP
9	Lagan Valley	38.20	16,925	APNI
10	Antrim South	41.33	16,611	SDLP

Democratic Unionist seats

		%maj	votes	2nd
1	Belfast East	17.31	6,754	UU
2	Antrim North	22.89	10,574	UU

SDLP seats

		%maj	votes	2nd
1	Newry and Armagh	9.18	4,889	UU
2	Down South	20.07	9,933	UU
3	Foyle	28.58	13,664	SF

Sinn Fein seats

		%maj	votes	2nd
1	Ulster Mid	3.72	1,883	DUP
2	Belfast West	17.24	7,909	SDLP

UKU seat

	%maj	votes	2nd
Down North	3.96	1,449	UU

Glossary

The variety of UK electoral systems

REGIONAL LISTS
European Parliament election, Great Britain, 10 June 1999
Regional lists are to be used for the European Parliament elections in Great Britain. There will be 11 regions, each returning between 3 and 11 MEPs depending on the size of their electorates. The entire nations of Scotland and Wales will form single electoral regions. Parties will supply a list of candidates for each region in the order in which they wish them to be elected. Electors will be able to cast their single vote either for a party or for an independent candidate. It will not be possible to make distinctions between individual candidates on a party's list. The votes of those candidates not on the list of a registered party will each be treated separately.

The first stage in the allocation of seats in each region will be to total the votes cast for each party list and for each individual candidate. The first seat is then allocated to the party with the highest vote and to the candidate in first place on that party's list. The remaining seats are decided having taken into account the number of seats a party has already won within the region. To do this it is necessary to divide the total votes cast for each party by the number of constituencies it has won **plus one**. Each time a party gains a seat the number by which its total vote is to be divided increases by one. The party with the largest remaining vote after each calculation is awarded the next seat, and so on until all the vacancies have been filled. A worked example of an election count using this system can be found in chapter 1.

To be certain of securing a European Parliament seat in Great Britain a party or an individual must receive a proportion of the vote equal to 100 divided by the total number of seats in the region **plus one**. This threshold will vary from 20% (100÷4+1) in the North East region to 8.3% (100÷11+1) in the South East region. It is possible to secure a seat with a lesser share of the vote depending on the way votes are distributed between the competing parties. Every EU country with the exception of Ireland (and Northern Ireland – see below) will use a form of list system for the European Parliament elections.

SINGLE TRANSFERABLE VOTE
European Parliament election, Northern Ireland, 10 June 1999
Northern Ireland Assembly election, 25 June 1998
Northern Ireland local elections
The Single Transferable Vote (STV) system is to be used to elect 3 Members of the European Parliament for Northern Ireland, as it has been at every election since 1979. Electors are required to vote for at least one candidate, and then to declare their preferences for as many or as few of the other candidates as they wish. Preferences are declared numerically, with '1' being written alongside the voter's first preference candidate, '2' alongside the second choice and so on. All candidates are listed individually and it is possible to choose among candidates and thus between parties as well.

To be elected a candidate must receive a minimum number of votes – the 'quota'– determined by a set formula. In Northern Ireland the formula known as the 'Droop quota' is used. It is calculated by dividing the total number of valid voting papers cast by the number of seats to be filled **plus one**. Candidates who reach the quota with their first preference votes are elected at once. The surplus votes of elected candidates, together with those of candidates who are excluded by virtue of their low support, are transferred to other candidates in accordance with the stated preference of voters. This process continues until all the vacancies have been filled. A worked example of an STV election count can be found in both chapters 1 and 4.

STV was also used to elect 108 members of the Northern Ireland Assembly in June 1998, and for elections to the 26 Northern Ireland district councils.

ADDITIONAL MEMBER SYSTEM
Scottish Parliament election, 6 May 1999
Welsh Assembly election, 6 May 1999
Greater London Assembly election, 4 May 2000
The Additional Member System to be used for the Scottish Parliament, Welsh Assembly and Greater London Assembly elections is a combination of the First Past the Post and Regional List systems. In each case the majority of representatives will be chosen by simple plurality within single member constituencies. The remainder of 'additional members', or 'top up' seats, are elected following the tallying of each party's vote within predetermined regions with the intention of counter-balancing any disparities between votes cast and seats won.

Electors have two votes. One for a candidate within their parliament/assembly constituency, and one for a 'party list' within their electoral region. Parties will supply a list of candidates for each region in the order in which they wish them to be elected. Electors will be able to cast their second vote either for a party or for an independent candidate. It will not be possible to make distinctions between individual candidates on a party's list. The votes of those candidates not on the list of a registered party will each be treated separately. Individuals may simultaneously be candidates both in a constituency and on *one* regional list, but those who win a constituency seat are no longer eligible to be an additional member.

Within each region the process of allocating the available additional seats begins by dividing the total list votes cast for each party by the number of first past the post constituencies it has won **plus one**. The first seat is then allocated to the party with the highest remaining vote and to the candidate in first place on that party's list. Each time a party gains a seat the number by which its total vote is to be divided increases by one. The party with the largest remaining vote after each calculation is awarded the next seat, and so on until all the vacancies have been filled. Worked examples of an election count using this system can be found in chapters 2, 3 and 5.

To be certain of securing a seat under this system a party or an individual must receive a proportion of the vote equal to 100 divided by the total number of seats, constituency plus additional members, in the region **plus one**. It is possible to secure a seat with a lesser share of the vote depending on the way votes are distributed between the competing parties. The distribution of constituency and additional member seats varies between each of the legislatures. In Scotland there will be 73 constituency representatives and 56 'top up' seats -a ratio of 57:43; in Wales the split is 40 and 20 -a ratio 67:33; and in London 14 and 11 -a ratio of 56:44. The greater the proportion of 'top up' as opposed to first past the post seats, the greater the likelihood that the distribution of seats within the legislature will be in proportion to the votes cast.

SUPPLEMENTARY VOTE
Greater London Mayor election, 4 May 2000
The Mayor of Greater London will be chosen in a cross-London ballot using the Supplementary Vote system of election. Electors will be asked to indicate by a 'X' in each of two columns their first and their second preference from among the candidates. A candidate is elected if s/he receives more than half the total number of first preference votes. If none of the candidates reaches this threshold, the two candidates with the greatest number of first preference votes remain in the contest and all the others are eliminated.

The second preferences indicated on the ballot papers of those candidates who have been eliminated are then inspected. Where such a second preference is for one of the two candidates remaining in the contest, it is added to that candidate's first preference votes. The candidate who has the greater total number of preference votes -that is, first preference votes plus second preference votes transferred from eliminated candidates- is deemed elected. A worked example of an election count using this system can be found in chapter 5.

ALTERNATIVE VOTE PLUS
System proposed by Independent Commission on the Voting System
Alternative Vote Plus, or Alternative Vote Top Up, was recommended by the Independent Commission on the Voting System (the Jenkins Commission) as the best alternative to First Past the Post for the election of the House of Commons. It is a combination of the Alternative Vote and Additional Member systems and would involve electors casting two ballots.

The Commission envisages that some 80-85% of MPs would continue to be elected on an individual constituency basis, but the Alternative Vote system would be used to choose them. For this election, the first vote, voters would mark their ballot papers in order of preference for the various candidates. If no candidate received a majority of first preference votes at the initial count, the candidate with the fewest votes would be eliminated and his/her second preference votes distributed between the other candidates. This process continues until one candidate has an overall majority of the votes.

The remaining 15-20% of MPs would be chosen in a way designed to correct any disparities between votes cast and seats won thrown up by the first stage. Electors would cast a single 'X', the second vote, for a party or individual candidate to represent a pre-defined geographical area. Within each area the process of allocating the available additional seats would begin by dividing the total number of second votes cast for each party by the number of individual constituencies it has won **plus one**. The first seat is then allocated to the party with the highest remaining vote and to the candidate in first place on that party's list. Each time a party gains a seat the number by which its total vote is to be divided increases by one. The party with the largest remaining vote after each calculation is awarded the next seat, and so on until all the vacancies have been filled.

The government has pledged that there will be no change to the system used for elections to the House of Commons without the approval of the electorate in a referendum. The next general election will be fought under current rules.

FIRST PAST THE POST
United Kingdom general elections
Great Britain local elections
First past the post (FPTP) is the name given to the plurality system used for electing Members of the House of Commons and local councillors in Great Britain. Voters mark the ballot paper with a 'X' and the candidate with the most such votes wins even if s/he has only a minority of the total votes cast. A single member is chosen in this way for each parliamentary constituency, but in local government it is common for two or three (and occasionally more) representatives to be elected for each electoral unit. In these cases voters cast as many 'X's as there are vacancies and, again, it is the candidates with the largest number of votes who win.

Appendix 1: Alphabetic listing of election candidates

European Parliament Elections 1999 – candidates*

Candidate	Party	Region	Number on list
Abbott, J.	Green	Eastern	5
Adam, G.*	Labour	North East	4
Adamson, C. Ms.	Lib Dem	Yorkshire & The Humber	6
Adamson, R.	Conservative	Yorkshire & The Humber	4
Ainley, S.	Green	Wales	5
Aldridge, R.	Lib Dem	Scotland	2
Alexander, P. Ms.	Green	Yorkshire & The Humber	1
Allan, K. Ms.	Green	Scotland	2
Anginotti, S. Ms.	Lib Dem	Yorkshire & The Humber	5
Arain, J.	Conservative	East Midlands	4
Armstrong, L. Ms.	Labour	South East	10
Armstrong-Braun, K.	Green	Wales	2
Atkins, R.	Conservative	North West	2
Attwooll, E. Ms.	Lib Dem	Scotland	1
Backhouse, G. Ms.	Green	East Midlands	1
Bagnall, R. Ms.	Labour	Eastern	8
Balfe, R.*	Labour	London	4
Ballance, C.	Green	Scotland	8
Baptie, P.	Green	West Midlands	3
Barber, S. Ms.	Lib Dem	East Midlands	2
Barton, R.*	Labour	Yorkshire & The Humber	4
Baxter, A.	Green	East Midlands	5
Bearder, C. Ms.	Lib Dem	South East	9
Beasley, J. Ms.	Lib Dem	South West	6
Beazley, C.	Conservative	Eastern	2
Bellotti, D.	Lib Dem	South East	4
Bennion, P.	Lib Dem	West Midlands	4
Berry, C.	Lib Dem	South East	10
Berry, J. Ms.	Green	Eastern	6
Best, N.	Green	North East	1
Bethell, B. Ms.	Conservative	South East	6
Bethell, N.	Conservative	London	3
Billingham, A. Ms.*	Labour	East Midlands	3
Blount, S. Ms.	Green	East Midlands	4
Bodfish, K.	Labour	South East	5
Boff, A.	Conservative	London	7
Bowe, D.*	Labour	Yorkshire & The Humber	2
Bowis, J.	Conservative	London	4
Bowles, S. Ms.	Lib Dem	South East	3
Bradbourn, P.	Conservative	West Midlands	4
Bradley, J.	Green	London	5
Bright, G.	Conservative	Eastern	7
Brown, K.	SNP	Scotland	7
Browne, R.	Lib Dem	Eastern	3
Buchanan, C.	Conservative	Scotland	4
Buchnor, V. Ms.	Labour	Eastern	6
Buckland, R.	Conservative	Wales	4

European Parliament Elections 1999 – candidates (continued)

Candidate	Party	Region	Number on list
Buckle, S. Ms.	Conservative	East Midlands	5
Bullock, J. Ms.	Green	East Midlands	6
Burall, P.	Lib Dem	Eastern	7
Burgess, E. Ms.	Green	Eastern	3
Burnett, M.	Conservative	West Midlands	8
Busby, C.	Green	North West	3
Bushill-Matthews, P.	Conservative	West Midlands	2
Butler, C.	Conservative	Wales	2
Butt-Philip, A.	Lib Dem	South West	5
Calder, J.	Lib Dem	West Midlands	7
Callanan, M.	Conservative	North East	1
Calton, P. Ms.	Lib Dem	North West	4
Cameron, A.	Lib Dem	Wales	3
Cane, C. Ms.	Lib Dem	Eastern	6
Carmichael, N.	Conservative	North West	10
Cashman, M.	Labour	West Midlands	2
Cassidy, B.*	Conservative	South West	6
Chichester, G.*	Conservative	South West	2
Clark, J. Ms.	Green	Yorkshire & The Humber	7
Clawley, A.	Green	West Midlands	4
Clawley, H. Ms.	Green	West Midlands	6
Clayton, M.	Lib Dem	North West	9
Clegg, N.	Lib Dem	East Midlands	1
Clifford, J.	Labour	Scotland	7
Clucas, F. Ms.	Lib Dem	North West	2
Collins, S.	Green	London	4
Corbett, R.*	Labour	Yorkshire & The Humber	3
Cordwell, J.	Lib Dem	West Midlands	8
Corrie, J.*	Conservative	West Midlands	1
Coyne, M. Ms.	Green	Scotland	4
Crookes, L.	Green	North West	6
Cunningham, T.*	Labour	North West	5
D'Agrone, A.	Green	Yorkshire & The Humber	5
Dartmouth, W.	Conservative	Yorkshire & The Humber	5
Davies, C.	Lib Dem	North West	1
Davis, P.	Labour	West Midlands	6
Davison, A. Ms.	Labour	South East	8
Dawe, H. Ms.	Green	South East	5
Dawe, S.	Green	South East	6
Denis, J.	Green	South East	8
Deva, N.	Conservative	South East	5
Dewar, M. Ms.	Labour	South West	5
Dhanda, P.	Labour	South East	6
Dixon, J.	Lib Dem	Wales	5
Donnelly, A.*	Labour	North East	1
Dover, D.	Conservative	North West	4
Dowding, G. Ms.	Green	North West	4
Duff, A.	Lib Dem	Eastern	1
Dunbar, L. Ms.	Lib Dem	East Midlands	6

European Parliament Elections 1999 – candidates (continued)

Candidate	Party	Region	Number on list
Dykes, H.	Lib Dem	London	2
Elles, J.*	Conservative	South East	4
Elliott, M.	Labour	London	10
Enright, D.	Labour	South East	9
Eserrecchia, L. Ms.	Green	South East	9
Evans, J.	Conservative	Wales	1
Evans, J. Ms.	Plaid Cymru	Wales	1
Evans, R.*	Labour	London	3
Facey, P.	Lib Dem	London	10
Farmer, G.	Green	Scotland	6
Farron, T.	Lib Dem	North West	3
Fewster, B.	Green	East Midlands	3
Field, R.	Green	North West	5
Fitz-Gibbon, S.	Green	North West	2
Flack, J.	Conservative	London	9
Flanagan, T. Ms.	Labour	South East	11
Fletcher, K. Ms.	Lib Dem	North West	8
Foote Wood, C.	Lib Dem	North East	1
Forbes, J. Ms.	Green	London	8
Ford, G.*	Labour	South West	1
Forse, G.	Green	East Midlands	2
Foster, J. Ms.	Conservative	North West	5
Francis, A.	Green	South East	3
Freel, K. Ms.	Lib Dem	Scotland	8
Fryer, J.	Lib Dem	London	4
Gabriel, L. Ms.	Lib Dem	East Midlands	4
Gilbey, A.	Conservative	Scotland	8
Gill, N. Ms.	Lib Dem	Eastern	8
Gill, R. Ms.	Labour	West Midlands	3
Gillies, A. Ms.	SNP	Scotland	3
Goldie, I.	SNP	Scotland	8
Goodwill, R.	Conservative	Yorkshire & The Humber	3
Gordon, R.	Conservative	Eastern	5
Green, P. Ms.*	Lib Dem	South West	7
Green, S.	Labour	London	1
Greenburgh, M.	Conservative	West Midlands	7
Greveson, M.	Green	North East	4
Griffin, T. Ms.	Labour	North West	10
Hall, F. Ms.	Lib Dem	North East	2
Hallam, D.*	Labour	West Midlands	5
Hannan, D.	Conservative	South East	3
Harbour, M.	Conservative	West Midlands	3
Hardstaffe, V. Ms.*	Labour	Yorkshire & The Humber	6
Harper, A. Ms.	Conservative	Scotland	3
Harper, R.	Green	Scotland	1
Harris, A. Ms.	Lib Dem	Yorkshire & The Humber	3
Harvey, A. Ms.	Lib Dem	North East	4
Harvey, J. Ms.	Conservative	London	10

European Parliament Elections 1999 – candidates (continued)

Candidate	Party	Region	Number on list
Hawkins, J. Ms.	Lib Dem	South East	5
Hayward, E.	Conservative	Wales	5
Heaton-Harris, C.	Conservative	East Midlands	3
Helmer, R.	Conservative	East Midlands	1
Hendrick, M.*	Labour	North West	6
Hendry, L. Ms.	Green	Scotland	7
Hewett-Silk, B. Ms.	Lib Dem	South East	7
Hill, M.	Green	Yorkshire & The Humber	2
Hogg, J. Ms.	Green	North West	10
Holmes, A.	Green	Eastern	8
Holtham, A.	Green	West Midlands	7
Honeyball, M. Ms.	Labour	London	7
Howard, A.	Labour	South East	7
Howitt, R.*	Labour	Eastern	2
Hudghton, I.	SNP	Scotland	1
Hughes Hallett, D.	Lib Dem	Wales	4
Hughes, J. Ms.	Lib Dem	Scotland	5
Hughes, S.*	Labour	North East	2
Huhne, C.	Lib Dem	South East	2
Hume, J.*	SDLP	Northern Ireland	
Hutt, J. Ms.	Labour	Wales	5
Inglewood, W.	Conservative	North West	1
Jackson, C. Ms.*	Conservative	South West	1
Jago, H.	Green	London	7
Jenny, J. Ms.	Green	North West	9
Jones, J. Ms.	Green	London	3
Jones, T. Ms.	Lib Dem	South West	3
Juned, S. Ms.	Lib Dem	West Midlands	3
Kaleta, R. Ms.	Green	Wales	4
Kellett-Bowman, E.*	Conservative	South East	7
Kelly, B. Ms.	Labour	Eastern	7
Khanbhai, B.	Conservative	Eastern	3
Kinnock, G. Ms.*	Labour	Wales	1
Kirk, M. Ms.	Lib Dem	Yorkshire & The Humber	7
Kirkhope, T.	Conservative	Yorkshire & The Humber	2
Knight, J.	Labour	South West	4
Kortvelyessy, N. Ms.	Green	London	2
Kramer, S. Ms.	Lib Dem	London	3
Lambert, J. Ms.	Green	London	1
Latham, P. Ms.	Conservative	East Midlands	6
Law, J. Ms.	SNP	Scotland	5
Lawson, R.	Green	South West	2
Leighter, H. Ms.	Lib Dem	London	5
Leslie, S.	Conservative	Scotland	5
Lisgo, L. Ms.	Labour	South West	7
Littman, L.	Green	South East	10
Llywelyn, O.	Plaid Cymru	Wales	5
Lucas, C. Ms.	Green	South East	1
Ludford, S. Ms.	Lib Dem	London	1

European Parliament Elections 1999 – candidates (continued)

Candidate	Party	Region	Number on list
Lyall, H. Ms.	Lib Dem	Scotland	4
Lynne, L. Ms.	Lib Dem	West Midlands	1
MacCormick, N.	SNP	Scotland	2
Macgregor, G.	Conservative	North East	4
Malik, M.	Labour	London	8
Mallory, S. Ms.	Labour	South West	3
Mann, J.	Labour	East Midlands	6
Marland, P.	Conservative	South West	7
Martin, A.	Green	Yorkshire & The Humber	4
Martin, D.	Conservative	South West	5
Martin, D.*	Labour	Scotland	1
Marwa, S.	Lib Dem	West Midlands	6
Maughan, P.	Lib Dem	North East	3
May, C. Ms.	Labour	Scotland	4
Mayhew, J.	Conservative	South East	9
McAvan, L. Ms.*	Labour	Yorkshire & The Humber	1
McCarthy, A. Ms.*	Labour	North West	1
McMahon, H.	Labour	Scotland	5
McMillan-Scott, E.*	Conservative	Yorkshire & The Humber	1
McNally, E. Ms.*	Labour	Eastern	1
Miller, B.*	Labour	Scotland	2
Mitchell, I.	Conservative	Scotland	6
Mitchison, N.	Lib Dem	Scotland	3
Moraes, C.	Labour	London	2
Morgan, E. Ms.*	Labour	Wales	2
Mountford, R.	Green	West Midlands	5
Murphy, B.	Conservative	North East	3
Murphy, S.*	Labour	West Midlands	1
Najabat Hussain, R.	Conservative	Yorkshire & The Humber	7
Nangle, C. Ms.	Labour	North West	8
Needle, C.*	Labour	Eastern	3
Newns, D.	Conservative	North West	6
Newton Dunn, B.	Conservative	East Midlands	2
Niblett, B.	Lib Dem	East Midlands	5
Nicholls, G.	Green	North West	8
Nicholson, E. Ms.	Lib Dem	South East	1
Nicholson, J.*	UU	Northern Ireland	
Norman, F. Ms.	Green	West Midlands	1
Normington, R.	Conservative	West Midlands	5
Nuttall, D.	Conservative	Yorkshire & The Humber	6
O'Brien, P.	Green	Scotland	5
O'Kane, N. Ms.	Labour	West Midlands	8
O'Toole, M. Ms.	Labour	North East	3
Oddy, C. Ms.*	Labour	West Midlands	7
Olliver, V. Ms.	Green	London	6
Orchard-Doughty, S. Ms.	Lib Dem	London	7
Otten, J.	Green	Yorkshire & The Humber	6
Paisley, I.*	DUP	Northern Ireland	
Parish, N.	Conservative	South West	4

European Parliament Elections 1999 – candidates (continued)

Candidate	Party	Region	Number on list
Parry, A. Ms.	Conservative	South East	8
Parry, J.	Green	North West	7
Paton, J.	Labour	Scotland	6
Pearce, A.	Conservative	North West	9
Pearcey, J. Ms.	Lib Dem	North West	10
Perkins, S. Ms.	Plaid Cymru	Wales	4
Perry, R.*	Conservative	South East	2
Phillips, M.	Plaid Cymru	Wales	3
Pickering, S.	Green	South West	3
Pinfield, N.	Lib Dem	London	6
Pitts, M.	Lib Dem	Yorkshire & The Humber	2
Pollack, A. Ms.*	Labour	South East	3
Popat, A.	Conservative	London	6
Powell, M.	Green	Eastern	4
Price, P.	Lib Dem	Wales	2
Provan, J.*	Conservative	South East	1
Purvis, J.	Conservative	Scotland	2
Putman, R.	Lib Dem	North West	5
Quinnell, J.	Green	South West	6
Ramsay, P.	Conservative	Scotland	7
Read M. Ms.*	Labour	East Midlands	1
Reid, A.	Lib Dem	North West	7
Reid, K.	Conservative	North West	7
Roberts, R.	Lib Dem	Wales	1
Rose, C.	Conservative	Eastern	8
Ross, C.	Lib Dem	Yorkshire & The Humber	4
Ruff, A.	Conservative	North East	2
Salmon, J.	Green	South East	11
Scheimann, M.	Green	Eastern	2
Scott Cato, M. Ms.	Lib Dem	Eastern	2
Scott, E. Ms.	Green	Scotland	3
Scott, R. Ms.	Green	Wales	1
Scrase, R.	Green	South West	4
Seal, B.*	Labour	Yorkshire & The Humber	5
Seaton, S. Ms.	SNP	Scotland	6
Shellard, D.	Labour	Yorkshire & The Humber	7
Shepherd, J.	Labour	South West	6
Simpson, B.*	Labour	North West	4
Skene, D.	Lib Dem	Scotland	7
Skinner, P.*	Labour	South East	1
Smith, V. Ms.	Green	Yorkshire & The Humber	3
Sneddon, C.	Lib Dem	Scotland	6
Snellgrove, A. Ms.	Labour	South East	4
Soutar, H.	Green	South West	5
Speight, B. Ms.	Green	North East	3
Spencley, L. Ms.	Lib Dem	Eastern	4
Spiers, S.*	Labour	London	6
Stanton, E. Ms.	Green	West Midlands	8
Stark, A.	Green	South East	7

European Parliament Elections 1999 – candidates (continued)

Candidate	Party	Region	Number on list
Steinberg, B.	Conservative	London	8
Stevenson, S.	Conservative	Scotland	1
Stimson, M.	Green	London	10
Stockton, A.	Conservative	South West	3
Sturdy, R.*	Conservative	Eastern	1
Sumberg, D.	Conservative	North West	3
Tannock, C.	Conservative	London	2
Tanswell, B.	Conservative	South East	10
Tappin, M.*	Labour	West Midlands	4
Taylor, C. Ms.	Labour	Scotland	3
Taylor, D.	Conservative	West Midlands	6
Taylor, V. Ms.	Green	South West	1
Teverson, R.*	Lib Dem	South West	2
Thomas, D.*	Labour	Eastern	5
Thomson, A. Ms.	Lib Dem	London	9
Thomson, N. Ms.	Green	Eastern	7
Tilsley, P.	Lib Dem	West Midlands	2
Titley, G.*	Labour	North West	2
Tongue, C. Ms.*	Labour	London	5
Truscott, P.*	Labour	Eastern	4
Turner, R. Ms.	Labour	North West	7
Twinn, I.	Conservative	London	5
Twitchen, K. Ms.	Conservative	Eastern	6
Vadher, A.	Lib Dem	East Midlands	3
Van Orden, G.	Conservative	Eastern	4
Vaz, V. Ms.	Labour	East Midlands	5
Vernon-Jackson, G.	Lib Dem	South East	8
Villiers, T. Ms.	Conservative	London	1
Waddington, S. Ms.*	Labour	East Midlands	4
Walker, S. Ms.	Green	Wales	3
Walker-Shaw, K. Ms.	Labour	Scotland	3
Wallis, D. Ms.	Lib Dem	Yorkshire & The Humber	1
Walmsley, J. Ms.	Lib Dem	West Midlands	5
Walsh, J.	Lib Dem	South East	6
Walton, D.	Green	London	9
Ward, M.	Labour	North West	9
Watson, G.*	Lib Dem	South West	1
Watts, M.*	Labour	South East	2
Webb, D. Ms.	Lib Dem	South East	11
West, P.	Green	South East	4
Wharfe, P. Ms.	Labour	London	9
White, C.	Lib Dem	Eastern	5
White, I.*	Labour	South West	2
Whitehead, P.*	Labour	East Midlands	2
Whitelegg, J.	Green	North West	1
Whiteside, R. Ms.	Green	North East	2
Wiggin, B.	Conservative	North West	8
Williams, O.	Conservative	Wales	3
Wilson, G.	SNP	Scotland	4

European Parliament Elections 1999 – candidates (continued)

Candidate	Party	Region	Number on list
Wilson, J.*	Labour	Wales	4
Wiseman, A.	Lib Dem	London	8
Woodford, G.	Green	West Midlands	2
Woodin, M.	Green	South East	2
Wright, M. Ms.	Green	Eastern	1
Wyn, E.	Plaid Cymru	Wales	2
Wynn, T.*	Labour	North West	3
Yates, P. Ms.	Lib Dem	South West	4
Zalzala, Y. Ms.	Lib Dem	North West	6

* Current Member of the European Parliament

Scottish Parliament Elections 1999 – candidates*

Candidate	Party	Constituency	Region	Number on list
Ackland, R.	LD	Clydebank & Milngavie	West of Scotland	3
Adam, B.	SNP	Aberdeen North	North East Scotland	3
Ahmed-Sheikh, T. Ms.	Con	Glasgow Govan		
Aitken, J. Ms.	Lab	Inverness East, Nairn & Lochaber		
Aitken, W.	Con	Glasgow Anniesland		
Alexander, W. Ms.	Lab	Paisley North		
Allan, K. Ms.	Green		Glasgow	1
Anderson, E. Ms.	LD	Aberdeen Central	North East Scotland	7
Arbuckle, A.	LD		Mid Scotland and Fife	2
Ardrey, A.	SNP	Hamilton South		
Ascherson, N.	LD	Renfrewshire West		
Aslam Kahn, M.	LD		Glasgow	3
Baillie, J. Ms.	Lab	Dumbarton		
Bain, C.	Con	Glasgow Shettleston		
Baird, S. Ms.	Green		North East Scotland	1
Balfour, J.	Con	Edinburgh East & Musselburgh		
Ballance, C.	Green		West of Scotland	1
Barrett, J.	LD	Linlithgow		
Barrie, S.	Lab	Dunfermline West		
Beamish, C.	Lab		South of Scotland	2
Bell, J. Ms.	LD	Ayr	South of Scotland	5
Boyack, S. Ms.	Lab	Edinburgh Central		
Brady, J.	SNP	Glasgow Springburn	Glasgow	6
Brankin, R. Ms.	Lab	Midlothian		
Brocklebank, E.	Con	Fife North East		
Brodie, C.	LD	Perth	Mid Scotland and Fife	6
Brown, I.	LD	Glasgow Anniesland		
Brown, K.	SNP	Falkirk East	Central Scotland	6
Brown, R.	LD	Glasgow Rutherglen	Glasgow	1
Buchan, G.	Con	Dundee West		
Buchan, G.	Con	Dunfermline West		
Byrne, J.	SNP	Glasgow Shettleston		

Scottish Parliament Elections 1999 – candidates (Continued)

Candidate	Party	Constituency	Region	Number on list
Campbell, C.	SNP	Renfrewshire West	West of Scotland	1
Cashley, C.	SNP	Dundee West		
Chisholm, M.*	Lab	Edinburgh North & Leith		
Coleshill, P.	LD	Dumbarton		
Cormack, C.	Con	Clydesdale		
Coyne, M. Ms.	Green		South of Scotland	1
Craig, M. Ms.	LD	Glasgow Kelvin	Glasgow	2
Craigie, C. Ms.	Lab	Cumbernauld & Kilsyth		
Crawford, B.	SNP		Mid Scotland and Fife	5
Crawford, D.	SNP		Highlands and Islands	7
Crawford, S.	SNP	Roxburgh & Berwickshire		
Creech, C. Ms.	SNP	Tweeddale, Ettrick & Lauderdale	South of Scotland	4
Cunningham, R. Ms.*	SNP	Perth	Mid Scotland and Fife	4
Curran, M. Ms.	Lab	Glasgow Ballieston		
Currie, R.	LD		Highlands and Islands	4
Dana, A. Ms.	SNP	Edinburgh North & Leith	Lothians	4
Davidson, D.	Con	Banff & Buchan		
Deacon, S. Ms.	Lab	Edinburgh East & Musselburgh		
Dewar, D.*	Lab	Glasgow Anniesland	Glasgow	1
Dick, E. Ms.	LD	Dundee West	North East Scotland	6
Eadie, H. Ms.	Lab	Dunfermline East		
Elder, D. Ms.	SNP	Glasgow Ballieston	Glasgow	2
Elder, J.	LD	Midlothian		
Elrick, M.	Lab	Aberdeen South		
Ewing, A. Ms.	SNP	Stirling	Mid Scotland and Fife	6
Ewing, F.	SNP	Inverness East, Nairn & Lochaber	Highlands and Islands	4
Ewing, M. Ms.*	SNP	Moray	Highlands and Islands	2
Ewing, W. Ms.	SNP		Highlands and Islands	1
Fabiani, L. Ms.	SNP	East Kilbride	Central Scotland	5
Falconer, M.	Green		Central Scotland	1
Farmer, G.	Green		Mid Scotland & Fife	1
Farquhar-Munro, J.	LD	Ross, Skye & Inverness West		
Farquharson, A. Ms.	Lab	Moray		
Ferguson, C.	Con	Strathkelvin & Bearsden		
Ferguson, P. Ms.	Lab	Glasgow Maryhill		
Fergusson, A.	Con	Galloway & Upper Nithsdale		
Findlay, A.	Con	Moray		
Findlay, R. Ms.	SNP	Eastwood	West of Scotland	7
Finnie, R.	LD	Greenock & Inverclyde	West of Scotland	1
Fitzpatrick, B.	Lab		Glasgow	2
Ford, M.	LD		North East Scotland	3
Fox, C. Ms.	Lab	Edinburgh West		
Foxley, M.	LD		Highlands and Islands	1

Scottish Parliament Elections 1999 – candidates (Continued)

Candidate	Party	Constituency	Region	Number on list
Fraser, D.	LD	Inverness East, Nairn & Lochaber	Highlands and Islands	3
Fraser, M.	Con	Tayside North		
Fry, M.	Con	Glasgow Maryhill		
Fryer, J. Ms.	LD	Glasgow Shettleston		
Galbraith, S.*	Lab	Strathkelvin & Bearsden	West of Scotland	1
Gallie, P.	Con	Ayr		
Geddes, K.	Lab		South of Scotland	1
Gibb, S.	SNP	Edinburgh Pentlands	Lothians	6
Gibson, I.	LD	Edinburgh Pentlands	Lothians	5
Gibson, K.	SNP	Glasgow Pollok	Glasgow	3
Gibson, W.	Con	Motherwell & Wishaw		
Glenn, M. Ms.	Lab		North East Scotland	2
Godman, P. Ms.	Lab	Renfrewshire West		
Goldie, A. Ms.	Con	Renfrewshire West		
Gorrie, D.*	LD		Central Scotland	1
Gray, I.	Lab	Edinburgh Pentlands		
Grieve, S. Ms.	LD	Clydesdale	South of Scotland	4
Hamblen, C. Ms.	LD		West of Scotland	5
Hamilton, D.	SNP	Argyll & Bute	Highlands and Islands	3
Hamilton, I.	SNP	Greenock & Inverclyde	West of Scotland	6
Hannay, D.	LD		South of Scotland	2
Harding, K.	Con	Fife Central		
Harper, R.	Green		Lothian	1
Harris, E. Ms.	LD		Mid Scotland and Fife	3
Harris, M. Ms.	Lab	Banff and Buchan		
Harris, R.	Con	Angus		
Haughie, I.	Con	Aberdeen North		
Hawthorn, E.	LD	East Kilbride		
Hayman, J. Ms.	LD	East Lothian	South of Scotland	3
Hendry, J.	Lab	Caithness, Sutherland & Easter Ross		
Henry, H.	Lab	Paisley South		
Higgins, K. Ms.	SNP		South of Scotland	6
Home Robertson, J.*	Lab	East Lothian		
Hook, J. Ms.	LD		Glasgow	5
Horne, J.	LD	Western Isles		
Hosie, S.	SNP	Kirkcaldy		
Hughes, J. Ms.	Lab	Glasgow Rutherglen		
Hutton, A.	Con	Roxburgh & Berwickshire		
Hyslop, F. Ms.	SNP		Lothians	3
Ingram, A.	SNP	Carrick, Cumnock & Doon Valley	South of Scotland	3
Jackson, G.	Lab	Glasgow Govan		
Jackson, S. Ms.	Lab	Stirling		
Jamieson, C. Ms.	Lab	Carrick, Cumnock & Doon Valley		
Jamieston, M. Ms.	Lab	Kilmarnock & Loudoun		

Scottish Parliament Elections 1999 – candidates (Continued)

Candidate	Party	Constituency	Region	Number on list
Jenkins, I.	LD	Tweeddale, Ettrick & Lauderdale		
Jenkins, R.	Con	Caithness, Sutherland & Easter Ross		
Johnston, M.	Con	Cunninghame North		
Johnston, N.	Con	Ochil		
Johnstone, A.	Con	Gordon		
Kearney, P.	SNP	Coatbridge & Chryston		
Kenton, P. Ms.	LD	Moray	Highlands and Islands	5
Kerr, A.	Lab	East Kilbride		
Laidlaw, S. Ms.	Con	Paisley South		
Lamont, J.	Lab	Glasgow Pollok		
Lawrie, R.	LD	Dundee East		
Leishman, M. Ms.	Con	Glasgow Cathcart		
Lind, G.	Con	Coatbridge & Chryston		
Lindhorst, G.	Con	Linlithgow		
Liston, J-A. Ms.	LD	Fife Central		
Livingston, M. Ms.	Lab	Kirkcaldy		
Lochhead, R.	SNP	Aberdeen Central	North East Scotland	4
Low, J. Ms.	Con	Edinburgh Central		
Luckhorst, D. Ms.	Con	Clydebank & Milngavie		
Lyon, G.	LD	Argyll & Bute		
MacAskill, K.	SNP	Edinburgh East & Musselburgh	Lothians	2
MacDonald, G.	LD	Falkirk East	Central Scotland	5
MacDonald, L.	Lab	Aberdeen Central		
MacDonald, M. Ms.	SNP	Edinburgh South	Lothians	1
MacFarlane, I.	LD	Stirling	Central Scotland	4
MacKay, A.	Lab	Edinburgh South		
MacKay, I.	SNP	Paisley North		
Mackie, M.	LD	Banff & Buchan	North East Scotland	2
MacLaren, M. Ms.	LD		Lothians	3
MacLean, K. Ms.	Lab	Dundee West		
MacMahon, M.	Lab	Hamilton North & Bellshill		
MacNeil, D.	Lab	Greenock & Inverclyde		
Mainland, J.	LD	Kirkcaldy		
Mair, R.	LD		Highlands and Islands	7
Mar & Kellie, J.	LD	Ochil	Mid Scotland and Fife	5
Martin, B.	SNP	Paisley South		
Martin, P.	Lab	Glasgow Springburn		
Martin, R.	Lab	Falkirk West		
Marwick, T. Ms.	SNP	Fife Central	Mid Scotland and Fife	3
Mason, T.	Con	Aberdeen Central		
Mather, J.	SNP	Ross, Skye & Inverness West	Highlands and Islands	5
Matheson, M.	SNP	Falkirk West	Central Scotland	3
McAllion, J.*	Lab	Dundee East	North East Scotland	1
McAlorum, K. Ms.	SNP	Hamilton North & Bellshill		
McAveety, F.	Lab	Glasgow Shettleston		
McCabe, T.	Lab	Hamilton South		

Scottish Parliament Elections 1999 – candidates (Continued)

Candidate	Party	Constituency	Region	Number on list
McCarra, G.	SNP	Livingston		
McCarthy, D.	SNP	Dunfermline East		
McCartin, E. Ms.	LD		West of Scotland	2
McConnell, J.	Lab	Motherwell & Wishaw		
McCurley, A. Ms.	LD	Eastwood		
McFatridge, I.	Lab	Angus		
McGregor, G.	Lab	Tweeddale, Ettrick & Lauderdale		
McGrigor, J.	Con	Western Isles		
McGugan, I. Ms.	SNP	Aberdeen South	North East Scotland	6
McGuigan, J.	SNP	Motherwell & Wishaw		
McInnes, C. Ms.	LD		West of Scotland	7
McIntosh, K.	Lab	Eastwood		
McIntosh, L. Ms.	Con	Kilmarnock & Loudoun		
McKee, I.	SNP	Edinburgh Central	Lothians	7
McKie, A.	LD		Highlands and Islands	6
McLean, B.	Lab		Lothians	2
McLeish, H.*	Lab	Fife Central	Mid Scotland and Fife	1
McLeod, F. Ms.	SNP	Strathkelvin & Bearsden	West of Scotland	4
McLeod, S. Ms.	Lab	Roxburgh and Berwickshire		
McLetchie, D.	Con	Edinburgh Pentlands		
McMillan, M. Ms.	Lab		Highlands and Islands	2
McNeill, P. Ms.	Lab	Glasgow Kelvin		
McNulty, D.	Lab	Clydebank & Milngavie		
Millar, C.	SNP	East Lothian		
Miller, D.	LD	Airdrie & Shotts		
Miller, G.	Con	Falkirk West		
Miller, M. Ms.	Lab		Mid Scotland and Fife	2
Milne, C.	Lab	Fife North East		
Milne, N. Ms.	Con	Aberdeen South		
Mitchell, I.	Con	Dundee East		
Mitchell, J. Ms.	LD	Galloway & Upper Nithsdale		
Mitchell, M. Ms.	Con	Hamilton South		
Monteith, B.	Con	Stirling		
Morgan, A.*	SNP	Galloway & Upper Nithsdale	South of Scotland	1
Morrison, A.	Lab	Western Isles		
Morrison, J.	LD		West of Scotland	6
Mowat, J.	SNP	Orkney		
Muldoon, B.	Lab	Livingston		
Mulligan, M. Ms.	Lab	Linlithgow		
Mullin, R.	SNP	Ayr	South of Scotland	7
Mundell, D.	Con	Dumfries		
Munro, D.	Lab	Ross, Skye & Inverness West		
Murray, E. Ms.	Lab	Dumfries		
Myles, A.	LD	Edinburgh Central	Lothians	4
Napier, C. Ms.	LD		South of Scotland	6
Neary, K. Ms.	SNP		Central Scotland	7
Neil, A.	SNP	Kilmarnock & Loudoun	Central Scotland	1
Nicholson, A.	SNP	Western Isles	Highlands and Islands	6

Scottish Parliament Elections 1999 – candidates (Continued)

Candidate	Party	Constituency	Region	Number on list
Norris, S.	SNP	Dumfries	South of Scotland	5
O'Brien, R.	Con	Glasgow Pollok		
O'Donnell, H.	LD	Cumbernauld & Kilsyth		
Oldfather, I. Ms.	Lab	Cunninghame South		
Oliver, M.	LD	Livingston		
Orr, A.	Con	Falkirk East		
Paris, M. Ms.	LD		Glasgow	4
Paterson, G. Ms.	SNP	Airdrie & Shotts	Central Scotland	4
Peacock, P.	Lab		Highlands and Islands	1
Peattie, C. Ms.	Lab	Falkirk East		
Petrie, D.	Con	Argyll & Bute		
Pickering, C. Ms.	Con	Glasgow Ballieston		
Pringle, M.	LD	Edinburgh South	Lothians	2
Quinan, L.	SNP	Dumbarton	West of Scotland	3
Radcliffe, N. Ms.	LD	Gordon		
Raffan, K.	LD		Mid Scotland and Fife	1
Ramsey, P.	Con	Paisley North		
Rasul, A.	Con	Glasgow Kelvin		
Raven, H.	Lab	Argyll & Bute		
Reece, D.	Con	Dumbarton		
Regent, P.	LD	Tayside North	Mid Scotland and Fife	7
Reid, G.	SNP	Ochil	Mid Scotland and Fife	2
Richard, C. Ms.	Con	East Lothian		
Richards, J. Ms.	Lab	Perth		
Robertson, A.	SNP	Midlothian		
Robertson, J. Ms.	LD		Mid Scotland and Fife	4
Robinson, G.	Con	Shetland		
Robison, S. Ms.	SNP	Dundee East	North East Scotland	5
Robson, E.	LD	Roxburgh & Berwickshire		
Ross Scott, J.	LD		South of Scotland	1
Ross, W.	SNP	Shetland		
Ross-Taylor, W.	Con	Airdrie & Shotts		
Roxburgh, M.	Con	Glasgow Springburn		
Rumbles, M.	LD	Aberdeenshire West & Kincardine	North East Scotland	4
Russell, M.	SNP	Cunninghame South	South of Scotland	2
Ruxton, C. Ms.	Con	Dunfermline East		
Salmond, A.*	SNP	Banff & Buchan	North East Scotland	1
Scanlon, M. Ms.	Con	Inverness East, Nairn & Lochaber		
Scott, E. Ms.	Green		Highlands & Islands	1
Scott, J.	Con	Carrick, Cumnock & Doon Valley		
Scott, J.	Con	Ross, Skye & Inverness West		
Scott, P.	SNP		Lothians	5
Scott, T.	LD	Shetland		
Scott-Hayward, M.	Con	Kirkcaldy		
Selkirk, Lord	Con	Edinburgh West		
Sempill, J.	Con	Edinburgh North & Leith		

Scottish Parliament Elections 1999 – candidates (Continued)

Candidate	Party	Constituency	Region	Number on list
Sewel, Lord	Lab		North East Scotland	3
Shiels, L. Ms.	Lab		Lothians	1
Simpson, R.	Lab	Ochil		
Slack, R.	Con	Cumbernauld & Kilsyth		
Smith, A.	LD	Falkirk West		
Smith, E. Ms.	Lab	Coatbridge & Chryston		
Smith, I.	LD	Fife North East		
Smith, M. Ms.	LD	Edinburgh West		
Speirs, D.	LD	Angus		
Spillane, R.	LD	Motherwell & Wishaw	Central Scotland	6
Starbuck, M.	Con	Glasgow Rutherglen		
Steel, D.	LD		Lothians	1
Stephen, N.	LD	Aberdeen South	North East Scotland	1
Stevenson, C.	Con	East Kilbride		
Stevenson, I.	Con	Perth		
Stevenson, S.	SNP	Linlithgow		
Stewart, J.	LD	Kilmarnock & Loudoun	Central Scotland	2
Stewart, K.	SNP	Glasgow Anniesland		
Stone, J.	LD	Caithness, Sutherland & Easter Ross		
Stronach, S.	SNP	Gordon	North East Scotland	7
Sturgeon, N. Ms.	SNP	Glasgow Govan	Glasgow	1
Sutherland, G.	SNP	Edinburgh West		
Sutherland, L. Ms.	Lab.		Central Scotland	2
Swinney, J.*	SNP	Tayside North	Mid Scotland and Fife	1
Thomas, M. Ms.	LD	Edinburgh East & Musselburgh		
Thomson, E. Ms.	Lab	Aberdeen North		
Thomson, S.	Con	Hamilton North & Bellshill		
Thurso, J.	LD		Highlands and Islands	2
Tombs, S.	LD	Edinburgh North & Leith		
Tosh, M.	Con	Cunninghame South		
Tough, A.	LD		West of Scotland	4
Turnbull, G.	Con	Midlothian		
Turnbull, K. Ms.	Lab	Clydesdale		
Tynan, B.	Lab.		Central Scotland	1
Ullrich, K. Ms.	SNP	Cunninghame North	West of Scotland	2
Urquhart, J. Ms.	SNP	Caithness, Sutherland & Easter Ross		
Utting, K. Ms.	LD		Lothians	6
Waddell, R.	LD		Central Scotland	3
Wallace, B.	Con	Aberdeenshire West & Kincardine		
Wallace, J.*	LD	Orkney		
Wallace, N.	LD	Dumfries		
Watson, M.	Lab	Glasgow Cathcart		
Watt, M. Ms.	SNP	Aberdeenshire West & Kincardine		
Welsh, A.*	SNP	Angus	North East Scotland	2

Scottish Parliament Elections 1999 – candidates (Continued)

Candidate	Party	Constituency	Region	Number on list
Welsh, C.	SNP	Fife North East	Mid Scotland and Fife	7
Welsh, I.	Lab	Ayr		
White, S. Ms.	SNP	Glasgow Kelvin	Glasgow	4
Whitefield, K. Ms.	Lab	Airdrie & Shotts		
Whitehead, M. Ms.	SNP	Glasgow Cathcart	Glasgow	5
Whyte, I.	Con	Edinburgh South		
Wilkinson, R.	Con	Greenock & Inverclyde		
Wilson, A.	SNP	Cumbernauld & Kilsyth	Central Scotland	2
Wilson, A.	Lab	Cunninghame North		
Wilson, B.	SNP	Glasgow Maryhill	Glasgow	7
Wilson, N. Ms.	Lab		West of Scotland	2
Winning, A. Ms.	SNP	Clydesdale		
Young, J.	Con	Eastwood		
Younger, D.	Con	Livingston		
Yuill, I.	LD		North East Scotland	5
Yuill, J.	SNP	Clydebank & Milngavie	West of Scotland	5
Zawadski, C.	Con	Orkney		

*Current Member of the House of Commons

Welsh Assembly Elections 1999 – candidates*

Candidate	Party	Constituency	Region	Number on list
Al-Nuaimi, M.	Lab		South Wales East	4
Andrew, S.	Con	Vale of Clwyd		
Aubel, F.	Con	Preseli Pembrokeshire	Mid and West Wales	4
Ash, A. Ms.	Lab		South Wales Easr	1
Ball, J.	PC	Swansea East		
Barrett, L. Ms.	Lab	Cardiff South & Penarth		
Bates, M.	LD	Montgomeryshire		
Battle, M. Ms.	Lab	Ceredigion		
Black, P.	LD	Swansea East	South Wales West	1
Bone, P.	Con	Newport East		
Bourne, N.	Con	Brecon & Radnorshire	Mid and West Wales	1
Bowen, D.	PC		South Wales West	4
Bradney, D.	Green		Mid and West Wales	1
Brown, G.	LD		Mid and West Wales	3
Bryant, C.	PC	Preseli Pembrokeshire		
Brynach, S.	PC	Vale of Clwyd	North Wales	2
Burnham, E. Ms.	LD	Delyn	North Wales	2
Bush, E. Ms.	PC	Cardiff West	South Wales Central	3
Butler, R. Ms.	Lab	Newport West		
Cairns, A.	Con	Bridgend	South Wales West	1
Cameron, A.	LD	Newport East	South Wales East	3
Canning, J.	PC	Bridgend		
Chambers, J. Ms.	Con	Neath		
Chapman, C. Ms.	Lab	Cynon Valley		
Clarke, J.	LD	Alyn & Deeside		
Clarke, J.	LD	Ynys Mon		
Coghill, R.	Green		South Wales East	1
Cox, A.	PC	Merthyr Tydfil & Rhymney		
Dafis, C.*	PC		Mid and West Wales	2
David, W.	Lab	Rhondda		
Davidson, J. Ms.	Lab	Pontypridd		
Davies, A.	Lab	Swansea West		
Davies, D.	LD	Neath		
Davies, D.	Con	Monmouth	South Wales East	1
Davies, G.	Con	Montgomeryshire	Mid and West Wales	1
Davies, G.	PC	Rhondda		
Davies, J.	PC		South Wales East	1
Davies, J. Ms.	PC	Aberavon	South Wales West	1
Davies, K.	LD	Aberavon	South Wales West	4
Davies, M. Ms.	Con	Aberavon		
Davies, M. Ms.	Con	Cardiff South & Penarth		
Davies, R.*	Lab	Caerphilly		
Dixon, J.	LD	Cardiff West		
Drakeford, M.	Lab	Cardiff Central		
Dumper, T.	LD	Llanelli		
Edwards, D.	Con	Carmarthen West & South Pembrokeshire		
Edwards, R.	Lab	Preseli Pembrokeshire		
Elis Thomas, D.	PC	Meirionnydd Nant Conwy		

Welsh Assembly Elections 1999 – candidates (continued)

Candidate	Party	Constituency	Region	Number on list
Elis, M. Ms.	PC	Delyn		
Elphick, F. Ms.	Con	Wrexham		
Essex, S. Ms.	Lab	Cardiff North	South Wales Central	2
Evans, D.	LD	Ceredigion		
Evans, D. Ms.	Lab		Mid and West Wales	2
Evans, H.	LD	Gower	South Wales West	3
Feeley, R. Ms.	LD	Clywd West	North Wales	4
Feld, V. Ms.	Lab	Swansea East		
Formstone, N.	Con	Alyn & Deeside		
Francis, H.	Lab		South Wales West	2
Francis, M. Ms.	Lab		South Wales West	1
Franks, C.	PC	Vale of Glamorgan		
Garrard, A. Ms.	Lab	Llanelli		
Gasson, J. Ms.	LD		South Wales Central	3
German, M.	LD	Caerphilly	South Wales East	1
Gething, V.	Lab		Mid and West Wales	3
Gibbons, B.	Lab	Aberavon		
Gough, R.	PC	Caerphilly		
Graham, W.	Con	Newport West	South Wales East	2
Gray, J. Ms.	LD	Torfaen	South Wales East	4
Greenwood, J. Ms.	Con	Cardiff West		
Gregory, J. Ms.	Lab	Ogmore		
Griffiths, J.	Lab	Newport East		
Griffiths, P.	Lab		South Wales West	4
Grigg, B.	Green		South Wales West	1
Gwyther, C. Ms.	Lab	Carmarthen West & South Pembrokeshire		
Halford, A. Ms.	Lab	Delyn		
Hancock, B.	PC	Islwyn		
Hancock, B. Ms.	PC	Pontypridd	South Wales Central	4
Harding, B.	Con	Llanelli		
Harris, K.	LD	Clwyd South		
Hart, E. Ms.	Lab	Gower		
Hayward, E.	Con	Cynon Valley		
Hewitt, C.	Lab	Montgomeryshire		
Hobbins, P.	Con	Rhondda		
Holland, C.	PC	Newport East		
Hopkins, K.	Lab		South Wales Central	3
Hubbard, M.	PC	Monmouth		
Hughes, B.	Con	Swansea East	South Wales West	3
Hughes, J. Ms.	LD	Carmarthen East & Dinefwr	Mid and West Wales	2
Humphreys, C. Ms.	LD	Conwy	North Wales	1
Humphreys, R.	LD	Bridgend	South Wales West	2
Hutt, J. Ms.	Lab	Vale of Glamorgan		
Huxley, L.	PC		Mid and West Wales	4
Hyde, C. Ms.	Con	Merthyr Tydfil & Rhymney	South Wales East	3
Inglefield, S. Ms.	Con	Pontypridd	South Wales Central	4
Jakeway, K.	Green		South Wales Central	1
Janes, I.	Lab	Brecon & Radnorshire		

Welsh Assembly Elections 1999 – candidates (continued)

Candidate	Party	Constituency	Region	Number on list
Jarman, P. Ms.	PC		South Wales Central	1
Jones, A.	Con	Gower		
Jones, A. Ms.	Lab	Vale of Clwyd		
Jones, C.	Lab	Bridgend		
Jones, D.	Con	Clwyd South		
Jones, D.	Con	Conwy	North Wales	3
Jones, D. Ms.	Lab	Meirionnydd Nant Conwy		
Jones, E.	LD	Merthyr Tydfil & Rhymney		
Jones, E. Ms.	PC	Ceredigion		
Jones, G.	PC	Conwy		
Jones, G. Ms.	PC		South Wales East	3
Jones, H. Ms.	PC	Llanelli	Mid and West Wales	1
Jones, I.*	PC	Ynys Mon		
Jones, S.	Con	Cardiff Central	South Wales Central	3
Jones, T.	Lab	Caernarfon	North Wales	1
Jones, T.	PC	Neath		
Killock, J.	Green		North Wales	1
Law, P.	Lab	Blaenau Gwent		
Lewis, H.	Lab	Merthyr Tydfil & Rhymney		
Lines, C.	LD	Monmouth		
Little, F.	LD	Vale of Glamorgan		
Llewelyn, C.	Lab	Carmarthen East & Dinefwr		
Llewelyn, R.	PC	Carmarthen West & South Pembrokeshire		
Lloyd Davies, H.	Con	Ceredigion		
Lloyd, D.	LD	Preseli Pembrokeshire	Mid and West Wales	4
Lloyd, D.	PC	Swansea West	South Wales West	2
Lloyd, P.	LD	Vale of Clwyd	North Wales	3
Lumley, K. Ms.	Con	Delyn	North Wales	4
Mann, C.	PC	Cardiff North		
Marek, J.*	Lab	Wrexham		
Maw-Cornish, J. Ms.	LD	Cardiff South & Penarth		
Meikle, A.	LD	Cardiff North		
Melding, D.	Con	Vale of Glamorgan	South Wales Central	2
Michael, A.*	Lab		Mid and West Wales	1
Middlehurst, T.	Lab	Alyn & Deeside		
Morgan, J.	Con	Cardiff North	South Wales Central	1
Morgan, R.*	Lab	Cardiff West	South Wales Central	1
Morgan, W. Ms.	Lab		South Wales Central	4
Naish, B. Ms.	Con	Caernarfon		
Neagle, L. Ms.	Lab	Torfaen		
Newbury, J.	LD	Swansea West		
O'Toole, C. Ms.	LD	Wrexham		
Orsi, G.	LD	Pontypridd	South Wales Central	2
Owen A.	Lab	Ynys Mon		
Owen, A. Ms.	PC	Alyn & Deeside		
Owen, G.	PC		North Wales	4
Peterson, D.	PC	Brecon & Radnorshire		
Pritchard, M. Ms.	Lab		North Wales	2

Welsh Assembly Elections 1999 – candidates (continued)

Candidate	Party	Constituency	Region	Number on list
Pugh, A.	Lab	Clywd West		
Randerson, J. Ms.	LD	Cardiff Central	South Wales Central	1
Reid, S. Ms.	PC		South Wales West	3
Rhys Jones, D.	PC	Gower		
Richards, D. Ms.	PC		Mid and West Wales	3
Richards, P.	PC	Cynon Valley		
Richards, R.	Con	Clywd West	North Wales	1
Richards, S. Ms.	Lab		Mid and West Wales	4
Roberts, F. Ms.	PC		North Wales	3
Roberts, N. Ms.	Lab		North Wales	4
Rogers, J.	PC	Ogmore		
Rogers, K.	LD	Blaenau Gwent		
Rogers, P.	Con	Ynys Mon	North Wales	2
Rowlands, J.	PC	Cardiff South & Penarth		
Ryder, J. Ms.	PC	Wrexham	North Wales	1
Senior, D.	PC	Montgomeryshire		
Shankland, D.	LD	Caernarfon		
Sherrington, C. Ms.	Lab	Conwy		
Short, C. Ms.	Lab	Monmouth	South Wales East	3
Sinclair, K. Ms.	Lab	Clwyd South		
Smart, C.	Con	Ogmore	South Wales West	2
Smith, B.	Lab		South Wales East	2
Smith, R.	Lab		South Wales West	3
Stevens, C.	Con	Islwyn		
Stoddart, H. Ms.	Con	Carmarthen East & Dinefwr		
Taylor, M. Ms.	Con	Caerphilly	South Wales East	4
Thomas, D.	Con	Blaenau Gwent		
Thomas, G. Ms.	Lab	Neath		
Thomas, K. Ms.	Con	Torfaen		
Thomas, O.	PC	Cardiff Central	South Wales Central	2
Thomas, R.	PC	Carmarthen East & Dinefwr		
Turner, N.	PC	Torfaen		
Valerio, P.	Con	Swansea West	South Wales West	4
Vickery, B.	PC	Newport West		
Watkins, V. Ms.	LD	Newport West	South Wales East	2
Waye, S. Ms.	LD	Ogmore		
Whittle, L. Ms.	PC		South Wales East	4
Wigley, D.*	PC	Caernarfon		
Williams, E.	Lab		North Wales	3
Williams, E. Ms.	PC	Clywd West		
Williams, H.	PC	Clwyd South		
Williams, K. Ms.	LD	Brecon & Radnorshire		
Williams, M. Ms.	LD	Rhondda		
Williams, O.	Con	Meirionnydd Nant Conwy	Mid and West Wales	2
Williams, P.	PC	Blaenau Gwent	South Wales East	2
Williams, R.	LD	Carmarthen West & South Pembrokeshire	Mid and West Wales	1
Williams, S.	Lab	Islwyn		
Willott, A. Ms.	LD	Cynon Valley	South Wales Central	4
Worley, G.	LD	Meirionnydd Nant Conwy		

*Current Member of the House of Commons

Appendix 2: Alphabetic list of Northern Ireland Assembly Members

Candidate	Party	Constituency
Adams, G.	SF	Belfast West
Adamson, I.	UUP	Belfast East
Agnew, W.	UU	Belfast North
Alderdice, J.	AP	Belfast East
Armitage, Ms. P.	UUP	Londonderry East
Armstrong W.	UUP	Mid Ulster
Attwood, A.	SDLP	Belfast West
Beggs, R.	UUP	Antrim East
Bell, Ms. E.	AP	North Down
Bell, W.	UUP	Lagan Valley
Benson, T.	UUP	Strangford
Berry, P.	DUP	Newry and Armagh
Birnie, J.	UUP	Belfast South
Boyd, N.	UKU	South Antrim
Bradley, P.	SDLP	South Down
Byrne, J.	SDLP	West Tyrone
Campbell, G.	DUP	Londonderry East
Carrick, W.	DUP	Upper Bann
Carson, Ms. J.	UUP	Fermanagh and South Tyrone
Close, S.	AP	Lagan Valley
Clyde, S.	DUP	South Antrim
Cobain, F.	UUP	Belfast North
Coulter, R.	UUP	North Antrim
Dallat, J.	SDLP	Londonderry East
Dalton, D.	UUP	South Antrim
Davis, I.	UUP	Lagan Valley
De Brun, Ms. B.	SF	Belfast West
Dodds, N.	DUP	Belfast North
Doherty, A.	SDLP	Londonderry East
Doherty, P.	SF	West Tyrone
Douglas, B.	Union	Londonderry East
Durkan, M.	SDLP	Foyle
Empey, R.	UUP	Belfast East
Ervine, D.	PUP	Belfast East
Farren, S.	SDLP	North Antrim
Fee, J.	SDLP	Newry and Armagh
Ford, D.	AP	South Antrim
Foster, S.	UUP	Fermanagh and South Tyrone
Gallagher, T.	SDLP	Fermanagh and South Tyrone
Gibson, O.	DUP	West Tyrone
Gildernew, Ms. M.	SF	Fermanagh and South Tyrone
Gorman, J.	UUP	North Down
Hanna, Ms. C.	SDLP	Belfast South
Haughey, D.	SDLP	Mid Ulster

Northern Ireland Assembly Members (continued)

Candidate	Party	Constituency
Hay, W.	DUP	Foyle
Hendron, J.	SDLP	Belfast West
Hilditch, D.	DUP	Antrim East
Hume, J.	SDLP	Foyle
Hussey, D.	UUP	West Tyrone
Hutchinson, B.	PUP	Belfast North
Hutchinson, R.	UKU	Antrim East
Kane, G.	DUP	North Antrim
Kelly, G.	SF	Belfast North
Kelly, J.	SF	Mid Ulster
Kennedy, T.	UUP	Newry and Armagh
Leslie, J.	UUP	North Antrim
Lewsley, Ms. P.	SDLP	Lagan Valley
Maginness, A.	SDLP	Belfast North
Mallon, S.	SDLP	Newry and Armagh
Maskey, A.	SF	Belfast West
McCarthy, K.	AP	Strangford
McCartney, R.	UKU	North Down
McClelland, D.	SDLP	South Antrim
McCrea, R.	DUP	Mid Ulster
McDonnell, A.	SDLP	Belfast South
McElduff, B.	SF	West Tyrone
McFarland, R.	UUP	North Down
McGimpsey, M.	UUP	Belfast South
McGrady, E.	SDLP	South Down
McGuinness, M.	SF	Mid Ulster
McHugh, G.	SF	Fermanagh and South Tyrone
McLarty, D.	UUP	Londonderry East
McLaughlin, M.	SF	Foyle
McMenamin, E.	SDLP	West Tyrone
McNamee, P.	SF	Newry and Armagh
McWilliams, Ms. M.	NIWC	Belfast South
Molloy, F.	SF	Mid Ulster
Morrice, Ms. J.	NIWC	North Down
Morrow, M.	DUP	Fermanagh and South Tyrone
Murphy, C.	SF	Newry and Armagh
Murphy, M.	SF	South Down
Neeson, S.	AP	Antrim East
Nelis, Ms. M.	SF	Foyle
Nesbitt, D.	UUP	South Down
O'Connor, D.	SDLP	Antrim East
O'Hagan, Ms. D.	SF	Upper Bann
O'Neill, E.	SDLP	South Down
Paisley, I. Jnr.	DUP	North Antrim
Paisley, I. Snr.	DUP	North Antrim
Poots, E.	DUP	Lagan Valley
Ramsey, Ms. S.	SF	Belfast West

Northern Ireland Assembly Members (continued)

Candidate	Party	Constituency
Robinson, I.	DUP	Strangford
Robinson, P.	DUP	Belfast East
Robinson, S.	DUP	Belfast South
Roche, P.	UKU	Lagan Valley
Rodgers, Ms. B.	SDLP	Upper Bann
Savage, G.	UUP	Upper Bann
Shannon, R.	DUP	Strangford
Steele, Ms. M.	UUP	Antrim East
Taylor, J.	UUP	Strangford
Tierney, J.	SDLP	Foyle
Trimble, D.	UUP	Upper Bann
Watson, D.	United	Upper Bann
Weir, P.	UUP	North Down
Wells, J.	DUP	South Down
Wilson, C.	UKU	Strangford
Wilson, J.	UUP	South Antrim
Wilson, S.	DUP	Belfast East

THE VACHER DOD PUBLISHING GROUP TITLES

Dod's Parliamentary Companion 1999
*Published since 1832. Parliament's leading annual reference book.
Over 1,300 pages.*

The Vacher Dod House of Commons Companion
*Focuses on the House of Commons. MPs' biographies,
constituency profiles and results. Government Departments,
Select Committees, Procedure and Standing Orders.
Over 1,000 pages.*

Vacher's Parliamentary Companion
*Published since 1832. Parliament's foremost quarterly guide.
Available in A5 or handy pocket size. 450 pages.*

Handbook of House of Commons Procedure 1999
*Written and now completely revised by a Clerk with fifteen years'
experience of working in the House. An essential reference work.*

Vacher's European Companion
*26th Anniversary. A wide-ranging European reference book.
UK MEPs and prominent European personalities' biographies.
Updated quarterly. 450 pages.*

New Britain: New Elections 1999
*An indispensable guide to the new constitutional and electoral
architecture of the United Kingdom.*

The Prime Ministers from Walpole to Macmillan
*Forty-four biographies covering 242 tumultuous years
which helped to shape the nation. 175 pages.*

Vacher Dod Publishing Limited
PO Box 3700, Westminster, London SW1E 5NP
Tel: 0171-828 7256   Fax: 0171-828 7269
E-mail: politics@vacherdod.co.uk

Appendix 3: Parliamentary Constituencies and the new Electoral Geography

No	Constituency	Member of Parliament	Party	European seat	Parliament/ Assembly area	Local authorities
1	Aberavon	John Morris	Lab	Wales	South Wales West	Neath and Port Talbot
2	Aberdeen Central	Frank Doran	Lab	Scotland	North East Scotland	Aberdeen
3	Aberdeen North	Malcolm Savidge	Lab	Scotland	North East Scotland	Aberdeen
4	Aberdeen South	Anne Begg	Lab	Scotland	North East Scotland	Aberdeen
5	Aberdeenshire West & Kincardine	Robert Smith	LD	Scotland	North East Scotland	Aberdeenshire
6	Airdrie & Shotts	Helen Liddell	Lab	Scotland	Central Scotland	North Lanarkshire
7	Aldershot	Gerald Howarth	Con	South East	—	Hampshire, Hart, Rushmoor
8	Aldridge – Brownhills	Richard Shepherd	Con	West Midlands	—	Walsall
9	Altrincham & Sale West	Graham Brady	Con	North West	—	Trafford
10	Alyn & Deeside	Barry Jones	Lab	Wales	North Wales	Flintshire
11	Amber Valley	Judy Mallaber	Lab	East Midlands	—	Derbyshire, Amber Valley, Erewash
12	Angus	Andrew Welsh	SNP	Scotland	North East Scotland	Angus, Perthshire and Kinross
13	Antrim East	Roy Beggs	UU	Northern Ireland	Antrim East	Carrickfergus, Larne, Newtonabbey
14	Antrim North	Ian Paisley	DUP	Northern Ireland	Antrim North	Ballymena, Ballymoney, Moyle
15	Antrim South	Clifford Forsythe	UU	Northern Ireland	Antrim South	Antrim, Newtonabbey
16	Argyll & Bute	Ray Michie	LD	Scotland	Highlands and Islands	Argyll & Bute
17	Arundel & South Downs	Howard Flight	Con	South East	—	West Sussex, Arun, Chichester, Horsham, Mid Sussex
18	Ashfield	Geoff Hoon	Lab	East Midlands	—	Nottinghamshire, Ashfield, Broxtowe
19	Ashford	Damian Green	Con	South East	—	Kent, Ashford
20	Ashton under Lyne	Robert Sheldon	Lab	North West	—	Oldham, Tameside
21	Aylesbury	David Lidington	Con	South East	—	Buckinghamshire, Aylesbury Vale, Chiltern, Wycombe
22	Ayr	Sandra Osborne	Lab	Scotland	South of Scotland	South Ayrshire
23	Banbury	Anthony Baldry	Con	South East	—	Oxfordshire, Cherwell
24	Banff & Buchan	Alex Salmond	SNP	Scotland	North East Scotland	Aberdeenshire
25	Barking	Margaret Hodge	Lab	London	City and East	Barking and Dagenham

No	Constituency	Member of Parliament	Party	European seat	Parliament/ Assembly area	Local authorities
26	Barnsley Central	Eric Illsley	Lab	Yorkshire & the Humber	—	Barnsley
27	Barnsley East & Mexborough	Jeff Ennis	Lab	Yorkshire & the Humber	—	Barnsley, Doncaster
28	Barnsley West & Penistone	Michael Clapham	Lab	Yorkshire & the Humber	—	Barnsley
29	Barrow & Furness	John Hutton	Lab	North West	—	Cumbria, Barrow-in-Furness, South Lakeland
30	Basildon	Angela Smith	Lab	Eastern	—	Essex, Basildon, Thurrock
31	Basingstoke	Andrew Hunter	Con	South East	—	Hampshire, Basingstoke and Deane
32	Bassetlaw	Joe Ashton	Lab	East Midlands	—	Nottinghamshire, Bassetlaw, Mansfield
33	Bath	Don Foster	LD	South West	—	Bath and North East Somerset
34	Batley & Spen	Mike Wood	Lab	Yorkshire & the Humber	—	Kirklees
35	Battersea	Martin Linton	Lab	London	Merton and Wandsworth	Wandsworth
36	Beaconsfield	Dominic Grieve	Con	South East	—	Buckinghamshire, South Buckinghamshire, Wycombe
37	Beckenham	Jacqui Lait	Con	South East	—	Bromley
38	Bedford	Patrick Hall	Lab	Eastern	—	Bedfordshire, Bedford
39	Bedfordshire Mid	Jonathan Sayeed	Con	Eastern	—	Bedfordshire, Bedford, Mid Bedfordshire, South Bedfordshire
40	Bedfordshire North East	Nicholas Lyell	Con	Eastern	—	Bedfordshire, Bedford, Mid Bedfordshire
41	Bedfordshire South West	David Madel	Con	Eastern	—	Bedfordshire, South Bedfordshire
42	Belfast East	Peter Robinson	DUP	Northern Ireland	Belfast East	Belfast, Castlereagh
43	Belfast North	Cecil Walker	UU	Northern Ireland	Belfast North	Belfast, Newtonabbey
44	Belfast South	Martin Smyth	UU	Northern Ireland	Belfast South	Belfast, Castlereagh
45	Belfast West	Gerry Adams	SF	Northern Ireland	Belfast West	Belfast, Lisburn

No	Constituency	Member of Parliament	Party	European seat	Parliament/ Assembly area	Local authorities
46	Berwick-upon-Tweed	Alan Beith	LD	North East	–	Northumberland, Alnwick, Berwick-upon-Tweed, Castle Morpeth
47	Bethnal Green & Bow	Oona King	Lab	London	City and East	Tower Hamlets
48	Beverley & Holderness	James Cran	Con	Yorkshire & the Humber	–	East Riding of Yorkshire
49	Bexhill & Battle	Charles Wardle	Con	South East	–	East Sussex, Rother, Wealden
50	Bexleyheath & Crayford	Nigel Beard	Lab	London	Bexley and Bromley	Bexley
51	Billericay	Teresa Gorman	Con	Eastern	–	Essex, Basildon
52	Birkenhead	Frank Field	Lab	North West	–	Wirral
53	Birmingham Edgbaston	Gisela Stuart	Lab	West Midlands	–	Birmingham
54	Birmingham Erdington	Robin Corbett	Lab	West Midlands	–	Birmingham
55	Birmingham Hall Green	Stephen McCabe	Lab	West Midlands	–	Birmingham
56	Birmingham Hodge Hill	Terry Davis	Lab	West Midlands	–	Birmingham
57	Birmingham Ladywood	Clare Short	Lab	West Midlands	–	Birmingham
58	Birmingham Northfield	Richard Burden	Lab	West Midlands	–	Birmingham
59	Birmingham Perry Barr	Jeff Rooker	Lab	West Midlands	–	Birmingham
60	Birmingham Selly Oak	Lynne Jones	Lab	West Midlands	–	Birmingham
61	Birmingham Sparkbrook & Small Heath	Roger Godsiff	Lab	West Midlands	–	Birmingham
62	Birmingham Yardley	Estelle Morris	Lab	West Midlands	–	Birmingham
63	Bishop Auckland	Derek Foster	Lab	North East	–	Durham, Sedgefield, Teesdale, Wear Valley
64	Blaby	Andrew Robathan	Con	East Midlands	–	Leicestershire, Blaby, Harborough
65	Blackburn	Jack Straw	Lab	North West	–	Blackburn with Darwen
66	Blackpool North & Fleetwood	Joan Humble	Lab	North West	–	Lancashire, Blackpool, Wyre
67	Blackpool South	Gordon Marsden	Lab	North West	–	Blackpool
68	Blaenau Gwent	Llew Smith	Lab	Wales	South Wales East	Blaenau Gwent
69	Blaydon	John McWilliam	Lab	North East	–	Gateshead
70	Blyth Valley	Ronnie Campbell	Lab	North East	–	Northumberland, Blyth Valley

No	Constituency	Member of Parliament	Party	European seat	Parliament/ Assembly area	Local authorities
71	Bognor Regis & Littlehampton	Nick Gibb	Con	South East	–	West Sussex, Arun
72	Bolsover	Dennis Skinner	Lab	East Midlands	–	Derbyshire, Bolsover, North East Derbyshire
73	Bolton North East	David Crausby	Lab	North West	–	Bolton
74	Bolton South East	Brian Iddon	Lab	North West	–	Bolton
75	Bolton West	Ruth Kelly	Lab	North West	–	Bolton
76	Bootle	Joe Benton	Lab	North West	–	Sefton
77	Boston & Skegness	Richard Body	Con	East Midlands	–	Lincolnshire, Boston, East Lindsey
78	Bosworth	David Tredinnick	Con	East Midlands		Leicestershire, Hinckley and Bosworth
79	Bournemouth East	David Atkinson	Con	South West	–	Bournemouth
80	Bournemouth West	John Butterfill	Con	South West	–	Bournemouth
81	Bracknell	Andrew Mackay	Con	South East	–	Bracknell Forest, Wokingham
82	Bradford North	Terry Rooney	Lab	Yorkshire & the Humber	–	Bradford
83	Bradford South	Gerry Sutcliffe	Lab	Yorkshire & the Humber	–	Bradford
84	Bradford West	Marsha Singh	Lab	Yorkshire & the Humber	–	Bradford
85	Braintree	Alan Hurst	Lab	Eastern	–	Essex, Braintree
86	Brecon & Radnorshire	Richard Livsey	LD	Wales	Mid and West Wales	Powys
87	Brent East	Ken Livingstone	Lab	London	Brent and Harrow	Brent
88	Brent North	Barry Gardiner	Lab	London	Brent and Harrow	Brent
89	Brent South	Paul Boateng	Lab	London	Brent and Harrow	Brent
90	Brentford & Isleworth	Ann Keen	Lab	London	South West	Hounslow
91	Brentwood & Ongar	Eric Pickles	Con	Eastern	–	Essex, Brentwood, Epping Forest
92	Bridgend	Win Griffiths	Lab	Wales	South Wales West	Bridgend, Vale of Glamorgan
93	Bridgwater	Tom King	Con	South West	–	Somerset, Sedgemoor, West Somerset

No	Constituency	Member of Parliament	Party	European seat	Parliament/ Assembly area	Local authorities
94	Brigg & Goole	Ian Cawsey	Lab	Yorkshire & the Humber	–	East Riding of Yorkshire, North Lincolnshire
95	Brighton Kemptown	Desmond Turner	Lab	South East	–	East Sussex, Brighton and Hove, Lewes
96	Brighton Pavilion	David Lepper	Lab	South East		Brighton and Hove
97	Bristol East	Jean Corston	Lab	South West		Bristol
98	Bristol North West	Douglas Naysmith	Lab	South West		Bristol, South Gloucestershire
99	Bristol South	Dawn Primarolo	Lab	South West		Bristol
100	Bristol West	Valerie Davey	Lab	South West		Bristol
101	Bromley & Chislehurst	Eric Forth	Con	London	Bexley and Bromley	Bromley
102	Bromsgrove	Julie Kirkbride	Con	West Midlands		Worcestershire, Bromsgrove
103	Broxbourne	Marion Roe	Con	Eastern		Hertfordshire, Broxbourne, Welwyn Hatfield
104	Broxtowe	Nick Palmer	Lab	East Midlands		Nottinghamshire, Broxtowe
105	Buckingham	John Bercow	Con	South East		Buckinghamshire, Aylesbury Vale
106	Burnley	Peter Pike	Lab	North West		Lancashire, Burnley
107	Burton	Janet Dean	Lab	West Midlands		Staffordshire, East Staffordshire
108	Bury North	David Chaytor	Lab	North West		Bury
109	Bury South	Ivan Lewis	Lab	North West		Bury
110	Bury St Edmunds	David Ruffley	Con	Eastern		Suffolk, Mid Suffolk, St. Edmundsbury
111	Caernarfon	Dafydd Wigley	PC	Wales	North Wales	Gwynedd
112	Caerphilly	Ron Davies	Lab	Wales	South Wales East	Caerphilly
113	Caithness, Sutherland & Easter Ross	Robert Maclennan	LD	Scotland	Highlands and Islands	Highland
114	Calder Valley	Christine McCafferty	Lab	Yorkshire & the Humber		Calderdale
115	Camberwell & Peckham	Harriet Harman	Lab	London	Lambeth and Southwark	Southwark
116	Cambridge	Anne Campbell	Lab	Eastern		Cambridgeshire, Cambridge

No	Constituency	Member of Parliament	Party	European seat	Parliament/ Assembly area	Local authorities
117	Cambridgeshire North East	Malcolm Moss	Con	Eastern	—	Cambridgeshire, East Cambridgeshire, Fenland, Peterborough
118	Cambridgeshire North West	Brian Mawhinney	Con	Eastern	—	Cambridgeshire, Huntingdonshire, Peterborough
119	Cambridgeshire South	Andrew Lansley	Con	Eastern	—	Cambridgeshire, Cambridge, South Cambridgeshire
120	Cambridgeshire South East	James Paice	Con	Eastern	—	Cambridgeshire, East Cambridgeshire, South Cambridgeshire
121	Cannock Chase	Tony Wright	Lab	West Midlands	—	Staffordshire, Cannock Chase, South Staffordshire
122	Canterbury	Julian Brazier	Con	South East	—	Kent, Canterbury
123	Cardiff Central	Jon Owen Jones	Lab	Wales	South Wales Central	Cardiff
124	Cardiff North	Julie Morgan	Lab	Wales	South Wales Central	Cardiff
125	Cardiff South & Penarth	Alun Michael	Lab	Wales	South Wales Central	Cardiff, Vale of Glamorgan
126	Cardiff West	Rhodri Morgan	Lab	Wales	South Wales Central	Cardiff
127	Carlisle	Eric Martlew	Lab	North West	—	Cumbria, Carlisle
128	Carmarthen East & Dinefwr	Alan Wynne Williams	Lab	Wales	Mid and West Wales	Carmarthenshire
129	Carmarthen West & South Pembrokeshire	Nicholas Ainger	Lab	Wales	Mid and West Wales	Carmarthenshire, Pembrokeshire
130	Carrick, Cumnock & Doon Valley	George Foulkes	Lab	Scotland	South of Scotland	East Ayrshire, South Ayrshire
131	Carshalton & Wallington	Tom Brake	LD	London	Croydon and Sutton	Sutton
132	Castle Point	Christine Butler	Lab	Eastern	—	Essex, Castle Point
133	Ceredigion	Cynog Dafis	PC	Wales	Mid and West Wales	Ceredigion
134	Charnwood	Stephen Dorrell	Con	East Midlands	—	Leicestershire, Blaby, Charnwood, Hinckley and Bosworth
135	Chatham & Aylesford	Jonathan Shaw	Lab	South East	—	Kent, Medway Towns, Tonbridge and Malling
136	Cheadle	Stephen Day	Con	North West	—	Stockport

No	Constituency	Member of Parliament	Party	European seat	Parliament/ Assembly area	Local authorities
137	Chelmsford West	Simon Burns	Con	Eastern	—	Essex, Chelmsford
138	Cheltenham	Nigel Jones	LD	South West	—	Gloucestershire, Cheltenham
139	Chesham & Amersham	Cheryl Gillan	Con	South East	—	Buckinghamshire, Chiltern, Wycombe
140	Chester, City of	Christine Russell	Lab	North West	—	Cheshire, Chester
141	Chesterfield	Tony Benn	Lab	East Midlands	—	Derbyshire, Chesterfield
142	Chichester	Andrew Tyrie	Con	South East	—	West Sussex, Chichester
143	Chingford & Woodford Green	Iain Duncan Smith	Con	London	Havering and Redbridge North East	Redbridge, Waltham Forest
144	Chipping Barnet	Sidney Chapman	Con	London	Barnet and Camden	Barnet
145	Chorley	Lindsay Hoyle	Lab	North West	—	Lancashire, Chorley
146	Christchurch	Christopher Chope	Con	South West	—	Dorset, Christchurch, East Dorset
147	Cities of London & Westminster	Peter Brooke	Con	London	City & East, West Central	City of London, Westminster
148	Cleethorpes	Shona McIsaac	Lab	Yorkshire & the Humber	—	North East Lincolnshire
149	Clwyd South	Martyn Jones	Lab	Wales	North Wales	Denbighshire, Powys, Wrexham
150	Clwyd West	Gareth Thomas	Lab	Wales	North Wales	Conwy, Denbighshire
151	Clydebank & Milngavie	Tony Worthington	Lab	Scotland	West of Scotland	West Dunbartonshire, East Dunbartonshire
152	Clydesdale	Jimmy Hood	Lab	Scotland	South of Scotland	South Lanarkshire
153	Coatbridge & Chryston	Tom Clarke	Lab	Scotland	Central Scotland	East Dunbartonshire, North Lanarkshire
154	Colchester	Bob Russell	LD	Eastern	—	Essex, Colchester
155	Colne Valley	Kali Mountford	Lab	Yorkshire & the Humber	—	Kirklees
156	Congleton	Ann Winterton	Con	North West	—	Cheshire, Congleton
157	Conwy	Betty Williams	Lab	Wales	North Wales	Conwy, Gwynedd
158	Copeland	Jack Cunningham	Lab	North West	—	Cumbria, Copeland
159	Corby	Philip Hope	Lab	East Midlands	—	Northamptonshire, Corby, East Northamptonshire

No	Constituency	Member of Parliament	Party	European seat	Parliament/ Assembly area	Local authorities
160	Cornwall North	Paul Tyler	LD	South West	—	Cornwall, North Cornwall, Restormel
161	Cornwall South East	Colin Breed	LD	South West	—	Cornwall, Caradon, North Cornwall, Restormel
162	Cotswold	Geoffrey Clifton-Brown	Con	South West	—	Gloucestershire, Cotswold, Stroud
163	Coventry North East	Bob Ainsworth	Lab	West Midlands	—	Coventry
164	Coventry North West	Geoffrey Robinson	Lab	West Midlands	—	Coventry
165	Coventry South	Jim Cunningham	Lab	West Midlands	—	Coventry
166	Crawley	Laura Moffatt	Lab	South East	—	West Sussex, Crawley
167	Crewe & Nantwich	Gwyneth Dunwoody	Lab	North West	—	Cheshire, Crewe and Nantwich
168	Crosby	Clare Curtis-Tansley	Lab	North West	—	Sefton
169	Croydon Central	Geraint Davies	Lab	London	Croydon and Sutton	Croydon
170	Croydon North	Malcolm Wicks	Lab	London	Croydon and Sutton	Croydon
171	Croydon South	Richard Ottaway	Con	London	Croydon and Sutton	Croydon
172	Cumbernauld & Kilsyth	Rosemary McKenna	Lab	Scotland	Central Scotland	North Lanarkshire
173	Cunninghame North	Brian Wilson	Lab	Scotland	West of Scotland	North Ayrshire
174	Cunninghame South	Brian Donohoe	Lab	Scotland	South of Scotland	North Ayrshire
175	Cynon Valley	Ann Clwyd	Lab	Wales	South Wales Central	Rhondda/Cynon/Taff
176	Dagenham	Judith Church	Lab	London	City and East	Barking and Dagenham
177	Darlington	Alan Milburn	Lab	North East	—	Darlington
178	Dartford	Howard Stoate	Lab	South East	—	Kent, Dartford, Sevenoaks
179	Daventry	Timothy Boswell	Con	East Midlands	—	Northamptonshire, Daventry, South Northamptonshire
180	Delyn	David Hanson	Lab	Wales	North Wales	Flintshire
181	Denton & Reddish	Andrew Bennett	Lab	North West	—	Stockport, Tameside
182	Derby North	Bob Laxton	Lab	East Midlands	—	Derby
183	Derby South	Margaret Beckett	Lab	East Midlands	—	Derby
184	Derbyshire North East	Harry Barnes	Lab	East Midlands	—	Derbyshire, Chesterfield, North East Derbyshire
185	Derbyshire South	Mark Todd	Lab	East Midlands	—	Derbyshire, Derby, South Derbyshire

No	Constituency	Member of Parliament	Party	European seat	Parliament/ Assembly area	Local authorities
186	Derbyshire West	Patrick McLoughlin	Con	East Midlands	—	Derbyshire, Amber Valley, Derbyshire Dales
187	Devizes	Michael Ancram	Con	South West	—	Wiltshire, Kennet, North Wiltshire, West Wiltshire
188	Devon East	Peter Emery	Con	South West	—	Devon, East Devon
189	Devon North	Nick Harvey	LD	South West	—	Devon, Mid Devon, North Devon
190	Devon South West	Gary Streeter	Con	South West	—	Devon, Plymouth, South Hams, West Devon
191	Devon West & Torridge	John Burnett	LD	South West	—	Devon, Torridge, West Devon
192	Dewsbury	Ann Taylor	Lab	Yorkshire & the Humber	—	Kirklees
193	Don Valley	Caroline Flint	Lab	Yorkshire & the Humber	—	Doncaster
194	Doncaster Central	Rosie Winterton	Lab	Yorkshire & the Humber	—	Doncaster
195	Doncaster North	Kevin Hughes	Lab	Yorkshire & the Humber	—	Doncaster
196	Dorset Mid & North Poole	Christopher Fraser	Con	South West	—	Dorset, Poole, East Dorset, Purbeck
197	Dorset North	Robert Walter	Con	South West	—	Dorset, East Dorset, North Dorset
198	Dorset South	Ian Bruce	Con	South West	—	Dorset, Purbeck, West Dorset, Weymouth and Portland
199	Dorset West	Oliver Letwin	Con	South West	—	Dorset, West Dorset
200	Dover	Gwyn Prosser	Lab	South East	—	Kent, Dover
201	Down North	Robert McCartney	UKU	Northern Ireland	Down North	Ards, North Down
202	Down South	Eddie McGrady	SDLP	Northern Ireland	Down South	Banbridge, Down, Newry and Mourne
203	Dudley North	John Gilbert	Lab	West Midlands	—	Dudley
204	Dudley South	Ian Pearson	Lab	West Midlands	—	Dudley
205	Dulwich & West Norwood	Tessa Jowell	Lab	London	Lambeth and Southwark	Lambeth, Southwark
206	Dumbarton	John McFall	Lab	Scotland	West of Scotland	Argyll and Bute, West Dunbartonshire

No	Constituency	Member of Parliament	Party	European seat	Parliament/Assembly area	Local authorities
207	Dumfries	Russell Brown	Lab	Scotland	South of Scotland	Dumfries and Galloway
208	Dundee East	John McAllion	Lab	Scotland	North East Scotland	Dundee
209	Dundee West	Ernie Ross	Lab	Scotland	North East Scotland	Dundee
210	Dunfermline East	Gordon Brown	Lab	Scotland	Mid Scotland and Fife	Fife
211	Dunfermline West	Rachel Squire	Lab	Scotland	Mid Scotland and Fife	Fife
212	Durham North	Giles Radice	Lab	North East	—	Durham, Chester-le-Street, Derwentside
213	Durham North West	Hilary Armstrong	Lab	North East	—	Durham, Derwentside, Wear Valley
214	Durham, City of	Gerald Steinberg	Lab	North East	—	Durham, City of Durham
215	Ealing Acton & Shepherd's Bush	Clive Soley	Lab	London	Ealing and Hillingdon, West Central	Ealing, Hammersmith and Fulham
216	Ealing North	Stephen Pound	Lab	London	Ealing and Hillingdon	Ealing
217	Ealing Southall	Piara Khabra	Lab	London	Ealing and Hillingdon	Ealing
218	Easington	John Cummings	Lab	North East	—	Durham, Easington
219	East Ham	Stephen Timms	Lab	London	City and East	Newham
220	East Kilbride	Adam Ingram	Lab	Scotland	Central Scotland	South Lanarkshire
221	East Lothian	John Home Robertson	Lab	Scotland	South of Scotland	East Lothian
222	Eastbourne	Nigel Waterson	Con	South East	—	East Sussex, Eastbourne, Wealden
223	Eastleigh	David Chidgey	LD	South East	—	Hampshire, Eastleigh
224	Eastwood	Jim Murphy	Lab	Scotland	West of Scotland	East Renfrewshire
225	Eccles	Ian Stewart	Lab	North West	—	Salford
226	Eddisbury	Alistair Goodlad	Con	North West	—	Cheshire, Chester, Crewe and Nantwich, Vale Royal
227	Edinburgh Central	Alistair Darling	Lab	Scotland	Lothians	Edinburgh
228	Edinburgh East & Musselburgh	Gavin Strang	Lab	Scotland	Lothians	East Lothian, Edinburgh
229	Edinburgh North & Leith	Malcolm Chisholm	Lab	Scotland	Lothians	Edinburgh
230	Edinburgh Pentlands	Linda Clark	Lab	Scotland	Lothians	Edinburgh
231	Edinburgh South	Nigel Griffiths	Lab	Scotland	Lothians	Edinburgh
232	Edinburgh West	Donald Gorrie	LD	Scotland	Lothians	Edinburgh
233	Edmonton	Andy Love	Lab	London	Enfield and Haringey	Enfield

No	Constituency	Member of Parliament	Party	European seat	Parliament/ Assembly area	Local authorities
234	Ellesmere Port & Neston	Andrew Miller	Lab	North West	—	Cheshire, Chester, Ellesmere Port and Neston
235	Elmet	Colin Burgon	Lab	Yorkshire & the Humber	—	Leeds
236	Eltham	Clive Efford	Lab	London	Greenwich & Lewisham	Greenwich
237	Enfield North	Joan Ryan	Lab	London	Enfield and Haringey	Enfield
238	Enfield Southgate	Stephen Twigg	Lab	London	Enfield and Haringey	Enfield
239	Epping Forest	Eleanor Laing	Con	Eastern	—	Essex, Epping Forest
240	Epsom & Ewell	Archie Hamilton	Con	South East	—	Surrey, Epsom and Ewell, Mole Valley, Reigate and Banstead
241	Erewash	Elizabeth Blackman	Lab	East Midlands	—	Derbyshire, Erewash
242	Erith & Thamesmead	John Austin-Walker	Lab	London	Bexley and Bromley, Greenwich & Lewisham	Bexley, Greenwich
243	Esher & Walton	Ian Taylor	Con	South East	—	Surrey, Elmbridge
244	Essex North	Bernard Jenkin	Con	Eastern	—	Essex, Colchester, Tendring
245	Exeter	Ben Bradshaw	Lab	South West	—	Devon, Exeter
246	Falkirk East	Michael Connarty	Lab	Scotland	Central Scotland	Falkirk
247	Falkirk West	Dennis Canavan	Lab	Scotland	Central Scotland	Falkirk
248	Falmouth & Camborne	Candy Atherton	Lab	South West	—	Cornwall, Carrick, Kerrier
249	Fareham	Peter Lloyd	Con	South East	—	Hampshire, Fareham
250	Faversham & Mid Kent	Andrew Rowe	Con	South East	—	Kent, Maidstone, Swale
251	Feltham & Heston	Alan Keen	Lab	London	South West	Hounslow
252	Fermanagh & South Tyrone	Ken Maginnis	UU	Northern Ireland	Fermanagh & South Tyrone	Dungannon, Fermanagh
253	Fife Central	Henry McLeish	Lab	Scotland	Mid Scotland and Fife	Fife
254	Fife North East	Menzies Campbell	LD	Scotland	Mid Scotland and Fife	Fife
255	Finchley & Golders Green	Rudolph Vis	Lab	London	Barnet and Camden	Barnet
256	Folkestone & Hythe	Michael Howard	Con	South East	—	Kent, Shepway
257	Forest of Dean	Diana Organ	Lab	South West	—	Gloucestershire, Forest of Dean, Tewkesbury
258	Foyle	John Hume	SDLP	Northern Ireland	Foyle	Derry

No	Constituency	Member of Parliament	Party	European seat	Parliament/ Assembly area	Local authorities
259	Fylde	Michael Jack	Con	North West	—	Lancashire, Fylde, Preston, Wyre
260	Gainsborough	Edward Leigh	Con	East Midlands	—	Lincolnshire, East Lindsey, West Lindsey
261	Galloway & Upper Nithsdale	Alasdair Morgan	SNP	Scotland	South of Scotland	Dumfries and Galloway
262	Gateshead East & Washington West	Joyce Quin	Lab	North East	—	Gateshead, Sunderland
263	Gedling	Vernon Coaker	Lab	East Midlands	—	Nottinghamshire, Gedling
264	Gillingham	Paul Clark	Lab	South East	—	Medway Towns
265	Glasgow Anniesland	Donald Dewar	Lab	Scotland	Glasgow	Glasgow
266	Glasgow Baillieston	James Wray	Lab	Scotland	Glasgow	Glasgow
267	Glasgow Cathcart	John Maxton	Lab	Scotland	Glasgow	Glasgow
268	Glasgow Govan	Mohammed Sarwar	Lab	Scotland	Glasgow	Glasgow
269	Glasgow Kelvin	George Galloway	Lab	Scotland	Glasgow	Glasgow
270	Glasgow Maryhill	Maria Fyfe	Lab	Scotland	Glasgow	Glasgow
271	Glasgow Pollok	Ian Davidson	Lab	Scotland	Glasgow	Glasgow
272	Glasgow Rutherglen	Thomas McAvoy	Lab	Scotland	Glasgow	Glasgow, South Lanarkshire
273	Glasgow Shettleston	David Marshall	Lab	Scotland	Glasgow	Glasgow
274	Glasgow Springburn	Michael Martin	Lab	Scotland	Glasgow	Glasgow
275	Gloucester	Tess Kingham	Lab	South West	—	Gloucestershire, Gloucester
276	Gordon	Malcolm Bruce	LD	Scotland	North East Scotland	Aberdeenshire, Moray
277	Gosport	Peter Viggers	Con	South East	—	Hampshire, Fareham, Gosport
278	Gower	Martin Caton	Lab	Wales	South Wales West	Swansea
279	Grantham & Stamford	Quentin Davies	Con	East Midlands	—	Lincolnshire, South Kesteven
280	Gravesham	Chris Pond	Lab	South East	—	Kent, Gravesham
281	Great Grimsby	Austin Mitchell	Lab	Yorkshire & the Humber	—	North East Lincolnshire
282	Great Yarmouth	Tony Wright	Lab	Eastern	—	Norfolk, Great Yarmouth
283	Greenock & Inverclyde	Norman Godman	Lab	Scotland	West of Scotland	Inverclyde
284	Greenwich & Woolwich	Nick Raynsford	Lab	London	Greenwich & Lewisham	Greenwich
285	Guildford	Nick St Aubyn	Con	South East	—	Surrey, Guildford, Waverley

No	Constituency	Member of Parliament	Party	European seat	Parliament/ Assembly area	Local authorities
286	Hackney North & Stoke Newington	Diane Abbott	Lab	London	North East	Hackney
287	Hackney South & Shoreditch	Brian Sedgemore	Lab	London	North East	Hackney
288	Halesowen & Rowley Regis	Sylvia Heal	Lab	West Midlands	—	Dudley, Sandwell
289	Halifax	Alice Mahon	Lab	Yorkshire & the Humber	—	Calderdale
290	Haltemprice & Howden	David Davis	Con	Yorkshire & the Humber	—	East Riding of Yorkshire
291	Halton	Derek Twigg	Lab	North West	—	Halton
292	Hamilton North & Bellshill	John Reid	Lab	Scotland	Central Scotland	North Lanarkshire, South Lanarkshire
293	Hamilton South	George Robertson	Lab	Scotland	Central Scotland	South Lanarkshire
294	Hammersmith & Fulham	Iain Coleman	Lab	London	West Central	Hammersmith and Fulham
295	Hampshire East	Michael Mates	Con	South East	—	Hampshire, East Hampshire, Havant
296	Hampshire North East	James Arbuthnot	Con	South East	—	Hampshire, East Hampshire, Hart
297	Hampshire North West	George Young	Con	South East	—	Hampshire, Basingstoke and Deane, Test Valley
298	Hampstead & Highgate	Glenda Jackson	Lab	London	Barnet and Croydon	Camden
299	Harborough	Edward Garnier	Con	East Midlands	—	Leicestershire, Harborough, Oadby and Wigston
300	Harlow	Bill Rammell	Lab	Eastern	—	Essex, Epping Forest, Harlow
301	Harrogate & Knaresborough	Phil Willis	LD	Yorkshire & the Humber	—	North Yorkshire, Harrogate
302	Harrow East	Tony McNulty	Lab	London	Brent and Harrow	Harrow
303	Harrow West	Gareth Thomas	Lab	London	Brent and Harrow	Harrow
304	Hartlepool	Peter Mandelson	Lab	North East	—	Hartlepool
305	Harwich	Ivan Henderson	Lab	Eastern	—	Essex, Tendring
306	Hastings & Rye	Michael Foster	Lab	South East	—	East Sussex, Hastings, Rother

No	Constituency	Member of Parliament	Party	European seat	Parliament/ Assembly area	Local authorities
307	Havant	David Willetts	Con	South East	—	Hampshire, Havant
308	Hayes & Harlington	John McDonnell	Lab	London	Ealing and Hillingdon	Hillingdon
309	Hazel Grove	Andrew Stunell	LD	North West	—	Stockport
310	Hemel Hempstead	Tony McWalter	Lab	Eastern	—	Hertfordshire, Dacorum
311	Hemsworth	Jon Trickett	Lab	Yorkshire & the Humber	—	Wakefield
312	Hendon	Andrew Dismore	Lab	London	Barnet and Camden	Barnet
313	Henley	Michael Heseltine	Con	South East	—	Oxfordshire, South Oxfordshire
314	Hereford	Paul Keetch	LD	West Midlands	—	Herefordshire
315	Hertford & Stortford	Bowen Wells	Con	Eastern	—	Hertfordshire, East Hertfordshire
316	Hertfordshire North East	Oliver Heald	Con	Eastern	—	Hertfordshire, East Hertfordshire, North Hertfordshire
317	Hertfordshire South West	Richard Page	Con	Eastern	—	Hertfordshire, Dacorum, Three Rivers
318	Hertsmere	James Clappison	Con	Eastern	—	Hertfordshire, Hertsmere
319	Hexham	Peter Atkinson	Con	North East	—	Northumberland, Castle Morpeth, Tynedale
320	Heywood & Middleton	Jim Dobbin	Lab	North West	—	Rochdale
321	High Peak	Tom Levitt	Lab	East Midlands	—	Derbyshire, High Peak, Derbyshire Dales
322	Hitchin & Harpenden	Peter Lilley	Con	Eastern	—	Hertfordshire, North Hertfordshire, St. Albans
323	Holborn & St Pancras	Frank Dobson	Lab	London	Barnet and Camden	Camden
324	Hornchurch	John Cryer	Lab	London	Havering and Redbridge	Havering
325	Hornsey & Wood Green	Barbara Roche	Lab	London	Enfield and Haringey	Haringey
326	Horsham	Francis Maude	Con	South East	—	West Sussex, Chichester, Horsham, Mid Sussex
327	Houghton & Washington East	Fraser Kemp	Lab	North East	—	Sunderland
328	Hove	Ivor Caplin	Lab	South East	—	Brighton and Hove

No	Constituency	Member of Parliament	Party	European seat	Parliament/ Assembly area	Local authorities
329	Huddersfield	Barry Sheerman	Lab	Yorkshire & the Humber	—	Kirklees
330	Hull East	John Prescott	Lab	Yorkshire & the Humber	—	Kingston upon Hull
331	Hull North	Kevin McNamara	Lab	Yorkshire & the Humber	—	Kingston upon Hull
332	Hull West & Hessle	Alan Johnson	Lab	Yorkshire & the Humber	—	Kingston upon Hull, East Riding of Yorkshire
333	Huntingdon	John Major	Con	Eastern	—	Cambridgeshire, Huntingdonshire
334	Hyndburn	Greg Pope	Lab	North West	—	Lancashire, Hyndburn, Rossendale
335	Ilford North	Linda Perham	Lab	London	Havering and Redbridge	Redbridge
336	Ilford South	Mike Gapes	Lab	London	Havering and Redbridge	Redbridge
337	Inverness East, Nairn & Lochaber	David Stewart	Lab	Scotland	Highlands and Islands	Highland
338	Ipswich	Jamie Cann	Lab	Eastern	—	Suffolk, Ipswich
339	Isle of Wight	Peter Brand	LD	South East	—	Isle of Wight
340	Islington North	Jeremy Corbyn	Lab	London	North East	Islington
341	Islington South & Finsbury	Chris Smith	Lab	London	North East	Islington
342	Islwyn	Don Touhig	Lab	Wales	South Wales East	Caerphilly
343	Jarrow	Stephen Hepburn	Lab	North East	—	Gateshead, South Tyneside
344	Keighley	Ann Cryer	Lab	Yorkshire & the Humber	—	Bradford
345	Kensington & Chelsea	Alan Clark	Con	London	West Central	Kensington and Chelsea
346	Kettering	Philip Sawford	Lab	East Midlands	—	Northamptonshire, Daventry, Kettering
347	Kilmarnock & Loudoun	Desmond Brown	Lab	Scotland	Central Scotland	East Ayrshire
348	Kingston & Surbiton	Edward Davey	LD	London	South West	Kingston upon Thames
349	Kingswood	Roger Berry	Lab	South West	—	Bristol, South Gloucestershire
350	Kirkcaldy	Lewis Moonie	Lab	Scotland	Mid Scotland and Fife	Fife

No	Constituency	Member of Parliament	Party	European seat	Parliament/ Assembly area	Local authorities
351	Knowsley North & Sefton East	George Howarth	Lab	North West	–	Knowsley, Sefton
352	Knowsley South	Eddie O'Hara	Lab	North West	–	Knowsley
353	Lagan Valley	Jeffrey Donaldson	UU	Northern Ireland	Lagan Valley	Banbridge, Lisburn
354	Lancashire West	Colin Pickthall	Lab	North West	–	Lancashire, West Lancashire
355	Lancaster & Wyre	Hilton Dawson	Lab	North West	–	Lancashire, Lancaster, Wyre
356	Leeds Central	Derek Fatchett	Lab	Yorkshire & the Humber	–	Leeds
357	Leeds East	George Mudie	Lab	Yorkshire & the Humber	–	Leeds
358	Leeds North East	Fabian Hamilton	Lab	Yorkshire & the Humber	–	Leeds
359	Leeds North West	Harold Best	Lab	Yorkshire & the Humber	–	Leeds
360	Leeds West	John Battle	Lab	Yorkshire & the Humber	–	Leeds
361	Leicester East	Keith Vaz	Lab	East Midlands	–	Leicester
362	Leicester South	James Marshall	Lab	East Midlands	–	Leicester
363	Leicester West	Patricia Hewitt	Lab	East Midlands	–	Leicester
364	Leicestershire North West	David Taylor	Lab	East Midlands	–	Leicestershire, North West Leicestershire
365	Leigh	Lawrence Cunliffe	Lab	North West	–	Wigan
366	Leominster	Peter Temple-Morris	Con*	West Midlands	–	Worcestershire, Herefordshire, Malvern Hills, Wyre Forest
367	Lewes	Norman Baker	LD	South East	–	East Sussex, Lewes, Wealden
368	Lewisham Deptford	Joan Ruddock	Lab	London	Greenwich & Lewisham	Lewisham
369	Lewisham East	Bridget Prentice	Lab	London	Greenwich & Lewisham	Lewisham
370	Lewisham West	Jim Dowd	Lab	London	Greenwich & Lewisham	Lewisham
371	Leyton & Wanstead	Harry Cohen	Lab	London	Havering & Redbridge, North East	Redbridge, Waltham Forest

No	Constituency	Member of Parliament	Party	European seat	Parliament/Assembly area	Local authorities
372	Lichfield	Michael Fabricant	Con	West Midlands	—	Staffordshire, East Staffordshire, Lichfield
373	Lincoln	Gillian Merron	Lab	East Midlands	—	Lincolnshire, Lincoln, North Kesteven
374	Linlithgow	Tam Dalyell	Lab	Scotland	Lothians	West Lothian
375	Liverpool Garston	Maria Eagle	Lab	North West	—	Liverpool
376	Liverpool Riverside	Louise Ellman	Lab	North West	—	Liverpool
377	Liverpool Walton	Peter Kilfoyle	Lab	North West	—	Liverpool
378	Liverpool Wavertree	Jane Kennedy	Lab	North West	—	Liverpool
379	Liverpool West Derby	Robert Wareing	Lab	North West	—	Liverpool
380	Livingstone	Robin Cook	Lab	Scotland	Lothians	West Lothian
381	Llanelli	Denzil Davies	Lab	Wales	Mid and West Wales	Carmarthenshire
382	Londonderry East	William Ross	UU	Northern Ireland	Londonderry East	Coleraine, Limavady
383	Loughborough	Andy Reed	Lab	East Midlands	—	Leicestershire, Charnwood
384	Louth & Horncastle	Peter Tapsell	Con	East Midlands	—	Lincolnshire, East Lindsey
385	Ludlow	Christopher Gill	Con	West Midlands	—	Shropshire, Bridgnorth, South Shropshire
386	Luton North	Kelvin Hopkins	Lab	Eastern	—	Luton
387	Luton South	Margaret Moran	Lab	Eastern	—	Bedfordshire, Luton, South Bedfordshire
388	Macclesfield	Nicholas Winterton	Con	North West	—	Cheshire, Macclesfield
389	Maidenhead	Theresa May	Con	South East	—	Windsor and Maidenhead, Wokingham
390	Maidstone & The Weald	Ann Widdecombe	Con	South East	—	Kent, Maidstone, Tunbridge Wells
391	Makerfield	Ian McCartney	Lab	North West	—	Wigan
392	Maldon & East Chelmsford	John Whittingdale	Con	Eastern	—	Essex, Chelmsford, Maldon
393	Manchester Blackley	Graham Stringer	Lab	North West	—	Manchester
394	Manchester Central	Tony Lloyd	Lab	North West	—	Manchester
395	Manchester Gorton	Gerald Kaufman	Lab	North West	—	Manchester
396	Manchester Withington	Keith Bradley	Lab	North West	—	Manchester
397	Mansfield	Alan Meale	Lab	East Midlands	—	Nottinghamshire, Mansfield

No	Constituency	Member of Parliament	Party	European seat	Parliament/ Assembly area	Local authorities
398	Medway	Robert Marshall-Andrews	Lab	South East	–	Medway Towns
399	Meirionnydd Nant Conwy	Elfyn Llwyd	PC	Wales	Mid and West Wales	Conwy, Gwynedd
400	Meriden	Caroline Spelman	Con	West Midlands	–	Solihull
401	Merthyr Tydfil & Rhymney	Ted Rowlands	Lab	Wales	South Wales East	Caerphilly, Merthyr Tydfil
402	Middlesbrough	Stuart Bell	Lab	North East	–	Middlesbrough
403	Middlesbrough South & East Cleveland	Ashok Kumar	Lab	North East	–	Middlesbrough, Redcar and and Cleveland
404	Midlothian	Eric Clarke	Lab	Scotland	Lothians	Midlothian
405	Milton Keynes North East	Brian White	Lab	South East	–	Milton Keynes
406	Milton Keynes South West	Phyllis Starkey	Lab	South East	–	Milton Keynes
407	Mitcham & Morden	Siobhain McDonagh	Lab	London	Merton and Wandsworth	Merton
408	Mole Valley	Paul Beresford	Con	South East	–	Surrey, Guildford, Mole Valley
409	Monmouth	Huw Edwards	Lab	Wales	South Wales East	Monmouthshire, Torfaen
410	Montgomeryshire	Lembit Opik	LD	Wales	Mid and West Wales	Powys
411	Moray	Margaret Ewing	SNP	Scotland	Highlands and Islands	Moray
412	Morecambe & Lunesdale	Geraldine Smith	Lab	North West	–	Lancashire, Lancaster
413	Morley & Rothwell	John Gunnell	Lab	Yorkshire & the Humber	–	Leeds
414	Motherwell & Wishaw	Frank Roy	Lab	Scotland	Central Scotland	North Lanarkshire
415	Neath	Peter Hain	Lab	Wales	South Wales West	Neath and Port Talbot
416	New Forest East	Julian Lewis	Con	South East	–	Hampshire, New Forest
417	New Forest West	Desmond Swayne	Con	South East	–	Hampshire, New Forest
418	Newark	Fiona Jones	Lab	East Midlands	–	Nottinghamshire, Bassetlaw, Newark and Sherwood
419	Newbury	David Rendel	LD	South East	–	West Berkshire
420	Newcastle-under-Lyme	Llin Golding	Lab	West Midlands	–	Staffordshire, Newcastle-under-Lyme
421	Newcastle upon Tyne Central	Jim Cousins	Lab	North East	–	Newcastle upon Tyne
422	Newcastle upon Tyne East & Wallsend	Nick Brown	Lab	North East	–	Newcastle upon Tyne, North Tyneside

No	Constituency	Member of Parliament	Party	European seat	Parliament/ Assembly area	Local authorities
423	Newcastle upon Tyne North	Doug Henderson	Lab	North East	—	Newcastle upon Tyne
424	Newport East	Roy Hughes	Lab	Wales	South Wales East	Monmouthshire, Newport
425	Newport West	Paul Flynn	Lab	Wales	South Wales East	Newport
426	Newry & Armagh	Seamus Mallon	SDLP	Northern Ireland	Newry and Armagh	Armagh, Newry and Mourne
427	Norfolk Mid	Keith Simpson	Con	Eastern	—	Norfolk, Breckland, Broadland
428	Norfolk North	David Prior	Con	Eastern	—	Norfolk, North Norfolk
429	Norfolk North West	George Turner	Lab	Eastern	—	Norfolk, King's Lynn and West Norfolk
430	Norfolk South	John MacGregor	Con	Eastern	—	Norfolk, South Norfolk
431	Norfolk South West	Gillian Shephard	Con	Eastern	—	Norfolk, Breckland, King's Lynn and West Norfolk
432	Normanton	Bill O'Brien	Lab	Yorkshire & the Humber	—	Wakefield
433	Northampton North	Sally Keeble	Lab	East Midlands	—	Northamptonshire, Northampton
434	Northampton South	Tony Clark	Lab	East Midlands	—	Northamptonshire, Northampton, South Northamptonshire
435	Northavon	Steven Webb	LD	South West	—	South Gloucestershire
436	Norwich North	Ian Gibson	Lab	Eastern	—	Norfolk, Broadland, Norwich
437	Norwich South	Charles Clarke	Lab	Eastern	—	Norfolk, Norwich, South Norfolk
438	Nottingham East	John Heppell	Lab	East Midlands	—	Nottingham
439	Nottingham North	Graham Allen	Lab	East Midlands	—	Nottingham
440	Nottingham South	Alan Simpson	Lab	East Midlands	—	Nottingham
441	Nuneaton	Bill Olner	Lab	West Midlands	—	Warwickshire, Nuneaton and Bedworth, Rugby
442	Ochil	Martin O'Neill	Lab	Scotland	Mid Scotland and Fife	Clackmannan, Perthshire and Kinross, Stirling
443	Ogmore	Ray Powell	Lab	Wales	South Wales West	Bridgend, Rhondda/Cynon/Taff
444	Old Bexley & Sidcup	Edward Heath	Con	London	Bexley and Bromley	Bexley
445	Oldham East & Saddleworth	Phil Woolas	Lab	North West	—	Oldham, Rochdale
446	Oldham West & Royton	Michael Meacher	Lab	North West	—	Oldham
447	Orkney & Shetland	Jim Wallace	LD	Scotland	Highlands and Islands	Orkney Islands, Shetland Islands

No	Constituency	Member of Parliament	Party	European seat	Parliament/Assembly area	Local authorities
448	Orpington	John Horam	Con	South East	—	Bromley
449	Oxford East	Andrew Smith	Lab	South East	—	Oxfordshire, Oxford
450	Oxford West & Abingdon	Evan Harris	LD	South East	—	Oxfordshire, Cherwell, Oxford, Vale of White Horse
451	Paisley North	Irene Adams	Lab	Scotland	West of Scotland	Renfrewshire
452	Paisley South	Douglas Alexander	Lab	Scotland	West of Scotland	Renfrewshire
453	Pendle	Gordon Prentice	Lab	North West	—	Lancashire, Pendle
454	Penrith & The Border	David Maclean	Con	North West	—	Cumbria, Allerdale, Carlisle, Eden
455	Perth	Roseanna Cunningham	SNP	Scotland	Mid Scotland and Fife	Perthshire and Kinross
456	Peterborough	Helen Brinton	Lab	Eastern	—	Peterborough
457	Plymouth Devonport	David Jamieson	Lab	South West	—	Plymouth
458	Plymouth Sutton	Linda Gilroy	Lab	South West	—	Plymouth
459	Pontefract & Castleford	Yvette Cooper	Lab	Yorkshire & the Humber	—	Wakefield
460	Pontypridd	Kim Howells	Lab	Wales	South Wales Central	Cardiff, Rhondda/Cynon/Taff
461	Poole	Robert Syms	Con	South West	—	Poole
462	Poplar & Canning Town	Jim Fitzpatrick	Lab	London	City and East	Newham, Tower Hamlets
463	Portsmouth North	Syd Rapson	Lab	South East	—	Portsmouth
464	Portsmouth South	Mike Hancock	LD	South East	—	Portsmouth
465	Preseli Pembrokeshire	Jackie Lawrence	Lab	Wales	Mid and West Wales	Pembrokeshire
466	Preston	Audrey Wise	Lab	North West	—	Lancashire, Preston, South Ribble
467	Pudsey	Paul Truswell	Lab	Yorkshire & the Humber	—	Leeds
468	Putney	Anthony Colman	Lab	London	Merton and Wandsworth	Wandsworth
469	Rayleigh	Michael Clark	Con	Eastern	—	Essex, Chelmsford, Rochford
470	Reading East	Jane Griffiths	Lab	South East	—	Reading, Wokingham
471	Reading West	Martin Salter	Lab	South East	—	Reading, West Berkshire
472	Redcar	Mo Mowlam	Lab	North East	—	Redcar and Cleveland
473	Redditch	Jacqui Smith	Lab	West Midlands	—	Worcestershire, Redditch, Wychavon

No	Constituency	Member of Parliament	Party	European seat	Parliament/ Assembly area	Local authorities
474	Regent's Park & Kensington North	Karen Buck	Lab	London	West Central	Kensington and Chelsea, Westminster
475	Reigate	Crispin Blunt	Con	South East	—	Surrey, Reigate and Banstead
476	Renfrewshire West	Thomas Graham	Lab	Scotland	West of Scotland	Inverclyde, Renfrewshire
477	Rhondda	Allan Rogers	Lab	Wales	South Wales Central	Rhondda/Cynon/Taff
478	Ribble South	David Borrow	Lab	North West	—	Lancashire, South Ribble, West Lancashire
479	Ribble Valley	Nigel Evans	Con	North West	—	Lancashire, Preston, Ribble Valley, South Ribble
480	Richmond (Yorks)	William Hague	Con	Yorkshire & the Humber	—	North Yorkshire, Hambleton, Richmondshire
481	Richmond Park	Jenny Tonge	LD	London	South West	Kingston upon Thames, Richmond upon Thames
482	Rochdale	Lorna Fitzsimmons	Lab	North West	—	Rochdale
483	Rochford & Southend East	Teddy Taylor	Con	Eastern	—	Essex, Rochford, Southend-on-Sea
484	Romford	Eileen Gordon	Lab	London	Havering and Redbridge	Havering
485	Romsey	Michael Colvin	Con	South East	—	Hampshire, Eastleigh, Southampton, Test Valley
486	Ross, Skye & Inverness West	Charles Kennedy	LD	Scotland	Highlands and Islands	Highland
487	Rossendale & Darwen	Janet Anderson	Lab	North West	—	Lancashire, Blackburn with Darwen, Rossendale
488	Rother Valley	Kevin Barron	Lab	Yorkshire & the Humber	—	Rotherham
489	Rotherham	Denis MacShane	Lab	Yorkshire & the Humber	—	Rotherham
490	Roxburgh & Berwickshire	Archy Kirkwood	LD	Scotland	South of Scotland	Scottish Borders
491	Rugby & Kenilworth	Andy King	Lab	West Midlands	—	Warwickshire, Rugby, Warwick
492	Ruislip – Northwood	John Wilkinson	Con	London	Ealing and Hillingdon	Hillingdon
493	Runnymede & Weybridge	Philip Hammond	Con	South East	—	Surrey, Elmbridge, Runnymede
494	Rushcliffe	Kenneth Clarke	Con	East Midlands	—	Nottinghamshire, Rushcliffe

No	Constituency	Member of Parliament	Party	European seat	Parliament/ Assembly area	Local authorities
495	Rutland & Melton	Alan Duncan	Con	East Midlands	—	Leicestershire, Harborough, Melton, Rutland
496	Ryedale	John Greenway	Con	Yorkshire & the Humber	—	North Yorkshire, Ryedale, Scarborough
497	Saffron Walden	Alan Haselhurst	Con	Eastern	—	Essex, Braintree, Uttlesford
498	St Albans	Kerry Pollard	Lab	Eastern	—	Hertfordshire, St. Albans, Three Rivers
499	St Helens North	Dave Watts	Lab	North West	—	St. Helens
500	St Helens South	Gerry Bermingham	Lab	North West	—	St. Helens
501	St Ives	Andrew George	LD	South West	—	Cornwall, Kerrier, Penwith, Isles of Scilly
502	Salford	Hazel Blears	Lab	North West	—	Salford
503	Salisbury	Robert Key	Con	South West	—	Wiltshire, Salisbury
504	Scarborough & Whitby	Lawrence Quinn	Lab	Yorkshire & the Humber	—	North Yorkshire, Scarborough
505	Scunthorpe	Elliot Morley	Lab	Yorkshire & the Humber	—	North Lincolnshire
506	Sedgefield	Tony Blair	Lab	North East	—	Durham, Darlington, Easington, Sedgefield
507	Selby	John Grogan	Lab	Yorkshire & the Humber	—	North Yorkshire, Selby, City of York
508	Sevenoaks	Michael Fallon	Con	South East	—	Kent, Sevenoaks
509	Sheffield Attercliffe	Clive Betts	Lab	Yorkshire & the Humber	—	Sheffield
510	Sheffield Brightside	David Blunkett	Lab	Yorkshire & the Humber	—	Sheffield
511	Sheffield Central	Richard Caborn	Lab	Yorkshire & the Humber	—	Sheffield
512	Sheffield Hallam	Richard Allan	LD	Yorkshire & the Humber	—	Sheffield

No	Constituency	Member of Parliament	Party	European seat	Parliament/ Assembly area	Local authorities
513	Sheffield Heeley	Bill Michie	Lab	Yorkshire & the Humber	–	Sheffield
514	Sheffield Hillsborough	Helen Jackson	Lab	Yorkshire & the Humber	–	Sheffield
515	Sherwood	Paddy Tipping	Lab	East Midlands	–	Nottinghamshire, Ashfield, Gedling, Newark and Sherwood
516	Shipley	Christopher Leslie	Lab	Yorkshire & the Humber	–	Bradford
517	Shrewsbury & Atcham	Paul Marsden	Lab	West Midlands	–	Shropshire, Shrewsbury and Atcham
518	Shropshire North	Owen Patterson	Con	West Midlands	–	Shropshire, North Shropshire, Oswestry
519	Sittingbourne & Sheppey	Derek Wyatt	Lab	South East	–	Kent, Swale
520	Skipton & Ripon	David Curry	Con	Yorkshire & the Humber	–	North Yorkshire, Craven, Harrogate
521	Sleaford & North Hykeham	Douglas Hogg	Con	East Midlands	–	Lincolnshire, North Kesteven, South Kesteven
522	Slough	Fiona Mactaggart	Lab	South East	–	Slough
523	Solihull	John Taylor	Con	West Midlands	–	Solihull
524	Somerton & Frome	David Heath	LD	South West	–	Somerset, Mendip, South Somerset
525	South Holland & the Deepings	John Hayes	Con	East Midlands	–	Lincolnshire, South Holland, South Kesteven
526	South Shields	David Clark	Lab	North East	–	South Tyneside
527	Southampton Itchen	John Denham	Lab	South East	–	Southampton
528	Southampton Test	Alan Whitehead	Lab	South East	–	Southampton
529	Southend West	David Amess	Con	Eastern	–	Southend-on-Sea
530	Southport	Ronnie Fearn	LD	North West	–	Sefton
531	Southwark North & Bermondsey	Simon Hughes	LD	London	Lambeth and Southwark	Southwark
532	Spelthorne	David Wilshire	Con	South East	–	Surrey, Spelthorne

No	Constituency	Member of Parliament	Party	European seat	Parliament/ Assembly area	Local authorities
533	Stafford	David Kidney	Lab	West Midlands	–	Staffordshire, South Staffordshire, Stafford
534	Staffordshire Moorlands	Charlotte Atkins	Lab	West Midlands	–	Staffordshire, Newcastle-under-Lyme, Staffordshire Moorlands
535	Staffordshire South	Patrick Cormack	Con	West Midlands	–	Staffordshire, South Staffordshire
536	Stalybridge & Hyde	Tom Pendry	Lab	North West	–	Tameside
537	Stevenage	Barbara Follett	Lab	Eastern	–	Hertfordshire, East Hertfordshire, North Hertfordshire, Stevenage
538	Stirling	Anne McGuire	Lab	Scotland	Mid Scotland and Fife	Stirling
539	Stockport	Ann Coffey	Lab	North West	–	Stockport
540	Stockton North	Frank Cook	Lab	North East	–	Stockton-on-Tees
541	Stockton South	Dari Taylor	Lab	North East	–	Stockton-on-Tees
542	Stoke-on-Trent Central	Mark Fisher	Lab	West Midlands	–	Stoke-on-Trent
543	Stoke-on-Trent North	Joan Walley	Lab	West Midlands	–	Staffordshire, Staffordshire Moorlands, Stoke-on-Trent
544	Stoke-on-Trent South	George Stevenson	Lab	West Midlands	–	Stoke-on-Trent
545	Stone	William Cash	Con	West Midlands	–	Staffordshire, Newcastle-under-Lyme, Stafford, Staffordshire Moorlands
546	Stourbridge	Debra Shipley	Lab	West Midlands	–	Dudley
547	Strangford	John Taylor	UU	Northern Ireland	Strangford	Ards, Castlereagh, Down
548	Stratford on Avon	John Maples	Con	West Midlands	–	Warwickshire, Stratford-on-Avon
549	Strathkelvin & Bearsden	Sam Galbraith	Lab	Scotland	West of Scotland	East Dunbartonshire
550	Streatham	Keith Hill	Lab	London	Lambeth and Southwark	Lambeth
551	Stretford & Urmston	Beverley Hughes	Lab	North West	–	Trafford
552	Stroud	David Drew	Lab	South West	–	Gloucestershire, Stroud
553	Suffolk Central & Ipswich North	Michael Lord	Con	Eastern	–	Suffolk, Ipswich, Mid Suffolk, Suffolk Coastal
554	Suffolk Coastal	John Gummer	Con	Eastern	–	Suffolk, Suffolk Coastal, Waveney
555	Suffolk South	Tim Yeo	Con	Eastern	–	Suffolk, Babergh, St. Edmundsbury

No	Constituency	Member of Parliament	Party	European seat	Parliament/ Assembly area	Local authorities
556	Suffolk West	Richard Spring	Con	Eastern	—	Suffolk, Forest Heath, St. Edmundsbury
557	Sunderland North	William Etherington	Lab	North East	—	Sunderland
558	Sunderland South	Chris Mullin	Lab	North East	—	Sunderland
559	Surrey East	Peter Ainsworth	Con	South East	—	Surrey, Reigate and Banstead, Tandridge
560	Surrey Heath	Nick Hawkins	Con	South East	—	Guildford, Surrey Heath
561	Surrey South West	Virginia Bottomley	Con	South East	—	Surrey, Waverley
562	Sussex Mid	Nicholas Soames	Con	South East	—	West Sussex, Mid Sussex
563	Sutton & Cheam	Paul Burstow	LD	London	Croydon and Sutton	Sutton
564	Sutton Coldfield	Norman Fowler	Con	West Midlands	—	Birmingham
565	Swansea East	Donald Anderson	Lab	Wales	South Wales West	Swansea
566	Swansea West	Alan Williams	Lab	Wales	South Wales West	Swansea
567	Swindon North	Michael Wills	Lab	South West	—	Wiltshire, North Wiltshire, Swindon
568	Swindon South	Julia Drown	Lab	South West	—	Swindon
569	Tamworth	Brian Jenkins	Lab	West Midlands	—	Staffordshire, Lichfield, Tamworth
570	Tatton	Martin Bell	Ind	North West	—	Cheshire, Macclesfield, Vale Royal
571	Taunton	Jackie Ballard	LD	South West	—	Somerset, Taunton Deane, West Somerset
572	Tayside North	John Swinney	SNP	Scotland	Mid Scotland and Fife	Angus, Perthshire and Kinross
573	Teignbridge	Patrick Nicholls	Con	South West	—	Devon, Teignbridge
574	Telford	Bruce Grocott	Lab	West Midlands	—	Telford and Wrekin
575	Tewkesbury	Laurence Robertson	Con	South West	—	Gloucestershire, Cheltenham, Tewkesbury
576	Thanet North	Roger Gale	Con	South East	—	Kent, Canterbury, Thanet
577	Thanet South	Stephen Ladyman	Lab	South East	—	Kent, Dover, Thanet
578	Thurrock	Andrew MacKinlay	Lab	Eastern	—	Thurrock
579	Tiverton & Honiton	Angela Browning	Con	South West	—	Devon, East Devon, Mid Devon
580	Tonbridge & Malling	John Stanley	Con	South East	—	Kent, Sevenoaks, Tonbridge and Malling
581	Tooting	Tom Cox	Lab	London	Merton and Wandsworth	Wandsworth

No	Constituency	Member of Parliament	Party	European seat	Parliament/ Assembly area	Local authorities
582	Torbay	Adrian Sanders	LD	South West	–	Torbay
583	Torfaen	Paul Murphy	Lab	Wales	South Wales East	Torfaen
584	Totnes	Anthony Steen	Con	South West	–	Devon, South Hams, Teignbridge, Torbay
585	Tottenham	Bernie Grant	Lab	London	Enfield and Haringey	Haringey
586	Truro & St Austell	Matthew Taylor	LD	South West	–	Cornwall, Carrick, Restormel
587	Tunbridge Wells	Archie Norman	Con	South East	–	Kent, Tunbridge Wells
588	Tweeddale, Ettrick & Lauderdale	Michael Moore	LD	Scotland	South of Scotland	Scottish Borders, Midlothian
589	Twickenham	Vincent Cable	LD	London	South West	Richmond upon Thames
590	Tyne Bridge	David Clelland	Lab	North East	–	Gateshead, Newcastle upon Tyne
591	Tynemouth	Alan Campbell	Lab	North East	–	North Tyneside
592	Tyneside North	Stephen Byers	Lab	North East	–	North Tyneside
593	Tyrone West	William Thompson	UU	Northern Ireland	Tyrone West	Omagh, Strabane
594	Ulster Mid	Martin McGuinness	SF	Northern Ireland	Ulster Mid	Cookstown, Dungannon, Magherafelt
595	Upminster	Keith Darvill	Lab	London	Havering and Redbridge	Havering
596	Upper Bann	David Trimble	UU	Northern Ireland	Upper Bann	Banbridge, Craigavon
597	Uxbridge	John Randall	Con	London	Ealing and Hillingdon	Hillingdon
598	Vale of Clwyd	Chris Ruane	Lab	Wales	North Wales	Denbighshire
599	Vale of Glamorgan	John Smith	Lab	Wales	South Wales Central	Vale of Glamorgan
600	Vale of York	Anne McIntosh	Con	Yorkshire & the Humber	–	North Yorkshire, Hambleton, Harrogate, Ryedale, City of York
601	Vauxhall	Kate Hoey	Lab	London	Lambeth and Southwark	Lambeth
602	Wakefield	David Hinchliffe	Lab	Yorkshire & the Humber	–	Kirklees, Wakefield
603	Wallasey	Angela Eagle	Lab	North West	–	Wirral
604	Walsall North	David Winnick	Lab	West Midlands	–	Walsall
605	Walsall South	Bruce George	Lab	West Midlands	–	Walsall
606	Walthamstow	Neil Gerrard	Lab	London	North East	Waltham Forest

No	Constituency	Member of Parliament	Party	European seat	Parliament/ Assembly area	Local authorities
607	Wansbeck	Dennis Murphy	Lab	North East	—	Northumberland, Castle Morpeth, Wansbeck
608	Wansdyke	Dan Norris	Lab	South West	—	Bath and North East Somerset, South Gloucestershire
609	Wantage	Robert Jackson	Con	South East	—	Oxfordshire, South Oxfordshire, Vale of White Horse
610	Warley	John Spellar	Lab	West Midlands	—	Sandwell
611	Warrington North	Helen Jones	Lab	North West	—	Warrington
612	Warrington South	Helen Southworth	Lab	North West	—	Warrington
613	Warwick & Leamington	James Plaskitt	Lab	West Midlands	—	Warwickshire, Stratford-on-Avon, Warwick
614	Warwickshire North	Michael O'Brien	Lab	West Midlands	—	Warwickshire, North Warwickshire, Nuneaton and Bedworth
615	Watford	Claire Ward	Lab	Eastern	—	Hertfordshire, Three Rivers, Watford
616	Waveney	Robert Blizzard	Lab	Eastern	—	Suffolk, Waveney
617	Wealden	Geoffrey Johnson Smith	Con	South East	—	East Sussex, Wealden
618	Weaver Vale	Mike Hall	Lab	North West	—	Cheshire, Halton, Vale Royal
619	Wellingborough	Paul Stinchcombe	Lab	East Midlands	—	Northamptonshire, East Northamptonshire, Wellingborough
620	Wells	David Heathcote-Amory	Con	South West	—	Somerset, Mendip, Sedgemoor
621	Welwyn Hatfield	Melanie Johnson	Lab	Eastern	—	Hertfordshire, Welwyn Hatfield
622	Wentworth	John Healey	Lab	Yorkshire & the Humber	—	Rotherham
623	West Bromwich East	Peter Snape	Lab	West Midlands	—	Sandwell
624	West Bromwich West	Betty Boothroyd	Speaker	West Midlands	—	Sandwell
625	West Ham	Tony Banks	Lab	London	City and East	Newham
626	Westbury	David Faber	Con	South West	—	Wiltshire, Salisbury, West Wiltshire
627	Western Isles	Calum Macdonald	Lab	Scotland	Highlands and Islands	Western Isles
628	Westmorland & Lonsdale	Tim Collins	Con	North West	—	Cumbria, South Lakeland
629	Weston-Super-Mare	Brian Cotter	LD	South West	—	North Somerset

No	Constituency	Member of Parliament	Party	European seat	Parliament/ Assembly area	Local authorities
630	Wigan	Roger Stott	Lab	North West	–	Wigan
631	Wiltshire North	James Gray	Con	South West	–	Wiltshire, North Wiltshire
632	Wimbledon	Roger Casale	Lab	London	Merton & Wandsworth	Merton
633	Winchester	Mark Oaten	LD	South East	–	Hampshire, Winchester
634	Windsor	Michael Trend	Con	South East	–	Bracknell Forest, Slough, Windsor and Maidenhead
635	Wirral South	Ben Chapman	Lab	North West	–	Wirral
636	Wirral West	Stephen Hesford	Lab	North West	–	Wirral
637	Witney	Shaun Woodward	Con	South East	–	Oxfordshire, Cherwell, West Oxfordshire
638	Woking	Humphrey Malins	Con	South East	–	Surrey, Guildford, Woking
639	Wokingham	John Redwood	Con	South East	–	West Berkshire, Wokingham
640	Wolverhampton North East	Kenneth Purchase	Lab	West Midlands	–	Wolverhampton
641	Wolverhampton South East	Dennis Turner	Lab	West Midlands	–	Wolverhampton
642	Wolverhampton South West	Jenny Jones	Lab	West Midlands	–	Wolverhampton
643	Woodspring	Liam Fox	Con	South West	–	North Somerset
644	Worcester	Michael Foster	Lab	West Midlands	–	Worcestershire, Worcester
645	Worcestershire Mid	Peter Luff	Con	West Midlands	–	Worcestershire, Wychavon
646	Worcestershire West	Michael Spicer	Con	West Midlands	–	Worcestershire, Malvern Hills, Wychavon
647	Workington	Dale Campbell-Savours	Lab	North West	–	Cumbria, Allerdale
648	Worsley	Terry Lewis	Lab	North West	–	Salford, Wigan
649	Worthing East & Shoreham	Tim Loughton	Con	South East	–	West Sussex, Adur, Worthing
650	Worthing West	Peter Bottomley	Con	South East	–	West Sussex, Arun, Worthing
651	Wrekin, The	Peter Bradley	Lab	West Midlands	–	Shropshire, Bridgnorth, Telford and Wrekin
652	Wrexham	John Marek	Lab	Wales	North Wales	Wrexham
653	Wycombe	Ray Whitney	Con	South East	–	Buckinghamshire, Wycombe
654	Wyre Forest	David Lock	Lab	West Midlands	–	Worcestershire, Wyre Forest
655	Wythenshawe & Sale East	Paul Goggins	Lab	North West	–	Manchester, Trafford
656	Yeovil	Paddy Ashdown	LD	South West	–	Somerset, South Somerset

No	Constituency	Member of Parliament	Party	European seat	Parliament/ Assembly area	Local authorities
657	Ynys Mon	Ieuan Wyn Jones	PC	Wales	North Wales	Anglesey
658	York, City of	Hugh Bayley	Lab	Yorkshire & the Humber	—	City of York
659	Yorkshire East	John Townend	Con	Yorkshire & the Humber	—	East Riding of Yorkshire

*Peter Temple-Morris was elected as a Conservative, but subsequently defected to Labour.

NOTES

NOTES

NOTES

Data Processing and Typesetting by
Vacher Dod Publishing Limited

Printed in Great Britain by
The Cromwell Press, Trowbridge, Wiltshire